VOICES:
Letters From World War II

VOICES:
Letters From World War II

By KEN SCHARNBERG

PREMIUM PRESS AMERICA
NASHVILLE, TENNESSEE

PREMIUM PRESS AMERICA
P.O. Box 159015 (37215)
5604 Knob Road
Nashville TN 37209-4522
(615) 352-3922

PREMIUM PRESS AMERICA is a division of Schnitzer Communications, Inc.

ISBN 0-9637733-0-5

Library of Congress Catalog Card Number
93-85481

PREMIUM PRESS AMERICA books are available at special discounts for bulk purchases for sales promotions, premiums, fund-raising, or educational use. For information contact PREMIUM PRESS AMERICA.

| Book editing and design | Armour&Armour |
| Cover design | L. Mayhew Gore Art |

Photographs provided by The American Legion Archives and where noted by individual contributors.

Printed in the United States of America
Horowitz/Rae Book Manufacturers, Inc.

Limited Contributors' First Edition
1 2 3 4 5 6 7 8 9 10 ★ 93 94

ACKNOWLEDGMENT

*To the members of The American Legion,
without whom this book would not
have been possible.*

FROM THE AUTHOR

This book is a collaboration.

It was written by my wife Nancy, who typed hundreds of handwritten letters into the computer and put up with endless weekends dedicated to "the book."

It was written by George Schnitzer, Jr., the book's publisher, who held unswerving faith in the project and was more than understanding over deadlines.

It was written by the National Executive Committee and the national officers of The American Legion, who authorized its creation.

It was written by my boss, Daniel Wheeler, publisher of *The American Legion Magazine,* who encouraged me, let me run with an idea, and allowed me the time to see it to completion.

Most of all, it was written by the contributors, the men, women, and children who heroically worked their way through an era of terrible risk, tragic events, and unspeakable upheaval—the people of the World War II years. More than anyone, it was they who wrote this book with their blood, with their toil, and with their pain, and with their victory.

I am proud to have been allowed to collaborate, associate, and learn. Thank you.

ABOUT THE AUTHOR

Ken Scharnberg was born in Iowa in 1947 and attended college in Nebraska for a year before entering the Army in 1966. A scout dog handler in the Army, he served with the 173rd Airborne Brigade in 1968 and 1969.

After being wounded, he continued his college education while hospitalized at Camp Drake, Japan, and later in California.

Scharnberg's career has been somewhat varied and includes experience as a radio announcer, truck driver, advertising copy writer, and hog confinement manager. However, he has always had a passion for writing. Beginning as a freelance writer, and after selling nearly 400 stories and articles to various magazines and publications, including a Hardy boys mystery and a book on careers in trucking, he became an assistant editor for *THE AMERICAN LEGION MAGAZINE* in 1990.

He is married, has four children and one granddaughter, and is the national contender for the title of Worst Golfer Of The Decade.

DEDICATION

For those who served . . .
For those who waited . . .
And for those who never came back . . .
This book is dedicated.

CONTENTS

INTRODUCTION

They are the warriors of the forties. They fought battles in Anzio and Atlanta, New Guinea and New Mexico, in Fortresses and factories. They came from every walk of life and served in every capacity. They held front lines and assembly lines, suffered loss and celebrated victory, buried their dead and birthed a new generation.

Most of them who are still with us are in their late 60s and early 70s now. More than half a century ago they answered their country's call, won the war, and returned home—never to be the same. And to this day, most will tell you the friends they made and the experiences they shared in the foxholes, the aircraft, and the ships they manned are irreplaceable.

Those poignant memories are recalled in excerpts from nearly 1,000 letters that appear in this book. No, these letters cannot capture the full experience of World War II. Only those who were there know the full flavor of those times. But for anyone who went through those blood-and-guts years, these letters can bring cause to remember.

The experiences related in this book come mostly from members of The American Legion. The book belongs, however, to all 15 million Americans who proudly served during World War II. This is their story, told by them.

PUBLISHER'S NOTE
The letters that follow give you the opportunity to hear eyewitnesses share their memories in their own words. Therefore, the letters have not received the customary editing for style, grammar, and spelling that published material usually undergoes.

Chapter 1
Prelude To War

The war clouds that hung over Europe in the 1930s were not lost on the United States, but the country had suffered a long, hard climb from the depths of the Great Depression. By 1939, the consensus of public opinion was largely one of isolation. Even The American Legion, whose membership was veterans of World War I, propounded an isolationist stance. Two decades had not healed the scars of the last war and "what happens in Europe is none of our business" was the predominate viewpoint.

On September 1, 1939, German Fuehrer Adolph Hitler invaded Poland, and the earth shook.

Constance Krasowska Gray *of Union, New Jersey, was in the wrong place at the wrong time.*

I WAS THRILLED TO LEARN that I would be studying for a year at the Jagiellonian University in Cracon, Poland, as a Kusciunszko Foundation scholar.

The passing weeks were filled with excursions to concerts, museums, and more, as well as attending classes. But the best part was meeting students from all over the world who had also come to the university where Copernicus had studied centuries before.

A handsome Swedish student named Eric Svenson told me I reminded him of his sister. I'm so glad I remembered.

The rumblings of World War II were already easy to hear and see, so the American Embassy warned Americans to leave Poland at once. We boarded the train—the last one out of Warsaw!—and zig-zagged across Bulgaria, Hungary, Czechoslovakia, Austria to Germany.

My most vivid memory is Adolph Hitler Platz in Berlin, Sept. 1, 1939. This was the worst place for Americans to be on the first day of World War II. German tanks and troops were everywhere.

The embassy had told us to keep a low profile, so when a German officer asked me my name, I blurted out, "Helga Svenson." There was too much military commotion in the Platz, so my blonde, blue-eyed features allowed me to pass as a Swede.

*In the U.S., Hitler's invasion of Poland was met with shock. The reactions and memories of **Robert E. Barton** of Garden City, Kansas, may be typical.*

1

Our family was much into baseball. We never missed seeing the locals play and followed the teams to the surrounding towns. Exhibition games were always a big treat.

The House of Davids and the Kansas City Monarchs with Satchel Paige were playing at Stockton, Kansas in September 1939. They played major league caliber baseball.

Mother prepared a basket lunch for the outing. It was a beautiful Sunday for picnics and baseball and when we arrived at the Saline River, Dad pulled into a roadside clearing and lunch was served.

The radio continued playing, then a special announcement was made. "German troops have invaded Poland."

As a 17 year-old, I was shocked. I felt I would be called. On November 19, 1942, I entered the service, to eventually serve with the 45th division in North Africa, Sicily and Italy.

Hitler's march across Europe did not end at Poland. As the German Fuehrer became bolder and bolder, Western Europe geared up for war.

In spite of the isolationist attitude that prevailed within the US at that time, the United States had European allies and President Franklin Roosevelt had no intention of abandoning them. In October 1940, Congress authorized the draft. When the Lend/Lease Act was passed in 1941, the legislation allowed the US to sell war materiel to our European friends, primarily Great Britain.

Overall, Lend/Lease met with national approval because it not only offered support to our friends, but it also supplied employment to a workforce that had known deprivation and bread lines during the Great Depression.

But a frightening parallel was beginning to take place. The 1915 sinking of the passenger liner Lusitania *by a German submarine had eventually led the United States into World War I.*

Now this form of warfare had now developed into a terrifyingly effective force. By 1940, German wolf packs had become the terror of the Atlantic. U-boats sent hundreds of thousands of tons of materiel to the bottom of the sea within just a few months' time. Residents of New York's Long Island had even been able to see the fires aboard the ships sinking just outside of New York Harbor.

To provide protection for the convoys bound for England, Roosevelt authorized the use of US Navy ships to escort the poorly armed Merchant Marine cargo vessels. Even this was ineffective as **Philip Kaminsky** *of Wantagh, New York, discovered.*

IN 1939, I WAS LOADING war supplies (Bundles for Britain, etc.) as a longshoreman. The grapevine indicated that the Navy would welcome volunteers to move the ships to England, Iceland, Murmansk and other ports. Several longshoreman became merchant seamen overnight.

After experiencing action along the coasts of Cuba, the Gulf, then

South and East Africa, I was signed on the "Norwalk" and made several North Atlantic crossings to Rekjavick, Iceland while parts of the convoy continued on to Murmansk.

One trip we spotted wooden orange crates floating, but the sunshine betrayed the shiny periscope lenses and the convoy flags signaled "Disperse!"

We got out our available "heavy armor" — Colt .45s — and attacked (?) the wolf pack as we scooted away.

On another Icelandic crossing, our convoy escorts, wooden Canadian corvettes, sounded the alarm and catapulted depth charges around the convoy.

The damned U-boats ducked right under the convoy to escape detection, bumping and scraping the bottom of our ship until they eventually escaped the corvettes.

As Hitler's list of conquests grew, people with ties to folks in Europe, like **Charlene Buckman Gordon** *of Camp Point, Illinois, found it increasingly difficult to keep in contact.*

W E STARTED CORRESPONDING in fourth grade. Over the years, we traded little girl talk, then dreams of the future.

Her letters stopped after the German invasion of Holland. Many months later, at Christmas-time, my best gift was a letter from my friend in Occupied Netherlands. It had been censored and stamped with a Nazi swastika. It simply said that she was well and that she thought of me often. I still have that last letter.

I often wondered what happened to my little Dutch pen pal. Then, after the war, a friend traveling in Europe found the answer. She and her family were Jewish, which I had not known. They had disappeared in a death camp.

Now, with this 50th anniversary, and as so many remember loved ones gone to war, I join them in sad thoughts of a little lost Dutch girl.

It would not be until many years later that the true extent of the horrors of this war would be known. In truth, the war was not going well. Hitler's troops were well organized and by the time Western European powers had mobilized, it was too late to prevent the German advance. Tiny England was beleaguered and the US responded by sending aid.

Yet, bombings that occurred almost nightly rapidly changed the lifestyles of the British civilian. **Jean Taylor Kraynik,** *now of Holley, New York, found a unique way to express the gratitude felt by the people of England in those early days.*

A S A CHILD in England, let me give tribute to all you "Yanks" who gave of yourself so that your sacrifice of the 40s would allow us to be strong and free.

England: 1941
We carry only the cat
and scramble, night gowned and barefoot
over black bricks.
An acrid smell of sulfur there is
Flashes of vermilion
Screams and curses to Hitler
Who doesn't hear.
Someone yells, "The orphanage is hit!"
And Matron, significant with rage,
Shakes her fist at the blameless sky
As we children are herded, bewildered, sleep warm
To a dank cellar.
With steeled-in calm we endure
Our blistered feet to be bathed
By people, self-conscious of their pity,
Who murmur, "Poor bairns. Poor bairns,"
And give us sugarless cocoa, hot and bitter.
Lying beneath moth-balled blankets One-eyed, not moving
We wonder only
If spiders lurk in dark corners
And will they feed the cat?

Some Americans chose not to wait for the US to become involved directly with the war. Many, like Milford, Iowa's **Ken Herbster** *joined the armies and navies of our allies.*

I VOLUNTEERED TO SERVE in the Canadian army and arrived in England in September 1941. I had a degree in physical training and political science. I was awarded an honorary rank and given a job as swimming instructor at Cosford, England.

After Pearl Harbor, I went to the American Embassy in London and applied for transfer into the US forces, where I was assigned into the 8th Air Force and later to 306th Bomb Group, and eventually volunteered as an Aerial Gunnery Officer.

More and more Americans were becoming involved in the war. When the Germans invaded Norway, ships in port were considered fair game. Some, like the father of **Michael E. Bailey** *of Orange, California, discovered first-hand what that meant.*

MY FATHER, JACK BAILEY, went into the Merchant Marine in 1933 and served until 1944. He saw service in the North Atlantic, the Russian run, and North Africa.

His most vivid memory of World War II was being shelled and captured by the Germans at Bergen, Norway, in 1940.

Jack was an ordinary seaman on the freighter "Charles R. McCormick." His ship had left Baltimore in March, bound for Scandinavia. When the Germans reached Bergen, his ship was in port unloading cargo.

The ship attempted to flee the harbor and was assailed by German shore artillery. At the same time, two German torpedo boats gave chase and overtook the tramp, and fired a shot across her bow.

The vessel was taken back to the pier and the ship and crew were held there for two months. (The Captain of the ship died while in Bergen and is buried there.) The Germans accused the steamship of trying to smuggle out machinery and spare parts.

When released, the ship returned to New York under the command of the First Officer.

By 1941, the war against merchant vessels was becoming intense. In October, two incidents within weeks of each other would act as a catalyst. **William J. Flynn** *of Philadelphia was involved in one of those incidents.*

I N OCTOBER 1941, I WAS on convoy duty with the Navy in the North Atlantic.

The destroyers USS Plunket, Livermore, Kearney (DD432), Decatur (DD341) and Greer were ordered to the rescue of Convoy SC 48, which consisted of 45 fully loaded vessels bound for England with much needed supplies for the war. They were being escorted by British, Canadian and Free French naval vessels.

The American destroyers, upon reaching the convoy, found a wolf pack of German U-boats methodically picking off the merchant ships, which were traveling at a speed of less than 10 knots.

The USS Kearney and Decatur were stationed to the rear of the convoy to intercept the U-boats. Early in the morning on 17 October, 1941, a U-boat attack was launched from the rear of the convoy. Torpedoes fired from the starboard side of the convoy missed the Decatur and struck the Kearney number one boiler room amidships. Seven men were killed at their battle stations and four more were killed on the bridge.

I was severely burned and scalded when equipment in the engine room ruptured from depth charge explosions. However, the Navy said there was no war, so no Purple Heart.

While the news of the Decatur *drew anger from the American people, events two weeks later enraged them.* **Wayne Glick** *of Wichita, Kansas, tells what happened.*

O N OCTOBER 17, 1941, the destroyer USS Tarbell (DD142) sailed from Boston for Argentia, Newfoundland, where she took on fuel and stores and prepared for a long session at sea.

Four or five days later, the Tarbell, along with the USS Bensen, Niblack, H.P. Jones, and Reuben James got underway for a mid-ocean meeting point where they would join a convoy of 35 or 40 ships en route to Great Britain.

At noon the following day, the convoy was sighted and the five destroyers took their positions. The Bensen headed the convoy, the H.P. Jones was stationed at the upper left corner, the Reuben James at the lower left corner, the Tarbell at the right-rear corner and the Niblack at the upper right corner.

The convoy was taking a new route to Britain, hoping to avoid the usual shipping lanes which were infested with Nazi submarines. After cruising for two or three days, the convoy was attacked by one or two submarines. The destroyers dropped a few depth bombs and continued on their way, never knowing if they had sunk the subs or not.

On the night of October 30/31, the moon was hidden by clouds and it was very dark. At 5:37 a.m., Oct. 31, general quarters sounded aboard the Tarbell. We rushed to our duty stations, but on the way, we noticed the dull red glare in the sky on the left hand side of the convoy. After we had been at our battle stations for two or three minutes, we sighted a second red glare where the Reuben James was supposed to be located.

We kept our course and stayed at general quarters for two or three hours, dropping depth charges and scouting for more submarines.

We finally learned that the first glare was when the Reuben James was hit. It sank in seven minutes.

The second flare, we learned, came from the life raft which carried the majority of the survivors. It didn't seem possible that one minute, she was afloat and the next she was at the bottom of the sea. All in all, only about 35 of the crew of 142 survived.

The press items said that the USS Reuben James was sunk west of Iceland, but at the time, we were about 350 miles north of the Azore Islands and about 300 or 400 miles off the tip of Great Britain.

The sinking of the USS Reuben James *was a hint of things to come. But while American eyes focused on Europe, the final action that would open the gates of war would take place at a little-known military base far to the east called Pearl Harbor.* **Thomas D. Campbell Sr.** *of Junction City, Kansas, remembers.*

I WAS A 19-YEAR-OLD Army sergeant, participating in the "Battle of the North Atlantic."

We arrived in Iceland in September 1941 after a hazardous crossing in which we lost troop and cargo ships and untold sleepless hours on deck due to German submarines and sea sickness aboard one of Kaiser's troop ships.

Before December 7, 1941, our tour was supposedly for six months. As we stood in the early morning cold, fog and drizzle of Iceland for breakfast, the PA system announced that Japan had attacked Pearl Harbor and we were at war with the Japanese and Germany.

The Iceland tour became 27 months, then a tour in England and Normandy, France on D-Day, Omaha Red for a total of 42 months.

Fifty years later, that PA announcement is as vivid as if it were this morning.

The United States was once again at war.

Chapter 2
Infamy!

Arguments within the US pitting isolationists against those who thought the United States should enter the conflict were becoming heated. But almost all dissension to US involvement ended on a warm Sunday morning in December on the US territorial islands of Hawaii when suddenly, without warning, the military installations in and around Pearl Harbor were attacked by Japanese aircraft.

The Japanese military, especially the air wing of its navy, had been building since 1939 under the direction of Admiral Isoruko Yamamoto. The ultimate aim of the Japanese was to build an impenetrable defense perimeter around their expanding island empire to the point that they would control all raw materials needed for industry. With this in mind, they sent troops to various points in Southeast Asia and planned attacks to take over strategic islands of the Central and South Pacific.

Once secure, the Japanese leaders felt that the Allies, especially the United States, would sue for peace rather than conduct war against an enemy so well entrenched.

However, once this strategic plan was put into action, and to ensure success, Yamamoto and his senior officers felt it was imperative to keep the US out of the war for a minimum of six months. To accomplish this, plans were made to deliver a surprise attack on the United States's primary naval installation at Pearl Harbor, Hawaii. Once the ships, repair facilities, and fuel dumps were destroyed at Pearl Harbor, the US would be left without an effective Pacific fleet and no means of resupplying what did remain of its forces until the Hawaiian base was rebuilt.

American military and political strategists were not unaware of Japan's imperialistic goals, but most believed that the primary targets would be Hong Kong and Singapore.

In addition, Pearl Harbor was a shallow port. At that time, aircraft-launched torpedoes were useless in shallow waters, or so most experts believed. Unbeknown to US experts, the Japanese had solved this problem.

On the morning of December 7, 1941, six Japanese aircraft carriers, the Akagi, Soryu, Zuikaku, Shokaku, Kaga, *and* Hiryu, *along with their escort and support ships, were within 200 miles of Hawaii. The task force was under the command of Vice-Admiral Chuichi Nagumo. The carriers, loaded with 423 aircraft, launched their attack against Pearl Harbor under heavily overcast skies.*

Originally, the attack was planned in three waves, but Nagumo, a torpedo expert, was overly cautious and canceled the third assault. Had the third wave been launched, and the vital base repair and supply facilities and fuel dumps destroyed, it is quite possible, according to some military historians, that the Japanese plan would have succeeded.

The military leaders at Pearl Harbor did, however, have a little warning of what was to come. In addition to the aircraft carriers and their attendant escort, the Japanese launched five midget submarines with the intention of sinking ships in the main channel of the harbor, thereby making the port unusable.

None of the subs accomplished its mission. Again, had the winds of fate blown in another direction, history may have been recorded differently.

The destroyer USS Ward *responded to a message it received at 0342 that morning from the minesweeper* Condor, *which had sighted a sub's conning tower but failed to make contact. At 0630, the* Ward *again received word of the submarine, this time from the supply ship* Antares. *A Navy patrol plane, a PBY designated 14-P-1, piloted by* **Ensign William P. Tanner** *is dispatched to the scene. At 0645, the* Ward *spots the sub, opens fire, closes, then drops depth charges. Immediately afterward, the PBY attacks the submarine.*

In Tanner's report, he said that at first he thought the sub was in distress and being escorted by the destroyer. The sub was about a mile south of Pearl Harbor when Tanner dropped two lighted buoys to mark the spot for the Ward. *The* Ward *changed course and when within 100 yards, opened fire. The gun crew thought both shots had missed. It was later determined that one shell had passed through the submarine's conning tower.*

The Ward *was forced to change course to avoid a collision, but as it turned, it dropped two depth charges immediately in front of the submarine.*

As the craft began to submerge, Tanner also dropped a depth charge. He felt certain the submarine had been destroyed and sent a coded message to both the communication centers at the air wing and the US task force at sea, Comtaskforce 3. Only the air wing, Compatwing 2, responded and 15 minutes later, asked for verification.

Tanner's second message read, "Sunk one enemy submarine one mile south of Pearl Harbor."

At about the same time Tanner took off on his patrol, Opiana radar station reported a flight of incoming planes to their headquarters, but the report was discounted as a flight of our own aircraft. At 0739, the blips are within 20 miles of Oahu and disappear from the radar screen after entering a "dead zone" created by the hills surrounding the radar site.

The situation at Pearl Harbor from a military standpoint in those last few seconds before the attack was dismal. On Sunday, December 7, the military command at Pearl Harbor had canceled the "war warning" alert that had been issued two weeks earlier. As is the custom of the US military in peacetime, ammunition, including the type used in anti-aircraft guns, and most small arms and automatic weapons were held under lock and key in base arms rooms and munitions lockers.

The Japanese intelligence services had excellent information on the combat status of the military in Hawaii at that time and in fact had received a confirmation at 0739 that morning from a scout plane launched from the Japanese cruiser Chikuma *that the main US fleet was at anchor in Pearl Harbor.*

This, coupled with the fact that traditionally Americans view Sunday as a day of rest, offered the ideal window of opportunity for the Japanese and they took advantage of it.

*At 7:55 a.m. a rift in the overcast skies opened up and the first wave of 181 dive bombers, bombers, and fighter planes attacked Pearl Harbor. This is what **David Montgomery** of Petersburg, Illinois, witnessed.*

A S SUPERVISOR of communications, in the Administration building, for Commander Patrol Wing Two, I was waiting in the radio room for an answer from Patrol plane 14-P-1 verifying his previous message that he had sunk a submarine off the entrance to Pearl Harbor, when a plane was heard diving on the Air Station.

My assistant Supervisor and I stepped outside the Radio Room and watched as a Japanese plane leveled off and dropped a bomb on one of our hangars, which immediately burst into flames.

Returning to the Communication office I was handed the message "AIR-RAID ON PEARL HARBOR X THIS IS NO DRILL" by our Operation Officer Lt. Cmdr. Logan Ramsey.

This message was sent to all stations by our radio operators and signaled the start of World War II and a very long and hectic day for me.

*The first wave of aircraft streaked in from the north shore of Oahu. Torpedo planes concentrated on the ships in the harbor while bombers and fighters attacked airfields and military targets at Kaneho, Ford Island, Hickam, Bellows, Wheeler, and Ewa. The surprise is total as **William J. Agen** of Wrightstown, Wisconsin, describes.*

I WAS ABOARD the USS Honolulu and was in the crews washroom getting ready to catch the first liberty Party ashore. On the main deck the bugler was playing Colors. Suddenly everybody in the washroom realized that the bugler was playing General Quarters, and the General Alarm went off throughout the ship.

In unison we all said, "Hell! not a drill on Sunday morning."

We stood and listened as a voice came over the ship's intercom. "General Quarters! General Quarters! Men this is no shit, General Quarters!"

We heard gunfire. Gunfire in the harbor? I was on main deck in seconds. I can still see the red ball on the wing of this flaming airplane as it headed for the water.

That Sunday there was no liberty on the Honolulu. For over 2000 sailors, soldiers and Marines there was no tomorrow.

Miles J. Leigh of Sioux City, Iowa, went for an unplanned swim that morning.

MY FIRST SHIP the USS Oklahoma, went down at Pearl Harbor. I was four decks below, making out Christmas cards when all hell broke loose. Over the intercom came the words, "Abandon ship! This is not a drill."

I made it to my gun station, and it was under water. Then the last torpedo hit and I was thrown into the water. I was one of the lucky ones. I was picked up by a motor launch. Me and my buddies proceeded to pick up bodies, putting them into the launch.

I remember one fellow we picked up. I started to pump him out, and he started breathing, but unconscious. I covered him with my tee shirt and we took him and the other guys to a make shift hospital.

That done, my buddy and I found a launch and headed out to pick up other bodies.

The war was on...God bless all my buddies and shipmates that did not make it.

The shock and horror of that morning are still vivid to those who were there, like Joel E. Bachner of Reading, Pennsylvania.

I WAS A NAVY RADIOMAN on the USS California and witnessed the USS Oklahoma as it turned over and also the Japanese torpedo planes as they made a run on my own ship. I saw the smoke and flames as they erupted from the USS Arizona. My memories are still vivid of my swim to shore after the USS California was hit and observing my comrades as they also abandoned ship.

It is hard to imagine what it must have been like to be on board one of the ships in the harbor. Unfortunately, David W. Gillmartin of Sag Harbor, New York, didn't have to imagine.

MY SHIP, the USS Utah, was rolling over. I climbed to the main deck. I tried to climb up to the starboard rail twice, but slid back amidships.

A sailor nearby told me to throw away the cigarettes. To my amazement I was holding a carton of cigarettes in one hand. I dropped them and went over the side.

One of the sailor's wristwatch was stopped at 8:06.

Melvin Delaine Bacon *of Cape Girardeau, Missouri, tells another harrowing tale of that morning.*

I WAS ON WATCH aboard the USS Utah in the water distilling plant, called "evaporators". I had just finished taking the 0800 water meter reading when the first torpedo hit. It shook the whole plant.

Gauges, pumps and all equipment went haywire. The air-compressor, reciprocating engine with large flywheel started pounding as if a dozen war drums were beating it out. Other pump voltages were going up and down. There was no longer any way to control the power to the machinery.

Next torpedo put a list toward portside. I started to secure the plant, which was proper procedure during a major crisis. Our sleeping quarters were just to the starboard side divided by an open hatch. I saw a buddy asleep in his bunk and yelled to awaken him. He made it out OK.

The auxiliary steam valve was a six inch valve. I got it about half closed, when all power and lights went out. The ship was tilting to port fairly fast.

Went through our living compartment to get to the ladder to the next deck, had to pull myself up the ladder. Water was gushing in about twelve feet away. I staggered to next ladder up and pulled myself up the ladder to topside which was half engulfed in dark, churning water. The ship continued rolling over. I crawled up the remaining deck to the side of the bottom of the ship which was by now completely out of the water.

As I slid into the water, I heard cries of sailors already in the water. "Help! Save me!" etc. I started to swim toward shore. A motor launch was near and a sailor yelled, "Are you hurt?" I shook my head and continued toward shore.

I climbed upon a mooring platform on my first try, being about 8 feet out of the water. I looked around, then jumped back in the water and swam the rest of the distance to land.

A large pipe-line ditch was just a short distance away and I jumped into it. Some of my shipmates were in the ditch, too. I saw another run of Jap planes go over and saw one slow and drop a bomb on the ship aft of the Utah. If I had a rock or baseball I believe I could have come near hitting this Jap plane.

I tried, along with other sailors, to get a change of clothes from a nearby building, but no success. A first-aid station, after a fashion, was set up in this building. I did get my scratches covered with Mercurochrome, then went looking for water with a group in a truck to a couple of houses, which were for Navy personnel and family.

We stopped after two houses. A little water was obtained from iceboxes.

Next, on a motor launch which had a depth charge on the bow, we went looking for midget subs. Sure was glad to get off the motor launch.

Next, a shipmate I knew slightly, and I went with a group given rifles—old 30-30s and some ammunition—to an open area. It was thought there might be a parachute drop. Stayed there until dark. Only one cracker and applesauce and one cracker and peanut butter sandwich and a bottle of orange soda, chow for the day.

Stayed in Marine dining hall the rest of the night. Went aboard the USS Argonne, our division flagship, just before dusk, the 8th of December. Got a good meal then and also signed and "checked" two postcards, which were to be sent to the next of kin. These two postcards never got home.

I sent a telegram 24 December to my mother—the first news she had about me.

We helped put dead sailors into wooden boxes for burial. This was no fun.

A few days later I was assigned to the destroyer USS A.B. Cummings #365 and finished the war with 77 months overseas and 13 battle stars.

*Imagine how shocking the attack must have been to the youngsters that had just recently signed up like **Adolph Kuhn** of Manteca, California.*

FRESH FROM A KANSAS WHEAT FARM in 1940, this 18-year-old sailor found himself in an Aviation Metalsmith School in Pensacola, Florida. Shortly thereafter, in January 1941, I was shipped to Pearl Harbor to the US Naval Air Station, Ford Island, unaware of what lay ahead in eleven months.

I was blasted out of a motor launch with 11 other seamen on December 7, 1941, into the oil burning on the waters of Pearl Harbor Channel. Dog paddling and groping through debris of human bits, etc. I reached hangar 39 amidst exploding ships and planes.

Experienced in tractor driving, I mounted a Minneapolis Molene, and started towing burning planes to a safer area, when a Japanese bomb crashed the runway ahead of me. I ran to the flaming USS Arizona to aid wounded sailors. My leather shoe soles smoked from the hot decks as I scampered about, pulling charred bodies from under scorching debris.

***John H. McGoran** of Corte Madera, California, like hundreds of others, was occupied in trying to rescue the survivors.*

I WAS ONE of the three sailors standing on the tiller deck of a small boat that escaped when the battleship USS California's anti-aircraft ammunition magazine exploded, killing 50 men. The boat left the ship with 10 volunteers in search of anti-aircraft ammunition.

First we went to the battleship USS Maryland, but her crew was too busy to accommodate us. Then, we went around the over-turned battleship USS Oklahoma to the port bow of the USS West Virginia, where Warrant Officer Applegate went aboard with several of the volunteers. Mr. Applegate delegated me to stay in the boat to receive and stack the ammunition, if available. (Mr. Applegate received a commendation for his efforts.)

Soon an explosion happened on the forecastle of the West Virginia. An officer on board warned our coxswain to pull away, as he thought the entire ship could blow-up. In pulling back our boat nearly crashed into the Oklahoma's propeller. That is the reason two of us "extra" sailors were on the tiller deck. We had jumped up to the tiller deck and on over the taffrail. By hanging on to the taffrail, stretching out our legs to push against the Oklahoma's propeller, we avoided a crash and damage to our boat's propeller.

As soon as our attention was free of the Oklahoma, our coxswain noticed a man in the water, with flames drifting toward him. He said: "We're going after him."

With full power ahead our boat sped to the sailor. He was picked from the water and after he was safely aboard, we headed for Ten-Ten dock in the Navy yard, where we all landed ashore.

Peacetime meant strict controls on the weapons of war and on that Sunday morning, the rules had disastrous consequences. **Gilbert A. Goodwin Jr.** *of East Dennis, Massachusetts, has personal remembrances of what that was like.*

I WAS ON WATCH (4 to 8) with the OD on the fantail of the USS Curtiss. We had just arrived back in Pearl Harbor from a trip to Wake and Midway where we delivered fuel, Marines and pilots to shore up the defenses.

All of a sudden planes came roaring by us with large orange balls on their wings. By the many bomb explosions that followed, we realized that we were being attacked by Japan.

I ran to the port side of the bridge and manned my 50 caliber machine gun but no ammunition was available. Everything was locked up and secured. In addition, 50% of the crew was on liberty. I took a huge nozzle off the bulkhead and broke the lock off the ammo box and commenced firing.

One bomber crashed right behind me on the boat deck and another into the water nearby. The five-inch gun down in front of me also shot right through the conning tower of a miniature sub which was about to torpedo us. One bomb went down through the radio room into the hangar and exploded, killing all the handling crew in number three five-inch.

That is the way World War II started for us on the USS Curtiss.

Close calls were common, as **Edward W. Stone** *of Syracuse, New York, knows too well.*

A S I WAS RELIEVING the radioman for the 8 to 12 watch aboard USS Pyro AE-1, Japanese planes were sighted flying 100 feet off the water heading for battleship row. It was unbelievable and shocking to know we were under an enemy attack. This was not the best place to be since the Pyro was a fully loaded ammunition ship, tied up to the Naval Ammunition Depot Dock in West Lock, Pearl Harbor.

One bomber got through our heavy anti-aircraft fire, but missed the ship with his bomb by 12 feet. The bomb exploded on the concrete dock and caused only superficial damage repaired by the ships force. The ship's radio antenna was shot away by our own machine guns while firing at the attacking planes.

Luckily, we had no casualties.

Carlos D. Barrera of San Antonio, Texas, was in church when the attack started.

I WAS OUTSIDE a small church at Pearl Harbor waiting for 8:00 Mass. We heard a lot of planes in the distance towards Hickam Field. Moments later we heard their machine guns as they headed down the channel towards the harbor. We heard loud explosions and we started running toward our ships.

I was assigned to the USS Argonne tied up to dock across the channel from all the battleships. Shrapnel was falling everywhere. When I got to my ship, the USS Ogalala next to us was already on its side and sinking fast. Four of the battleships had already been torpedoed, were on fire and smoking badly. The USS Nevada and Arizona were trying to get under way when a wave of dive bombers dove on them scoring one direct hit after another. The USS Shaw in drydock took a direct hit and went up in a ball of fire.

Then the boatloads of wounded and burned were being brought to our dock and loaded into trucks and ambulances—a sight I hate to remember, but can never forget. The saddest part was that the ones who were still alive and trapped in those ships died never knowing what had happened.

As the attack was taking place, no one was thinking about retaliation, but Ted Tupper of Massapequa, New York, takes great satisfaction in knowing that he and his ship would later get a chance to strike back.

M Y SHIP, the cruiser USS San Francisco CA-38 was in the Navy Yard at Pearl Harbor. I was below deck getting ready to go to church when general quarters sounded. Going topside I could see the battleship Arizona blowing up and the Oklahoma rolling over.

I was issued a Springfield rifle and proceeded to fire at the oncoming planes.

Ironically, almost a year later on Friday 13th of November 1942, in a night action at Guadalcanal our 13-ship task group, USS San Francisco, Flagship, Adm. Daniel J. Callaghan in command, engaged a superior Japanese force consisting of the battleships Hiei and Kirishima that were in the Pearl Harbor attack group.

The San Francisco sailed right into the enemy fleet and at point-blank range silenced and disabled the Hiei. We were heavily damaged by 15 large-caliber hits, suffered 190 casualties including Adm. Callaghan and most of the officers killed.

The San Francisco and I recovered from our wounds to fight again.

Chapter 3
Total Surprise

For the people working in the hospitals near Pearl Harbor, December 7 was a living, dying nightmare. **John B. "Burt" Amgwert** *of Lincoln, Nebraska, describes the scene.*

BURNED INTO MY MEMORY never to be erased are the first Japanese planes shot down, crashing on the Naval Hospital lawn at 0805; the Jap submarine periscopes in channel entering Pearl Harbor; tremendous smoke, burning oil and explosions of ships bombed and torpedoed in the harbor. Being part of the staff of outstanding doctors, nurses and hospital corpsmen who handled an onslaught of casualties beyond belief. Indescribable burns, traumatic wounds and amputations.

The Naval Hospital normal bed capacity of 400, overloaded with 545 battle casualties, to a midnight census of 960 Patients, plus 313 dead, stacked like cord-wood outside the buildings.

Five minutes after the Japanese aircraft crashes on the lawn in front of the hospital, the forward magazine of the USS Arizona *ignites. There is a tremendous explosion and a huge fireball climbs into the sky. Nine minutes later, the* Arizona *is gone.*

At 0812, a message is sent from Pearl Harbor, and Washington is notified of the attack.

Robert J. Lee, *who still resides in Kailua, Hawaii, had a bird's eye view of the attack.*

I WAS JUST 20. Our house was on a headland up above the Navy boat landing at Aiea in Pearl Harbor. We looked directly at Battleship Row and East Loch. To the left was the main shipyard.

I awoke early Sunday to the shocking sight of our ships under attack. There were heavy explosions and geysers of water shooting up beside the tethered ships. Soon, those ships and the smaller ones in East Loch were firing at anything in the sky.

Many fires broke out and there was much smoke. The latticework mast of the Oklahoma canted more and more as that ship slowly turned over. Then the Arizona blew up with a great explosion. The whole ship turned a bright red. Then big tongues of flame gushed out. There was tremendous noise and black smoke. Much more destruction went on around us. It was a terrible beating.

My life was changed from that moment on. More than four years in uniform would follow. I can never adequately express to anyone who didn't experience 1942/1943 just how desperate and uncertain the time was for us. Historians tend to gloss over this period to fit their own theories. These were tough times and not easily forgotten or forgiven.

In addition to the harbor, there were other targets for Japanese planes that day, as **Earl J. Bangert** *of Hillside, New Jersey, can attest.*

I AWOKE to the sound of gunfire and bombs at my barracks at Schofield. Words cannot explain the confusion that occurred that fatal morning. We had just come off an alert that ran from around Thanksgiving to December 6th. We were totally taken by surprise and to say that confusion was rampant is an understatement.

Most of our officers were off base, and most of our non-coms were as shaken as we were. Japanese planes flew over our barracks on their way to bomb Wheeler Field, an Army Air Force base adjacent to Schofield.

In years since, I've forgotten many events, but even until this day I can recall everything that happened that day. We went from peace to war in a matter of seconds.

For men who work with aircraft, the destruction of the airfields must have been overwhelming. Yet, **John A. Diefenbach** *of San Antonio, Texas, says that his people were back at work already that night.*

SUNDAY MORNING I was relieved from the guard post. After a good breakfast several of us were sitting, talking over a cup of coffee when an airplane flew over the barracks right at roof-top. We remarked that the Navy pilot was violating safety regulations. There was a big explosion, we thought the pilot had failed to pull-up. Then another plane came over, again at roof-top.

Someone outside yelled "Japs—Japs—!"

After what seemed like an awful long time, the planes stopped strafing, bombing the flight line and hangars. We made our way out to the flight line. Most of our P-40's were burned but at the very end, 3 were missed and before night we put two more together.

No one could believe that anyone would dare attack the most powerful military nation on earth. But men like **Ira W. Southern** *of Princeton, West Virginia, know from hard experience that isn't true.*

ALL HELL broke loose! From the third floor of our new barracks I heard the first bomb explosions and thought the Navy was firing at target sleeves being towed across Pearl Harbor. From the west window I saw the "Rising Sun" emblem on the wings of a Japanese plane pulling out of a dive over the Hawaiian Air Depot.

This was it! We were under attack and at war. With shaking hands, I unlocked the combination lock on my locker to retrieve my civilian gas mask, then rushed to the basement supply to get a gun and ammunition.

We had been on a double alert for two weeks, but the alert was called off on Saturday the 6th, and my riot gun was turned into the supply room. I had stood guard duty with a 12-gauge riot gun with fixed bayonet, but no ammunition. I was aware that Gen. Short would not issue ammunition, even during the alert for fear of sabotage.

The supply room was locked and it was necessary to break down the door. The gun racks were also locked and we had to break these locks to get guns. I grabbed a bolt action '03 Springfield rifle and a 45 automatic pistol, filled my front pockets with 45 ammo and two bandoliers with 30-06 ammo and rushed to the front lawn of my barracks.

I was shocked at the damage already inflicted. The entire hangar line was on fire and destroyed along with the aircraft. A glance backward brought another surprise. My barracks was ablaze.

The Japanese planes were bombing and strafing at tree-top altitudes. I could fire one shot into the plane on its attack approach and get one shot into the rear as it departed. I could not tell if I inflicted any damage even though I was a good shot with a rifle. The situation was chaotic. We were without leadership. Every man was on his own.

The headquarters building was under attack and the planes were trying to destroy the American flag bravely waving in the breeze from atop the flag pole, even though it was battered and torn. I hid in the shrubbery beside the building and fired at the attacking planes as fast as I could.

The entire harbor was a column of black boiling smoke. The Japanese planes used it for cover from what little fire-power there was from our ships and ground forces.

The attack ended as suddenly as it began somewhere around 10 a.m. A blaring loud speaker from a military vehicle ordered all women and children from the base. I assisted in the search for women and children in all residences and buildings and helped them to waiting vehicles to transport them from the base.

I was near the USS Shaw when it violently exploded. Ships and buildings were still exploding and burning. The attack was ended, but the war had begun. Where and when would it all end?

Memory is a series of impressions, and that's how **Richard F. Ferguson** *of Carthage, Missouri, describes his morning in 1941.*

W E FINISHED CHOW at the mess hall of Battery E, 64th Coast Artillery (AA), Fort Shafter, Territory of Hawaii and I was walking back to the barracks with a fellow artilleryman when we caught sight of black puffs of ack-ack smoke in the early morning sky over Pearl Harbor way.

I remember suddenly seeing strange planes overhead, red balls painted on their fuselages. Then the alarm, "The Japs are attacking Pearl"—thunderous explosions, our own outfit hit . . . one killed, three wounded.

Flashes of memories. On my belly to a field phone to call in the post fire department to fight fire in our wooden barracks. Signing for Springfield 03 ammo. Catching a detail as secondary infantryman to search for and detain suspected Jap saboteurs and sympathizers in the area surrounding our post. Moving to field position that night in the cane fields overlooking Pearl Harbor's West Loch. Burning ships.

Good God, we're at war.

The chaos of December 7 was, in part, created by leaders who had never been tested under battle. **Edward W. Powell** *of Aurora, Colorado, knows what that's like.*

AT HICKAM FIELD only a partial alert was on, so half could be off base at once. Outside the barracks I noticed aircraft with fixed landing gears carrying torpedoes. The explosions, spouts of water and black smoke at Pearl made the football players on the parade ground uneasy. One was yelling, "It was only the Navy practicing."

A torpedo-carrying aircraft passed over the flag pole. Ground defense men were shooting rifles but a sergeant was ordering them to hold their fire.

Later, our First Sergeant came with a roster and some had a zero behind their names—they were the first to die. Being professional soldiers, it was all in a day's work but I did get a ring side seat to the very first moments of the start of our entry into a first class war.

One reason people remember disasters is that you travel from commonplace, everyday interests to something totally out of any index of human experience. That's what happened to **Edward Park** *of Big Pine, California, and his friends.*

OUR MOTORCYCLE CLUB had spent the night in the building where we met. On Sunday morning we heard planes flying over and we ran to the rooftop, thinking it was the usual visitor's salute. We could see the pilots' faces, and the rising sun on the wings.

A second squadron flew over. In the direction of flight, smoke was coming from Hickam Field and Pearl Harbor. One of the guys ran upstairs yelling, "Take cover, we're being attacked!" We thought it was a joke, until he shouted "No kidding!"

Cars were speeding, tires screeching and radios bellowed "This is war, take cover!"

As a volunteer motorcycle messenger between posts for the Army, I drove at night with only a small spot of blue light shining. It was scary driving in the blackout and hearing gunfire, not knowing where it came from. Everyone was jittery, especially me.

*It wasn't until **Anthony Solomon** of Glenshaw, Pennsylvania, saw a pilot's face that he knew who was attacking.*

I HEARD a lot of noise and not knowing what was going on, I ran out of our second-floor porch and saw planes dropping bombs on Pearl Harbor. The first thing that came to my mind was that the Marine Air Force were having practice.

As I was standing on the porch, a plane came very close to me, peeling off after it dropped its bombs. It was so close that I saw the pilot laughing and then I realized they were Japs.

*Disbelief was the order of the day, as described by **John O. Thach** of Westminster, Colorado.*

I WAS STATIONED at Schofield Barracks with the 24th Division. It was Sunday, a day off and I was sleeping in when I heard the first bomb fall on Wheeler Field and thought we were having an earthquake. I jumped up and ran outside and could see the smoke bellowing up at Wheeler Field.

The men were in the chow line, one of them said, "The Navy must be having maneuvers."

I said, "Maneuvers, hell, can't you see the Rising Sun on that plane?"

About that time this plane peeled off and dove down to strafe us, but he pulled up as he started strafing to avoid the trees and his bullets hit the top of the barracks. A ricochet caught me below the right knee and barely broke the skin. It was a .25 caliber bullet that dropped to the curb, spent.

*Who would have believed that something as innocent as going to church could get you killed? **William T. Wall** of Sun City, Arizona, had at least one buddy who died that way.*

WE HAD A CHURCH PARTY of six leave the USS Vestal at 7:45, as we approached the gate at Mary Point Landing the war started. We saw the plane drop bombs on Hickam Field and said, "Look the Army even painted red balls on the planes." When the first torpedo plane flew over us it was so low we jumped. When the second one flew over, we saw the bullets along side of us.

We ran for cover and the rear gunner in the third plane hit one of our men. Ray Kerrigan died the next day.

After getting under cover we saw the torpedo planes drop their torpedoes like clockwork, starting with the Oklahoma then through battleship row.

The rest of the day we spent our time in a machine gun nest.

*It's a safe bet that **Ernie Carroll** of Ticonderoga, New York, probably thought twice about sleeping in after December 7.*

I AWOKE with a start. Strange sounds were coming from the bay and in my sleep, it took me a moment to orient myself. "Oh, the engineers must be blasting the channel," I thought. I quickly jumped out of bed and looked out the window of my quarters, just in time to see a fighter plane diving toward the house. Flashes sputtered from its wings and as it passed I noticed a large red ball marking the plane's fuselage.

I quickly realized the engineers weren't blasting the channel and ran out of the house and up the road toward the dispensary. A plane approached from the rear kicking up dirt at my feet—50 caliber dirt!

I dove under the power station which was built off the ground, on concrete stilts. "If they hit this I am cooked," I thought. The plane passed and I continued running to the dispensary, hoping to stay alive.

Everyone remembers their 21st birthday. **Richard B. Anderson** *of Toms River, New Jersey, recalls his, perhaps better than most.*

I T WAS MY TWENTY-FIRST BIRTHDAY and I was trying to figure out what I wanted to do. We were back on peacetime status, so there would be no trouble getting to town. I had a big day planned, dinner with a friend, then off to the beach for the rest of the day.

So, I took it easy Saturday night and got in early and was up bright and early Sunday morning. After breakfast I watched some planes circling around. I thought the Marines were having maneuvers.

One of these planes came close to the barracks. I could see the guy in the back cockpit and the torpedo clearly. Well, I wave at the guy, he thumbs his nose at me, swings the machine gun around, aims at me and starts firing.

I figure blanks. Wrong! Live ammo and close. This is Sunday, the seventh of December 1941, Fort Kamehameha, Defenses of Pearl Harbor. What a way to celebrate my "Twenty-first Birthday"!

Even as the planes at Hickam and other airfields are being destroyed, a flight of B-17s flying in from the mainland arrive over the islands. Unarmed, low on fuel, they are caught between friendly ground fire and the withering attack of the Japanese.

At the same time, aircraft from the carrier USS Enterprise *arrive. They, too, are unaware of the fury they are about to enter.*

There were few safe places that morning, and almost certainly being in the air inbound for Pearl Harbor, as was **Jack Leaming** *of Wildwood, New Jersey, was about the last place anyone would want to be.*

W E COULD SMELL the acrid aroma of explosives 50 miles at sea at 2,000 feet. Minutes later, we could see the columns of smoke rising over Oahu as we neared the completion of our search mission and return from Wake. We were almost shot down by our own forces attempting to land at the Marine Base at Ewa. As the landing was aborted, the scene at Ewa was unbelievable, planes destroyed and smoldering, hangars afire, machine gun fire and 1.1 fire whizzing by our plane. Fires burned on all the battleships.

All hell had broken loose. We never, ever, received a lei greeting, but this? War! Who? Why?

My frantic attempts to get even for all this ended on 4 March 1942 when dive-bombing Marcus Island. After dumping 700 pounds of explosives, we were hit by AA setting sixty gallons of gas on fire. The hiss of its extinguishment hitting the water heralded 42 months of hell as uninvited guests of Emperor Hirohito.

Ah, freedom!

*In spite of the initial surprise, and the fact American forces were caught almost flat-footed, at least two P-40 aircraft did make it into the skies over Oahu, and **Maurice Harmelink** of Grand Rapids, Michigan, was proud of those pilots' efforts.*

I WAS AT WHEELER FIELD when, above the billowing smoke, exploding ammunition in the hangars, and the high whine of the engines of the strafing Japanese Zeros, I heard the sound of an American P-40 pursuit plane on the tail of a Japanese Zero.

That sound of an American plane's engine above the chaos below was heartening to us all at the very start of World War II.

*Pearl Harbor was a disaster—some even said a national disgrace—but the actions of our forces that day made men like **James P. O'Grady** of Rochester, New York, proud.*

I WAS A 23-YEAR-OLD private in the Signal Company Aircraft Warning, when the Japs bombed, strafed, killed and wounded many sailors, Marines and soldiers.

I was proud when my buddies on the radar scope at Opiana picked up the Jap planes 144 miles away, but disappointed that this info was disregarded at the Information Center where I was on duty.

I was proud again when two Army Air Force pilots, Lieutenants Welch and Taylor, managed to get into the air and knock down several Nips each.

*Pearl Harbor was an inferno. From such flames, heroes are created. **Joseph Rutkowski** of New York, describes one.*

A T 7:55 AM, as I lay sleeping in my bed in Schofield Barracks on Oahu, Hawaii, I was awakened by a loud noise that sounded like thunder. The Island was actually shaking. Someone yelled that it must be an earthquake.

As everyone was scurrying about trying to get organized, word came that the Japanese was attacking Pearl Harbor. Everyone ran to the windows, where we could see the Japanese planes diving down on the Navy ships and Hickam and Schofield Barracks. We had front row seats.

But the incident that stands out most in my mind while the Japanese were attacking, was that our bugler was standing out in the middle of the barracks quadrangle, an easy target for the Japanese planes, and was blowing that we were being attacked. He did not miss a note nor did he move while the Japanese planes were flying around bombing and strafing.

Yet, at best, the resistance is merely token. At 0854, the second wave of Japanese aircraft, consisting of 54 high level bombers, 78 dive bombers, and 36 fighter planes begins its run on the island.

*Local radio stations have been blaring the warning that this was no drill and telling all service people to return to their posts for almost an hour. Word of mouth was how **Michael R. Rush** of Clifton Springs, New York, found out what was going on.*

ON SUNDAY MORNING, we were on a trip around the Island. A civilian stopped us. We were to report to our post immediately.

Coming into Honolulu, we saw planes in the air and people in the streets. We turned our radio on and heard, "This is no maneuver, No sham battle! It's the real McCoy. Japanese planes are bombing Pearl Harbor & Hickam Field."

We hurried to our positions. All we had were rifles and 30 caliber machine gun ammo. Our 50 caliber and 37 millimeter ammo was at the Dump and it came too late. They were gone. We overlooked Pearl to the right and Hickam to the left. All you could see were ships on fire and smoke, hangars and planes burning.

The words of the Broadcast never left me. I still hear them today.

*Timing is everything, and it's a safe bet that **Lawrence C. Katz** of Blytheville, Arkansas, is happy he didn't arrive at his ship any earlier that morning.*

I WAS HURRYING back to Ford Island on the highway leading back to the Navy Yard to catch the motor launch back to my base. While passing Hickam Field, I heard what sounded just like this typewriter. Not knowing what the noise was, I turned in my seat of the cab, looked over my shoulder and saw a Japanese plane strafing us with the cherry tracers coming right at me. About a dozen cars back, it banked to the right, came across the cab and headed down the runway at Hickam Field, strafing the planes trying to take off and hitting them.

We jumped out of the cab and ran to the main gate of the Navy Yard in time to see the Nevada get hit and run up on the beach.

*If an Army lives on its belly, **Walter R. Gorr** of Tracy, California, and his buddy did exactly what any good GI would do.*

I WAS STANDING in line at Schofield Barracks, Oahu, along with the rest of the men in "C" Company of the 34th Combat Engineer Regiment, at the back door of the mess hall and waiting to get fried eggs right off the griddle.

We looked up and saw fighter planes coming over the mountains. At first, we thought that the Air Force was out early, until they dove down at us and we saw the "meat ball".

Someone yelled that we were at war with Japan. My buddy and I went in and ate breakfast. We said it might be the last meal we would have for some time.

Within an hour or so, we were camped in the brush at Hickam Airfield to clean up so incoming planes could land.

*Walter's buddy was, in a sense, correct. Sunday morning, December 7, 1941, life changed for both military and civilians alike. The aftermath of the Pearl Harbor attack would touch an entire nation as it affected **Irving Whitney** of Pembroke, Massachusetts.*

ALTHOUGH I WAS NOT in the service at the time, I had arrived at Pearl Harbor on Dec. 1 to start work as an electrician's helper in the electric shop. The shop was located adjacent to the dry dock that contained the destroyers Cassen and Downs and the battleship Pennsylvania. I arrived at the shop just as the last wave of Japanese planes were flying over.

The most memorable sight besides the devastation at the dry docks was the burning of the USS Shaw, the USS West Virginia and the USS Arizona and to see the battleship USS Oklahoma laying bottom-up.

*Confusion reigned and officials feared attacks in addition to the aerial bombardment, as **James Cocarus** of Rochester, New Hampshire, relates.*

I WAS ON DUTY at Hickam Field and recall hearing a lot of explosions from nearby Pearl Harbor. All at once, I remember seeing many "red ball" insignias on Japanese planes strafing and bombing our hangars and barracks.

We were being attacked by the Japanese. Many heroic men died while trying to repel this merciless and unexpected raid. Our rifles and machine guns were no match for the enemy's well-planned aerial attacking planes.

Pearl Harbor was a flaming inferno of sinking ships, and here at Hickam Field, we GI's were also on our enemy's "hit list".

I and other GI's were sent to strategic areas to repel "supposed attacks" from parachuting and landing troops.

Fortunately none came and later we returned to our base to survey the damage.

*As the Japanese attack groups departed, the one-time Paradise of Oahu lay in ruins. Take a drive with **Harold F. Cook** of Seminole, Florida, and see the devastation.*

THE SKIES OVER Schofield Barracks, Oahu, Territory Hawaii, blackened with planes with rising suns painted on their wings, strafing, bombing, and torpedoing our military personnel, planes, ships at Pearl Harbor and other military installations.

The death and wounding of men; the blood, tears and agonies; the devastation; the nauseous odors of burning flesh and oil; the fear of explosion, invasion, and yes, life; the total destruction. This was Pearl Harbor!

It was a long drive into the unknown that day as I drove through Schofield Barracks, Wheeler Field (dead lay on the walks), Pearl City and Pearl Harbor (the smoke and explosions) on my journey to Waikiki Beach and my defense position. The images of this day are instilled in my mind and will be in my memory forever. This was truly the Hell of war, undeclared!

That night, Hawaii stood on a war footing and the lives of its residents changed forever. **Harry Giles Adams** *of Blackshear, Georgia, found that out very quickly.*

I WAS QUARTERED at Fort Armstrong, stationed at the Finance Office, US Army, in downtown Honolulu. I reported to my office and when I returned to Armstrong for lunch, I was issued a .45 with two clips of ammo. Our commanding officer authorized the enlisted men to spend the night at the Army Navy YMCA on that Sunday night. The building was almost full of evacuees from the various bases on Oahu, plus the normal group of enlisted men who were quartered there.

I was the only one with a weapon and when there was a report of flashing lights on the roof, I was the logical one to investigate.

I rode the elevator to the fifth floor, climbed a ladder into the upper Part and then stepped out on the roof. Five stories up, a slanting roof, and pitch dark. I saw no lights so turned to retrace my steps and there in front of me were the flashing lights: the mechanism of the electric elevator was flashing every time the elevator moved.

I reported this and the next day they covered the open parts with blackout curtains. That night and for several nights thereafter, the police radio would tell of lights showing; many times the police and Army personnel had to shoot lights out. Those first few days and especially the nights, were very tense ones for those of us in Hawaii.

Chapter 4
America Reacts

When news of the sneak attack on Pearl Harbor reached the mainland United States, reactions ranged from shock and surprise to rage. Regardless of how the message was conveyed, the ultimate result was to unite the country. Talk of isolationism died away almost immediately.

But in 1941, mass communications, by today's standards, were very primitive. News was received by newspapers, radio, telegraph, and telephone, by word of mouth, and even by announcements at the local theater. Two telephone operators relate what happened when the attack was first announced. This is what **Jeanne Reho** *of Williamstown, Pennsylvania, remembers.*

I WAS A RECENT HIGH SCHOOL GRADUATE, working in a small town telephone office, the lone operator on duty. It was a manually operated 150-jack switchboard with plug-in cords. Sometimes there were as many as 15 customers on one line. That is, 13-R12, 13-R11 and so on. The "R" meant the number of rings, all done by hand.

When the bombs fell Sunday morning in Hawaii, it was afternoon in our town in Pennsylvania. I thought the switchboard had exploded! Every key on the board dropped open. That meant customers were ringing the operator.

I pushed them back, thinking it was maybe a short circuit. No way! They all rang again.

After 15 minutes of frantic answering, mostly for long-distance calls to relatives, I realized that something had happened outside my office.

I called the chief operator and she said, "I'm on my way to the office. The Japanese just bombed Pearl Harbor."

Reho's counterpart in Hartford, Connecticut, **Helen Rivard** *now of Lake Worth, Florida, was also on duty that day.*

I T WAS A WARM, LOVELY DAY in Hartford, Conn., and I was a long-distance operator at the telephone company.

I was anxious to get off work and enjoy the nice day. I would be getting off at 9 p.m.

When the boards lit up like a Christmas tree, we didn't know why. Finally, a customer told us.

We ate at the board that day, which was usually a "no-no." Our manager marked tickets for long distance calls with his young daughter and I thought of my brother in Camp Blandering, Florida.

My life, like millions of others, changed, but we survived and tried to return to a life before Dec. 7, 1941.

In the 30 years preceding World War II, the United States had come to look to radio as a source of both news and entertainment. What should have been a pleasant Sunday of music and entertainment was suddenly interrupted by sinister news.

Just how remarkable was the impact of this news? Like a handful of major events—the assassination of President John F. Kennedy or the explosion of the space shuttle Challenger—*young or old, everyone who was around on December 7 can tell you with startling clarity exactly where they were and what they were doing. Pearl Harbor marked a major change in lifestyle for America.* **William H. Cameron** *of Nashville, Tennessee, tells what happened to him.*

I WAS ONLY EIGHT years old when the announcement came over the radio. Moments afterward, my father instructed my brother and I to go invite the neighbors who didn't own radios to our home so they could listen to the incoming reports.

Little did I realize this was the beginning of a new way of life for our entire family. Dad worked in Washington, DC as a welder and mother, who did not work, went to work for the War Department. We lived in the country, about 45 miles from Washington and it soon became apparent that my parents would have to room in the city because of the gas shortage.

A neighbor saw to my brothers and me and got us off to school and made sure we had food on the table.

I remember war ration books, air raid drills at school, dark shades hung over our windows that had to be pulled down each night and watching my mother put colored lotion on her legs to resemble nylons.

I grew up thankful for what we had and for being born in this great nation.

In 1941, radio was what cable television is to people today. For those who didn't own a radio, news was not always timely. **J. Oreo White** *of Kaplan, Louisiana, may be the ultimate example.*

I WAS CAMPED OUT in the marsh in a tent with an old trapper. We were there about a month when I met another old trapper one day and he started telling me the news. We had no radio and we had not seen anybody since we had been out in the marsh.

When he saw I did not know what he was talking about, he said, "Do you know that we are in war?"

That sure was a surprise to me. I served in the US Coast Guard 3 years and 9 months.

*Of course, Mr. White's example may have been a bit extreme. Other people's experiences, like that of **Ross Barbs** of Newburgh, Indiana, were more common.*

I WAS IN THE 5TH GRADE—we lived on a farm and had no radio. I didn't know about the war until I went to school the next day and the teacher told us. We were asking questions like, "Where is Pearl Harbor?" and "How come we don't hear bombs?"

*It's strange what people recall more than 50 years after the event. **Robert W. Gilliom** of Paoli, Indiana, remember a pair of soiled pants and his grandmother.*

I WAS SO EMBARRASSED a few minutes after hearing the radio announcement of the Pearl Harbor bombing.

This eight year old boy just knew his grandmother would not be listening to her radio, so I just had to run to her house and give her the news. Throwing caution to the wind, I raced down the snow-softened mud lane.

With her back door in sight, I lost my footing and executed a face-down slide.

Suddenly, I had two urgent missions: Inform Grandmother the Japs had bombed some unknown group of islands and explain the mud coating my prized corduroy knickers.

I knew my parents had sacrificed for those britches and soiling or damaging them was unthinkable.

Grandma and my parents somehow understood. Fortunately for everyone, both the United States and my britches survived their dastardly attacks.

*For those who received the word early, the day's normal activities were placed on the back burner. For **Mrs. Robert D. Wright's** father, that meant a special prayer service. Here's what the Venice, Florida, resident has to say.*

MY FAMILY had arisen early that morning, preparing for Sunday services at our local church. After hearing the tragic words of President Roosevelt delivered over the radio, we attended with heavy hearts, saddened and fearful for what our nation and the world might have to face in the days ahead.

My father, who was pastor of that church, led his congregation in a special prayer service that morning.

I was just 10 years old on that December morning and the following years would hold memories of the CC camp just down the road, of rationing stamps for gasoline, sugar and tire, of sons of our congregation being killed in battle, of Mother's cousin being killed in the Bataan Death March and of those small flags hanging in living room windows.

I shall never forget.

*For those families with draft-age members or with family members already in the service, the Pearl Harbor attack was devastating news. **Lois Sockol** of Needham, Massachusetts, recalls the shock the news of Pearl Harbor produced within her family.*

I WAS ONLY NINE years old, sitting with my family riveted to the radio listening to President Roosevelt's emotionally charged voice as he addressed the nation. My heart raced at his pronouncement of war and a weight of resounding fear and resentment was descending on us.

Mom's gasp echoed through the room as she turned toward her 19-year-old kid brother, my Uncle Jim.

Dad rose, put his arms around Mom and told her not to worry, that everything would be OK. Then he looked at my Uncle Jim and said, "Come on. We've got some talking to do."

But everything wasn't OK. All our lives were drastically changed and for me, that afternoon is frozen in time, sealed forever as the day of infamy.

*Sunday afternoons in 1941 were favorite times to attend the movies. But even here, there was no escaping the news, and again, the memories seem to be seared in the minds of those who witnessed the event. Like many other Americans, that's where **Norbert Zelinski** of Manitowoc, Wisconsin, first got the word.*

F IVE GUYS I "pal"ed around with went to a movie called "Tin Pan Alley." Now get this: This movie was centered around World War I.

On the way home, the newspaper boy was going by us on his bicycle and we hollered at him and asked him what's up?

He said there's a new edition out and something about the Japanese bombing a place called Pearl Harbor.

One of the guys in our gang asked, "Where in the hell is Pearl Harbor?"

Nobody knew and we walked on for about five minutes. Then I said, "Holy God! Lenny, my brother, is at Pearl Harbor. That's in the Hawaiian Islands." Lenny was a sea-going Marine.

As it turned out, he was on escort duty 500 miles south of Pearl Harbor when it was hit. But I never forgot this.

*People who didn't receive phone calls or have radios received the word in other ways. For **Donald B. Justice** of Lusby, Maryland, it meant an interruption to a Sunday routine.*

W E WERE GOING out to dinner on Sunday afternoon. My parents lived in Bethesda, Maryland at the time and we used to go to Harvey's Restaurant next door to the Mayflower Hotel every Sunday.

I can remember that Sunday as if it were yesterday. As usual, Dad drove down Wisconsin Avenue to Massachusetts Avenue, then onto Connecticut to DuPont Circle. There was a big traffic jam on Mass. Ave. at the Japanese Embassy and we wondered what it was all about.

After we got to the restaurant, some people came in after the ball game—the Redskins played the Giants that day and lost—and they had a portable radio with them. That's when we learned what the traffic jam was all about. Even though I was only seven, I somehow knew what it was all about.

*Instinctively, young marrieds, like **Irma M. Schwantes** of Fulda, Minnesota, knew that war meant they would be separated from their loved ones.*

I REMEMBER the chilling apprehension that tingled down my spine as the lady across the hall brought me the news of the Japanese attack.

My sister and I had been quietly visiting while her toddlers played at our feet and my five-month old daughter slept in a nearby crib.

Our husbands were involved in a weekly Sheephead card tournament at one of the taverns uptown. Before the war ended, both would be drafted and serve in the South Pacific. Our brothers and dear ones served in theaters of war throughout the world while at home, we stretched ration coupons and mended our silk stockings with nail polish.

The world shrank that infamous Sunday and life never again held that pre-war innocence.

*For the very young, like **William Dolan** of Owego, New York, war is a very hard thing to comprehend.*

THE ELDERLY PEOPLE were out in the streets, hugging and crying. I was too young to really understand that this was their way of sharing sorrow. They knew what was going to happen. They had lived through the horror of World War I and now it was happening again.

Many years later, at memorial services, I, too, quietly weep and the young child standing beside me wonders why.

***L. Everett Hawkes** of Windham, Maine, had just gotten out of the hospital that morning.*

I WAS 11 and had been in the hospital suffering from a strep infection in my right leg. I had gone through the rigors of exercise and rehabilitation that was so necessary to get me to walk again.

The day came when I was released and Dad drove me home that Sunday morning. After getting into bed and Mom had served me dinner, Dad asked if I would like my radio on to see if one of our favorite Sunday afternoon adventure shows might be on.

Ten minutes into the broadcast, a special bulletin was announced—the attack on Pearl Harbor was announced!

This, to me, will always be a day that will "live in infamy."

*A bottle of milk and a newspaper hawker's message that changed the world—that's what **Robert G. Olson** of Park Hill, Oklahoma, experienced in Chicago that morning.*

I T WAS A BEAUTIFUL SUNDAY, the sunshine was warm as I took my morning walk to the neighborhood store for the Sunday Chicago Tribune and a bottle of milk. Crossing 12th and Wrightwood Avenue, the world exploded with a shouting newsboy's "Extra! Extra! Japs bomb Pearl Harbor."

That was instantly followed by, "Sneak attack kills thousands of Americans. Pacific fleet destroyed!"

The news was impossible to believe. Not the United States of America, my country, my friends, my relatives among the civilian and service personnel. My Uncle Jiggs was a 19-year-old seaman aboard the battleship Arizona.

I bought a newspaper and rushed into the little grocery store. A radio on the countertop confirmed every word. Stunned and angered, my heart, soul and guts were cold with aching pain. Nothing would ever be the same and it was the first scar I was to carry from World War II.

The sheer brutality of the attack enraged and stunned the nation. As more and more people heard the news, crowds began to form. **A.G. McCallion** *of New York City witnessed what happened that morning in the "Big Apple."*

I WAS 15 and I remember the masses of men milling about the New York Times building watching the sign report the damage and casualties of Pearl Harbor. It was my second year of high school and every Sunday my friend Bob Burns and I would usually go from the Bronx to 42nd Street to catch a movie and a couple hot dogs.

When we came out of the Robert Taylor picture about a Navy flier and the military and saw the crowds and heard the comments, we were overwhelmed. The men were yelling, "We'll kill them bastards!" and "It'll be over in four weeks." and all kinds of comments.

Needless to say, it was four years and not four weeks. Bob Burns would enlist in the Marines in 1943 and I in the Coast Guard. We would both be 17.

We would win the war, but somehow, I felt we lost the peace. Often, I think the sacrifices that were made of necessity, though not in vain, were a higher order, culling the ranks of America's youth.

In an instant, all things familiar seemed to have disappeared, including people you took for granted as part of your everyday life, according to **Thomas R. Atkinson Sr.** *of Lakeville, Pennsylvania.*

I HAD GONE to the movies with my mother and father. Ten minutes into the film, the manager announced the Pearl Harbor news and that the United States was at war.

A few minutes later, Mother literally yelled at my father, "Ralph, that was real. We are at war!"

I don't remember what was playing, only my mother's shocked realization that the announcement was not part of the movie. I would soon learn what war meant as teachers, firemen, policemen, the milkman and other people you get to know so well went off to fight. . . . and so many who would not come back to deliver our milk or respond to fires anymore.

*For those with loved ones overseas, like **Jewel Brown** of Anna, Texas, the announcement of war was especially hard.*

I WOKE UP Sunday morning and turned on the radio. Instead of my regular program, I heard the very distinctive voice of President Roosevelt. Needless to say, his announcement captivated my attention and I called out to my mother. We both listened in horror and disbelief as he described the attack on Pearl Harbor and Midway Island. My only brother, a Marine, was stationed on Midway.

It took a month for us to receive any word from him.

*In spite of the war clouds on the horizon, some things, like having a baby, still went on. But even births were affected that day, says **Patricia P. Garate** of Beowawe, Nevada.*

A LL DAY, the radio blared the war news. At the same time, my uncle's sister-in-law was trying to have her baby.

I was 11 years old and my job was to keep the little kids away from the window while ideas of the stork were dispelled once and for all.

The doctor had to travel 20 miles from Alturas to Likely, California, and he just wasn't showing. Finally, my mom and Mrs. Olsen delivered the baby.

When the doctor did arrive, he was so drunk he could only drink coffee and curse the Japanese.

*According to **Carlton B. Sprague Sr.** of Island Pond, Vermont, everyone was affected in some way.*

I WORKED in a dairy and on Sunday morning, my boss came in screaming about Japs and thousands killed and our Navy destroyed.

I've never seen anything like it before or since. The whole country was red-hot mad! Boys 16 and younger were lying about their age to get into the service. Some made it, others were caught and sent home. Of course, at 18 you were drafted. Older men also lied about their age and more often than not, it worked.

Those who couldn't serve quickly got into defense work. People were so upset and angry, they all wanted to be part of the "great effort."

We'd been caught with our defenses down. The car pool was born and quiet nights were no more.

*War came, and with it, those stars in the windows, recalls **Veda Du-Clos** of Prairie du Rochet, Illinois.*

I WAS SITTING in a '39 Ford, stuck in the mud, when we heard the news. By January, the first of three uncles I had been raised with was called up. All three were like brothers to me and we placed the banner with the little blue star in our window that showed we had someone in the service. Gold stars were for families with a deceased soldier, and we would eventually have it in our window.

Some Americans had grown up with Japanese children for playmates, like **Bayard T. Read** *of Brunswick, Maine. For people like him, the news was especially incredible.*

DURING MY HIGH SCHOOL YEARS, I lived at Ft. Kamehameha, Hawaii at the entrance channel to Pearl Harbor. I attended Roosevelt High School with a mix of Caucasian, Oriental, Filipino and Hawaiian students. My family had a Japanese cook and used to joke that she was a spy because she liked to watch the battleships and cruisers enter and exit the harbor.

Six years later, I was a student at Duke University when news reached us that the Japanese had attacked my old playground.

It seemed so foolhardy of the Japanese, and so unlike those with whom I had competed and against in high school. Four years later, I would walk into Tokyo still wondering why.

Chapter 5
In Uniform

Anger turned to action. By early Monday morning, every military re-cruiting center in the country was swamped with volunteers. The Milwau-kee Sentinel *reported that 457 men showed up at the Marine recruiting station alone.* **William A. Schoewe** *of Milton, Florida, may have been one of them.*

JIM, A HIGH SCHOOL CHUM and I were playing catch with a foot-ball on the school grounds across from where he lived. It was a pleas-ant, clear day, not too cold for a day early in December in Milwaukee, Wisconsin.

When we tired of playing catch, we decided to go back to Jim's house for lunch. It was after we'd finished eating that Jim's mom turned on the radio and we heard the news.

My thoughts turned from extreme anger to great concern for my sister's boyfriend, who was in the Navy and attached to the Pacific fleet. (We found out later that, though his ship had been in port, it did not suf-fer any damage.)

I was enraged, wondering what I could do to even the score. I left Jim's house to go home and find out if my parents had heard the terrible news, wondering how my sister would react. The rest of the day was spent lis-tening to the radio, my sister teary-eyed, not knowing if her boyfriend was hurt or killed.

I spent a sleepless night. The next morning, a school day, I met Jim on the way to school. We talked of the possibility of war and I could tell by the look on Jim's face that he, too, was thinking, "Let's join the Navy."

We had entertained this thought all summer long, but our parents wanted us to finish high school first. Would they understand? Since we were not quite 18, we needed our parents' consent.

Instead of continuing on to school, we headed downtown to the Navy recruiting office. It was packed with men with the same intentions. The day was spent signing papers, taking tests and submitting to a prelimi-nary physical. On my way home, my mind was filled with one thought: Would my parents sign?

After supper, my father said to me, "Son, if this is what you want to do, then I will sign for you. I know that we are going to be at war very soon and I am too old to go. The least I can do for our country is to let you go in my place and pray for your safe return."

I kissed him and thanked him, for in my heart, I knew this was the right thing to do.

While the attack on Pearl Harbor would eventually have major effects on families and friends throughout the world, perhaps those who felt the most immediate impact, other than those who were at Pearl Harbor that morning, were the men who were already in the service. Before December 7, draftees could expect to work for Uncle Sam for a one-year hitch. **Howard F. Wiseman** *of Dauphin, Pennsylvania, was one of them.*

I WAS DRAFTED on May 13, 1941, sent to Ft. Meade, Md., assigned to an anti-tank company and sent to two communications schools.

We were coming back from maneuvers and had stopped at Black Hills, Va. for dinner. While sitting in the command care with my SCR245, copying the news that came across the wireless in the dit-dah's of Morse Code, anxious buddies gathered around to learn of happenings.

Alas! Came over the wireless "Pearl Harbor bombed."

I said, "Call the company."

"Aw, there's nothing to it. . . ." Remember that one year hitch? Well, it ended four years later.

Leonard A. Krashefski *of Moodus, Connecticut, was another who found his plans disrupted.*

I WAS INDUCTED in April of 1941 and eventually wound up at Ft. Ethan Allen, Vermont. After North Carolina maneuvers in late Fall of '41, we were back at Ethan Allen and it was about this time that inductees over the age of 29 were being discharged. My brother had already received his discharge and was home.

That Sunday after Mass I was writing a letter home telling the folks how much I was looking forward to getting home in the next few days. Just about that time the news flash came in on the radio: Pearl Harbor.

I arrived home four years and six months later.

Often, fate would play a role in a person's future, as it did with **Earl D. Bell** *of Hartford City, Indiana.*

I VOLUNTEERED for the one-year draft in 1940 and was accepted November 20, 1940. On Nov. 20, 1941, we had been on maneuvers in Louisiana and North Carolina, but they wouldn't let me out until we returned to Ft. Knox.

The day we got back to Ft. Knox, the Japs bombed Pearl Harbor and I didn't get out until June 15, 1945.

But the draft was not the overriding concern of many of the active duty *military. For them, when the news came, it meant an immediate and often drastic change in lifestyle. In those first few hours, confusion and disbelief were rampant. That's how **Joseph R. Sadow** of Tacoma, Washington, tells it.*

I WAS ON LIBERTY in Portland, Ore. and flying with my wife, who had a private pilot's license. After landing and on our way home in the car, the radio reported the Pearl Harbor news. I tried to call a shipmate I'd ridden down with, but he was already gone.

I took the bus to Seattle where my ship was, but it was gone and the Navy OD officer told me to go to the Coast Guard base at Port Angeles and wait there for it.

She came in on a "slow bell." She had only one boiler in use. They were rebricking the other boiler and had not finished working on it when the Pearl Harbor news reached them.

__James E. Knight__ of Brunswick, Maine, was the one who broke the news to his commanding officer.

I WAS ON DUTY in the Philadelphia Navy Yard in the radio lab. I serviced the ECM coding machines used by the Navy. I had the radio turned on when I heard the Japs had bombed Pearl Harbor and I called my commander, Lt. Cmdr. Gustoff, and asked him if his radio was on.

He said, "Why?" and when I told him the news, was he surprised.

Of course, it does help if you know where Pearl Harbor is, according to **Eugene E. Plank** *of Honolulu, Hawaii.*

I WAS A COOK'S INSTRUCTOR stationed at Ft. Belvoir, Virginia. We had served dinner and were relaxing for a few minutes when the radio blasted the news of Pearl Harbor.

We weren't particularly impressed. But a few minutes later, a sergeant burst into the mess hall shouting, "Did you guys hear Pearl Harbor has been bombed?"

Someone called out, "Where the hell is Pearl Harbor?"

When he explained it was Honolulu, a hush fell over the group as we began to understand what this meant.

__Peter Karetka__ of Chicopee, Massachusetts, and the men aboard his ship had a close call within hours of the Pearl Harbor announcement.

THE DESTROYER USS HUGHES was anchored outside Portland, Me. when the boatswains mate went through the ship piping all hands to the after mess hall. While assembled there, the executive officer arrived holding several manuals.

He took a good, long puff on his pipe, then said, "Gentlemen, we are now at war with Japan."

It made one's hair stand on end.

He told the boatswain to post an armed guard on the fan tail and the forecastle with live ammunition as a stunned silence fell over the crew.

We sailed for Boston that evening and were greeted with a three letter challenge for identity. There was nobody on the bridge available to respond. Then came the bellow from the bridge.

"Damn it, get a signalman to respond or we'll get blown out of the water!" Response was quick.

It would not take long before GIs learned who possessed leadership and who did not, as **Arthur V. Bornn** *of Victoria, Texas, describes.*

WE HAD THE OLD B-18 bombers at Coolidge Field, Antigua, British West Indies, where I was an enlisted radio operator/gunner. The peace of that lovely and historic Caribbean island was shattered on December 7.

I was in my barracks and a young lieutenant came rushing through the building shouting hysterically that the Japs had attacked Pearl Harbor. A seasoned sergeant had to forcibly quiet and eject the young officer, who was out of control. The sergeant feared the effect this "seven-day-wonder" would have on the rest of his young troops.

Like many others, **Robert F. Ellis** *of Nashua, New Hampshire, can recall what movie he was watching that day, but it would be many years before he could tell anyone how it ended.*

I WAS A MARINE stationed at the Philadelphia Navy Yard when war broke out. I was uptown in a movie house watching "Sundown" starring Gene Tierney and George Sanders when the manager of the theater stopped the movie and got up on the stage.

He said, "All servicemen are to report to their stations right away. Japan just attacked Pearl Harbor."

It would be 30 years later, on the late, late show, before I got to see the parts of "Sundown" I missed.

Seemingly within hours, a wave of patriotism and nationalism galvanized the country. And that spirit would have a terrific effect on things to come. A sampling of that spirit is shown in the experience of Brookfield, Wisconsin, resident **William M. Pokrass.**

I WAS A MEMBER of the "Red Arrow" Infantry Division of the Wisconsin National Guard. I had been activated a year earlier and sent to Louisiana to train. Sunday night, I was attending a play at Alexandria High School with two buddies when the Pearl Harbor attack was announced. All the military personnel were ordered back to camp.

As we left, the entire audience stood and applauded!

The events of that day changed my life forever, but that moment of intense patriotism in a high school gym would sustain me through the hazards of three years in the Pacific.

*The war would have its effect on everyone, young, old, famous or unknown. To the credit of the military, once the hammer fell, it was quick to respond as **Charles Lucas** of Detroit, Michigan, can verify.*

O N DEC. 5, 1941, I was stationed at Ft. Bliss, Texas. About 10 of our draftees were over 28 years of age, married and had children. They were sent home leaving us short on manpower.

I was a 22 year-old staff sergeant who knew everything, so on Sunday, a group of us decided to visit Mexico. As we dressed, the musical program on my radio was interrupted by a hysterical radio announcer who was shouting that Japan had attacked Pearl Harbor.

By 3 p.m. we were on a troop train. We wound up on the HMS Queen Elizabeth bound for Sydney, Australia.

Our 28-year-olds rejoined us and the unit completed its basic training on the Queen.

*Of course, the draft wasn't always perfect, and war, as **Joe R. Hardy** of Ft. Worth, Texas, will tell you, changes things considerably.*

I WAS IN THE NATIONAL GUARD of the US Army, but they discharged me, saying that I was unfit for military service. I went to the draft board, they examined me and they, too, declared me unfit for military service.

When Pearl Harbor was hit by the Japs, I was sent a draft card and I reported to the draft board. They ask me if I felt like I was fit for service and when I replied yes, they said I was A-1 and drafted me. I was as an ambulance driver for the duration of the war.

A.F. Munk *of Baltimore, Maryland, has an economy of words.*

I VOLUNTEERED for the Army on March 19, 1941 for one year. I came out 4 years later.

*For green recruits, like **Raymond L.H. Menker Jr.** of Dayton, Ohio, the service was full of surprises, not all of them war-related.*

O UR TORPEDO GROUP was shipped to Oahu, Hawaii, to be assigned Pacific theater duties. Five of us were told we were to be stationed on the USS Ford Island, and I thought, "Great! We got a ship."

But when we asked where she was tied up, the fellow said, "See that ferry boat? See that island in the center of Pearl Harbor? That island is the USS Ford Island."

In spite of repeated efforts to be reassigned to a real ship, I wound up with two years' duty "aboard" the USS Ford Island.

Jasper "Jeep" Camarata *of Souderton, Pennsylvania, was about as green as green can get when he signed up.*

W HEN I WAS READY to be sworn in, I was asked to do a chore by an acting PFC. I declined, as I had not yet raised my hand to be sworn in. "I cannot make you do this," he retorted, "but you will be sorry later!"

Needless to say after washing what seemed to be, three million stainless trays, I learned to obey and respect authority.

__Ralph A. Casperson__ of Niles, Michigan, didn't have any problem finding his post, but apparently others did.

I WAS ASSIGNED to Camp Roberts and was walking guard on a post manned only when the camp was on alert. Because this guard post was manned infrequently, I was forgotten when the other guards were relieved. When the roll call was taken I was missing. A search of the camp was unsuccessful, but at last the sergeant of the guard remembered the special guard post.

He and the officer of the guard walked up the hill where I was still walking my post in a military manner. I was properly relieved in accordance with the fifth general guard order, "To quit my post only when properly relieved."

The officer asked me how long I would have stayed on my post had I not been relieved. I, remembering our terms of enlistment, replied, "For the duration and six months, Sir."

Then again, __Frank Mace__ of Providence, Rhode Island, learned a valuable lesson about volunteering in 1941.

I WAS WAITING for my discharge. I had volunteered for the draft for one year. Beginning November 20, 1940, I was in the Army. While waiting for my discharge papers in 1941, the war broke out and four years, nine months and 21 days later I finally got my discharge.

I have never again volunteered for anything.

For a young soldier, the simple separation from loved ones and the stress of not knowing can be traumatic. Some, like __Martin G. Freim__ of Zephyr Cove, Nevada, were lucky. They had someone to guide them.

EARLY RECRUIT DAYS in the 1st Bomb Wing, March Field, GA, in 1941, were exciting and a bit stressful to a young farm boy from South Dakota.

An "Old Soldier" by the name of Bartnick, sensitive to my anxieties, guided me in those early days. The advice he gave me then, guided my life through the war years, and still does to this day.

He told me, "Do your job well, don't worry, and everything will be alright."

Many months later, I saw a "Pathe" news story of wounded and repatriated Air Corps Personnel. One of those repatriated soldiers coming down the ship's gang plank, in a wheel chair, I'm quite certain, was Bartnick and Bartnick was smiling as he usually was.

*While most of us would think of the pain and sacrifice of the young people that always fight our wars, some, like **Howard L. Buse** of Hershey, Pennsylvania, recalled the pain of his parents.*

I REMEMBER THE NIGHT before I was to go and be inducted into the Army at Fort Snelling Army Camp in Minnesota.

I was never away from home so this made me very sad, to see my mother and father show that great sacrifice they were about to make. To see their son off to war was surely a memory I shall never forget. I know I went to fight in a war and if had to be give my life for my country.

But we must always remember our father and mother also made that big sacrifice for their country. It may have been in a different way, but just as great as our fighting men and women.

*No parent who has ever sent a son or daughter off to war has to be told how difficult this was to do. **Edward Rosmarin** of West Hartford, Connecticut, remembers his father's pain.*

MY FATHER was a Vet of WWI, 77th Div. My brother a vet of World War II, also of 77th. So our family knows of the military.

I enlisted in the Navy as a kid of 17 years of age. After 5 weeks of boot camp, I shipped out to the South Pacific for a tour of duty. After a year or so, I was sent back to the States for a new construction assignment and a 30 day leave. My leave went quickly and little did I realize till then how much I loved family and home.

The day came for me to leave and go back to active duty. My dad accompanied me to Grand Central Station and as I entered the gate, I looked back for a wave and my last good-bye.

There, in the great crowd of the station stood my dad, tears flowing down his cheeks.

To this day, I can still see that scene, my Dad showing in his own way, the love that can only come in such times.

*Of course, love takes many forms. **Sirl Myhand** of Orleans, California, would find a lifetime cure for loneliness.*

IN EARLY 1942 I was a sailor and a patient in the Naval Hospital at San Diego, California, due to an injury I received while stationed at the Naval Air Station on North Island.

In the hospital I met Elza Edwards, another sailor who had been injured aboard his ship. One day Elza asked me if I would like some good "home cooked" food. Naturally I said yes, since we all know that GI food gets a little monotonous after awhile.

So, Elza told me there was a family now living in San Diego from his hometown of Plains, Montana, that had a daughter named Dorothy who was in his grade all through high school and the following Sunday we had some fine home cooking at these folks home.

That is how I met Dorothy, my wife now for 48 years.

But it would be four long years before anyone really had anything to really smile about.

Chapter 6
War Comes to the Young

*All across the country, radios were tuned in classrooms while an anxious nation listened with growing anger and concern as the President addressed Congress and the American people. For some, like **Gordon F. DeHart** of Aurora, Illinois, the simple act of volunteering to stay in the classroom that day would be indelibly imprinted in his memory.*

I RAISED MY HAND in a grade school class with two or three other students to volunteer to stay in class to listen to a noon radio broadcast. The teacher said something to the effect that it would be an important event. I was curious enough to raise my hand and did not go to lunch. Instead, I listened to the radio.

I heard President Roosevelt speak and the Congress declare War. I have many memories of WORLD WAR II, but somehow that noon December 8, 1941, live radio broadcast sticks most in my mind.

*War carries an impact that affects young and old alike. After more than half a century, children of the '40s, like **Carmen Olson-Foust** of Booneville, Arkansas, remember those days as affecting and directing their life in later years.*

I WOULD SIT QUIETLY beside my grandfather, listening to radio war news, with our three starred window flag hanging nearby, and standing at attention with him when the National Anthem played.

My grandfather instilled patriotism and love of country so deeply in me that I enlisted in the US Marine Corps for the Korean War.

*An era, a way of life, and one person's effect on a young mind. The entire country, seemingly, caught the spirit, like **Mary Farmer**, now of Leesburg, Florida, who still remembers what it was like.*

O N THE MORNING of Dec. 8 our high school class assembled in the auditorium to hear President Roosevelt address the nation. A chill went through us as we heard his voice ring out, "a day in infamy" and "we are at war."

By our June '42 graduation, of the 10 classmates who had rushed to enlist, two were killed in action.

I joined soon after in the WAC following after my brothers and cousins already in uniform.

In our town, Perth Amboy, New Jersey (population 38,000) 6,000 men and women were in armed services for that war. Our casualty rate was 163 dead, of them 87 graduates during the war's four years.

*For those Americans already over the age of 18 who were attending college, like **Jack B. Morris** of Cape Coral, Florida, the morning of Dec. 8, 1941, would alter the course of their lives forever.*

M ANY OF US had gone home for the weekend. Returning to college on Monday, December 8, we were informed that a convocation for all male students was the initial item of activity that day.

The president of the college spoke to us, advising not to do anything rash, be patient, and that we would be advised when the government needed our services. He then excused us from classes to hear President Roosevelt's message to Congress. We retired to our rooms in the fraternity houses and dormitories anticipating that we were to hear "a declaration of war." When we emerged from our rooms, there were few dry eyes and many questions in our minds.

Who would go?

Who would come back?

How long and when?

Would we be effective in helping direct changes in the world we then knew?

*Effective in directing changes in the world? Yes, that would prove correct. But it would be many years before the enormity of this conflict could be appreciated. For people who were born after World War II, their memories of a time they were nine years old are almost certainly very different from those of Brooklyn, New York's **Tom Knapp.***

I WAS YOUNG. We were sheltered from the realities to an extent, but the concept of war filtered through. The gold stars hung in shade drawn windows, the blackout curtains. The air raid drills in school, where we sat in the halls and sang, "God Bless America".

Karl, my 3rd grade classmate, whose mother, a German immigrant, cried with happiness for her son's being here.

The endless passing of uniforms who returned a 9 year old's salutes as they went off to far places, perhaps not to return. To know and do their duty to our country.

The party for cousin Jon McCambridge who came home on crutches.

And the flags! Everywhere on every holiday—the Flag flew as it does no more. Indeed we need the flag again, it starts at home. That's America—Home!

*In this modern age of Nintendo and MTV, many kids still complain about being bored. This did not seem to be the case with the kids of the war years, as **Kathryn David** of Sandusky, Ohio, describes.*

I SAW THE WAR through the eyes of a grade school child.

I eagerly participated in paper drives, where all my comic books went, scrap drives, piling all that scrap on our school playground, buying savings stamps each week in school, one or two 10-cent stamps at a time, then proudly redeeming my full book for a war bond.

Rationing: long lines, coupon books, recipes without sugar, meatless Tuesdays and Thursdays. Grocery shopping, my folks never complained, because they were TRUE AMERICANS.

My pride in our large victory garden. Writing letters often to our five relatives overseas, and the V-Mail I received, which I still have. Oh yes, a little girl, grown-up, remembers World War II very well.

*And another school kid of the 40s, **Lester B. Abbott** of Somerset, Kentucky, tells about those busy years.*

SCRAP METAL was collected and stored from corner to corner of the one-acre school yard surrounding our one-room country school (enrollment approx. 35) deep in the hills of southeastern Kentucky.

Each of us had diligently and enthusiastically done our part to help "OUR BOYS AT THE FRONT". Everyone of us seemed to have at least one close relative; uncle, cousin or brother fighting in Africa, Europe or the Pacific.

This was a very personal war. For a month we had spent every spare minute scrounging for and bringing in every old buggy wheel, shackle line rod, abandoned oil well power unit, old stove, piece of pipe or miscellaneous scrap of metal.

As the County Superintendent presented our school the award for the most scrap collected in the county, as a 9 year old, I saw myself, personally delivering every ton of it to the factory in Detroit to be reformed into airplanes and tanks.

*A personal war, indeed, but the price would be enormously high. **James F. Hawkins** of Fresno, California, tells of what came next.*

ON SUNDAY NIGHT December 7, 1941, I was a 9 year old, and my family and I were listening to the radio. The Jack Benny program was on when the announcement was made that Pearl Harbor had been attacked by the Japanese.

I remember that we were sad and angry at the same time. I also remember watching the front page of the Chattanooga Times every day for enemy and friendly progress. My home town of Summerville, Georgia (population Approx. 2,000 at that time), lost most of the men 18-38 years of age to the war effort.

My dad was a rural letter carrier and was allowed to purchase an early 1942 model car and tires whenever he needed them.

Imagine being able to get tires whenever you needed them. Rationing did not happen all at once, but lifelong habits would develop because of rationing. Today, in the age of synthetics and giant shopping complexes, the idea of being "allowed" to buy a car or tires seems very strange, but almost immediately after war was declared, the phenomenon of rationing was put in place.

It wasn't so much that the United States was not the land of plenty, but rather that peacetime industries were converting from peacetime production to the war machine. And shipping—especially for products that had to come from locales outside of the United States—was becoming very chancy. In addition, some items would, indeed, become scarce.

*It takes an enormous amount of metal to build machines of war. And there was a special feeling of accomplishment and camaraderie for being a part of the war effort. Young, old, men, women, and even children, all were affected. And children like **Tom Davenport** of Bellevue, Ohio, who must have been only about 7 years old, learned young. In Tom's case, his experiences would last him a lifetime.*

M Y THIRD GRADE CLASS in Castalia, Ohio, walked to Resthaven Wildlife Area and picked milkweed pods for naval aviators life jackets when we learned they were short of Kapok. I rode my bike on an 8 mile paper route and trapped mink, muskrat and 'coon.

By 1943, my friends and I were drawing US and Nazi aircraft in combat. This last experience evidently stuck. March 1951 at 17 I joined Co. B Fremont 34th Infantry and to this day 50 years later I draw and design for military.

One more thing, from the first, I was very aware of the selfless sacrifice the men and women who fought World War II made for us all. If there was a lasting lesson the 1941 American GI leaves with us, it is that self government only works with self discipline.

If we can remember that and MacArthur's "Duty, honor, country," we have a shot at surviving the 21st century.

*Another youth at that time, **Alexander M. Rackiewicz** of Greensboro, North Carolina, tells of his persistence to help the war effort.*

I PARTICIPATED in grammar school in the scrap metal drive for National Defense. In less than one year I collected 30 plus pounds of cigarette wrapper paper, I turned into a ball every day. The school got money for needs.

*Sometimes students themselves earned money from the scrap drives. So, what did they spend it on? Columbus, Ohio's **Betty Sekerak** recounts how she spent hers.*

STUDENTS from our small country school would gather burlap bags of milkweed pods from which the inner filling was used to fill life jackets.

We also purchased at our school each week, 25-cent savings stamps that we placed in a bond book and when it was filled we turned it in for a $25.00 war bond.

We were proud to do our part for the war effort.

That pride would carry over in future years and sustain the United States through other wars and hardships. Yet, these were not easy times, especially for children. Blackout was a new word on everyone's lips. In 1942, no one knew if or when the enemy might actually strike on American soil. **Mildred Smith Hathaway** *of Edgartown, Massachusetts, shared a fear that was probably common to all children of that era.*

I WAS ABOUT 10 YEARS OLD, living in the city. Our front room window had a banner in it with a star—my father was somewhere overseas in Europe. I recall going to the grocery store with my mother and her using little tokens for coffee, butter and sugar.

One hot summer night the air-raid sirens went off. I remember my mother going to all the windows and pulling down black shades—going outside and see search lights light up the sky.

I had on a white pinafore and I asked my mother if they (the airplanes) could see me because of it.

Today, it's chilling to think a small child could worry about bombers seeing her white pinafore, but as **Walton E. Wells** *of Arivaca, Arizona, points out, those childhood fears were very real, and the news media did not help allay them.*

WINTER OF 1942, Viola, a small town in northern Idaho. Here was a small boy glued to the radio news broadcasts. The news was not very good for the allies. It seems that Hitler had his armies moving everywhere. However, the place of most concern was the advance on Moscow.

I was that small boy and I was sure that the end was near as I had visions of white clad troops slowly advancing on through the snow covered fields of northern Idaho, killing men, women and children in their path.

Gosh, just about everyone knew that Viola was only 9 miles from Moscow and the radio said that the German soldiers were in the outskirts of Moscow!

Finally, I gathered up enough courage to ask my folks about these fears and to my relief was told that the Moscow that was on the news was on the other side of the world.

The thought of little girls wondering if enemy aircraft could see to bomb her in her pinafore and little boys worrying about Nazi troops nine miles down the road would make modern-day child psychologists cringe. Yet, *like Ravenel, South Carolina, resident **Betty L. Simmons**, these are all part and parcel of the times. This is what she remembers.*

THE NIGHTMARES of incendiary bombs burning everything around me.

Headlights on cars painted half way down, black.

Dad was a civilian in Civil Engineers, so I remember activity on base, especially being invited to Thanksgiving and Christmas in the mess hall where we enjoyed foods and treats we were unable to afford or could not get due to rationing.

Mom and my aunts taking jobs to replace a man, in railroad yards and the shipyard. Seen through the eyes of a 10 year old. These recollections brought a flood of memories for me. Most happy and a few troublesome.

James R. Jorgensen still lives in Sioux Falls, South Dakota, but he remembers a train ride.

I WAS 8 YEARS OLD, when my mother and I took a train from Sioux Falls to Oakland, California to join my father, who was in the Seabees.

On the train from Omaha, it was packed, some sitting in the aisle. I gave my seat to a sailor with one leg missing, and I spent most of the trip in the luggage rack, above everyone else.

We shared our large packed lunch with several. I remember it was very well received, as it was put together by my grandmother on the farm.

When we reached Oakland I saw my Dad in a sea of white hats, but Mom said, "We'll go to the downtown station."

Dad beat us downtown, somehow. What a great reunion.

*War has been romanticized by writers, television, movies, and more. It's unsurprising that girls like Aberdeen, Mississippi's **Sarah Peugh** would get stars in their eyes.*

AFTER PRESIDENT FRANKLIN DELANO ROOSEVELT declared war December 7, 1941, everyone had a spirit of nationalism. I was in the cafeteria at college—17 years old, a country girl who'd never had seen a soldier—when the announcement was made.

The excitement of war, enhanced with soldiers in creased uniforms made the situation romantic. I was swept off my feet. I quit college and married the first Army private who asked me, a mistake ending in divorce.

I worked at different USOs where I lived. During this time my second husband-to-be, an Air Force Sergeant, was flying 20 heavy sortie strikes in the South Pacific, receiving many metals.

We married in 1947.

Dorothy Shannon of Clinton, Indiana, experienced something that many in this new, mobile America would share.

I WAS A TEENAGER when we moved to the South side of Chicago (Mayor Dailey's) neighborhood from the country. Before we came to town, we didn't have electricity or indoor plumbing. We were the butt of a lot of Hick-from-the-sticks jokes, but for the first time we had a little money.

My favorite memory was the Englewood neighborhood Block Parties. Flowers were planted on a designated corner and a billboard with all the servicemen's names on it was erected. Then a big party in the street was held to honor the men.

The street was closed for dancing and celebrating like one big family, very united.

I also remember watching flags in the windows with blue stars for each man in service. Some homes had several stars. Sometimes they changed to gold. This always made me sad.

Victory gardens, war bonds, loose lips—these small phrases are enough to evoke memories in those who lived through the trying times. **Norman A. Richards** *of Fort Wayne, Indiana, remembers how everything changed so fast.*

I RECALL how quickly we learned the location of Pearl Harbor and immediately resolved to win at any cost. How fast we mobilized and all pitched in with paper and scrap drives. The shortages which called for rationing and the many bond drives. Our Victory Garden. The blackouts and walking with my father, the Civil Defense Block Warden.

As the war dragged on, we wondered if it will ever end?

And I recall the horrible news of a friend missing or killed in action and how everyone listened to the news on the radio and read the newspaper accounts of the major battles.

And I remember how proud we were of the servicemen wearing their uniforms when they came home on their last leave and the flag waving and patriotism of us all in one common cause.

Finally, I remember hearing my mother cry when letters to our family in France were returned "NOT DELIVERABLE".

Perhaps it sounds naive, but being unable to join the military was a crushing blow to many. When turned away, some, like **Michael Rusinich** *of Queens, New York, found other ways to serve until they could get in.*

I WENT DOWN to my Army Recruiting Center and they told me I could not join up because I was too young. They said that I had to get my father's permission, but my father would not give me his consent, so what could I do now.

The next day I read in the Daily News, there was a great shortage of rubber in the United States. I lived in Bay Ridge, Brooklyn at the time of the war and there was a United States Armory near where I lived. I went down there one day and asked to see the captain in charge.

I said, "Captain, is it true that the United States is short on rubber?" and the captain said yes. "Captain," I said, "I am going home to get my wagon and I will get you some of that rubber. Is it all right if I bring all this rubber to your Armory?"

"Son," the Captain said, "that's a great idea."

So, I went with my wagon door to door and asked the people for any type of rubber which they can't use. To my surprise, those people helped me out. They ask why I wanted this rubber. I said, "It was the war effort. I am taking all this rubber to the United States Armory here in Bay Ridge."

I got old rain coats, rubber gloves, hot water bottles, old bicycle tires, rubber mats and I brought all these things to the armory. Then I took my wagon to some empty lots in the neighborhood and a lot of old rubber tires were all over the place and I took these to the armory, too.

The Captain said, "Bless you. You're doing your country a great service."

A year and a half later I went into the United States Air Force and served until 1946.

Rationing, saving, contributing to the war effort—these would all become common catch-phrases in the United States in the early '40s. And, as **Barbara R. Douglas** *of Emerson, Iowa, describes, the sight of uniforms became very common.*

I REMEMBER saving cooking grease, paper bags for reuse, planting a victory garden, buying saving stamps at the post office, collecting milkweed pods for life jackets in a countywide competition between country schools and how the war came alive as we sat with friends in the movie theater watching for a glimpse of husbands and fathers in the news reels.

One memory is standing in the steel yard and silently watching the soldier daily exercising his dog. The dust puffed with each step and the soldier cautioned us to be quiet as they passed. This team was a paratrooper home on leave with his constant companion, a German Shepherd jumper. We knew the dog was highly trained and he was doing his part to end this war. We certainly didn't want the dog to attack us as the enemy. So, no running, jumping, screaming or teasing this four-footed friend.

I will never forget the silence on Main Street of our town when the ladder and paint were carried to a large sign on the wall of the local grocery store. Everyone watched in reverence. Had another young man joined the service of his country? Some even cutting short their education to end this war. Or was there to be sadness in another neighbor's home as a star was added beside a present name on the list?

Every serviceman became "our boy" lost when the stars were added. Every town lost but we wanted the world to gain peace.

*In some cases, a "curtailed education" might have been an understatement, as **Luther J. Jarrett** of St. Alban's, West Virginia, describes.*

W HEN WORLD WAR II STARTED I was only 15 years old. So, I lied about my age and went to work in shipyard in Portsmouth, Virginia. I came back at 16, lied about my age again and went into the Navy during World War II. I felt I wanted to do my part in the worse way, and I hope I did my best, while serving in the Navy.

I had a brother in the Battle of Bulge, and a brother in the Marine Corps. I am sure my brothers and I felt we were doing a good thing for our country.

*America was mobilizing. Men and women who'd never been more than a few miles away from home were traveling across country to military bases and duty stations and debarkation depots. Children like **Raymond E. Kalthoff** of Marshall, Missouri, were caught up in the excitement.*

M Y MOST VIVID MEMORY of World War II is of troop trains passing our home. As kids my two brothers, my sister and I would run out to the front fence at the sight of a troop train coming and yell, jump and wave at the "boys" who mom had told us were going to war.

Many of the men waved at the rag-tag three of us and often threw out paper plates with hellos or their home towns written on them. We thought this was great.

We were quite young and did not really understand the war or its implications but would hope that some of the men who passed were cheered by the smiling, laughing children who, in their own way, saluted them in appreciation.

We lost one uncle of six who perhaps rode troop trains much like the ones which passed our house.

*We lost one uncle. . . . Such simple words to describe a loss that, especially for the very young like **Marilyn Lane Wagner** of Columbus, Ohio, was at the time, would continue to cause trauma and pain for the rest of their lives.*

W HEN THE WAR BROKE OUT, we were living near Washington, D.C. I was only 6, when a letter arrived. My mother cried. My father said be good and help your mother, and I'll write you letters. Watch for the mailman.

My father was an officer with General Patton. My own letters arrived from Africa, Italy, England, Germany, and France.

Some of the special mail on our street came by telegram delivered by a man on a bicycle. When these telegrams arrived my friends were very sad, didn't come out and play and some moved away.

Near the end of the war everyone was feeling very happy, especially my mother. One morning a man on a bicycle delivered a special telegram to my mother. She screamed, the neighbors came, I didn't go out and play any more, and we moved away. I helped my mother a lot . . . and no more letters came.

Chapter 7
Life Changes

Was rationing really necessary? It wasn't so much that the United States was not the land of plenty, but rather that peacetime industries were converting from peacetime production to the war machine. And because shipping—especially for products that had to come from locales outside of the United States—was becoming very chancy. In addition, some items would, indeed, become scarce.

The end result was that, in addition to draft boards, rationing boards were created, and **Gladys Jordan** *of Robbinsville, North Carolina, served on one of them.*

I WAS CHIEF CLERK during the rationing program to the Local Rationing Board.

The program was implemented in January, 1942, and extended to October, 1945. Rationing was necessary because essential commodities became so scarce they could not be fairly distributed by means of the usual buying and selling practices.

The following commodities were rationed: Tires and tubes, automobiles, typewriters, sugar, gasoline, bicycles, rubber footwear, fuel oil, coffee, heating stoves, shoes, processed foods, meats and fats.

The government had ration books, coupons and certificates printed and sent to local boards. The boards received applications from consumers to determine their needs and issued books, coupons and certificates which the consumers used to purchase commodities from the retailers.

Although the program was an inconvenience to consumers, there were few complaints, as that was the public's contribution to the War effort.

Of course, rationing changed dramatically the way people lived, as did so many other things, like service stars. Those stars meant that someone who normally lived there was now gone, a part of the war effort. For **Lola M. Hudson** *of Ferndale, Pennsylvania, it was a high contribution indeed, for after her husband left for war she became a mother.*

A FTER PEARL HARBOR was attacked, I went to work for the government in Washington D. C.

I'll never forget how the government buildings (roof tops) were manned with soldiers holding firearms in case of an enemy attack.

Later, I recall going down to the train station to say farewell to my husband, (I met him while working in D.C.), who was boarding a train to some strange land to fight for our freedom. There were tears everywhere.

I went back to Pittsburgh to wait the arrival of our firstborn. Living there, I got the first taste of food stamps & gasoline rationing, and trying to make the margarine look like butter with those yellow capsules.

Mary B. Lashley of Hagerstown, Maryland, was in a similar position.

W HEN GEORGE boarded a train, it left me with three children under 5 years of age. Flashes of memories of those days include: on payday, $120.00 a month, they got an ice cream cone; coffee, sugar rations; ration books; making children's clothing out of feed bags.

We living on the second floor with a cook stove in the kitchen. We carried coal up, ashes down. Our telephone was on a party line, with maybe eight other families on the line.

I planted a garden, tended it with a hoe and a garden plow and canned a lot of fruits and vegetables.

I remember taking my children to Christmas Eve service. What did we see but old Santa himself walking up the hill with a pack on his back. Did we believe in Santa?

You bet we did!

Still another who remembers those gallant stars is **Helen Sponaugle** *of Fontana, California.*

A S A PRE-TEEN, then teenager during the war, I was afraid like everyone else of losing someone in my family, but we were all proud that they were doing their share, and so we put the blue stars on a white field, with red fringe in the window.

The three blue stars in our window were for Red in Italy, Ed in the 8th Air Force in England and Dad in the Aleutians.

Everywhere you looked there were blue stars in the windows and then—some stars changed to gold. Everyday more and more gold. Just one of those stars was eighteen year old Jimmy, a neighbor.

For Winside, Nebraska's **Marlin A. H. Westerhaus,** *memories consist of both enterprise and tragedy.*

I REMEMBER the rationing and the local county draft boards. I gathered up all the old scrap iron/rubber and even picked milkweed pods all for the war effort and bought saving stamps with the money I earned selling scrap iron.

Also, one Sunday morning about 8 a.m. we had a plane—a B-26— in trouble. It crashed about 2 miles from our home, killing all the crew. I'll never forget the eerie sound it made and the fireball of the explosion.

*GIs were everywhere. Military camps and bases sprang up across the country. Paonia, Colorado's **Margie Cooke Porteus's** life was affected by it.*

S OME GIs were sent for schooling at the small college I was attending, Southwestern State at Weatherford, Oklahoma. Our two college dorms were turned over to the soldiers; they attended classes on campus and marched to meals in the school cafeteria. It was the first time most of us had met persons from different areas of the country. We laughed at their accents, made friends with them, dated them and some married them.

The presence of GIs on campus, as well as our classmates going off to war, brought home the changes in our life and foretold changes to come that we could not have imagined.

*Changes brought about by war are often dangerous, but war itself was not the only thing that was risky. The training itself was often perilous. **Harold E. Pruett** of Gainesville, Florida, can attest to this.*

I WAS UNDERGOING transition training as a member of a six-man crew assigned as a radio-operator gunner. Immediately after entering training, I found myself in the Base Hospital with the German measles. I was placed in an isolation ward. It was dark. I was alone.

After I began to feel better, my crew was allowed to visit. They wished me a speedy recovery and a swift return to duty. I was disappointed.

The following afternoon, a friend arrived with a copy of the local newspaper. He asked had I heard the news. "What news?" I inquired. He silently handed me the paper, pointing to the following headline:

12 BARKSDALE FLYERS KILLED
TWO BOMBERS CRASH AND BURN AFTER MID-AIR COLLISION

There were no survivors. My entire crew was gone. It was dark. I was alone.

*Whether volunteer or draftee, it would be four long, terrible years before war's end and the losses would continue. During that time, some would live, others die, and as **Jack Snowden** of Upland, California, describes, some would simply separate and never meet again.*

W E WERE PLAYING BRIDGE when the announcement about Pearl Harbor was made. During our conversation I predicted that we would never get together again. How true that was!

In a short time Ken was in Navy officer's school. Mac got drafted, and Stan and I applied for pilot training.

Stan was accepted but I wasn't because of loss of hearing in my right ear.

I saw him once more when he was home on leave between flying Spitfires over England and going to the South Pacific. He survived the war but died of polio later.

I enlisted in the Army but didn't last long because of loss of hearing and my prediction came true. We were scattered to the four winds and never did get together again.

*The United States, seemingly overnight, geared up for war and more stars appeared in windows. No one will ever forget those very special stars, or those special times, including **Harold Kavonian** of Milford, Massachusetts, who offers his impression of those times. This is what he remembers:*

SEEING YOUR NEIGHBORHOOD go silent for days and grown up people whispering and crying. Then a gold star flag would be in someone's window.

When the air raid wardens would make sure you were in your house with all the lights out and the curtains down at night.

Older people going to fight those, "Slant Eye Japs" wearing your loved ones hat or patch.

Buying stamps in school one or two at a time to get a complete War Bond.

Cars with headlights painted black with a little slit for light—putting metal in a large pile for someone to pick up.

Going to the movies and cheering for the American side and cussing the Jap pilot who was shot down with blood coming out of his mouth.

*Movies were almost a way of life at that time, and for some, one way of seeing as well as hearing and reading the news. **Margie Ann Bridges** of Harrisburg, Arkansas, collected metal, saved bonds, and watched movies with the rest of America.*

I HAVE MEMORIES of Saturday afternoons at our local theater seeing newsreel of US servicemen in land and sea battles, movie stars and people entertaining our troops, nurses and doctors working with the wounded.

Here in town sadly seeing our men off on a bus to camp and even sadder when I heard of two of our local boys killed on the Battleship Arizona, two shot down over the Pacific, one later died of wounds received in battle.

Happy moments when men returned from overseas, one later who would be my husband.

*The demand and drain of males from the workforce led to something America had never seen before: Women in traditional male jobs. **Patricia Cotten** of Rio Oso, California, had one of them.*

I WAS WORKING in the office of our hospital and watching my newly uniformed friends dwindle away. I needed to do more—take part in bringing an end to the constant upheaval in everyone's lives. So I took a war-job at the Alameda Naval Air Station Salvage Yard.

2nd Lieutenant Dwight C. Brown's all-female warehouse crew worked in the forms warehouse at Jeffersonville Q.M. Depot in the summer of 1943. Ma Baker, far right, could lift 200 pounds.

We were the "Women Behind the Men". We learned the names of tools and how to use them, to buck rivets and drill them out, to mount gunsights without cracking windshields, install 50-caliber machine guns and adjust turnbuckles for synchronized bomb drops. In 3 months we graduated.

Before we ever got to work on the Navy Hellcats going "out" we had to take apart the ones that had come back "in" for recycling, so we were shuttled out to the Salvage Yard. The "ins" were strewn about looking like huge wounded birds fallen from flight.

I climbed into the lopsided cockpit of the ship assigned me and sat down. The gunsight wasn't broken and I started to remove it. I didn't have to worry about the windshield, most of it had been blown away.

I looked around me. Someone had flown this plane. Somebody in uniform had taken this plane up for its last flight. Who was it? Did he get out in time or had he died in the very seat where I was sitting? I touched the panel in front of me as if to find an answer.

We dismantled those planes piece by piece, rivet by rivet. It seemed backward, starting out there, like dying before you got to live. But it taught me an acute awareness of the work ahead which I might not have taken as seriously if I had not worked the Salvage Yard first.

"For the war effort" was the rallying cry, and if you couldn't contribute in one area, there was always another as **Violet White** *of Titusville, Florida, discovered.*

EVERYONE WAS WORKING together, doing anything to help the service men overseas. We worked twelve hours a day, seven days a week and over if we had to.

I tried so hard to join and enlist to any branch of service, but couldn't for I had two children, only thing that kept me from being in the service. So I joined the "Civil Air Patrol" and did what I could.

One war effort that many contributed to was the Victory Garden. With shortages or rationing on many essential items, Victory Gardens came into vogue. But being chic, then as now, was not always possible. **Elizabeth E. Crump** *of Albany, Georgia, reminds us that the Depression was not long over.*

I USED TO GO TO BED at night and actually pray for a Victory Garden and at the same time knowing we had no money to buy seed and supplies to plant such. We had a small garden but nothing as frivolous as one shaped in the V which I thought was the most patriotic of all. Gladly would I have sacrificed all of my share of war ration coupons just to have had a Victory Garden.

IF YOU HAD SOMEONE overseas, there was one thing you always wanted to see: Mail! To a GI, one of the most precious of commodities but no less precious to those who waited and wondered, like **Mary Villella Crudo** *of Erie, Pennsylvania.*

WE WOULD WAIT for the V-Mail, the small thin paper mail that we received from our boys overseas. Those V-Mail letters were like a God send each time we read one. Our hopes were raised and our relief was so great, the joy just exuded from my mother and father.

In the course of the years, my three brothers would serve, two in the Navy and one in the Army in Europe.

So you may very well know how grateful we were when we received those dear little letters.

Sometimes, the "war effort" took sort of an unusual turn. Just ask **Arthur J. Grothouse** *of Delphos, Ohio.*

I WAS PICKED OUT of a platoon, on the parade grounds, at Jefferson Barracks, Missouri and taken to a remote place, dressed in torn clothing, and then they took pictures of me swinging a rifle.

This picture was chosen to be used by the city of St. Louis for what they called a War Chest Campaign.

To my regret, I never saw the pictures used as I was shipped out to Alaska, then to the Aleutian Islands before the campaign began, but I heard that the picture was used for two years in all their ad's and posted all over St. Louis.

I had several calls from the newspaper, at that time, as they confirmed that both of the campaigns went over big.

Grothouse wasn't the only one used for "the war effort," at least, not according to **Thomas H. Komstohk** *of Indianapolis, Indiana.*

A S A MEMBER of the US Coast Guard Reserve my job was to do guard duty and fire watch aboard freighters and cargo ships at different harbors in the Norfolk, Virginia and Chesapeake areas. I was stationed in the Port Security Unit out of Portsmouth.

At the time I was watching the loading of boxes (wooden 4x4" and about 20" long). As I looked on a Chief Petty Officer accosted me and told me to put this jersey on. It was a 1st Class Boatswain Mate's navy blue jumper. Then he told me to stand and act as if I were supervising the loading and storing of these boxes for shipment overseas.

My curiosity got the best of me so I inquired as to what was in the wooden boxes. One of the loaders broke into a box and I viewed a large brass shell for cannon firing. His answer to my question was "Mustard Gas". Then he wanted to know if they were packing them right. I nodded in agreement.

The incident passed on and a camera took all the action of the loading. Two years later I was in Miami Beach learning to thread different types of cameras and how to splice the film when I suddenly found myself viewing the same filming that I had been a 1st class boatswain mate for 4 hours. The vocal part of the film announced, "Skilled Coast Guardsmen were supervising the loading of the cargo"—I had finally seen the filming of the loading.

Everyone wanted to do his or her part, and the simple memories of the little things are often the most poignant, like a barking collie and a cabby who wasn't greedy. These are some of the things **Earle R. Bee** *of Parkersburg, West Virginia, recalls.*

I LEFT A SEA of blue uniforms at Sampson Naval Base on my first furlough home after boot camp and still remember the sense of pride I felt marching to the beat of Anchors Aweigh.

The trip took all day with exchange of trains at Buffalo and Pittsburgh. It was two in the morning when we reached Parkersburg. I still thank the cabby who passed up more lucrative fares to drive me home six miles away.

I left the cab and started the short walk up the lane to my home. I could hear the watch dog bark of my collie that became one of ecstasy when he recognized me. I knelt, hugged him and put a hand on home soil.

The welcome continued inside with my wife and three sons. Those memories of home cooked meals shared with loved ones and, yes, the loving from my wife will always be with me.

Somehow, no matter how much happens, life seems to travel in full circles, says **John B. Bernice** *of Columbia, Maryland.*

I N SEPTEMBER 1939, Europe had gone to war, and in October of next year, America started the draft. At that time I was an eighteen year old member of the New York National Guard. On February 3, 1941, we were federalized and mobilized.

We assembled at our armory, and with family and friends looking on, the Regiment passed in review. We marched out of the armory doors to the steps leading to the I.R.T. subway, onto the waiting cars for the trip to Grand Central Station. We boarded railroad cars and the next morning arrived at Fort Ethan Allen, Vermont.

Thus began the great adventure with a subway ride.

Nearly five years later I was discharged at Fort Dix, and took the same I.R.T. subway to the same station which I left from, only this time I was alone.

Whether soldier, girl friend, wife, or parent, loneliness and fear became constant companions if someone you loved was gone. **Irene Minetola** *of Allentown, Pennsylvania, knows something about that.*

I REMEMBER NOW and have never really forgotten how lonesome and anxious we who were waiting at home were. We read about the Japanese who were put in camps and how difficult it was for them. It was very difficult for everyone in those years. We were worried and anxious everyday. Almost every male I knew was gone.

We had the radio and we were only told what they wanted to tell us. Sometimes I think the people today have forgotten we WERE bombed at Pearl Harbor and how bad it was.

The rationing was bearable. We walked everywhere we had to go. We went to church often and prayed daily. I was 18 at the time and I was scared. I remember waiting for the mailman and paper boy everyday.

That mobile sea of humanity in uniform would make a lasting impression on the young. In addition, in spite of the war segregation still existed, and that too would make an impression. **Anne E. Russell** *of Pontiac, Michigan, offers an excellent example.*

W E WOULD SEE CONVOYS of men, black and white, for days on end, being transported to the newly constructed Camp Rucker. We lived beside a main thoroughfare, in the country, and were not accustomed to so much traffic on the highway. On certain days all the men on the trucks would be black; on other days the men would be white. They would wave to us as they passed and sometimes throw apples or scraps of paper with a name and address. As we were not quite teens, these were very exciting times.

There was another group of people who would be affected by the war— people with names like **William Hohensee,** *of Munith, Michigan.*

T HE TIME THE FBI CAME to my home to question me about my nationality. Because I was born in Germany, the FBI questioned me at great length regarding many German activities that took place in various German Clubs and establishments in Detroit, Michigan.

All of this took place shortly after Pearl Harbor. From January 1942, until my induction into the Army in 1943, they harassed me periodically with their constant questioning. They were even instrumental in me losing my job as a Teamster employee in the trucking industry. Much to their dismay, I was unable to enlighten them on any German activities simply because I was never involved in anything. However, I do believe to the day that I had the last laugh. After being sent overseas in early 1945, I was assigned to the 9th Army, 16th Corps G-2 as an I.P.W. (Interrogator, Prisoner of War). After the conclusion of hostilities (May 8, 1945), I became an agent with a Military Intelligence Unit as an (I.I.T.). As an Interpreter, Interrogator and Translator (German of course), I carried a Top Secret clearance and remained at this job until I finally came home in late 1952.

While Mr. Hohensee may have had the last laugh on the FBI, the guys who may have overheard **Bob Vander Schaaf** *of Alton, Iowa, may have had a pretty good chuckle, too.*

O N MY SECOND DAY at Great Lakes Naval Training Center in early 1942, we were marching to chow but had to wait for another company which was singing, "Let's remember Pearl Harbor" etc. As they passed I whispered to my buddy, "You can tell that they were there— they've got vengeance in their eyes."

Later I found out they had only been in the Navy four days.

There were experiences like those of **K.W. Vanda** *of Endicott, New York.*

S EATED BACKWARDS in an A-6 Army Training plane, I was off to my first Air-to-Air Gunnery practice. There was no intercom so the pilot said, "When you finish firing, wave your hand and we'll go home."

I sighted the target, fastened the floor safety strap to the already loose fitting leg straps of my parachute harness, and stood up to fire. The firing went smoothly to the end and I waved my hand. The plane rolled over and fell away. I was hanging half out of the cockpit and the gun was swinging wildly. Ducking every swipe the gun made, I retained a white-knuckled hold on the cockpit. When the Gulf of Mexico returned to its rightful place under the plane, I got things together.

Lesson Learned: First, stow and lock the gun, sit down and fasten your seatbelt, then wave your hand.

*Lessons came hard, but it was best to learn them during training. Just ask **Robert F. Johnson** of Green Bay, Wisconsin.*

I WAS CALLED to active duty in October 1940 and sent to Camp Beauregard, Louisiana. The camp was not large enough to hold our 32nd Division so the artillery was sent to Camp Disregard as we called it about 5 miles into the boonies. We arrived about 8 at night and were assigned tents and after a meal went to bed. We had parked our trucks and guns in a field near the tent area.

When we awoke and went for training the first morning our trucks and guns were sunk in the mud of La. It took us all day to get our guns and trucks back on the road and to a gun park we called Blue Berry Hill.

The first lesson was, take the high ground.

*Tens of thousands of men and women inexperienced with war signed up to do their part. The flood of patriots enlisting after a time could make people like **Charles W. Sembower** of Bloomington, Indiana, wonder if their contribution really meant anything.*

A S AN ENLISTED MAN from March 21, 1942, to February 7, 1946, I often thought that what I did was insignificant and unimportant—even though maybe it wasn't but now I realize that just being "there" was important enough.

"There" is a noncom with the Military Police was Fort Harrison, Indiana and Fort Custer, Michigan.

"There" as a noncom with the Medics (227th General Hospital) was Camp Ellis, Illinois; and in France at Mourmelon-le-Grand, near Reims, and Marseilles.

Yes, now, whenever I get to feeling apologetic about what I did as a soldier—or did not do, such as something heroic—I force myself to realize that just being "there"—doing what I was expected to do—was indeed important enough and something worth remembering.

*Americans left for "there" by the thousands. It was impossible not to know someone in uniform. Perhaps no one's life changed more than for those who joined up, like **Raymond S. Gawriluk** of Naperville, Illinois, who recounts a memory from basic training.*

W HEN I WAS AT BOOT CAMP at Great Lakes, we needed to know how to swim. To qualify as a swimmer, we had to swim the perimeter of the pool and jump off a 50 foot tower wearing a Mae West life preserver. That tower was scary. Our favorite "out" was to reach for the side of the pool and pant.

One day our instructor, a Notre Dame football star, was wearing combat boots with his swimming trunks. We thought it was a silly get up, but when anyone started to reach for the side of the pool, the combat boot came crashing down. We all qualified that day.

Protesters today would call this brutality but many lives were spared knowing how to abandon ship.

*Of course, there are other aspects to training, like learning to do your job thoroughly, as **Charles William Stull** of Buchanan, Virginia, graphically relates.*

I WAS PRE-FLIGHTING an AT-6 at Duncan Field when the pilot in no uncertain terms ordered me to check out a chute. He was considerate enough to explain how to put it on and how to exit in case of trouble.

Climbing to 10,000 ft. he said, "Private, let's see if you have cleaned this bird."

Immediately I found myself upside down with dust and of all things a few bolts dancing on the canopy. With a quick glance I saw a grinning pilot.

Then I received the shock of my life. He wanted to smoke and I was to take over. Following a few instructions you have no idea what took place. Besides giving him a nervous smoke break, I was sure I didn't want to be a pilot.

Back on the ground, to a still nervous private, he confessed he planted the bolts, but not the dust.

*Others in training, like **C. Edwin Ward** of Little Falls, New Jersey, recall a single particular moment in time.*

THE DAY my flying career started, my instructor and I had flown over to an auxiliary field of Mustang Army Flying School just outside of El Reno, Oklahoma. We shot several take-offs and landings when my instructor told me to taxi to the edge of the field. With the engine idling, he climbed out on the wing of the open cockpit PT-19. He leaned over and hollered: "O.K. if you want to kill yourself, you'll do it without me," and he jumped down with the "Thumbs Up" sign.

I taxied out and took off on my first solo.

I vividly recall singing the Air Corps song: "Off we go, into the wild blue yonder ——— if you live to be a gray-haired wonder" ——— the lyric proved prophetic.

I survived and am gray-haired!

*Sadly, as **Harry Hillis Jr.** of Olney, Illinois, describes, some would not be coming home.*

HAROLD "COWBOY" VARNER had been killed in action. A pleasant, outgoing young man, he had been a printer and pressman at the Olney Daily Mail, a small town mid-America newspaper. "Cowboy" counted papers for me and the other carriers and often bought us treats of candy, ice cream or pop.

Paraphrasing the front page editorial that day: "Getting the Daily Mail to press today was more difficult than it has ever been, but the problems were emotional rather that mechanical." Following a poignant obituary that expressed the feeling of loss throughout the newspaper plant, the piece concluded: "Please excuse our show of emotion. We have lost the one and only "Cowboy."

As a young high school student, the terrible reality of war had hit me personally for the first time.

*Before it was over, the reality of war would hit many more, and many tears would fall. Shirley, Massachusetts, resident **Theodore A. Marion** remembers all too well.*

THAT NIGHT, there was a pounding on the back door. It woke me up. Then I heard my Mother cry, "Oh my God! June it's for you".

A telegram had come for my sister. "We regret to inform you ———". Harry was dead. My sister's husband, Harry, had gone down with his ship in the Pacific. My sister collapsed.

Harry couldn't swim, he was afraid of water, but when the enemy invaded Pearl Harbor, Harry crowded into line to join the Navy. They made him a machinist's mate—a "Snipe". He worked below deck. It didn't matter to Harry, he wanted to fight and fast.

His wife, my sister, had a baby boy. Harry knew what he had to do for his son and for his country. We were all proud of him—but his ship went down—Harry was lost.

Somehow, though, his spirit prevailed and we, America went on to defeat the enemy. Thank God for the thousands of Harrys. I'll never forget them and I'll never forget that night.

Yes, thank God for all the Harrys. Freedom carries a price and America was about to discover just how high that price could be.

Chapter 8
The Battle Is Joined

At the same time the Pearl Harbor disaster was taking place, the Japanese were also attacking or preparing to attack other areas of the Pacific. As news of Pearl Harbor splashed across the front pages of every American newspaper, the Japanese, within a seven-hour period of its attack in Hawaii, simultaneously landed in Malaya, launched aerial assaults on the Philippine island of Luzon and on the strategically located island of Wake, and attacked British-controlled Hong Kong.

Because of the International Dateline, only Pearl Harbor is recorded as being attacked on December 7. All other attacks were listed as taking place December 8, 1941, local time.

Gene A. Fleener *of Big Bear Lake, California, tells his story.*

WHEN THE JAPANESE attacked Pearl Harbor, I was a Marine stationed on Wake Island, and since we were across the International Date Line, the attack to us was on Monday. We had received word about Pearl Harbor.

At noon I was in the chow line to get food from a truck that had been dispatched from the mess hall to our five-inch gun position. Suddenly we heard planes. Someone said, "It's the Squadron from Midway."

When black objects began dropping from the planes, someone shouted that they were "just disposable gas tanks."

A crusty senior NCO put it all in perspective when he bellowed, "Hell, those are bombs and those are Jap planes!" There were 36 of them. Of the dozen fighter planes we had, they destroyed seven. Our tents and most everything else was destroyed as they made two passes over the Island.

It was scary. It was exciting.

*The total surprise of the attacks meant that some Americans would leave port at peace and sail into war. For men like **Ernest Schock** of Forbes, North Dakota, war was a matter of timing.*

OUR ORDERS were to depart Fort Ord, California, Nov. 16, 1941. We reached Pearl Harbor on Nov. 27, 1941, left again for Australia. On the way, war broke out.

We were not ready for war. We threw all our practice stuff overboard and I don't think we had 10 rounds of ammo to a soldier. We stuck out like a sore thumb. The ship was white with two American flags on each side.

It had to be painted gray that day, Dec. 7th.

We landed in Brisbane, Australia on Dec. 23, 1941, then on to Darwin. And on Feb. 19, 1942, Darwin, Australia was bombed by the same Japs that bombed Pearl Harbor.

*According to **Edward C. Cuddington** of Sparta, Michigan, the Americans were not the only ones who were unaware of Japan's intentions.*

A ROUND THANKSGIVING DAY in 1941, the USS Alden (DD 211) on which I was serving, and three other four stackers were ordered out of Manila, in the Philippines. We heading for Balakpapan, Borneo and arrived there around Dec. 1, 1941. The destroyer tender Blackhawk, was also in port.

On Dec. 8 we received the news of Pearl Harbor being bombed by the Japanese and that we were at war. Our four destroyers and the Blackhawk were ordered to Singapore. We arrived on Dec. 10, 1941 (three days after war with the Japanese was declared) and as we were about to enter the port, two Japanese fishing vessels were coming out. As they passed, they saluted us by dipping their colors, and passed on out of port.

We radioed the British, and they brought them back. They were either sneaking out or didn't even know we were at war.

Two days before Cuddington's ship arrived at Singapore, the Japanese had staged a small bombing raid on the city. At the same time, they landed troops at other points of Malaysia, including Kota Bharu, where they captured a British airbase intact, including fuel and munitions, and also landed troops in Thailand at Singora and Patani.

The British defenders were poorly trained, poorly prepared, and spread far too thin. On December 8, 1941, the British government dispatched the battleships Prince of Wales *and* Repulse *accompanied by four destroyers, all under the command of Adm. Sir Tom Phillips, from Singapore to Thailand. This move would prove extremely important to the Allied forces because at that time, the* Prince of Wales *and* Repulse *were the only battleships in the Pacific.*

On the afternoon of December 9 both battleships, which were headed north toward the Japanese landing sites, were sighted by a Japanese submarine. The next afternoon, Phillips's force was attacked by an estimated 90 Japanese aircraft and within two hours both battleships had been sunk. Though most of the British seamen were rescued, Phillips was lost.

Within little more than 72 hours, through skill, planning, and a little luck, the Japanese believed they had managed to clear the Pacific of any major threat to their navy.

*During peacetime, little is mentioned about luck or fate unless someone hits the lottery or otherwise has a close call of some sort. But war is different. The hand of fate touches everyone during wartime, as it did Jonesboro, Arkansas, resident **Elmer C. Holland.***

A FEW DAYS before the Japanese attack on Pearl Harbor, I got off the USS Curtiss AV-3 and went onto the USS Wright AV-1 November 16, 1941.

The Wright was due to arrive at Pearl Harbor, off a trip to Midway and Wake, due in Sunday, December 7, 1941. Not knowing till later we came through the Japanese fleet on Saturday night before the attack. We had to lay out and come in Monday, Dec. 8th. The USS Curtiss got bombed, 15 men were killed in the compartment I slept in when I was on it. If we had been in the harbor, I'm sure we would have been bombed along with the Curtiss.

That was the most horrible sight I saw during my 6 years in the Navy in World War II, and about the most scared, when the Japanese said they were coming back again to Pearl Harbor.

*Many worried that Japan would be back. Their fears were not without grounds, according to **Jerome Klein** of Sarasota, Florida.*

O NE OF THE HUSHED-UP STORIES of World War II is that after we supposedly learned how unprepared we were on Dec. 7, 1941, Japanese planes successfully penetrated Hawaii twice more—and got away both times!

In March, 1942, a half-dozen Japanese flying boats dropped bombs near Honolulu. American interceptors failed to catch them although they apparently had re-fueled in the same area as the December 7 invaders.

Again in October 1943, a Japanese plane got above Pearl Harbor and radioed back a report on the disposition of the US fleet there. It was caught in searchlights, but managed to get away nevertheless.

The Signal Corps confirms that just as on the original onslaught by the Japanese, neither attacker was identified until too late and neither time was there any air raid alert sounded.

*Japan's second and third visits to Hawaii may have caused concern, but for those islands and countries they actually invaded, the situation was much worse. **J. N. Kaper** of Westchester, California, is fortunate to be around to tell of it.*

I WAS BORN AND RAISED on the Island Java and the day Japan attacked Pearl Harbor our government declared war on Japan to stand on the side of the US.

I remembered the Battle of the Java Sea where the US and the Netherlands Navy fought side by side. When we capitulated all the Europeans were put in prison camps under inhumane and barbaric conditions.

My father died on the Burma railroad, under slave conditions and undernourished. During the first part of 1942 we heard the Japs were transporting American, English, Australian and Dutch POWs in baskets on trucks or trains in the tropical heat without food and water. In Soerabaja they were hoisted aboard boats and dumped in the Java Sea, alive and starving, to drown or be attacked by sharks. The Jap guards laughed while the men were dying.

I survived, as a teenager, 3 years in slavery, no clothing and hardly any food. We had to work 15 hours a day, 364 days a year and were supposedly paid 15 cents a day, which we never saw.

Mr. Kaper's nightmarish experiences and memories of the atrocities visited on POWs, especially those under Japanese control, are shared by many survivors of prison camps during World War II.

Few of those experiences equal what the survivors of the Bataan Death March went through.

In retrospect, the events that led to the collapse of Bataan and Corregidor seem inevitable. Gen. Douglas MacArthur, who was in charge of the United States Army in the Philippines, gambled that his troops would receive reinforcements from the United States before he was backed into the Bataan Peninsula. He ordered delaying actions beginning in December 1941, but the devastation of Pearl Harbor and the decimation of the Pacific fleet made it impossible for reinforcements or supplies to reach the Philippines.

On the other hand, the Japanese reinforced and supplied their troops in the Philippines as needed and were also able to make landings on surrounding islands, effectively cutting MacArthur's forces off from outside help. Finally, Roosevelt ordered MacArthur off the island, leading to the general's famous quote, "I shall return." That promise would not be kept for many months.

In the meantime, the forces remaining on the island, under the command of Gen. Jonathon Wainwright, continued to fight for every inch of ground. Incredibly, the troops made up of Australian, Filipino, Dutch, and American forces held on for months, slowly giving ground to the Japanese forces.

Supplies were hard to get. The Japanese had all but totally blocked all the defenders' supply lines. By April the Bataan defenders were in bad shape. An estimated 24,000 American and Filipino troops were sick from tropical disease and from living on quarter-rations. On April 7, General Wainwright withdrew as many troops as possible—about 15,000—to Corregidor from Bataan and the next day, April 8, the Bataan resistance collapsed.

At noon, April 9, 1942, troops on Bataan surrendered to the Japanese. An estimated 12,000 American were captured, and were among the total 75,000 men and women who were marched to San Fernando 100 miles away. The incident would be recorded in history as the Bataan Death March.

Almost a month later, on May 6, the island of Corregidor fell and Wainwright and the remaining defenders surrendered as well.

Emilio A. Sales *of Bacarra, Ilocos Norte, Philippines, was one of the Filipinos who remembers the fall of the islands.*

I WAS 2ND LIEUTENANT, reserve force, Philippine Army when World War II erupted and sporadic battles were fought by American-Filipino forces against Japanese invaders resulting with the fall of Bataan on April 9, 1941. From said battlefields followed the "death march" to Tarlac Concentration Camp some 100 miles away.

Then began the Japanese Imperial Occupation, and Filipino leaders were appointed government figureheads, with Jose P. Laurel as Philippine President, the governors, mayors down the Ho-Ko line. What a HELL with Japanese rule for almost four years of rampant killings of innocent Filipinos!

Last but not least, is my vivid memory of the Resistant Movement against Japan which meant great sacrifice for life and property of guerrillas and civilians.

Santiago Pasaporte *of Iloilo City, Philippines, was on the Death March.*

A N AIR RAID of high altitude bombers over Corregidor came from four directions. After five-ten minutes comes a low dive bomber destroys guns and antiaircraft emplacement. For two weeks those islands—Ft. Mills, Hudges, Drum and Frank—were silent.

An unknown number of guns from Bataan fired day and night, follows surrender.

Death March from Bataan to Capas, Tarlac was lonely to remember. Buildings in camp over crowded, food shortages were common. We received food only once for three days. All sickness in the camp. Once you are attacked, no hope to survive. Graves were dug for 20-25 dead. Burial from morning to late afternoon of not less than one hundred daily.

It is hard to imagine the suffering that took place with these prisoners. In some cases, many may have felt the dead were the lucky ones. According to another eyewitness, **Howard M. Vassey** *of Lancaster, South Carolina, there was no shortage of death.*

I WAS PLACED on a burial detail at Cabanatuan POW Camp by the Jap guards. The Japs had dug a grave 20' X 20' and since it had been raining for the past five days, the grave was about half full of water.

There were about 40 POWs that had died during the past five days and the Jap guards recruited about 50 able bodies to help with the burial.

We walked to the hole with the bodies and dumped them in. Then the guard wanted someone to straighten out the corpses. After being jabbed several times by the Jap guard, I finally jumped in. One of the worst things that I had to do was to get into the hole with those POW bodies.

Not everyone on the Death March became a POW. Some escaped, like **Florencio Esteban** *of Baguio City, Philippines.*

D URING THE DEATH MARCH, I knew I had no chance to survive. It was still a long way off to Capas and yet I had no more food or water. What was my only course? To escape whatever happens!

By noontime of 25 April 1942, I opened a hole under the barbwire fence of the camp. A Japanese guard saw me and came to close the hole. He was murmuring something I could not understand. But definitely, it was a warning to me not to do it again.

Undaunted in my failure in my first attempt, my inner self prodded me to make a second try. Thus, after saying my prayers, I bid good-bye to my wife and country and then I reopened the barbed wires. I slipped my body out, stood for a while with half-closed eyes, then I walked casually towards the west, back to freedom.

Escape was every prisoner's goal. For those who did, their nightmare must have been being recaptured. That's what happened to **Pedro P. Lagutan** *of San Jose, Montalban Rizal, Philippines, and he paid a price.*

I AM ONE of the several thousand Filipino veterans who survived World War II. I served with the "A" Co. 1st Bn. Anti Sabotage Regiment, USAFFE (United States Armed Forces In The Far East). We fought side by side with American GIs and despite the unfortunate deaths of thousands, I escaped during the Death March and later joined the Guerrilla Oct. 2, 1942, under Col. Hughes Straughn, Fil-American (FAIT).

After a year I was captured and imprisoned. I was tortured in ways that damaged my hearing and I lost some of my teeth. Fortunately, I escaped again by jumping into the Pasig River.

For those still left behind in the prison camps, every day was a fight. Because of the huge numbers of prisoners, the Japanese split some of the bigger units up. By all reports, conditions were the same no matter where the POWs were. **Blas B. Afos** *of Surallah, South Cotabato, Philippines, graphically describes life in a POW camp.*

I T WAS IN THE YEAR 1942. The USAFFE had surrendered already and concentrated in Bataan. Life there was very terrible. Acute food shortage, no medicine, water reservoir bombed. The remnants of the USAFFE are very sick, starving, very thin and hungry. The conquerors did not like to give them enough food. Food supply was also scarce. So the Japanese Imperial Forces decided to move the Filipino soldiers to another province Capaz, Tarlac.

Now the March. The poor sickly soldiers, about a thousand of them, were transferred to Capaz Tarlac hiking. They were weak, hungry, very thin and rugged. How can they endure to hike up to the third province! Bataan, Pampanga and Tarlac? A pitiful soldier was very thirsty walking under the hot sun. He saw a pond near the road and ran there to drink. Others followed him. Angrily the guard shot them and killed them. Many could no longer endure to hike. They were weak and dying. Many died on the way.

When they were in Capaz, Tarlac, the condition was even worse. They were fed with rice and boiled leaves of vegetables. The taste was terrible. Many died daily. Soon the news spread all over the country. Some of them were sent home. Some were taken by their relatives.

That was the Death March! One of the most terrible evil the Japs had done during the Japanese Occupation, 1942-1945.

Weak, ill, often wounded, it didn't matter. The Japanese used them for slave labor for various projects. Somehow the prisoners endured. This is how Cincinnati, Ohio, resident **Louis Kolger** *remembers it.*

IT WAS THE RAINY SEASON in June of 1942. There were 300 of us, half-naked, Japanese POWs building a road and a bridge in the Luzon jungle. We had absolutely no shelter from the rain and mosquitoes except for lean-tos each individual made from Nepa-Palm leaves. We worked everyday from daylight till dark in ankle-deep mud.

The wheels on the wheelbarrows would lock with mud, a vine was then looped through the wheel. Two men pulled on the vine as a third man lifted on the handles. With this arrangement we literally plowed a furrow through the mud to the dumping area.

Our rice was cooked in a steel wheelbarrow. Frequently the firewood was too wet to burn and on these occasions we were given two spoonfuls of uncooked rice for our meal.

The detail (Tyabas Detail) lasted two months, approximately 100 of us survived.

Conditions in the prison camps were deplorable and disease ran rampant. Yet, somehow, the spirit of these gallant men and women never broke. Note the pride that comes through as **Julian B. Piedad** *of Piddig, Philippines, comments on the fall of Bataan and Corregidor.*

THE DEFENSE OF BATAAN and the bastion of Corregidor has fallen but the spirit that made it stand under the banner of unshakable faith will never fail. They have fallen not with the weakness of the forces fighting (USAFFE) under the command of Gen. Douglas MacArthur but to preserve that spirit and strength of the men fighting including the lives and properties of the civilians in the area.

Although these forces surrendered to the enemy, such was not voluntary. It was a proclamation by President Franklin Delano Roosevelt of the US, and were herded down to the road of death march to the concentration camp and suffered the ignominy of surrender.

Despite of all the various types of sufferings like death and diseases suffered by these men, the spirit that made Bataan and Corregidor stand under the banner of unshakable faith did not fail and victory was attained and Japan bowed to her knees and drunk of the dregs of bitterness from the cup of defeat.

Perhaps the only thing worse than being an American prisoner of war was to have been a Japanese-American. **Richard M. Sakakida** *of Fremont, California, doesn't have to imagine what that experience would be like—he lived it.*

I WAS ORDERED to the Philippines as an undercover intelligence agent prior to outbreak of World War II, and accompanied General Wainwright's surrender team as the general's interpreter. I would later become the first and only Japanese-American POW.

When identified as being of Japanese extraction, I was removed from the general's group and beaten. The next six months were spent undergoing interrogation by Japanese Military Police, since they suspected that I was a member of Military Intelligence. Due to my steadfast denial of intelligence involvement, the interrogation eventually led to physical torture, beginning with cigarette burns, water treatment and ending with hands being tied behind and body lifted by rope until shoulders were dislocated.

I withstood weeks of torture to convince Japanese authorities that they had erred in their suspicion.

The plight of the prisoners was deplorable and though they didn't know it, it would be a long, long time before Japan would be defeated. And while most of America was horrified by the plight of the men captured at Bataan and Corregidor, very few realized that American women were among those POWs. But **Hattie R. Brantley** *of Jefferson, Texas, knew only too well.*

WE WERE JOLTED into reality on 8 December (across the date line) in the Philippine Islands. It's hard to describe how unprepared we were. I was an Army Nurse assigned to the Philippine Department. Our Chief Nurse assured us the Japanese would not get this far, and she instructed that we go about our usual business.

My friend and I had the morning off duty, so we went out and played nine holes of golf!

At noon, Clark Field was blown to bits, and on Christmas Eve, the first contingent of medical personnel went to Bataan to set up field hospitals. We served in these outdoor, poorly equipped facilities with limited staff, medicine and food. Everything was scarce except casualties which came by the hundreds.

When Bataan fell, we nurses were evacuated to Corregidor which likewise fell on 6 May 1942, and off we went to prisoner of war camp until February 1945.

My most vivid memory of this period was constant unabated hunger.

In the meantime, America kept on producing war goods, building ships, training young men and women . . . and birthing heroes. Perhaps Gen. Jonathon Wainwright's surrender doesn't seem heroic, but don't tell that to any of the survivors, like **George M. Groneck** *of Cloverdale, California.*

A FTER MY CAPTURE on Caballo Island in June 1942. We were lined up, ready to board a POW ship for transfer to Japan. In my association with soldiers from mid-west, one of them shouted the following orders, "Detail, right flank, left face. Left flank, right face, hand salute."

I was curious. I saw US military staff surrounded by Japanese officers and their guard. They too, were going to board the ship. The US troupe stopped near us, a tall Army officer stopped and spoke with the men.

As he came to me, he bent down, placed his left hand on my shoulder, shook my hand and said, "Son, I know you're tired."

At this gesture I froze and got tears in my eyes. He was Gen. "Skinny" Wainwright.

*Wainwright was shipped to Manchuria where he served out the rest of the war as a POW. In a footnote to the story of Bataan, **Peter Finnegan** of Caldwell, New Jersey, offers this memory of General Wainwright.*

I N MAY 1945, I was one of an honor guard for General Jonathan Wainwright, who was visiting his family outside Syracuse, New York for a week. We had two men on guard duty around the clock.

I had the luck to be on duty in the rear of the house when the General came out to look at the flowers and I had a chance to talk to him. This was a man bent over, walking with a cane, very frail, and very low voice. As I had some very close friends who were on Corregidor Island with him, I wanted to know if he knew if they made it.

He started to cry, and said to me, "I don't know how many made it, but I can tell you every man there was a hero, the best soldiers I had the privilege to command."

Chapter 9
Pacific Hell

Old timers call it "getting blooded" the first time a green GI faces combat, but when war came to his islands, good old-fashioned fear kept **Ramon F. Jimenez** *of Leyte, Philippines, safe.*

O N JANUARY 13, 1942, I experienced heavy bombing effected by twelve Japanese planes in Calonog, Iloilo, Philippines. I was then young and a first-timer in war, and I thought that the world will end that moment.

I ran hastily towards the thick bamboo groves and sought cover. After the bombing and the planes were all gone, I found myself heavily enclasped by thick thorny-bamboos, and it was hard for me to come out. I cannot imagine how I got in there, prickless. My comrades helped me to get outside. That's my first experience in the war.

United States forces were engaged in a number of actions in the Pacific during early 1942. While American ships attacked the Gilbert and Marshall Islands in February, the Japanese launched a massive attack against Java on February 3, where a number of Dutch bases were located. The attack destroys all aircraft at Surabaya. **Marion H. Mahnken** *of Port St. Lucie, Florida, witnessed it.*

I N THE EARLY DAYS of WORLD WAR II, we had no overseas hospitals, a shortage of doctors and medication, people in command "running scared" and not qualified, troops poorly trained and inadequately equipped.

I remember losing all our aircraft and supplies in harbor of Java, eating mutton and potatoes 3 times a day in Australia, the sight of my blood from Nebic-dysentery on truck seat when evacuating Rangoon, Chinese Colonel Woo executed, temporary lost hearing from Japanese bomb, run over by truck during air-raid alert, malaria with 108 fever.

I remember Roosevelt saying, "You fight the war and we'll take care of you", but after the war I was disabled and went to the VA for help but was told, "we can't help you because we can't find your medical records". (All records were destroyed by order of 14th air force command when personnel were evacuated by airlift from Hengyang.)

Java, Rangoon, Hengyang—all exotic sounding locales. But as the battle raged in the Pacific, Japan was also trying to push its way into Malaysia, Singapore and other Southeast Asian areas. The day after the attack on Java began, Japan demanded the surrender of Singapore. The British refused and on February 8, the Japanese launched a major attack against the city.

One week later, on February 15, the British surrender. They have lost 138,000 men, compared to 10,000 Japanese troops lost. It is the greatest military disaster in British history.

One vital supply line for the Chinese, who were allies with the U.S., was the China/Burma/India theater.

*The overland supply line was called the Burma Road and it ran from the sea through Burma, crossing heavy jungles and scaling nerve-wrackingly steep mountains. For **Lonnie Zywiec** of Columbus, Nebraska, a seemingly endless sea voyage, the inhumanity of war, and the Burma Road are all vivid in his memory.*

I RECALL the trip across the ocean, with so many soldiers in one place and the many days on ship wondering if I would ever see land again. Then landing in a foreign country, totally new and unknown to me.

I found a feeling of anger and anxiety. Anger because I felt, why couldn't this have been settled more humanly, instead of this fighting and killing of innocent lives. Anxiety to get this war over fast and returning to my great country of freedom.

The China-Burma-India road stands out most vividly, a convoy of Army trucks traveling a man-made road, winding through mountainous country, across rivers, seeing trucks shoved off the road into deep ravines, because of mountain slides. It took us 30 days to travel some 1100 miles, finally arriving in China and then transported by plane to Calcutta India for further duties.

The Burma Road was a vital supply link from the sea to China and even before the Americans officially came into the war, Maj. Gen. Claire Lee Chennault, who was serving as advisor and trainer for China's aviation program, had come back to the United States and recruited 100 of the nation's best flyers—a group that would become famous as the Flying Tigers.

*By March 1, 1942, Chennault saw that the situation in Rangoon was hopeless and pulled his forces back and by the 27th, he is forced to pull out of Burma completely. By April 18, the Allied Chinese troops at Lashio, the end of the Burma Road, are annihilated and by April 29, the only way Burma can receive supplies is by air from India. This would become known as "flying the hump" and if a pilot and crew went down, they often called on **Dominick C. Spadaccino** of Langhorne, Pennsylvania, to help.*

I SERVED in the Army Air Force with Captain Ormand Julian and Major Ralph Dewsup, both surgeons, with an airborne Surgical Rescue Unit, stationed on the Burma Border.

My biggest experience was bailing out over the Himalayan Mountains to rescue survivors of planes that were shot down or crashed into the mountains. I spent hundreds of days in the jungles, with the help of the Burmese natives, rescuing officers and enlisted men. I was awarded the Soldier's Medal and Presidential Citation for traveling behind Japanese lines to rescue a radio operator.

During these rescue missions, I encountered monkeys, king cobra snakes, many other poisonous snakes, leeches, elephants, tigers and many others.

I was also in the village of the head hunters tribe which was quite an experience. In addition I traveled over the Burma-Stillwell Road on the first convoy.

Flying the hump literally meant clearing the Himalayan Mountains to bring supplies to beleaguered troops in Burma. The flights were dangerous, and sometimes just a bit eerie, as **Robert C. Noack** *of Celina, Ohio, describes.*

I SERVED in the CBI with the 1346th Army Air Force Base Unit Air Transport Command. I was a flight engineer on a converted B-24 liberator known as a C19 tanker hauling gasoline over the Himalayan Mountains which was called "Flying the Hump."

One night we saw St. Elmo's fire while flying an altitude of 32,000 ft. A ball of fire rolled from one end of the wing to the other. It was a sight I will never forget

I was stationed at Tezpur in the Assam Valley India.

K.W. Vanda *of Endicott, New York, describes one flight quite well.*

A GIANT THUNDERHEAD lay directly in our line of flight. Stretching up to 50,000 ft, it was sending its purple, pink, yellow and red warnings into the night sky.

Our war-weary C-109 Tanker (converted B-24 Bomber) labored directly into the maelstrom. Turning on the overhead cockpit lights, the pilot wrapped both arms around the controls and we braced for the worst.

Hailstones roared against the fuselage, lightning flashed continuously, we were in the grip of something awesome. Updrafts were heart stopping; downdrafts were gut sucking. The props threw large chunks of ice against the plane while St. Elmo's fire outlined the aircraft with smoky blue fingers.

Charted mountains to the left and right; were there now mountains ahead as well? The altimeter whirred and the compass had a mind of its own.

Was this the fate of planes that mysteriously vanished in past months?

*Sometimes, introduction to combat can be misleading, as **Edward Warren Ledbetter** of Phoenix, Arizona, can attest.*

I WAS TRAINED as a gunner/radio operator after I enlisted in the Army Air Force in 1943, and was assigned to a combat crew in the 14th Air Force aboard a B-24 Liberator in China-Burma-India. We flew missions from Luliang, China, radar bombing enemy shipping from the Philippines to Japan.

My first mission was a night bombing run. We were a green crew, flying alone, and dropped 10 500 lb. bombs right on the Kowloon Harbor docks. There was no resistance and that first mission seemed so easy. Later ones didn't.

We flew numerous missions over the "Hump," but the mission I remember the most happened in 1945 when we dropped leaflets written in Japanese over Nagasaki a week before the atomic bomb was dropped on Hiroshima.

The leaflets warned the people to surrender or suffer the consequences.

The 14th Air Force bombs docks and railroad yards in Kowloon, China.

*It would be three long years before those leaflets would be delivered. Meanwhile, even though life in the air was hazardous, those on the ground like **Arthur I. Buckhout** of Sea Cliff, New York, discovered the enemy was not always the Japanese.*

BECAUSE OF OUR ISOLATED POSITION in North Burma, receiving supplies was very difficult, particularly food. When the work load could spare personnel, hunting for wild game was a necessity.

One bright moonlit night two buddies and I ventured into the jungle to a lake approximately three miles from camp where a salt-lick had been placed on a low tree branch. We spread out and proceeded to wait. Time passed, which seemed like hours, and no game appeared. The moon was low in the sky and it was now quite dark.

After a bit of haggling, it was decided that no deer were coming and we may as well leave. Because we had moved about to various positions, we now realized that the foot trail was not where we thought. At this point we heard a loud roar. It was a tiger roar for sure. I tried to stay calm but panic was taking over. I am sure the others felt the same. We now moved faster in an attempt to find the foot path.

Then the roar was heard again! Thick jungle was around us, the moon was now quite low and it was getting darker. Each attempt to locate the path would lead us to thick brambles. At one time we found a path and hurriedly ran along. It led us to a clearing where we saw elephant dung with steam rising from the many piles. Elephants had left this spot only minutes earlier.

We rapidly backed out and took another path. The roar was heard again and we faced more thick jungle. At one point we considered climbing a tree and wait for daylight.

About this time we ventured through some thick bramble and to our surprise we found the foot path. We ran and stumbled as fast as we could to make a quick retreat back to camp.

*Young men in strange places, even with a war raging around them, will still find time to play tourist. And in the CBI, that could be interesting, according to **Earl O. Pearson** of Fox Lake, Illinois.*

IT HAPPENED in the village of Dibrugarh, Assam, India where those of us stationed at Chabua, an air base for "hump flyers" went to purchase a few souvenirs. Most of us bought carved ivory, brass objects, and wood carvings. Sidney Spirer did not buy the usual.

On this day, while in the village, Sid and I went to a building, the Indian person came out from a back room with a small cloth bag. The contents were emptied onto another cloth. These were various cut shapes and sizes of Alexanderite stones. Sid looked carefully through, picked out, and purchased a few stones. Spirer said "His wife said these were worth money."

Today the Alexanderite is a rare and valuable precious stone. Only Sidney Spirer would know if these were the genuine article. Yes, I still wonder.......

As the Flying Tigers were pulling back from Burma and pilots searched for routes through the treacherous Himalayas, other forces in the Pacific were having a hard time of it.

Morale perked up briefly when Lt. Gen. James Doolittle, a famous air racer and aircraft instrument designer before the war, led his squadron of carrier-launched B-25s on a raid on Tokyo on April 18, 1942, and landed the aircraft at Chinese bases afterward. The raid did little real damage, but it gave US forces a much-needed boost in morale.

Then-Lt. Col. James Doolittle wires a Japanese medal to the fin of a 500-lb. bomb on the deck of the USS Hornet

But it would be hard to argue that Japan, at this point in history, did not rule the Pacific. Though not as effective as the German U-boats fighting the ongoing Battle of the Atlantic half a world away, the Japanese submarine force nevertheless was a Pacific presence not to be discounted. In fact, it was not until April 14, 1942, that a US ship, the USS Roper, *sunk the first Japanese submarine. The presence of an enemy submarine, whether in the Atlantic or the Pacific, was a force to be reckoned with.*

What was it like to cross the Pacific in those days? **John Hults** *of Liberty, Missouri, offers some insight.*

O UR UNIT was formed on what the Navy called Goat Island in the San Francisco Bay. Our ship was loaded and we boarded it in Oakland, California. The whole Base Roses Force left the states April 12, 1942, from different ports on the West Coast. Our ship was the Old President Tyler. The ships carried Army, Navy, and Marines, a hospital unit, torpedo unit, and the second half of the 1st CB Battalion.

After a few engine break downs, the ship was only able to make about half speed, six knots, through Pacific waters patrolled by the enemy submarines. Needless to say we were on edge most of the time.

It was hot below the decks and after the lavatories ran over, it was really smelly below. The convoy arrived off of the Coast of the Island of Efate in the New Hebrides Islands a day after the Coral Sea Battle. Of course, this was before the landing on Tulagi and the Guadalcanal battles.

I guess in a way we were a bunch of brave souls, because there wasn't much of a naval fleet or air force between us and the enemy.

There was, however, a good supply of enemy craft. Yet, according to **E.W. Stewart** *of San Francisco, it may be true that what you don't know won't hurt you.*

I N APRIL 1942 I was a 16 year old throttleman and my ship just had a Jap sub attack. The Chief Quartermaster hollered over the speaking tube, "They just fired two torpedoes at us, but missed!"

I told the Engineering Officer this and he said quietly, "Tell him thanks, but keep it a secret from us next time, please."

Then again, **Claude F. Dilks** *of Hawthorne, Florida, found another way to deal with the threat of Japanese submarines.*

W E WERE PUT on a troop ship at Treasure Island in San Francisco, heading for Guam, just one of a large convoy of maybe 15 ships and 2 destroyers.

It was very scary at night, no lights, no smoking etc. On the second day out I became seasick and stayed seasick for the next 30 days until we arrived in Guam.

There was about 3000 other sailors on board and it was hard to find a spot on the rails to unload my stomach. After a day or two of this they became dry heaves, as I was unable to eat any food. It was quite useless to use the heads as they were as busy as the rails with seasick sailors.

At least my condition took off some of the fear of being torpedoed because if you are seasick this long, you really don't care if you live or die.

Still, the situation in the Pacific was no laughing matter. US forces were at a disadvantage in nearly every category. However, one distinct advantage enjoyed by the Allies was the ability to break and read Japanese codes. Late in April, US intelligence discovered Japanese plans to take Port Moresby, New Guinea. The Japanese are aware of the presence of one aircraft carrier in the area, but don't know that there are two, the Yorktown *and the* Lexington, *both under the command of Adm. Chester Nimitz.*

The coming confrontation begins on May 2 and will be known as the Battle of the Coral Sea. During the battle, both aircraft carriers are hit. The Lexington *is abandoned and later sunk but the* Yorktown *will survive to fight again.*

In the confusion, both the American and Japanese fleets try to locate each other. On May 7, 21 Japanese aircraft will mistake the Yorktown *for a Japanese carrier and try to land on her. Meanwhile, US pilots were working hard.* **Robert J. Hodgens Sr**. *of Ridge, New York, tells what it was like that day.*

ON MAY 8, 1942, at age 17, I was flying in a SBD, Dauntless dive bomber, 5-B-19, bombing squadron 5, USS Yorktown CV-5.

At 0915 the Air Group launched the attack. Pilot Lt. Moan and I took off with full gas tanks and a 1000 lb. bomb. Jap ships were sighted and radio silence was broken.

"Go get the bastards."

We dove down on the Jap carrier "Shokaku" with a direct hit onto the forward flight deck. We encountered heavy anti-aircraft fire and Jap zeros blasting away at us. Although being wounded, I shot down one Zero. Lt. Moan was also wounded.

We made it back to the Yorktown and crashed on the deck with gas tanks empty. We were pulled from the plane and received medical attention. I received the Purple Heart and Distinguished Flying Cross.

*As the battle at sea took place, heavy fighting was still taking place on the surrounding islands, including the Philippines. Wainwright had surrendered, but some forces assigned to fight delaying actions never got the word. That's what happened to Pacoima, Californian **Pedro Y. Ylagan's** group.*

I WAS A PLATOON LEADER during our encounter at Bacolod, Lanao, Philippines, where we fought a delaying action on May 3, 1942, when the Japanese landed at Malaband, Cotabato.

On that delaying action we were outfought, but we stood our ground. My platoon experienced bombing from planes, artillery shells, and stoke mortar fire, while our troops returned fire with our machine guns and automatic rifles. Our reserved force at the rear of the defense line withdrew earlier to Dansalan, Lanao, but the message ordering us to withdraw never reached our line due to the advancing Japanese troops.

My platoon was reported missing in action. If some of us were able to survive it was God's will. Our only way out when darkness came on May 3 was to go up the hill. Only 10 of my enlisted men, two wounded, survived the onslaught.

*The Japanese were making determined efforts to gain complete control of the Pacific area, and still knew they must take Port Moresby, New Guinea. Daily bombings and attacks made life in the region miserable, but other things added to it as well, says **William W. Travis** of Birmingham, Alabama.*

THE DAY WE LANDED at Port Moresby, New Guinea, in May 1942 I was grazed on the forehead by a low flying Zero.

The next day we moved seven miles inland to our airstrip. At the first air raid warning, I took cover in a slit trench only to discover it was infested with more than 200 black widow spiders. I jumped into the trench with the spiders. They must have been as scared as I was. None bit me, but I stayed clear of the area from then on.

I came home from the Pacific ten weeks after the end of the war, with not a scratch after the first day. I now believe that crouching among venomous spiders makes a more vivid memory to a new soldier than the first sight of enemy fighters.

The Japanese are tenacious, and continue to land forces on islands across the Pacific. Mindinao, Philippines, is forced to surrender on May 10, leaving mostly small multi-national guerrilla groups on the Philippines to harass and ambush the Japanese occupation forces.

But on May 14, the Americans once again intercept and decode a Japanese message and discover Japan's plans for the invasion of Midway. Because of this, when Japan sends two aircraft carriers and two cruisers to Alaska's Aleutian Islands as a diversionary tactic on May 25, US forces are not fooled.

The Yorktown, *which had been heavily damaged in the Battle of the Coral Sea, reaches Pearl Harbor to undergo repairs on May 27. Through superhuman efforts, the repairs are completed and* Yorktown *joins a fleet heading for Midway to intercept the Japanese. Compared to the ships the Japanese have available it is a pitifully small force, though in total number of carrier-based aircraft, the forces are about equal. The battleships* Colorado *and* Maryland *are dispatched from San Francisco in a desperate attempt to reinforce the Midway task forces.*

The Japanese are unaware that the US ships have already departed Hawaii and are in position northeast of Midway. Believing themselves safe, the Japanese invasion fleet launches 108 aircraft against the American-held island on the morning of June 4.

The Americans detect the aircraft and launch their own planes and are massacred, though little damage is inflicted on the island base itself.

At dawn, aircraft from the three carriers in the two US task forces launch their own aircraft in an attempt to locate the Japanese fleet. At 0930, the fleet is attacked by 41 US dive bombers. Only six survive the attack and no damage is done.

Admiral Nagumo has most of his aircraft aboard, preparing to strike at the US fleet. He is ready to launch his planes against the Americans when a second wave of American aircraft attacks. Within five minutes, three of the four Japanese carriers are sunk, their decks loaded with planes. But the Japanese carrier Hiryu *is untouched and launches its planes, which find the USS Yorktown.* **Wesley Woodland** *of Lake Ronkonkoma, New York, was aboard that valiant ship.*

WHILE IN THE BATTLE of Midway, June 3-6 1942, while serving on the Aircraft Carrier USS Yorktown (CV5) we were hit by Japanese bombs. We had to abandon ship.

I was top side manning an anti-aircraft gun. Leaving the ship hand-over-hand by a knotted line into the oily waters. I had nothing on except a life jacket. I was in the water for about 3 hours and being very fortunate to be picked up by a passing Destroyer and even luckier not to be wounded during the attack.

*Another crew member was **James R. Ball** of Hertford, North Carolina. Even in disaster, American GIs seem to always retain some sense of humor.*

I WAS AN 18 YEAR OLD farm boy from Tennessee when I heard the word passed on the PA system, "Abandon ship, nearest land bares ___ degrees, distance ___ miles, depth of water 90 fathoms."

This was aboard the USS Yorktown CV5 in June 1942 at the Battle of Midway.

Unable to get to my abandon ship station on the port side because it was under water, I went over on the high starboard side, after placing my shoes in a neat line on deck beside those of my many shipmates.

While we were in the water for about two hours, our worries were not about sharks or drowning, but of enemy planes strafing us, as we had been told they did.

On the humorous side was the Chief MAA going by on a yellow aircraft raft yelling, "Taxi."

The Yorktown *will not sink until June 7, when a Japanese sub spots her and torpedoes the hulk, finally sending it to the bottom.*

Meanwhile, aircraft from the Hornet *and the* Enterprise *find the* Hiryu *late in the afternoon on June 4. In one day, the Japanese have lost four carriers, leaving only two major aircraft carriers in their fleet. Worse, they have lost many of their most experienced pilots. The Battle of Midway is one of the most decisive sea victories the Americans will experience during the war.*

Chapter 10
Pacific Toeholds

Allied forces in the Pacific were engaged in either trying to hold on to bases or attempting to retake those they had lost by late summer 1942. Production facilities in US factories and manufacturing companies had regeared seemingly overnight into war industries and almost daily, fresh—albeit green—troops were loaded aboard ships converted into troop carriers and sent overseas to bolster and reinforce the GIs already on station in the Pacific.

For the most part, America was supported by New Zealand and Australian troops in the South Pacific. Japanese forces are intent on taking and occupying a number of targets, including the strategic Port Moresby, New Guinea.

To gain that objective, Japanese troops land at Gona, New Guinea on July 21 and advance along the Kokoda Trail, a pathway through the mountainous jungle terrain that eventually leads to Port Moresby. By July 23, the Japanese have captured Buna. The fighting in the dense, primitive jungle areas and at the settlements along the trail will last for months.

The Americans have recognized the need to stop the advancing Japanese and also realize they, too, need operative air bases on the strategic islands of the South Pacific. On July 31, American bombers attack Tulagi and Guadalcanal in the Solomons, where Japanese forces are constructing air strips of their own.

Although they didn't know it at the time, **John J. Maguire** *of Wallingford, Pennsylvania, and his shipmates were about to participate in a historic event.*

A FTER A LONG, UNESCORTED TRIP to the New Hebrides in 1943, we were commanded by the Navy to a refueling detail. We sat there refueling destroyers as they came in from their runs and as we ran low, another tanker would pump us full again. Often we would have four destroyers tied up along side at a time. We even had an Australian raider stop for a fill-up. The yard oiler was our best customer. They transported fuel from us to the cruisers and carriers.

On one refueling detail, we were sent to a remote island to rendezvous with two troops carriers loaded with the first Marines destined to land at Guadalcanal.

When we returned to Espiritu Santo, we painted a big, black eight-ball on our bridge.

On August 7, the 1st Marine Division, under the command of Lt. Gen. Alexander Vandergrift, lands on Guadalcanal. At first, there is little reaction from the Japanese, though two smaller Marine detachments land on Tulagi and Gavutu where they immediately face strong resistance. The quiet on Guadalcanal is short-lived and what ensues is an epic land and sea battle. **Robert V. Delanoy** *of Kingston, New York, offers a reflection on just how inexperienced our forces really were.*

WE LANDED without much opposition early in the morning. Around noontime the Japanese Air Force bombed and strafed all the ships that supported the landing. We took the air strip without much action.

That night we were told to go into a coconut grove to dig fox-holes and sleep. All of a sudden we heard a lot of loud booming noises. My buddy next to me said, "Boy we're giving the Japs hell tonight," and he no more said that when the coconut trees in that grove began flying around just like toothpicks.

The Japanese were shelling us.

I'll tell you, that was a scary thing ...... that was my indoctrination to combat. From then on we knew we were in a serious situation and it was a case of survival. That was a rude awakening. Needless to say, foxholes were dug deeper from then on.

Meanwhile, forces on the other landing sites weren't faring much better. Here's what **Albert N. Garbarino** *of San Diego, California, remembers of Gavutu, where Japanese defenders were deeply entrenched in caves on the island.*

WHEN WE LANDED on the island of Gavutu, I was with the 1st Parachute Battalion, under command of Marine Col. Robert H. Williams.

The landing consisted of three waves. Two met heavy fire and became pinned down until "B" Company overran the enemy's position on hill 148, Gavutu's "Solitary Hill." Conquering Gavutu was a must.

Our leader Captain Harry L Torgerson. His strategy to oust the Japanese from their caves was to tie dynamite sticks together, demand surrender, then toss the charge into the caves.

Lying fifteen feet away, wounded and helpless amid the deafening sound of exploding dynamite and shaking earth, I feared further injury. The sound and fury of the explosions, so close and fierce, was an unforgettable experience.

The captain's scheme was a complete success.

Offshore, the Navy was shelling the islands and sending in a steady stream of supplies to support the Marine landing forces. On August 9, *however, Japanese cruisers enter Sealark Channel, which will later be nick-named Ironbottom Sound, and engage the Navy support ships. Four US ships are sunk, leaving the Marines short on supplies. **Joseph R. Tomaino** of Monroeville, Pennsylvania, tells of that fateful night aboard ship.*

THAT NIGHT, I lost my second home, the *USS Vincennes*. We lived and fought together. We were there on August 7, 1942 for our country's first successful offense against Japan. We bombarded the shores of Guadalcanal to ward off Japanese planes from attacking the Marines and supply ships.

Then came August 9 at 12:05 A.M. It was a very dark night. We were suddenly hit by heavy gunfire from Japanese ships and torpedoes from Jap submarines. Direct hits silenced our guns, started fires, wounding and killing. She started sinking.

Those who could abandoned ship. Fires on deck lit the sky. She slowly sank and I watched teary-eyed, sad of heart. Darkness returned. I had lost my second home, many of my friends and buddies. Survivors floated around for seven hours. Our destroyers dropped depth charges to ward off sharks and Japanese subs.

My ship, second home, and buddies will never be forgotten. A piece of my flesh went down with her.

It is small consolation that the next day a US submarine spots and sinks the Japanese cruiser Kako *as it was returning to Rabaul from the Sealark Channel engagement.*

*Another man involved in the fighting that fateful night was **William M. Stoessel Jr., Edith S. Landon's** brother. Landon now lives in Fay-etteville, North Carolina. She would discover that he, like thousands of other GIs, seldom talked about their wartime experiences.*

ONE DAY in September 1942 I answered the doorbell and there stood my 24-year-old brother who was a Machinist Mate First Class as-signed to the cruiser Astoria in the South Pacific. He said his ship was in for repair and he would be home for two weeks. We were elated to see him as a couple of weeks earlier, my mother had a bad dream about him so she started praying.

After a few days, the Navy issued a communiqué saying the Japanese had sunk the USS Astoria, Vincennes, Quincy and the Australian ship, Canberra on August 9, 1943.

My brother told us he abandoned ship one-half hour before she sank and was rescued a couple of hours later. He and my patriotism were the reasons I joined the WAVES in December 1943.

It was as though each disaster, each valiant action lent fuel to the fires of nationalism that grew hotter by the day. People cheered as America struck back, although the price of each offensive was very high.

A 600-man Marine Raider force attacks a Japanese base at Taivu on August 7, which disrupts Japanese plans to attack Guadalcanal, but on August 12 an attack known as "Bloody Ridge" does take place. After two days of fighting, the Japanese have nothing to show for their efforts but 1,200 dead.

In other areas, the Japanese are more successful. In New Guinea, they drive to within 30 miles of Port Moresby before American troops arrive to reinforce the Australian defenders. With reinforcements, the Allies take the offensive and by the end of the month, the Japanese troops are retreating down the Kokoda Trail.

Still, the battle would not be won overnight, as **Steve Disco** *of Chapmanville, West Virginia, would learn.*

FROM 7 AUGUST 1942 to 9 February 1943, in the Solomon Islands seven months on Tulagi and Guadalcanal. Went through more than we bargained for. Then on to Saipan in the Marianas. That wasn't bad enough, we got the news that was to join Douglas MacArthur's 10th Army Div. to hit Tokyo. All of a sudden we got news we were glad to hear: We dropped the bomb.

But that day was still a long way off.

It is vital that the forces on Guadalcanal not only complete Henderson Field air strip, but also hold it. To that end, Espiritu Santu in New Guinea receives large numbers of reinforcements to build a base and ensure support to the troops engaged in the Guadalcanal campaign. Of course, the Japanese were aware of American activities at Espiritu Santu and a number of serious attacks took place. In between, however, according to **Bru Mysak** *of Jackson Heights, New York, they were harassed on a regular basis.*

ON ESPIRITU SANTO in the New Hebrides, there was a certain Japanese airplane we used to call "Washing Machine Charlie." "Charlie" made nightly flights and dropped 100 lb. bombs on us just to keep us on edge.

I was taking a shower when I heard the alert. Wrapping a towel around my waist and slipping on my wooden sandals, I ran to our underground air raid shelter. I was gingerly walking down to the bottom because it had rained and it was muddy when I got a sudden boot in the rear and fell in the mud. I hollered at my buddy, saying look what you've done! He said, "Are you nuts, you SOB? My butt was exposed and you're worried about mud?"

By the August 18, the Japanese on Guadalcanal have received reinforcements, but they make a major error based on faulty intelligence. They believe there are only about 3,000 American troops on the island and on August 21, launch a number of fanatic attacks against Guadalcanal's defenders. Instead of 3,000, there are now 10,000 troops on the island and the attackers are annihilated near the Tenaru River. Meanwhile, other important actions take place in the Pacific Theater. The Battle of the Eastern Solomons on August 24 results in the sinking of a Japanese aircraft carrier, but the US carrier Enterprise *is badly damaged.*

On August 27, the carrier Saratoga *is badly damaged and temporarily out of action. The only major US carrier in the Pacific is the* USS Wasp.

Meanwhile, the Japanese try to land forces at Milne Bay, New Guinea, but find fierce resistance from both Australian and US forces. By August 31, the Japanese withdraw from Milne Bay to concentrate on Guadalcanal. The Milne Bay action has cost them 1,000 men.

While the fighting at Milne Bay eventually stopped, the Japanese didn't forget about it, says **L.J. Hawkins** *of Maxwell, Texas.*

I T WAS AROUND 5 P.M. and raining as it can only rain in the tropics when our minesweeper entered Milne Bay, New Guinea. It was already pitch dark and on our way into the bay we passed a sunken cargo ship.

When we anchored, we could hear guns on the far side of the mountain, and Tokyo Rose welcomed us to Milne Bay on the radio.

My thought was that no one could possibly know where we were. Time proved my thoughts wrong and we operated out of there for almost two years and became quite used to Tokyo Rose advising us to leave.

One way or another, the Japanese wanted the Allied forces out of the South Pacific islands. By early September, the fighting on Guadalcanal and the surrounding areas is becoming intense and air support from the Milne Bay base plays an important part in the defense of the Solomons. **Clifton L. White** *of Brewer, Maine, says his air group was well known by the Japanese.*

I T WAS AROUND SEPT. 42 and my outfit the 403rd Bomb Squadron was at Milne Bay, New Guinea.

We had just taken it from the Japs a while before and they were trying to get it back. They had it in for us because we played dirty tricks on them. We dumped our garbage on them after exhausting our bombs. We also wire-wrapped our anti-personnel bombs to make them more deadly. They were timed to explode 75 feet above ground.

The Japs vowed to get us and one day they came over in a tight V formation, 27 strong. They pattern-bombed our entire camp area. Never scratched a man. I had four bombs straddle me. Talk about Lady Luck.

The Japs nick-named us The Mareeba Butchers and we adopted that name.

Though he doesn't mention it, White's unit was probably kept very busy. During the entire month, sporadic fighting takes place on land, sea, and air.

On October 11 and 12, another major sea battle, the Battle of Cape Esperance, takes place. With help from the aircraft based at Henderson Field, the Japanese will eventually lose a cruiser and two destroyers. Aircraft launched from Henderson are a thorn in the side to the Japanese, but not all pilots return to base safely. **Andrew Schmidt** *of Iron River, Michigan, can take credit for one pilot's return.*

ONE SUNDAY I was on watch aboard our destroyer, the USS Trathen #530. I thought I saw a bird falling from the sky in the distance, but after watching closely, I decided it wasn't a bird and reported it over the microphone.

Later, our captain summoned me and congratulated me. What I had seen was one of our pilots who'd been shot down, coming down in his parachute. Our ship had radioed the carrier we'd been escorting and the pilot had been rescued.

This was the only time I recall being glad I was in the Pacific. We saw enemy planes every day, but the suicide planes were really memorable! The day before we headed back to the states, we were hit by a 55 lb. five-inch shell. Four of our boys never made it home. No branch of the service is really safe.

With each major conflict, those who survived helped to spur on support in the United States for the war effort. **Edmund Jantz** *of Heber Springs, Arkansas, remembers their reception.*

WE RETURNED to the states after the Battle of Cape Esperance. As we went up the river to the Philadelphia Navy Yard, it seemed as though every ship or boat that could float was there to greet us. People lined up everywhere and fire boats discharged their hoses and there were horns and sirens and church bells. If it made noise, they used it. It was a fantastic sight.

It made us feel proud, having your people turn out to pay their respects to the 107 men we lost and to our ship, the USS Boise, nicknamed the "One-Ship fleet."

I'm sure the six Jap ships painted on our superstructure helped fuel the fire, but now they were a part of the effort put forth by the Navy. The people of Philadelphia treated us like royalty. Thank you.

While the USS Boise *was making its way home, disaster strikes in the Pacific. On September 14, the last operational US carrier, the* USS Wasp, *is sunk and the battleship* North Carolina *is damaged by three torpedoes from a Japanese submarine. Replacements and rapidly repaired ships are outfitted and launched into the Pacific theater.*

On October 25 and 26, the Battle of Santa Cruz takes place, where the carrier Hornet *is sunk and the* Enterprise *severely damaged. However, the Japanese lose most of their attacking aircraft.* **George Marse** *of Harahan, Louisiana, offers some comments.*

THE JAPANESE suicide pilots inflicted great destruction on our Pacific fleets. Imagine a pilot voluntarily and intentionally killing himself by plunging his aircraft into our warships.

They brought fear to the entire fleet with their low-level flying and their dive bombing from great heights as they piloted a bomb to contact. They struck the Enterprise, Wasp and Franklin, to name just a few.

Regardless of our hatred for the Japs, you have to admire the devotion to country demonstrated by those pilots. Yet, when they were shot down, rescued and brought aboard our ship, we were surprised to find the pilots looked like ordinary, scared young men, not the wide-eyed fanatical "devils" we imagined them to be.

Whether or not they were "devils," it was clear the Japanese recognized Guadalcanal as a strategic threat. Two Japanese battleships shell Henderson Field on October 27 and destroy 50 aircraft. Both sides manage to land reinforcements during the engagement, including 3,000 men from the US Americal Division. The Japanese forces now number about 20,000 and will again go on the offensive. By October 27, the offensive collapses after the Japanese lose an estimated 3,500 troops. Both sides are exhausted from the nearly continuous fighting. In addition to aircraft, ship-to-ship confrontations were common, and sometimes fate played a role in the outcome, as reported by **William A. Derryberry** *of Columbia, Tennessee.*

WHILE SERVING aboard the USS Trever (DMS-16), a high speed converted "Flush Deck" destroyer minesweeper, we supported the Marines on Guadalcanal and Tulagi. After unloading munitions and supplies at Tulagi on October 25, 1942, we were informed of three Japanese destroyers standing down the "slot" to shell Henderson Field.

Our skipper, Cmdr. D.M. Agnew decided to make a run for it rather than be trapped in Tulagi Bay. The Trever and our companion ship the USS Zane, zigzagged to avoid the fire from the fast closing Japanese ships.

Within firing range and exchanging fire, the Zane (DMS-14), took a hit amidships at number 3 gun, killing three men including the "sightsetter". Had the Japs hit us instead of the Zane, I might have been killed. I was Trever's "sightsetter" on number 3 gun.

Life was certainly no better on land than at sea, according to **Carl M. (Bud) DeVere Sr.** *of Alexandria, Virginia.*

I WAS AT HENDERSON FIELD, Guadalcanal with a Marine Corps aviation squadron. I spent the entire day seeking shelter from strafing Japanese Zeros. My selections always seemed insecure. In one, I had been laying beside a 50 gallon drum of high octane fuel in a gasoline dump containing hundreds of such drums.

Another time I dove under an abandoned Japanese truck as a strafing plane came over the trees. When the run was over I found my shelter was a full gasoline tank just above my head. A short time later I arose from a muddy foxhole after a sneak attack to discover blood oozing down my face. A bullet crease? I thought back to before the firing began, and realized I had been snagged by a thorny vine in my jump to the hole as the rounds began plowing up the dirt at my feet.

Artillery and aerial bombardment will continue, however. The Japanese are determined to take or destroy Henderson Field, whose aircraft missions against Japanese targets have proven very successful.

Day and night, again and again, the Japanese hammered away at the Guadalcanal defenders. And the Americans grew hungry for retaliation, according to **Homer E. Draughn** *of El Centro, California.*

IT WAS NOVEMBER 1942 when A Battery 1st Battalion, 11th Regiment, 1st. Marine Division struck back, individually, at strafing Zeros at Henderson Field, Guadalcanal.

A-1-11's primary mission was supporting our infantry holding the front lines. Heretofore shortages of light weapon ammunition had allowed the Zeros to hit us with impunity, but today we had ammo.

A-1-11, tired, battered and demoralized from naval gun-fire went to breakfast—limp Rice Crispys, powdered milk, and coffee, no sugar!—then two pilots arrived: friend and foe.

The friend, too heavy laden, crashed into our hellish acre. Next came the enemy strafing, spilling milk, scattering mess-kits and Marines.

We saved our unconscious pilot, shot up the Zeros that followed their leader and our morale climbed faster than P-38s intercepting Mitsubishis.

Retrospectively, that Sunday is a brilliant, priceless and bloody GEM. R.I.P. Mates, Mount Austen is your living monument.

In will be in January that US forces will launch an attack against Gifu, the Japanese garrison stronghold on Mount Austen and the struggle will last well into the next month before the stronghold falls.

Before the Mount Austen assault, however, a number of other actions and events take place. The Navy is able to land Marine reinforcements on the island to help relieve the constant bombardment and shelling, but even that isn't easy, as **L.W. Brockman** *of Hinsdale, Illinois, tells it.*

AS WE APPROACHED Guadalcanal on a lone Liberty ship, sirens shrieked and horns honked warning of aircraft. Bedlam! GIs jam the passageways. Sailors couldn't get through to their gun turrets. One sailor grabbed a fire hose and shouted, "Make way or I'll wash you overboard!"

We hit the deck and literally walked over the Army to get to our posts.

Those airplanes were friendly, but God bless the Navy anyway.

And bless those faces I will never forget; strangers who became friends—Forseca from California, Schaf of Nebraska, Hayley of Kentucky and Hausmann of Illinois. Faces with chicken shit grins, sweaty noses, forced smiles—I'll never forget them.

The heat of battle and shared risk would create friendships that would last a lifetime. Many would reunite within service organizations like The American Legion. Many, however, would never return, like some of the men who fought at Guadalcanal.

Two days earlier, **Joseph M. Kowal** *of Reading, Pennsylvania, had gotten a preview of what was to come.*

THE 1ST AVIATION ENGINEERS, 1st Marines Reinforced, entered Sealark Channel on November 11, 1942 Solomon Islands and I never forgot the Convoy's arrival off Lunga. It was November 10, 1942 in the states, the anniversary of the founding of the Corps.

Captain of our transport, the Zeilin, gave a speech on Marine history. General Quarters sounded and we were attacked by Japanese dive bombers as the convoy's anti-aircraft guns began the frantic firing.

The planes roared in low and the Zeilin's hull was ruptured by near misses. The vessel was in no danger of sinking. Where our ship went that night for safety and repairs I do not know, but we landed in the morning. The greatest naval sea battle in history was starting and our outfit was in the middle of it.

That day, both Japanese and American ships intended to land reinforcements at Guadalcanal. Ironically, this was also the day that the US government lowered the draft age from 20 to 18.

On November 13, the Battle of Guadalcanal takes place. A Japanese convoy carrying 11,000 troops and escorted by 11 destroyers, plus two battleships, two cruisers and 14 destroyers, approaches Guadalcanal. The troops are reinforcements. The warships intend to add their firepower to the bombardment of Henderson Field.

A US force of five cruisers and eight destroyers moves in to intercept the enemy convoy and a late-night half-hour sea battle ensues. Most of the Japanese ships are damaged and two cruisers are sunk. The next morning one crippled Japanese battleship must be scuttled after American bombers torpedo her.

American losses include two cruisers and four destroyers. One of the cruisers is the USS Juneau. *Aboard this ship are five brothers, the Sullivans from Waterloo, Iowa, who had petitioned the Navy to serve together.*

The Juneau *is not sunk during the night action, but is badly crippled. The next morning, she and another ship are spotted by a Japanese submarine. Three torpedoes are launched. One eye-witness said that the* Juneau *didn't sink; it literally blew itself apart.*

Initial reports were that all hands were lost. While inaccurate, only about 140 of the 700 men aboard survive. The Sullivans are not among the survivors. Again, the hand of fate touches a number of people, including **M.D. Roberge** *of Rutland, Vermont.*

I TOOK MY BOOT TRAINING at Newport, Rhode Island in 1942, having been the first to volunteer from the bank where I was employed.

I was scheduled to embark for duty on the cruiser, "Juneau". At the last moment, this was canceled and our company left on February 12 for Panama, arriving there on February 22.

Not long afterward we got news in Panama that the "Juneau" was sunk—and all were lost.

I am 71 years old now, but I could have been doomed at 23.

For some, like **Delwood S. Jackson** *of Cincinnati, Ohio, the loss of the* Juneau *was even more important.*

MY DRAFT NUMBER was 158 but I was not drafted at once. My mother had a stroke when the war began and lay in bed for months. On 13 November 1942 she sat up in bed and said: "Something has happened to Bill", and had a second stroke and passed away in Durham, North Carolina.

I was drafted about 10 days later at Ft. Bragg and sent to Camp Lee (now Ft Lee), Virginia. On 20 December 1942, I wrote a letter to my brother, Aubrey Stancil "Bill" Jackson, at USS Juneau, and it was returned.

Later we learned that USS Juneau had been sunk on 13 November 1942, and Bill had been lost.

For one, the tragic sinking of the Juneau *would come back to haunt him more than 20 years later.* **Frank C. Perrelli** *of Hudson, Florida, understands too well what a loss this was to the parents of the Sullivan brothers.*

I TOOK RECRUIT TRAINING in the same barracks as the Sullivan brothers. They were in company 51 and I was in 52. All five brothers would later die in battle aboard the USS Juneau, along with Frank Hurban, a friend from my home town of Lodi, New Jersey.

The last time I saw them was in Panama, jut before they shipped out to the Pacific.

Yet, of all the war memories—the malaria, the wounded, the burials at sea—none would hurt me so much as when, a little more than 20 years later, I would lose my own son in Vietnam.

Marine Lance Corporal Keith F. Perrelli was killed in action 24 Sept. 1967.

For two Americans, November 13 would offer good news for one and horrid news for another. **Marjorie McDonough Lovejoy** *of Buffalo, New York, joined the ranks of working women after her husband shipped out. Like many wives before and after, she worked and worried. Her worries were tragically well-placed.*

W HEN MY HUSBAND'S CRUISER sailed in July 1942, I volunteered for "war work", joining other civilians working for the Aircraft Warning Service in a New York City Filter Center. Mrs. Eddie Rickenbacker was the distinguished lady who helped volunteers plot the courses of planes flying over New York. Her quiet dedication during the long search for her husband, whose plane had gone down in the Pacific, gave way to radiance when Capt. Rickenbacker was rescued after being adrift for a month in a rubber raft.

She made her way through the center thanking everyone for their encouragement during her ordeal and expressing the happiness we all shared with her.

I later learned that my husband's ship, the USS Juneau, had been sunk in the Battle of Guadalcanal and I was widowed on the same day as Capt. Eddie's rescue—Friday the 13th of November, 1942.

But the Juneau *is not the only ship to see action. For those ashore that night, the two naval forces put on quite a show, according to* **Edward Klisiewicz** *of Temple, Texas.*

O UR SQUADRON landed on Henderson Field, Guadalcanal in the Solomon Islands a few days before bloody Friday the 13th of November 1942, between the Japanese and American warships. Admiral King called this battle the fiercest Naval Battle ever fought. Even Henderson Field took a beating and I thought the whole Island was blowing up.

Two or three days later, under the hot sun bloated bodies, both American sailors and Japanese were washed up on the beach. I was one of the unlucky ones in a group that was told to carefully carry the Americans inland for proper burial. Then go back and bayonet the bloated Japanese bodies to let the air out so they could be buried where the Sea-bees had dug a long trench above the high tide-mark.

Desperate days require desperate measures.

And these were desperate days. Nor was Sergeant Klisiewicz the only one on burial duty. **Leo L. Varner** *of Rome, New York, knows about it.*

I WAS INVOLVED in carrying the litter baskets to the hanger deck of the aircraft carrier that I had help put in commission. These baskets were flag draped and held the bodies of Marines who had been killed on board my ship and they were prepared for burial at sea.

Why I remember it most, is that 2 of these Marines and I had become real friends, always kidding each other since we had all been on the ship since commissioning.

Now I was involved with burying them at sea.

The ceremony, the stillness, the basket tipped slightly, the splash of the weighted body hitting the water, then the ship would make a left or right turn with only the American flag remaining over the basket. We were real buddies and they served their country well.

The intense fighting on Guadalcanal will continue into the New Year, but the exhausted Marines who had first carried the initial battle are relieved by the XIV Corps and sent to Australia on December 9.

As Christmas approached, fighting in New Guinea and the Solomons showed no evidence of slowing down. On Christmas Eve, **Guy A. Bensinger Jr.** *of Palm Beach Gardens, Florida, flew his first mission.*

I T HAPPENED way back in 1942. The glow was not from lighting a giant Christmas tree or the Northern lights; just a much needed attack on a Jap Island.

Preparations for the longest heavy bomber raid began in Hawaii—26 B-24 bombers then flew to Midway Island. Bomb bay tanks with extra gas had been installed and bottoms of aircraft were painted black. Destination: Wake Island.

Crews were briefed. Takeoff in fog was a bit hairy! First phase of the trip was at a high altitude, with radio silence to avoid enemy sub detection. Several aircraft arrived ahead of the group alerting the Jap search lights and anti-aircraft guns. A concentrated fire welcomed us.

The glare was intense as we dove to low level and released our loads.

My first mission and a Christmas Eve I will never forget.

On New Guinea, fighting was still taking place along the Kokoda Trail, though Papua had been cleaned out of Japanese troops. Yet, even war cannot destroy the Christmas spirit. Here's what **Stan W. Carlson** *of Minneapolis, Minnesota, remembers of that Christmas.*

W E WERE IN COMBAT in the steamy jungles of New Guinea when Christmas arrived. There was little promise of a pleasant Yule until we decided to do our best to celebrate this great event.

We asked our colonel to cease combat patrols for Christmas and maintain only the necessary guard, and he agreed.

Both officers and enlisted men contributed food from home to provide a festive table and our cooks baked enough bread for two slices apiece. We had Spam and sardines, fruit including peaches and pineapple, and the well-known battery-acid lemonade. Our chefs also baked a huge decorated cake, and we had nuts and candy.

After the meal, we sang Christmas songs accompanied by the chaplain's wheezy organ and as dusk approached, we watched a movie in our theater perched on coconut log seats.

The Navy men from the ship in the harbor were invited and when it was dark, we had a real surprise. The sailors had strung lights—all blue bulbs—to outline their ship. In the darkness, the outlined ship was a thing of beauty.

For a few brief hours, the war had seemed far away and we knew the true meaning of "peace on earth, good will toward men."

Of course, not everyone's memory of Christmas is the same. For in-

*stance, **John U. Martinez** of Hemet, California, has a considerably different memory.*

WE WERE ATTACKED by a submarine Christmas day December 25, 1942 off of Christmas Island. We were loaded with bombs and P-38s @ 1130 hours. A US Navy KA ship.

*For others, the entire holiday season simply meant more fighting and more days at risk. That's the situation **Elmer Hangartner** of Fairfield, California, found himself in three days after Christmas.*

I WAS WITH H-COMPANY, 127 Inf. the whole time overseas. On December 28, 1942 at 4:30 PM, two combat engineers and I volunteered to repair a section of a foot bridge over Entrance Creek, in New Guinea. We were carrying a plank to replace the one that was blown out by artillery fire.

When we were about halfway across, a Jap machine gun opened fire on us. The end man was hit almost immediately He continued with us, and we got the plank in place.

The first man jumped off the right side of the bridge. I jumped off the left side. We both got to the Jap-held shore. The third man who was badly wounded, got his foot caught in the bridge and hung head down in the water.

We were unable to help him in any way. The other combat engineer and I hid on the Jap side, for over 5 hours, then swam across to the US side after dark. Since then, I often think of that day and relive the whole action.

In the South Pacific, there was little hope that the next year would be much better.

Chapter 11
Battle for the Islands

In New Guinea, the Allies are making headway, and by New Year a portion of the Japanese garrison at Buna is forced to leave.

Meanwhile, at Guadalcanal, US forces again mount attacks against Gifu on Mount Austen, but in spite of intense fighting Gifu still remains in Japanese hands. The fighting has taken its toll, however, and unknown to the Americans, the Japanese are planning to withdraw from Gifu. They are very short on food and each attempt at reinforcing and resupplying the Japanese garrison by sea is foiled by air and sea forces. American PT boats, light-hulled high-speed torpedo boats, are proving to be an extremely effective deterrent tool among the islands.

From March 2 to March 4, in what would become known as the Battle of the Bismark Sea, combined forces of US and Australian aircraft and PT boats would wreak havoc on a Japanese convoy en route to New Guinea. All eight Japanese transports are sunk along with four destroyers. The Japanese lose 3,500 men while losses for Allies amount to only five aircraft. It is a serious blow to the Japanese supply line.

*But the Japanese weren't the only ones experiencing supply problems, according to **Leland B. King** of Flora, Illinois.*

WE TOOK CONTROL of a small island inhabited by 18 natives. A few chickens still remained, though where they came from or how they got there, no one knew.

The natives were moved to a larger island and amphibious carriers came each day with water and rations. When a storm, bringing high winds and rough water, prevented us from receiving rations and water for four days, it presented a problem.

In emergencies, you learn to make do with the best of what you have. We began catching chickens and our mess kits saw action. Whether chicken is your first choice of food or not, we never tasted anything better.

As bases were secured, more and more troops poured into the South Pacific. Of course, "secured" is a relative term. On April 7, Admiral Yamamoto pulls his most seasoned and skilled pilots from the carrier fleet and brings them to the Solomons.

He launches a 180-aircraft raid against Tulagi and Guadalcanal. This attack will be followed by more. Yamamoto has taken a serious risk, because it has left his naval forces with only green pilots. **Ralph E. Rinehart** *of Decatur, Illinois, describes what it was like to experience one of the Japanese air raids.*

O N THE MORNING of April 13, 1943, the Japanese sent 100 planes over the Port Moresby area in New Guinea.

As I returned to the Small Ships Section building after delivering sailing orders to the SS Lorrina, the red alert was sounded. I ran for a ditch outside which overlooked the harbor. The planes were already overhead, filling the sky and all the anti-aircraft guns in the area were firing at them.

As some of the planes were hit by ground fire, they would break formation and head out to sea, pursued by our fighter planes. Thirty-six of the attacking Japanese were reported shot down.

To the surprise and relief of those of us sharing the ditch, not one bomb was dropped on the ships in the harbor or Tatana Island. They did destroy a gas dump outside Port Moresby where six men were reported killed.

Under Yamamoto's direction, the attacks continue and some are not as lucky as Ralph Rinehart and his buddies. **James V. Kruse** *of Elkhart, Indiana, experienced one such incident.*

W E HAD JUST EXPERIENCED a bombing raid on Rendova Island in the South Pacific.

Through the acrid smoke and flying, burning ammunition, we were carrying a man on a litter around the bomb craters. His right leg was shattered and he was propped up on his elbows. His right eye, eyebrow, cheekbone and ear were gone, as was most of his nose. He made no sound. Was not bleeding, but the left eye, dark brown in color, stared at me.

This was not the first or last casualty that I saw while in the Marine Corps, but this nameless face comes to me many times when I awaken in the night.

However, an event that may well have changed the course of the war took place April 18. US intelligence had cracked the Japanese code system. One decoded message announced Admiral Yamamoto's travel plans.

The US launched a special force of P-38 Lightnings and on April 18, 1943, Admiral Yamamoto's plane was shot down. Oddly enough, neither the US or the Japanese announce Yamamoto's death immediately. The US waited until 1944 because to announce what had happened would alert the Japanese that their code system had been broken. The Japanese waited until May before announcing his death because of the impact on morale.

Japan had lost a savvy leader. **Roger W. Rivers** *of Williamstown, Massachusetts, was involved with the incident. He says that 18 Guadalcanal-based P-38s made the attack with the loss of only one plane and pilot.*

W E CELEBRATED the destruction of Admiral Yamamoto's plane by our 13th Air Force fighters in the Northern Solomon Islands. Our intelligence had broken the Japanese code and we were aware of his impending visit to Bougainville, the last of the Solomons still under Japanese control.

Our fighters were sent to bring him down.

What made it so memorable was that we who were involved in the ambush were aware it was going to happen before it took place.

Peter Musso of Orland Park, Illinois, was on Guadalcanal that day repairing the airfield. As his memoir indicates, while Yamamoto's death was important, the war went on.

W HILE REPAIRING Henderson Field at Guadalcanal, in April 1943, we were told to hurry because a squadron of P-38's were to take off on a special mission. A few hours after returning we found out that they had shot down Admiral Yamamoto's plane.

Our next mission was to invade the Russell Islands, 70 miles away. I was to deliver an oral message to the outpost at 3:00 a.m. Our destroyer let us off on a rubber raft about 200 yards from shore. We were given the signal (prearranged with Navy personnel) to go on shore. The message was bombardment to start at 6:00 AM and landing of troops at 7:00. All went well, the Island was secured a few days later.

We took Rendova, Welombangara, Auvendel, New Georgia and others. We were told the Japanese Navy was coming down and for sure a night sea battle would take place. We were on top of a hill watching a fierce battle going on. We saw a Japanese Destroyer ram a PT boat. Later we found out it was PT 109, President Kennedy's boat.

Raymond E. Komro of Durand, Wisconsin, was one of those men who would go ashore at the Russell Island invasion.

M Y FIRST NIGHT on Russell Island I was standing guard over the supplies we had unloaded that day. It was March 1944, and the night and the jungle were very dark. I was scared anyway when, around 0100 hours, a series of nearby explosions made the situation worse.

In the morning I found out the Japs had dropped a few bombs on an air strip not far away.

I was only 16, but I had changed my birth certificate. I was still scared, so I went to my CO and told him I wasn't of age and wanted to go home.

He said, "Son, there isn't a ship headed home for a while, so make the best of it."

Twenty-three months later, after hopping around a few more islands like Guadalcanal, Manus and Emireau, I returned to the states to find I was now a man among men, though at a very early age.

While the Japanese faced problems with intelligence leaks, the US forces had their own problems with "loose lips," as **Thelma Montgomery** *of Des Moines, Iowa, relates.*

I WAS STATIONED in the Schofield Barracks area of Hawaii with the 21st Infantry Reg. It was quite a long time after the war had begun before we were allowed passes, but we did finally get a three day pass for the weekend of Easter 1943. Several of us got together and went to Honolulu.

We found a place to stay overnight and after registering the woman clerk made the remark we would be leaving before long. She looked at a notebook and said we would probably be leaving July 26 or 27.

This was news to us and we got to wondering how she knew the time and date. When we returned to base we told the 1st Sgt. what had happened. He questioned each of us, then called Captain Ringnose and he questioned us, too. Then he called other officers. It was apparent they thought something was wrong. They decided to look into it, and the next morning another fellow who'd been in our group and I took them to the place downtown.

When we entered the lobby, the same woman clerk was at the desk and when Captain Ringnose asked her if she recognized me, she said yes and wanted to know why.

Then he asked her about her remark and where she had gotten her information. She sort of hesitated, then said in a low voice that she wasn't sure, but it was "street talk" and she'd heard it sometime before. They talked a little more, then we returned to camp and the excitement died away.

Then, shortly after the first week of July, things changed. There were no more passes and there was a gradual tightening up. There were rumors, but no exact information until July 20, when they told us we would be leaving shortly.

We left on the 27th, just as the woman at the boarding house had said.

But intelligence leaks, shortages of supplies, even Yamamoto's death, did not stop the air raids and fighting. **Robert L. Roebuck** *of Port Angeles, Washington, describes the air action around Guadalcanal, two months after Yamamoto's death.*

I N ALL, there was only about five minutes of air action, but I still remember June 13, 1943 and Guadalcanal.

We were on yellow alert when I heard a burst of machine gun fire and then the sound of airplanes. I ran from my tent in time to see a Zero flash by just above the top of the palm trees, followed by a "wop-wop-wop" noise. A Navy fighter was firing at the Zero and his rounds were striking the tops of the palms.

Just then a formation of 16 Japanese Betty bombers flew into a cloud overhead, followed by five P-40s. When they emerged from the cloud, two bombers were falling and the formation was going in all directions.

Someone shouted, "Look over there," and I turned in time to see a Zero shoot the tail off a P-38. The P-38's nose pitched down, but in a second, a parachute appeared and a cheer rose from hundreds on the ground.

In all, we lost 11 planes and five pilots. The Japanese lost 93 planes and crews.

Obviously, New Guinea in 1943 was not the safest place in the world to be. Yet, not all who were stationed around there were combatants. In fact, some were downright friendly, according to **John A. Carl** *of Vestaburg, Pennsylvania.*

W HILE ON KIRIWINA ISLAND, 4 native girls, ages 14 to 18 would stop now and then at the orderly room and watch me at the typewriter. The orderly room was built by the natives with living and working quarters for 1st Sgt. Steiger and myself, plus a working area for Capt. Herbert.

After a time, I noticed each girl had her name tattooed on her arm, Nanager, Setawata, Elagula, and Emaete. One day I typed their names on a piece of paper and handed it to each of them. Their actions were unexplainable. I then had visitors 2 or 3 times a week.

Finally one came to the opening and reached in and put her finger on my chest and said, "You, me go bush I want your American baby."

I was sure glad only 1st Sgt. Steiger witnessed it or I would have been teased to death.

The islands weren't the domain of US males only. In fact, there was a fair contingent of females in uniform in the South Pacific, and they, too, faced problems, but of a different sort. **A.G. "Mark" Marquardt** *of Lancaster, California, relates some of them.*

I WORKED with the WACs.
I was the officer-in-charge of the base "G" Signal Center in Hollandia, New Guinea. A WAC detachment of about 200 women was attached to our signal unit as typists, teletype operators and code clerks.

Almost every WAC letter home contained an urgent plea for lipstick, lotions, panties, bras, needles and threads for those who could sew, and most of all, for sanitary napkins. Since they had left Australia, WAC clothing and supplies had not caught up to them. When necessary, the women were issued men's high-top GI shoes, khaki shorts with cute little ties on the side, T-shirts, and fatigue pants that were not designed for females, especially shapely ones.

Mail and packages did arrive intermittently, several truck loads of light-weight mail sacks would be delivered to the Signal Center or WAC compound. The napkins finally arrived, along with other much sought after personal items.

As far as I'm concerned, the WACs were good soldiers!

*WACs weren't the only women in uniform on New Guinea. **Phyllis T. (Santaglo) Galeaz** of Lynn, Massachusetts, was one of them.*

I WAS STATIONED at an evacuation hospital in New Guinea. On the moonlit night of April 23, 1943, a sudden roaring over our wood frame building where I lived drew me outdoors.

The sky was filled with white aircraft bearing the Japanese insignia. Bombs began dropping like rain. The airstrip about five miles away was their target.

My heart pounded as I was overwhelmed with a feeling of helplessness being confined to the ground with no place to hide. We were sitting ducks!

I immediately thought of the numerous patients in the hospital tents on the hill. I ran in that direction, intending to reassure them, only to discover that they, too, were watching the attack and worrying about the nursing staff.

Thereafter, every full moon brought a subsequent attack.

*Yet even in the midst of a war, like a flower growing through the cracks in concrete, romance could bloom. Sometimes, as with **Mrs. Anne Burke** of Hellertown, Pennsylvania, a former captain in the Army's Nursing Corps, World War II is a bittersweet memory of romance.*

D URING WORLD WAR II, I found, then lost my husband during the three years I spent overseas in the Pacific Theater with the Army Nursing Corps.

A wounded soldier is carried from the Advanced Dressing Station at House Banana in New Guinea.

I met him, a very special first lieutenant of the 1st Marine Division, who was commissioned on the battlefields of Guadalcanal, when his division came to Melbourne, Australia, my duty station in 1943.

We saw each other as much as possible for eight months and were married three weeks before his division left for their next campaign. We never spent a full 24-hours together.

At that time, nurses were not allowed to marry and I received a disciplinary reprimand. I could have been discharged from the service, but I was "fortunate" and confined to my quarters for two weeks when not on duty. My husband and I planned our future through the mail for the next three months, but we planned in vain. I was informed of his sudden death from typhus fever following the Cape Gloucester invasion. He was eventually laid to rest at the Manila National Cemetery and I moved on with my hospital unit to New Guinea.

Reading his letters still moves me. His photographs don't age; we were both in our 20s. His uniforms are packed away, but I will always be grateful for that one year of happiness we found in the midst of a terrible war.

Forever young, that's how Mrs. Burke remembers her husband, and sadly, wars are fought by the young. Yet sometimes youth itself allows for memories that, for a moment, relieve the pain and fear of war. **Frederick F. (Ted) Sack** *of Miami, Florida, shares one of those youthful wartime memories.*

I THINK it was sometime in May 1943. There were nine of us in the back of a 6-by-6 Jimmy—an Army truck—riding on a very rough dirt road away from Port Moresby and the ocean on New Guinea, some 12,000 miles away from home.

We had in common our youth and our training as horse mounted cavalry at Fort Riley, Kansas. I was a New Yorker but the others were genuine cowboys from the southwestern United States. We didn't know where we were or where we were going. No one had told us.

The air was very clear and hot and, except for the noise of the engine, very quiet. Suddenly, a sound that could only be attributed to an alien being. It was a cross between a sawmill and a defective police siren. The others looked panic stricken. My innocence saved me for the moment, because I'd never heard a mule bray.

Thus commenced a World War II New Guinea adventure. Fifteen enlisted men, one Lt. Colonel and 1,200 Army mules who would spend 18 months in the 241st Remount Squadron Advanced Echelon some 18 miles inland from the Coral Sea.

By mid-summer, a new term has entered the language of the Pacific theater GI. It's island hopping. Small island chains within island chains become important as allied bases are established and enemy bases are destroyed.

In an effort to block the Japanese supply pipeline, the Navy mines the waters off New Georgia, a chain of islands within the Solomons. On June 30, US forces land at Rendova and Vangunu on New Georgia, but face heavy resistance.

At the same time, fighting on New Guinea intensifies as a joint U.S./ Australian force, nicknamed the McKechnie Force, lands at Nassau Bay near Salamaua. They, too, face heavy resistance, but by July 1, Marines have captured Viru in New Guinea.

By mid-July, a small US force has landed at Vella Lavella in the Solomons, but it will not be secured until August 15. Vella Lavella is considered of strategic importance, partially because of its close proximity to Bougainville, a Japanese stronghold in the Solomons.

*The landing at Vella Lavella did not go smoothly, as **George B. Freeman** of Orangeburg, South Carolina, relates.*

W E WERE ABOARD a destroyer, supporting a troop landing on Vella Lavella and laying the longest smoke screen in military history and our guns blazed away at the Japanese aircraft overhead.

I was at my battle station with a repair gang when I saw our sister ship emerge from the smoke. She was sure to collide with us portside amidships. I yelled as loud as possible to alert a 20mm gun crew nearby, then sought refuge behind a large coil of towlines. I knew I would be torn to ribbons.

I could have reached out and touched the ship's bow as it swept the deck aft, wiping out the gun mount, several depth charges and caving in the side of our ship near the after engine room. Thank goodness the gun crew escaped.

The executive officer arrived on the double and he and I surveyed the damage. We had to wrestle with 400 lb. depth charges rolling around on the deck for a few minutes, then we able to determine that we had no leaks or disabling damages.

Things settled down for a while and I thought the worst was over. Then the skipper announced that we had received orders to intercept five Japanese destroyers. I became real scared. My knees literally knocked. All this time, our five-inch guns were firing and I had lost my ear-cotton. I still don't hear so good.

We never did find those destroyers.

*As ground forces waded ashore, the action offshore was anything but peaceful. It is unlikely that **Alvin H. McFerren** of Shreveport, Louisiana, will ever forget the Vella Lavella landing.*

W HEN WE TOOK the Solomon Island of Vella Lavella, known as the Slot, we were constantly under aerial attack from Japanese dive bombers based at Rabaul. During one attack, my 40mm gun crew was firing at a dive bomber that had just released a bomb. By sheer accident, one of our 40mm rounds struck the bomb in mid-air and it exploded. Then we got a solid hit on the plane and it exploded in a ball of fire.

The next morning, one of this Jap's buddies, bent on revenge, came right out of the sun straight for our gun pit. We were firing at him all the way down, but we were off target. He pulled out of his dive no more than 75 feet, and belly up, released a 135 lb. daisy cutter bomb.

The bomb hit about 40 feet from our gun pit and the explosion threw a coconut log into our pit that hit one of the crew, causing a severe, but not fatal back injury. A .50-caliber machine gun crew about a hundred yards from our pit hit the low flying bomber and it crashed in the interior of the island. They got credit for the kill.

The memory of that instant when I saw that bomb being released right over my head is burned into my mind. I wasn't afraid, I was terrified.

One of the primary goals of the allied forces in the islands of the Pacific was to create a dependable supply line. One major obstacle, especially for the Navy, was the lack of ship repair facilities in the region. **Arthur W. Johnson** *of Lynnwood, Washington, describes how some of these problems were eliminated.*

IN JULY 1943 I was a member of the US Navy C.B. Det. 1007. We were anchored off Espiritu Santo Island in the New Hebrides, ready to debark over the side of our ship, the USS Dashing Wave.

Down the rope netting we went and into the amphibian ducks. After reaching shore we went into a coconut grove, where our driver let us off. The first thing we did was talk a native into climbing a coconut tree and shaking a few down. We paid him in cigarettes for his efforts.

Using our trusty bayonets, we husked the coconuts, broke the shells open and drank the milk. We learned two things: Coconuts can break bayonets and coconut milk cures constipation.

From 1943 to 1945, our unit built the largest floating drydock in the world. It was large enough to repair any ship the Navy had at that time and may still be in operation at Subic Bay.

When the dock was finally together, Navy tugs pulled an aircraft carrier into it and then several Navy divers placed huge blocks beneath the ship. The water was pumped from the dock and the ship slowly rose out of the water.

I'll never forget the sight of the water gushing from the big hole in the side below the water line. It was the size of a three bedroom house, made by a Japanese torpedo.

After we patched the carrier, we repaired the cruisers Cleveland, Columbia and Mt. Peleir.

Fighting will continue throughout the summer and into the fall on various islands throughout the Pacific, but the Allies are targeting two major strongholds for attack before 1943 ends. One is Tarawa, in the central Pa-

cific. The other is a place called Bougainville in the Solomons. There are 40,000 Japanese ground troops here and an additional 20,000 Japanese sailors.

On November 1, 14,000 Marines land on Bougainville. **Ronald H. Veltman** *of New Hyde Park, New York, saw firsthand the horrid results of the fighting.*

I WAS A NAVY CORPSMAN assigned to the 3rd Marine Division during the invasion of Bougainville on November 1, 1943.

Several days after we landed, two Marines were brought into our medical dugout, both with bad wounds of their left legs, just above the knee. Infection had set in and we had to tell them both that we couldn't save their leg. We would have to amputate or they would die.

One Marine accepted our word but the other was dead-set against it. We went ahead with the operation anyway under very adverse conditions.

When the first Marine came to, he never said a word. He just stared at me as though he wanted to kill me.

We called for a Navy PBY Black Cat to land in the bay. They would be flown down to the base hospital at Tulagi. When the plane landed, I took them both out to the aircraft in a rubber raft. The whole time I was with them, the one Marine never said a word. To this day, I wonder how they both made out.

In spite of the losses, Bougainville was a vital stepping stone to other targets in the Pacific. **William E. Byrd** *of Redwood City, California, describes his mission.*

W E HIT BOUGAINVILLE, the largest of the Solomons, on November 1, 1943. The Marines took a five-mile beachhead where we were to build one of three airstrips. They would be used to neutralize Rabaul, where there was a big enemy base. We accomplished this, spending five months on the island where we were bombed and shelled continually.

Though the enemy had two airstrips on the island, we lost only seven men—a miracle!

As the Marines fought to secure Bougainville, the Navy began the next step, according to **Stephen Marrone** *of Maspeth, New York.*

I WAS A GUNNER'S MATE aboard the USS Essex (CV-9) in November 1943 when we came under attack while raiding Rabaul in the South Pacific. The fight lasted a long time and there were many casualties including my own shrapnel wounds.

Near misses lifted the ship out of the water. Several hundred feet of water hose was flung into the air and when it came down, a brass nozzle hit me in the head, leaving me lying semi-conscious on the deck.

When the attack ended, casualty reports were made and I kept hearing my name very faintly. "Steve... Steve...?"

For a moment I thought I was dead and the angels were calling, but it was the telephone operator reporting me missing. They thought I had gone overboard.

I was discovered under the heavy hoses very much alive. Funny, but I can still hear those angels.

Clyde "Pete" Wood *of Moorhead, Mississippi, found that the Japanese weren't the only problems at Bougainville.*

I VOLUNTEERED for the Marines on September 25, 1942 and eventually was sent to a very secret school to learn radar countermeasures. When our five-man team landed on Guadalcanal, the Corps really didn't know what to do with us as we were very technical men, but with no equipment.

Eventually they loaded us and 25 other Marines onto a gunboat and we set sail for Bougainville where we were assigned to the Navy air force.

On Bougainville, the planes had to land on steel mesh laid down for a runway. Rain and heat were the order every hour, day and night. The insects, snakes, lizards and plants were unbelievable.

But it is the natives I remember the most. They were only about three or four feet tall and constantly roaming through our area. The women wore nothing above their waist and their breasts hung down about a foot.

Finally one morning, our CO shouted, "Get some T-shirts on those women!" So we did.

Next morning, the women had cut holes in their shirts, pulled their breasts through them and were flopping about the camp once more.

The CO threw up his hands and said, "I give up."

With more than 60,000 personnel on Bougainville, the Japanese had ample time and resources to continue their attacks in other areas. The fighting on Bougainville is very heavy, but the Japanese are slowly being forced to withdraw. Meanwhile, US forces open a new front when they land ground forces in the Gilbert Islands. One of these landings is at Betio Island in a place called Tarawa Atoll. US intelligence, for once, has failed.

Betio is no more than nine feet above sea level and is half a mile wide at its widest point and only two miles long. But what is not known is that the Japanese have a complex system of tunnels and bunkers. In spite of more than 3,000 tons of naval artillery and untold aerial attacks, the heavy sand of the island has cushioned the protected bunkers and tunnels from the worst of the bombardments.

On November 20, the initial wave of 5,000 men is decimated. Some 1,500 die on the beach. The remainder are pinned down in a crossfire. A second landing attempt on November 21 results in more heavy casualties. Yet, the Americans fight on.

The price was very high, as **Charles Wysocki Jr.** *of Green Valley, Arizona, describes.*

WE WERE ON TARAWA on November 20, 1943. As viscious as the battle was for 76 hours, what sticks in my mind is the help that my partner and I were able to give to the wounded in our area, Red Beach 3 at the far left end of the beach.

There were already many wounded on the beach when we landed with the third wave. We gave emergency treatment for their wounds to as many as we could while under continuous enemy fire.

On the second day of the battle, we are able to get help and moved them to a medical aid station. I hope we were able to save some lives instead of destroying them.

After the battle, we took the time to bury our dead. It was the least we could do for our fallen comrades who had given their all in a place called Tarawa.

Dennis H. Olson *of Nevada City, California, not only had to battle the enemy, but he faced other problems as well.*

GETTING ASHORE at Tarawa involved several almost fatal accidents.

The first was getting down the cargo net to a Higgins boat which bounced up and down and slammed against the side of the troop ship. I was overloaded and lost my grip and came near being crushed.

The ride to shore was frightening but uneventful, but when the ramp lowered we were shocked to see the beach was still a long way off. I ran off the side of the ramp and fell into a bomb crater. My war almost ended there as I struggled out of my equipment just in time to avoid drowning.

I never expected to make it to land. Machine gun fire and artillery blasts hit the water all around me. Once ashore, I crouched behind the sea wall and looked back to the beach and out to the ocean. Bodies were strewn along the sand and floating in the water.

I wondered how it felt to be dead and how long it would be before I found out.

Tarawa and the other Pacific landings made strong impressions on those who were there. **Richard V. Morgan** *of Waynesburg, Pennsylvania, met a hero there.*

I DON'T KNOW who he was, that US Marine I only briefly encountered during the first night of the three-day bloody battle for Tarawa. More than 1,000 Marines died, even more would have perished and the battle possibly lost, except for this unknown Sergeant and others of his make-up.

The Sergeant, though badly wounded, crawled under a disabled Jap tank in a revetment, deep in enemy territory and requested a field telephone. Combat wire was strung and he must have succeeded in alerting our lines as Japanese troops assembled to overrun the thinly held beach seawall positions.

The attack was blunted and we won the shortest, costliest invasion battle in US history, all because of one of many valiant Marines—one of whom I think of whenever the going gets tough.

I hope he lived, but it's probable that he was not a survivor. But he's not forgotten.

Some things never change in war. **Benny Bensen** *of New Orleans reminds us of one that is almost a cliché.*

W E WERE IN THE PACIFIC AREA and had participated in several landings. With each landing, some of the soldiers would pray to the Lord for an uninjured landing, promising they would attend Sunday services and communion every Sunday thereafter.

But when the landing was secure and they found themselves uninjured and alive, they'd forget their promise until the next landing.

It's easy to remember the Lord when danger lurks, and equally as easy to forget Him once the all clear sounds.

Of course, for some, a religious experience may have saved their life. Some may question whether or not there is a God, but not **S. Parzy Rose II** *of Clackamas, Oregon.*

A T THIS TIME I was an Aviation Radar Specialist flying with the Commander of Torpedo 8, off the Carrier USS Bunker Hill, CV17.

The first time torpedo bombers flew against the Japanese Fleet only one man, Ensign Gay of Torpedo Squadron 8 lived.

This was the second encounter. Commander K.F. Musick, E.V. Helms and I had spent a long day, 19 June, while our fleet raced to catch the Japanese fleet. Late in the afternoon we were close enough to strike but our return was doubtful, because of the Grumman Avenger's short range.

We attacked anyway, torpedo scored, we parachuted at 2000 hours, Lat. 13.5 Long. 136. I shed my parachute and swam, losing consciousness frequently.

Dawn broke, stormy seas continued, and I could see no ships. At 1030 hours, I had been swimming in the Pacific for 13½ hours. The next time I filled up with sea water I would end it. As I started the Lord spoke these words, "Look over your shoulder."

I looked and there was a destroyer.

Later we three returned to the USS Bunker Hill, Torpedo Squadron 8.

Chapter 12
Blood In The Pacific

The South Pacific was not the only area where Japanese presence was felt. In the frigid waters and bleak coastlines of the Aleutian Islands, US servicemen would face a determined and entrenched enemy.

Even though the Japanese move to the Aleutians was a diversionary tactic, the presence of a heavily armed Japanese garrison in the island chain was a serious threat to the United States coastline, Hawaii, and to the Arctic Ocean supply lines, which were vital for the Soviet Union's continuing battle on the Eastern Front.

The situation there for American troops is less than ideal, according to **Delbert H. Defries** *of Bloomington, Minnesota.*

I N 1941 I was at Kodiak, Alaska with the 215th Coast Artillery Antiaircraft Reg. We were there in Sept. 1941, a young army made up of Minnesota National Guard.

We dug in our gun emplacements, time drug on, and on Dec. 7, 1941, when the war began, we were sitting there with our antiaircraft weapons and one round of ammo. We had 50-cal. and 30-cal. but no 37mm.

My buddies and I were grateful that the Japanese did not hit our island. A lot of thoughts went through our minds.

Mr. Defries was lucky the Japanese didn't strike Kodiak. **Leonard S. Levandoski** *of Wilkes-Barre, Pennsylvania, wasn't so fortunate.*

I AM ESPECIALLY PROUD of one man I served with in a combat engagement we had with the Japanese in the Aleutian Islands when they attacked Dutch Harbor.

We consisted of a detachment of 12 pilots, 12 crew chief mechanics, and 12 P-40 type aircraft out of the 11th Fighter Squadron. Our Squadron Commander was Col. Jack Chennault, the son of General Claire Chennault of Flying Tiger fame in China. We had adopted the logo of Flying Tigers also.

The detachment was literally dumped on the island of Umnak, adjacent to the island of Unalaska where Dutch Harbor is located, in May 1942, a few days before the attack on Dutch Harbor.

Our leader and organizer was a young man by the name of First Lt.

Cape. He organized the detachment into a cohesive unit and in a short time we were battle ready.

Our pilots patrolled the waters off the island in the lumbering P-40's which proved to be no match for the lighter carrier based Zeros in a low ceiling atmosphere.

The last time I saw Lt. Cape was when he buzzed the tent we shared on a prearranged signal that the Japanese were coming in. He flew so low that I could read the excitement on his face as he banked away and headed back for battle. We lost Lt. Cape and two aircraft in this engagement.

He was my hero and would have made a great leader in our society had he survived. I salute you Lt. Cape and God Bless you in your watery grave in the Cold North Pacific.

The Japanese strike against Dutch Harbor was devastating, but US servicemen were never known to simply sit back and absorb these attacks. Instead, they dug in and built bases of their own from which to strike back. **Chester Allender** *was one of the guys sent north to do just that. He's from Jeffersonville, Indiana.*

W E LANDED Cold Bay, stayed one month then went to Dutch Harbor. The bay was full of American ships sunk. Stayed on boat a week.

We knew our work was cut out for us then went to Adak which was unoccupied. Engineers drained a lake and we built airport. When completed a squad of our fighter planes landed. Next day or two the Japanese plane discovered we were there. Soon after this took over Attu.

I stayed in Aleutians 31 months. Cold, wind, rain and snow.

It was obvious from the beginning that the "green" troops that America was sending into battle were badly overmatched by the seasoned troops of both the Japanese and Germans. **John Harold Saeter** *of Fosston, Minnesota, can identify with that.*

I WAS SHIPPED OUT of Ft Lawton, Seattle, Washington aboard the Eli D. Hoyle, a converted cattle carrier to a troop carrier. I was a member of Company B, 375th. Port Battalion, of the Transportation Corp. In Alaska we unloaded lend-lease materials from US ships onto Russian vessels when they arrived at our docks and warehouses at Excursion Inlet.

None of us had received any basic training, but we were given the M-1 Rifle. Company C was sent down near the Aleutians and nearly all were killed by Japanese soldiers. Pulling payroll guard the first time was very embarrassing. Receiving my ammunition, the CO told me to load my rifle. I fumbled around until he asked, "Didn't you have basic training, soldier?"

"No Sir".

He then loaded it and said, "Follow me but don't touch that damn thing!"

It would not be until the next year before American forces would be able to root the Japanese out of the Aleutians. During that time, many GIs would gain experience the hard way.

On January 12, 1943, US forces manage to occupy Amchitka Island, but due to a mishap, the USS Worden *is lost in the process.* **Carl C. Postma** *of Sanborn, Iowa, remembers life on the island.*

A FTER WE LANDED on Amchitka Island, we helped build the airfield for planes to land after bombing Kiska Island. One rainy, snowy, cold afternoon Sergeant said, "On the hill there, is a big hospital tent. We have a Chaplain on our island. You may be excused for chapel if you wish, I'll recommend it."

We all went. The Chaplain said, "Fellows, my name is Autry, but, I won't sing. You may not know it is Sunday today, also it is Mother's Day. If you haven't written her, do it tonight and tell her you love her and you love her God."

We all walked out changed men—what a sermon.

Once established on the island, American forces begin a two-day naval bombardment beginning January 18, and again on February 18 and 19, of the Japanese-held island of Attu. The harbor of Attu itself is hit on April 26 and on May 11, elements of the 7th Division land on the island in the face of heavy Japanese resistance.

Attu is finally taken and sporadic strikes take place for the next two months. But by July, after heavy bombing on Kiska, the Japanese have, unknown to the Americans, evacuated most of their garrison on the island.

The USS Salt Lake City *bombards Kiska, Alaska.*

When 34,000 US troops land on Kiska in August, the Japanese are gone. Still, no one who ever served there will ever forget the island chain. **Charles B. Barnwell Sr.** *of Bamberg, South Carolina, even recalls an irreverent poem about the place.*

THE ALEUTIANS are a long string of little islands located in the Bering Sea consisting of Attu, Kiska, Shemya, Amchitka, Adak, Atka, and others.

"I hope I shall never see another island without a tree. A land like this with heaven's curse. The loneliest spot on God's earth, a spit in the sea all covered with snow where no one really wanted to go."

Upon leaving in 1941 from their home in fear of an approaching Japanese invasion, the residents scorched the island to include their Greek Orthodox Church. That's how I received the following orders:

Captain, we are sending you over to the island of Atka to assist in the rehabilitation of a small clan of Aleuts returning from Alaska to their home, Atka.

Above clouds, by plane, all was serene except the landing. Cross winds prevented the landing and forced us back to Adak, on alert to return the next day.

The pleasure, rapture, glow, and the happiness that dominated their faces as these 68 men, women and children wound their way up a rain drenched road to the church yard where they knelt in prayer to the Almighty God for deliverance safely to their home was moving.

Atka, home, sweet, home!

Even President Roosevelt would visit the Aleutians one day. **Russell L. Rice** *of Buffalo, Indiana, says that FDR wasn't always thinking about the war.*

FDR CAME ABOARD our ship, USS. Cummings 365 at Kiska Alaska and sailed with us down the inland passage to Seattle Washington.

The President wanted to anchor and do some fishing on the way. He wasn't getting any bites so he sent the whaleboat over to a small boat where an Eskimo and his boy were fishing close to two rock piles and brought them alongside.

FDR asked him where the fish were biting. He said you won't catch any where we were, but that he'd give him some fish if he wanted.

Roosevelt said "Hell, I don't want you to give them to me, I want to catch them."

So while the little boy was picking his nose we weighed anchor and headed for Seattle.

Of course, the Aleutians are pretty desolate, yet most who served there really don't seem to hate the place. Most, like **Raymond Bailey** *of Searcy, Arkansas, seem to have fond memories of the islands.*

I WAS SENT to Attu (Aleutian Island), assigned duty with Fleet Air Wing Four in a Disbursing Office. Aleutian weather: Snows, fog, rain, "williwaws".

Not all was dreariness: Movies, gym, very few USO shows came to Attu. Reading and writing letters and playing cards in the Quonset hut and listening to Popular War Hits on radio. "Don't Fence Me In", "Gotta, Accentuate the Positive, Eliminate the Negative", "Don't Mess With Mr. In-Between", "Coming in on a Wing and a Prayer" were my favorites.

I wrote four gospel hymns, now published, on Attu in 1944.

Of course, it may not have been the greatest duty station in the world. By the time the war ends, most GIs were more than happy to leave the place, says **E.A. Humphrey** *of Lodi, California.*

YOU SHOULD HAVE SEEN the sight of big, strong combat infantry men of the 201st Infantry Regiment, lined up and weeping freely at the railing of our troopship as it entered Puget Sound (Seattle) following 30 months duty in the Aleutian Islands.

Overwhelmed by the tree studded view of the beautiful shoreline, obliterated and almost destroyed by their many months overseas in one of the most remote, uninhabited and weathered theaters of operations better known as the cradle of the storms.

Bold and brave, yes, but bent on being home and allowing their emotions to spill over.

Meanwhile, though the Aleutians were clear of Japanese, the war was far from over in other parts of the Pacific and the GIs in the Pacific would see in yet another new year. But by early 1944, the Americans had reason to believe they were gaining on the stubborn Japanese resistance. Sometimes, there was some question as to who was on whose side, as **Roscoe Mosteller** *of Greenville, South Carolina, relates.*

FRAME 10 TOPSIDE is right at the bow aboard the battleship USS Washington (BB56). That was my duty station in January 1944. The PA blared, "All hands man your fire stations on the double!"

I took off. Topside, it was dark and while going around number one gun turret, the boatswain, using all his strength, grabbed me with both arms and held me in an iron grip.

"Just where in the hell do you think you're going?" he demanded. When I told him, he said, "You ain't got no fire station. We ain't got no bow. We've been in a collision and the whole bow is shorn off. Ain't nobody going up there."

We had collided with the USS Indiana. Had he not stopped me. . . .

In spite of freak accidents, US forces knew precisely who and why they were fighting.

Still, attacks on islands such as Kwajalien and Eniwetok in the

Marshall Islands carried a heavy price tag in men and material. **William R. "Bill" Yarwood** *of Anaheim, California, remembers what happened when his aircraft carrier took part on an attack against the Japanese strongholds of Truk and Rabaul.*

O N THE NIGHT of February 8/9, 1944, the carrier USS Intrepid was torpedoed off Truk Island. Ordnance men had spent the day (February 8) checking equipment and reloading until, after the last flight, we had just finished with all ordnance fully reloaded, both ammunition and bombs for a pre-dawn attack, when we were ordered, "Strike all bombs below."

We finally finished about 2300 and were permitted to get some sleep so we could again be up by 0300. Most of us just sacked out in the armories. I was on deck along side the workbench. Another man — a big fellow — was on the bench. At five minutes after midnight, a Japanese torpedo hit our starboard quarter. When I came to, I was standing at the bench and the 200-pounder had his feet firmly planted where my head had been.

Yarwood's ship will have a rough year in 1944. On April 16 and 17, the Intrepid *will be attacked by Kamikaze aircraft and heavily damaged. Nor is it the only ship that will face the fanaticism of the Kamikaze.* **Norman C. Bradford** *of La Habra, California, can certainly identify with Yarwood.*

W E WERE MAKING a landing at Hollandia, New Guinea, to cut the Island in half and separate the Japanese. I was standing the 4 AM to chow watch on the number one five-inch anti-aircraft battery. I was on lookout when our task force turned into the wind to launch Aircraft for softening up the beaches for our landing group.

I heard a loud roar and looking up I saw a torpedo bomber hit our ships yardarm, then dive toward our bow. The plane just grazed the bow as it went by and exploded, sending a big flame over the ship from its gasoline.

Luckily our only casualty was a gunners mate who had gone to his battle station on the bow in preparation of the ship going to general quarters, just prior to dawn.

Amid the stress and tension, most combat GIs will agree on one thing: You have to keep a sense of humor, no matter what is taking place around you. While President Roosevelt was well liked and admired, his wife Eleanor was fair game, as **Charles R. Thomas** *of Margate, New Jersey, recounts.*

I T WAS SOMETIME DURING 1944 in the South Pacific. PT Base 21 was stationed aboard a small island called Mios Woendi, off the western coast of New Guinea.

We were a repair and maintenance unit of the Navy.

One day while working on one of the boats, I looked up at the stern of one of the PTs. Overhanging the stern, was a sturdy wood chair with a hole cut out of the middle of the seat. Underneath were the words: "Eleanor sat here."

Speaking of sitting, **Edward J. Giusto** *of Augusta, Georgia, recalls another story that involved sitting.*

THE INCIDENT that happened in 1944 on Hollandia, New Guinea. This staging area provided a mess tent and a 10-hole latrine for every company-sized group, but it was the group's responsibility to provide KPs to man the mess tent and an orderly to keep the latrine sanitized. This was done by pouring gasoline over the accumulated waste and burning it.

I was enjoying an after-breakfast cigarette with my buddies, when an explosion sent us madly scrambling for the nearest slit trench. After the guards assured us it was not a Japanese attack, we headed back to our area to check on the rest of our group. We found four missing, so we checked the hospital tent.

They were in hospital gowns and lying on their stomachs. The doctor assured us their wounds were not critical. When I asked what happened, one of them replied, "How in the hell was I to know, when I threw my cigarette butt down the hole, the damned orderly hadn't burned off the gasoline."

I still often wonder what their replies were to, "Daddy, how did you get your Purple Heart?"

Snipers, bombers, torpedoes . . . and latrines—as far as **Homer K. Carrick** *of Oceanside, California, is concerned, these are all weapons of war.*

WHILE I WAS STATIONED in Saipan, we all slept in tents, they had latrines they put chemicals in, and the covers were to stay open during the night, someone pulled a crank trick, and closed the lids.

About 0430, we heard an explosion, everyone ran out of their tents, thinking a bomb went off. What a mess all over the tents, everywhere! No one got any more sleep that night.

I don't think anyone will ever forget that night. It's funny now but believe me, it wasn't then.

While there were some lighthearted moments, the war was still a very grim reality. A primary goal of US strategists was to regain the Philippines. To do that, other strategic islands had to be taken as bases of operation. The only problem was, the Japanese wanted to keep them as bad as the US wanted to take them away.

That's why, once US forces spotted a target of opportunity, they struck —even knowing that they might face difficulties later. That's precisely the *situation with the aircraft launched during the Battle of the Philippine Sea. **William A. Stevens** of Greensburg, Pennsylvania, was there.*

M Y SERVICE was on the USS BATAAN CVL-29 as part of the Fast Carrier Task Force of the US Pacific Fleet; specifically the 1st battle of the Philippine Sea. Our aircraft were dispatched at about 4 p.m. on June 20, 1944 to deliver a bombing and torpedo attack on the Japanese Fleet.

Our planes inflicted heavy damage on many of their warships, but returned after dark at about 9 p.m. It was pitch black and the Fleet Commander ordered all lights turned on so our aircraft could to land. This would be the first night landing on carriers in a war zone.

What an awesome sight — to have been top side to see this epic spectacular. All those lights and flares made it seem like day light, and not one pilot was lost in this operation.

We were congratulated by COMPAC Chief, Adm. Chester W. Nimitz.

*Experienced pilots claims that landing on an aircraft carrier is like trying to land on a moving postage stamp. Another eyewitness to this remarkable battle was **Walter H. Brown** of Tarpon Springs, Florida.*

D URING THE BATTLE of the Philippine Sea, we spent most of the day searching for the Japanese fleet. With only two hours of daylight remaining, we located them at the far range of our aircraft.

Adm. Mitscher decided to launch our aircraft and the Japanese were taken by surprise and with little air protection. Our planes destroyed most of the fleet, but returned in darkness and low on fuel.

The Admiral ordered the ships to turn on their spotlights to locate the returning planes that were landing in the water and we spent the night plucking pilots from a sea turned green from locating dye. The sky was lit with tracers as gun crews fired at Japanese planes trying to land on our carriers. They had no other place to land.

Happily, 75 percent of our pilots made it back safely.

*Some select Japanese pilots had their own methods of landing on US ships. The pilots were called Kamikazes, and they amazed Tonawanda, New York's **Ernest J. Kassay.***

I WAS ASSIGNED to the aircraft carrier USS Langley for duty in the South Pacific. In June of 1944 while off Formosa and on route to cover the Philippine Sea operation we were informed of possible Japanese pilot suicide attempts.

To me it was inconceivable that individuals would sacrifice their lives in such suicide attempts—until it was actually witnessed by myself. This suicide sacrifice continued until the end of the war.

At the time, at my age it was as if I was watching a movie and this was not actually taking place.

*Unfortunately, this was no movie. In March, an island in the Marshalls called Eniwetok is finally taken, but there is a price. Sometimes even after the main battle ends, there is still a price to pay, as **Joe M. Powalski** of Baton Rouge, Louisiana, describes.*

R.J. LUGO was a giant of a man — both in size and courage — he served with the 110th NCB on Eniwetok (Marshall Atoll). This island served as an advanced airfield.

One night a horrendous accident happened. While taking off on a bombing mission a B-24 blew a tire that caused it to swerve into a parking lot filled with other planes — all loaded with gasoline, bombs and ammunition. The resulting conflagration was the most costly single accident in the Pacific Theater.

Lugo's decision to act was a courageous one. Even before the peak of this inferno, he was operating his bulldozer to push these burning planes away from larger aircraft. Had he not been successful even more lives would have been lost along with more planes.

R.J. Lugo, E.W. Diegoli and E.R. Driggers received the Navy and Marine Corps medal for their efforts in this terrible accident. The three suffered burns and cuts for their heroic efforts — but were back on their respective jobs the next day.

*In May and June, ground forces are busy securing a small island called Biak in New Guinea, as well as a number of other areas. By June, Mokmer airbase has been captured, but resistance is still strong. The Japanese are holed up in caves and it is very difficult to dislodge them. This made an indelible impression on **Robert Erhardt** of Fort Plain, New York.*

WE HAD TRAPPED some Japanese infantry in a cave. Keeping them pinned inside with rifle fire we exploded a satchel charge in the mouth of the cave and sealed them inside.

As it was late in the day we were given orders to dig in nearby and, if necessary, keep them from tunneling out. Sometime after midnight we heard what must have been singing or chanting coming very faintly from the cave. Then, about dawn, we heard a series of single rifle shots, seven in all.

This episode points up the stupidity of war.

Any other time with men trapped below ground we would have torn at the earth with our bare hands in an attempt to save them. Now, fate made us their executioners. Too bad those who start the wars do not have to fight them.

*In spite of stubborn, often fanatic resistance, US forces are able to set up bases. And, as at any military installations, one or two individuals will be long remembered. **Tony Kozach** of Taunton, Massachusetts, tells of one such individual.*

I WAS STATIONED on Biak Island, in the Netherlands, East Indies. All flight personnel lived in one tent area. There wasn't much to do when not on duty. Most of the men slept, washed clothes or went to the PX tent for mail, a can of grapefruit juice or a candy bar.

The GI in charge of the PX was about fifty, a veteran of World War I. Most of the personnel were in their early 20s and they affectionately called him 'Pop' and occasionally needled him, by calling him a 'Section Eight' for sticking it out on the atolls.

One night an air attack, from the Japanese held Celebe Islands, hit our air-strip and tent area with anti-personnel bombs. Private, 'PX POP' took charge in our area by directing and guiding us in moving the wounded to the field hospital. The last time I saw him, he had a GI around his shoulders heading for the medic tent.

Our 'PX POP' who had taken our cocky remarks in mature stride, was awarded the 'Soldier Medal'. 'PX POP' was a soldiers-soldier, held in high esteem by all serviceman.

Obviously, in wartime, these islands weren't the tropical paradise that travel brochures show today. In fact, according to **George Becker** *of Skokie, Illinois, they were downright primitive.*

F OR THOSE OF US in Detachment 45 Army Airways Communication System stationed on Biak Island in the Dutch East Indies in 1944 who did not have the comforts of a spring bed to make life more tolerable in the jungle, we devised a DO-IT-YOURSELF spring bed made from truck tire tubes.

We would cut up discarded truck tire tubes into long 1" wide strips and stretch them over a 3x6 ft frame made from 2x4s and criss-crossed them like a lawn chair. It was really comfortable.

One night we heard a large crash in our tent, and low and behold one of the guys homemade bed collapsed, and he ended up on the floor. The rubber strips were not secured properly, and they came loose from the frame.

However, the only thing hurt was his pride.

Of course, GIs are renowned for their inventiveness. Belmont, Michigan's **O. Jerry Wagner** *offers a case in point.*

I WAS A MASTER/SGT. CREW CHIEF on a B-29, stationed on Guam. Daytime temps ranged 120 to 130 degrees. At night it cooled down to around 70.

We were rationed four beers and four Cokes twice a month. There was no ice available. By burying the beer and coke in a saw dust filled box, we sprayed them with a CO_2 fire extinguisher. They got frosty cold. This was a well guarded secret.

Washing clothes, we buried a steel drum two feet in the ground behind our aircraft parking area. With brackets welded to the rim of the barrel to hold an off-set crankshaft. We attached a wooden agitator to the off-set shaft and a propeller.

The sun heated the water, and a running aircraft engine's airflow turned the propeller and shaft, washing our clothes.

The sun dried our clothes.

No, life wasn't easy on the islands, no matter how inventive you were. According to **Sarah G. Child-Taylor** *of Aurora, Indiana, it might even have been a bit worse if you were female.*

A FTER CROSSING the Pacific on the converted luxury liner *SS Lurline,* we debarked at Milne Bay, New Guinea March 25, 1944. The personnel of the 35th General Hospital were among the thousands of troops aboard. We nurses, wearing field gear and back packs, descended from the service port by landing net to the amphibious vehicles alongside. Soldiers stood by to encourage and assist us.

Women were very scarce in that war and at that time.

After we were ferried ashore and quartered, we dug drainage ditches around our tents, used the slit trenches, drank from the Lister bag, laundered in the creek, and began wearing men's boots and fatigues. Once dispersed to the hospitals in the area, we went to work.

Thus began my tour of duty caring for the sick and wounded in New Guinea and the Philippines.

Sarah G. Child-Taylor and Helen Wheeler-Buchheit stand in front of the first quarters of the 35th General Hospital nurses at Milne Bay, New Guinea, in March 1944. (Photo provided by Sarah G. Child-Taylor.)

These were dangerous, deadly times. Life, even on a tropical island paradise, is very fragile. And the enemy was not always the Japanese, as **Harry J. Jarvis** *of Ayden, North Carolina, relates.*

I WAS THERE for the burial of my closest buddy, Sergeant Thomas Deason. This tough, combat seasoned infantryman was killed on Morotai Island by a falling tree limb. At the time of his death, the island had been secured and Tom, a mortar battalion sergeant, was temporarily assigned to our Quartermaster unit.

About three o'clock one afternoon, I left Tom alive and well at the airstrip where he worked on a PX supply building to serve pilots and layover passengers. Two hours later I attended his funeral.

As the mournful notes of Taps wafted through the humid jungle air and we stood at attention, I stared at his crude wooden coffin and the blood oozing through a crack and onto white coral in a clearing surrounded by coconut palms watching over stilled bodies of American heroes.

As 1943 dragged on, it seemed as though the war would never end. **Angus P. Robinson** *of Dolton, Illinois, remembers those first few months.*

IN LATE OCTOBER 1943, we joined a Marine air group on the island of Ondonga in the New Georgia Island group. For some of us, it was the first time away from loved ones at home. Christmas came and went, and then we were only a few minutes away from New Year 1944.

Though we were not certain what the officers would think, we were determined to give 1943 a rousing send off and welcome 1944 in by firing eight rounds from our M1 rifles. Afterward, we would make a hasty withdrawal—Marines NEVER retreat!—to our tents before the OD checked into who had broken the silence of his watch.

Without warning, we heard heavy weapons across the island open fire and saw hundreds of tracers from .30 and .50-caliber machine guns streak into the night sky. We could also hear the bark of the 40mm cannons, the racket of the 90mm guns, and the booms of the 105 and 155 cannons in the distance. We stood transfixed by the beautiful but deadly display of man-killing pyrotechnics.

It seemed to last several minutes, but was probably only one or two before the firing stopped and silence again reigned over the jungle. I have no idea what it cost to fire all those weapons that night, but the price was insignificant compared to the moral uplift it gave each of us. Afterward, almost to a man, we returned to our tents. We didn't know it then, but many men watching the display that night would never see another New Year.

Somehow, perhaps, you can never really believe that it can happen to you, especially if you are young. Yet young men will continue to volunteer, and too often the consequences are as **Vernon F. Cornish** *of Fort Worth, Texas, describes.*

MY BUDDY WAS KNOWN AS "O D". He volunteered as an MP to accompany a "Recon" outfit into the mountains of Southern Mindanao.

The next morning they brought him back full of Jap bullets, and I had to turn him over and go through his pockets for his personal possessions!

No, the war in the Pacific was far from over.

Chapter 13

The Return

*By the end of August, US forces have Guam, Tinian, Saipan and other islands under control, but the fighting was very heavy. When casualties run high, other things happen as well, as **Robert E. Bumpus** of Maynard, Massachusetts, recalls.*

I WAS AN 18 YEAR OLD RADIOMAN aboard a communications ship during the invasion of Saipan in the Marianas. I was off duty in mid-morning of the operation. A determined Japanese defense resulted in more American Marine casualties than had ever been anticipated. I was at the rail of my ship watching the landing craft return from the beach with their human cargo.

One boat came alongside asking if there was more room aboard for the dead and dying.

"We have about 30 wounded and 12 dead", shouted the small boat coxswain.

The response from my ship's spokesman was, "We'll take the wounded but there's no room for the dead!"

At that instant, my youth was behind me. Now, I knew what war is all about.

*War can be a cold and callous thing. **Hugh M. Davis** of Iselin, New Jersey, discovered that for himself.*

O N THE 2ND DAY after we landed on Guam. My Company, CO C305, 77th Division was on the attack and our squad was protecting the rear.

I saw two men fall. Believing they were wounded, I called for a medic. No one heard me for the Company had moved on. Realizing this, I went to their help. My squad leader, Sgt. Paul Flisher had passed out from the intense heat and Pvt. Lawrence Farr had a ruptured appendix.

I managed to get them under cover and went down to the beach for help. There was only one medical outfit there, and it was a Marine Battalion. With the help of two Marines, we brought them back which was a good mile and a corpsman attended to them immediately. The next morning they were sent to a hospital ship and I returned to my company.

By September 1944, the final steps take place for the invasion of the Philippine Islands. One vital target is Peleliu in the Palau Island chain of the Caroline Islands. It is not an easy task. **James Howard Fitzgerald** *of Lockport, New York, shares his experience.*

A BOARD THE LEONARD WOOD, a Coast Guard ship nicknamed the USS Lucky, had survived several landings in Europe and she was now taking us in a Palau. We were the 322 Infantry of the 81st Wildcat Div. We had been briefed on our assault on Angure Island. It was September 16, 1944, and the Marines had landed on Peleliu.

Resistance was so strong and tough at Peleliu that our landing at Angure was moved back one day, to the 17th.

Morning broke as we came above decks and climbed down the landing nets to our assigned LCVPs. I don't think any of us had slept. Most had spent the night praying and our nerves were on edge.

As the sun rose, we were greeted by the most wondrous sight of our lives. From one horizon to the other, as far as the naked eye could see, was our Navy. Every type of supporting craft manufactured was there to back us. It was truly inspiring—a panorama of United States might and determination to conquer—and it took some of our fears away.

Still, we didn't know what we would hit on the beach. Our craft was in the initial wave, but we were sustained by the powerful sight of the vast amount of strength behind us. We stepped from the hatches and headed for the nets.

During the course of combat, there often isn't time to bury the dead. **Joe L. Saia** *of Helena, Arkansas, probably has nightmares over that.*

A S WE WERE MAKING OUR WAY to the observation post behind the infantry, we came upon a group of about eight dead Japs. Their bodies were piled together and they were swollen as though they were going to burst any minute. Big green flies swarmed around them. It was a horrible sight and the smell was almost unbearable.

One of our boys spotted a Jap helmet under a bush. As he reached for it I yelled, "Don't touch it. It may be booby trapped!"

But it was too late. He grabbed the helmet and I got sick to my stomach as I saw the dead Jap's head come off with the helmet.

In an invasion situation, it's easy to work up a "case of the nerves." That's what happened to **Joseph Santos Gomes** *of Santa Maria, California.*

W E HAD SECURED the Island of Peleliu in the Islands of Palau. The night Cpl. Ralph and I were in the revetment patrol, we heard weird a noise like Japanese troops marching at the beach counterattack the US troops.

At that time I didn't know what to expect. As a true brave soldier, I got behind the machine gun and started shooting.

Much to my dismay what we heard was only the so called land crabs. To this day I've been allergic to crabs.

Hamburg, New York, resident **Reynold Anderson** *offers another fine example of "the nerves," this time with tragic results.*

O UR CARRIER, the USS Hornet CV12, was anchored at Elythe, Palau, Island. The crew was sitting on mess benches watching a movie on the hangar deck.

Suddenly we heard a loud noise coming from behind us and we began to look over our shoulders, and imagination began to take control.

A large spool of 2" wire was on deck. Was this rolling toward us? Was there live ammunition loose ready to explode? All of a sudden panic broke among us. Men walked and jumped over others fighting their way toward the open hatchways. Then, as suddenly as it started, the noise stopped. It was then we saw the collapsed benches with broken twisted legs and arms extended from under them. We also lost a Shipmate over the side.

What happened? The answer, a CO2 fire extinguisher canister had fallen to the deck, releasing the locking pin, causing the noise of acceleration. We had created a disaster with our imaginations. . . .

The outer islands were either secure or being taken. In early October, US forces landed on Mindinao in the Philippines. History says that there was little Japanese resistance to the landing. **Harry J. Whittaker** *of St. Johns, Michigan, might not agree.*

I T WAS IN THE JUNGLES of Mindinao in the Philippines that I found myself facing a Japanese soldier. He was armed with a rifle, its bayonet pointing right at my face. I had just my survival knife in its sheath.

When he made his thrust with his bayonet, automatic reflex and action saved me that day. I guess paying attention while being trained on how to survive and kill while I was still stateside saved my hide that day.

By October 1944, it was time to keep a promise. **R.e. Fetherlin** *of Lola, Kansas, remembers the part his ship and comrades played in the unfolding drama.*

W E WERE IN PHILIPPINE WATERS aboard the jeep carrier CVE77. Our mission was to enter Susagai Straights and wreck Jap airfields so they could not interfere with our landings on Leyte.

The brass decided to send small carriers because they were more expendable than the big ones. (We were within striking distance of 21 Jap airstrips.) Adm. Halsey had taken the main fleet up the Philippine coast after some dummy Jap carriers and left us unprotected.

The main Jap fleet came out of the straights after us. They hit some of our carriers, but did not sink them because they were using armor-piercing shells. They would go in one side and out the other of our thin-skinned ships without exploding.

We used all our torpedoes, large bombs and fire bombs and were down to 100 lb. bombs that fighter aircraft carried under their wings when the captain said, "Let's go after them with what we have left."

We had one five-inch gun on each carrier and a few destroyer escorts. As we turned toward them to get into the wind to launch our airplanes, the Japs, in spite of all their firepower, turned and fled.

*Task Force 38 would prove to be one of the largest naval operations of the war. **Raymond J. Schoener** of Ironton, Ohio, shares his impressions.*

I BECAME PART of Admiral Mitscher's carrier force one morning in 1944, as we were cruising the Philippine Sea, preparatory to beginning air operations against the Jap-held Philippine Islands.

I was a combat aircrewman aboard a jeep carrier heading west from Pearl; a replacement for casualties of past carrier activities.

We steamed westward for several days. Early one morning, I went up to the flight deck and saw an incredible sight; we were cruising amidst the ships of Task Force 38.

Even though I was later transferred to the USS Lexington and its Air Group 19 dive-bombing squadron, subsequently saw the unforgettable strikes on the Philippines, Okinawa, and Formosa and many attacks by Jap planes; even a Kamikaze hit off the coast of Luzon, the time I slept aboard a jeep carrier, pushing alone through the night, and then woke up in the middle of the greatest task force in naval history always stuck out in my mind as something extra special.

*For many, like **Robert W. Hartley** of Wellington, Kansas, service in the Pacific and the invasion of the Philippines would be a sort of coming of age.*

I WAS AN 18-YEAR-OLD punk kid from Kansas aboard the sea tug USS Chickasaw (ATF 83). We were at the invasion of the Marshall Islands where a Jap Betty mistook us for a cruiser. The three tin fish she dropped went too deep and missed us. We rescued 250 injured Marines on an LST at Tinian after it was beached by a storm. The operation took 12 hours.

We were part of the largest convoy of ships ever assembled when we took Leyte during the invasion of the Philippines. There we rescued the USS Ross from a mine field after they took two hits and lost all power.

We learned to dodge the suicide planes and put out the fires they started, helped with rescues after the fleet saw action and were in on the second invasion of Luzon.

After dry dock at Okinawa and repairs at Pearl harbor, I returned home after 28 months and kissed American soil after a tour that made you aware there was a lot of water out there.

Even though the United States played a primary role in the battles of the Pacific, other nations held a vested interest in the area as well. One of *those nations was the Netherlands, as **Mytro Mykita** of Carnegie, Pennsylvania, can attest.*

A SSIGNED AS US ARMY GUNNER on Dutch Ship with Dutch captain, a Dutch engineer and flying the Dutch flag, the MS Janssans, with a Japanese crew of 120, an Australian radioman and twenty US army gunners took part in the invasion of the Philippines in Leyte Gulf at Tacloban. My gun was the biggest on the ship. Used for anti-sub and anti-aircraft, the Australian Field Artillery gun moved the ship each time it fired.

Even in the Pacific, few people knew that gunners on ships flying Dutch Flags were Americans. The Army had taken over several ships operating in Java, Borneo, and the islands in the Pacific. The 365th Coast Artillery Transport Detachment attached to the 35th T.C. Service Group is the closest I can get to naming my outfit.

*On October 21, 1944, the Americans came back to the Philippines. **Francis W. Poirier** of Edgewater, Maryland, was in the third wave ashore.*

T HE NAVAL ARMADA that attacked Leyte Beach was something to behold. When they finished firing, there was hardly a palm tree left standing. My group, the 24th Infantry Division, were the third wave to land on Leyte Beach.

View of the Leyte Island shore line at the invasion point, October 20, 1944.

The landing craft did not take us far enough toward shore and before I even got into combat, I nearly drowned with all the heavy ammo and artillery I was carrying.

I managed to struggle to shore and after the beachhead was secured, Gen. MacArthur and his entourage walked ashore. I was directly in front of him when he walked in. It was a spectacular moment.

The moment may have been spectacular, but the Japanese were not about to give up the Philippines without a fight, and it would prove to be a long, bitter battle. Grantsburg, Wisconsin's **Alton C. Jensen** *tells of the price paid.*

O UT OF THE DENSE COASTAL SMOKE SCREEN the wounded destroyer crept slowly toward land, then anchored. Shortly afterward, several groups of bodies were lowered to the Higgins boats and brought to the beach.

After being neatly arranged in rows, the bodies and the area were disinfected. The Graves Registration unit examined and identified each, then enclosed it in a wrapping.

An Army chaplain came to our unit and requested a squad of six men with rifles and the company bugler. A temporary burial site on Red Beach had been selected for burial and it was here that the solemn rites were conducted until all were consecrated.

It was then that it came to me the tremendous price these Navy men had paid to preserve our slender hold on the beaches of Leyte. I softly voiced a prayer of thanksgiving as I returned to my unit.

As the battle raged on the land, it intensified at sea as well. **Leo C. Gavitt** *of Stanton, Michigan, was there.*

O UR TASK FORCE was charged with protecting the landing on Leyte. We were attacked in a battle off Samar by the central Jap fleet of four battleships, nine cruisers and 14 destroyers.

Our largest gun was a five-inch 38 and with two aircraft carriers, two destroyers and one 8E sunk, hundreds of 19, 20 and 21 year-old lads were in the water gulping oil and dying who hadn't yet had a chance to learn what life was all about.

The Jap fleet, thinking Halsey was nearing, retreated, leaving the ocean covered with lads in life jackets. As we picked them up, we received orders over the bullhorn.

"Just the live ones, boys. Just the live ones."

As they lay there in the water, their oil soaked eyes shut and mouths open as if to say, "I did my best," we took their dog tags and said good-bye, buddy and God bless.

Does this bring a tear to your eye? We did our job but couldn't help but shed tears as we picked up over 150 on our little 8E, the USS John C. Butler.

*The battle at sea would rage off and on for days. With each engagement, the price tag of war grew higher. **Anthony Mancini** of Boca Raton, Florida, tells of tragedy at sea.*

O N OCTOBER 24, 1944, the USS Birmingham tried to save its sister ship, the USS Princeton after she was hit by a Japanese dive bomber off Leyte, Philippines four days after the invasion.

It looked like we had the damage under control when enemy planes showed up on radar and we had to ease off. All our starboard guns were knocked out in the attack that followed.

As we moved in after the planes were gone, we were less than 50 feet away when her bomb magazine exploded. Observers say the ships leaped apart.

The Princeton broke in two, spraying the Birmingham's superstructure with shrapnel, killing sailors from the bow to the stern.

There were 229 dead and 420 wounded. I earned a Purple Heart that day when Princeton was sunk and the waterways ran red with blood.

Our dead were left on deck overnight on the darkened ship with burial the next day. We had blankets full of arms and legs and broken bones.

The Japs made out that day. One carrier sunk and one cruiser, one AA cruiser and two destroyers limped back to the states for repairs.

*But it wouldn't remain that way. **Louis J. Penzes** of East Chatham, New York, says that he and his fellow submariners managed to get in a few good licks.*

T HE SUBMARINE USS Seadragon was cruising along north of Manila one night in October 1944 when, halfway across the China Sea, we encountered a typhoon which tossed us around quite a bit.

We were patrolling in a wolf pack with the submarines Blackfish and the Shark and this mission would prove to be the most successful in the Seadragon's career.

About midnight, the captain, Cmdr. J.H. Ashley, ordered us to battle stations. In the ensuing attack against a fast Japanese task force, a carrier sustained three hits and one was scored on a cruiser. The Shark was lost during this encounter, presumably a victim of depth charges.

Intelligence reports from prisoners of war later revealed that a carrier had been sunk that night in that area.

*The hazards of the South China Sea are well known, but some of the risks are not directly related to enemy actions, as **Joseph P. Nicolai Jr.** of Charlevoix, Michigan, shares.*

W E HAD EXPERIENCED rough sailing in the China Sea for over 30 days.

The ship was transferring a shot down pilot to a large air craft carrier. Ted and I climbed a ladder on #1 stack to have a better view.

As we watched the proceedings, the bow of our destroyer seemed to sail under the flat top's flight deck. We tried to get down off the stack, before we were crushed.

The bridge crew had the ship put in full reverse. The aft end sank under the water as we pulled away from the carrier. The pilot did make it to the carrier. Everyone below decks had a salt water bath.

If the flat top landed on us, I would have never gotten this letter out.

Sometimes, fate would take a bizarre twist, as **Henry D. Gates** *of Middleboro, Massachusetts, relates.*

I STOOD on the after gun deck on watch aboard the SS Jose C. Barbarosa after the "all clear" was given. I was a Navy gunner and it was October 1944 and we, along with a hundred other ships, were at anchor in the bay on Leyte, Philippines.

About noon I observed a lone aircraft approaching which I assumed was one of ours. As it flew over us and banked about 500 feet away, I saw those two red meatballs of a Jap Zero.

I was shocked and my legs shook uncontrollably. I gave the signal to fire but the electrical system would not respond, so we were forced to fire our 3-inch 50 gun manually.

That Zero must have been lost and strayed over the mountains. He never fired a shot at us. Our ship and one other were the only ones to fire at him and we never touched him.

For the Filipino forces already on the island, MacArthur's return with US forces was the answer to a prayer. **Claro C. Morantte** *of Tanauan, Leyte, Philippines, describes the scene from his vantage point.*

O N OCTOBER 20, 1944, allied forces landed on Leyte. I remember the ear-splitting explosions. Enemy installations were the targets of massive and relentless strikes from the combined allied firepower. The skies rained bombs and missiles and soon Japanese forces were immobilized.

Our company was at Siloon Mountain, Burauen. Below us, the ocean swelled with countless warships. Above, warplanes in formation swarmed, roaring in to strike their targets with precision.

Dulag town was leveled to the ground. As the allies attacked the Japanese installations, guerrillas chased the enemy. We lost Jose Perez, Rufino Villaflor and Inocentes Gobenciong. Nicholas Jaca, Sofronio Meniano and Francisco Realino were wounded.

Filipino guerrillas had fought and harassed the Japanese for nearly four years. The occupation of their islands had not been pleasant and when the Allies landed, the pay-back for the Japanese was hell, according to **Alonzo E. Essick** *of Promise City, Iowa.*

A S WE APPROACHED this little village, the Filipino's were running out of town as fast as they could. We were told a Jap was in town looking for some food.

When we got in town a Filipino showed us the trail he left into the jungle with a Filipino after him with a bolo knife. We started down the trail and met the Filipino coming back. His face and chest were bloody all over.

He told us a story: "About two years ago this Jap broke into my house, tied me to a chair, raped then killed my wife, while I had to watch. I made an oath that someday I would eat that Jap's liver alive and I just ate it."

We needed no further evidence.

Filipino resistance forces were deep in the mountains and had operated from these hidden areas since Bataan fell. Resupplying them was a problem and even after the landings at Leyte, it was still necessary to get supplies to the guerrillas and regular Army forces. As Filipino forces assaulted various targets, US units did not take long to establish bases of operation, as **James Robert Davis** *of Mishiwaka, Indiana, relates.*

W E WERE ON TACLOBAN, LEYTE in the Philippine Islands on D-Day plus one, October 21, 1944, when Gen. MacArthur's forces "returned." I was a dentist assigned to the 46th Engineer Construction Bn. and we had gone ashore the day before.

Our primary mission was to rebuild the Tacloban airstrip so our fighter planes and bombers would be able to land there. About 9 a.m., wet, hungry and afraid, imagine my surprise to look around and find that Gen. MacArthur and some of his aides stood within 10 feet of me.

What a boost to morale to see this great and famous man with us at that time.

Though MacArthur was ashore, the Philippines were far from secure, as **John C. Frisby** *of Forestville, Maryland, was to learn.*

G EN. VERN D. MUDGE did firmly believe in radio communication and immediate contact with the brigades and regiments of the 1st Cav. Div. I was his radio operator, equipped with a radio recon vehicle and five receivers, their related transmitters and an SRC-300 backpack transceiver.

As I drove the vehicle off the landing barge at the beachhead that had been established at Leyte, I saw the general wading ashore with the shock troops. I ran to report that his requested vehicle was ashore.

He said, "OK, Sarge, but I've found a man with a SRC-300 on his back. Tune me in on channel A."

After all our preparation, you can imagine my frustration as I tried to determine what to "weed out."

We moved inland and established a command post near Tacloban. Soon after, a convoy passed along the road with jeeps flying stars and carrying Gen. MacArthur, Adm. Halsey and Adm. Kinkaid. They were on an inspection tour.

They returned to the beach and 30 minutes later a tank lumbered up the same road and a Japanese sniper in a tree opened fire on the tank.

My only thought was if that sniper had realized the importance of the three virtually unprotected officers in those open jeeps, the war may have had a different outcome.

Tanks and flame-throwers would eventually have to be used to route the Japanese from their strongholds in the Philippines and on islands like Peleliu. Working with tanks, however, has its own peculiar hazards, as **Lester R. Wilkum** *of Milwaukee, Wisconsin, recounts.*

I WAS IN THE PHILIPPINES and we were stalled by Japanese troops. My commanding officer came up to me and said he was bringing up two tanks to clear the road. My job was to walk in front of the tanks and pick up the shells that did not explode.

I walked in front of the two tanks for almost an hour. I would see the Japs behind the grass huts that were about three feet above the ground. I'd rap on the tanks and they would blow up the huts. I figure I must have walked at least a mile and a half.

I was eventually relieved of duty and turned around and walked back. I still walk a lot everyday but my walk in the Philippines, I will never forget.

The Japanese fought stubbornly for each inch of ground. After nearly a month of intense fighting and a number of landings at various points around the islands, there was no sign of a let up, as **Clifton R. Beard** *of Cumberland Furnace, Tennessee, was to learn.*

THE FIRST HILL we took on Leyte, the Japanese took back. Some of us had been sent around to Ormock Valley to set up a road block to keep them from coming into the valley. For 13 days we held fast, then they pulled two Banzai attacks. We used mortar and hand grenades until all we had left were small arms ammo.

Lt. Davis sent me and Thanuel to pull early outpost. We were helping a blind man across this river when we were hit by a crossfire and the blind man was killed. Thanuel was hit and died later that night. It was Thanksgiving 1944.

Another holiday had arrived. Even amidst the fighting, one thing is always paramount in a GI's mind, and that's food. Some, like **Thomas E. McKeown** *of Scituate, Massachusetts, took eating very seriously.*

ON THANKSGIVING DAY, in November 1944, we were on Leyte, Philippines. We had been promised a real turkey dinner with all the "fixins" including real birds flown in from Australia by plane, so they wouldn't be all tired out.

As usual I am near the end of the chow line when suddenly the sky above us fills up with about 25-30 Japanese bombers and fighters. They had come in very low and our not-so-hot radar did not pick them up. Everybody scattered to their fox holes 'cept me.

I saw their bombs falling towards a nearby air strip so I hurried to the end of the chow line and scooped up a full tray of cherry pie which I hustled back to my tent and put it in my foot locker. Then I quietly ambled back to the mess tent, went through the line, got a delicious meal, including a small square of cherry pie.

When my tent mates came back after chow they were talking about the air raid, how good the food was, and how small and chinchy the piece of pie was. Then I opened my foot locker and produced the full tray of pie. When asked how I got it, I simply said, "That was easy. I just called Room Service!"

Filipina **Amparo Quintos-Bonicillo** *of Queson City, Philippines, recalls a turkey dinner, as well.*

I SAW THE 500 US PLANES flying the "I have returned" formation over the Leyte area as Gen. MacArthur's promise was fulfilled on October 15, 1944. Atop a mountain grandstand, I saw the most beautiful fireworks in the vast Pacific on the eve of that memorable victory.

Shortly after October 20 the Liberation Forces broke the strong Yamashita Line, followed by the capitulation of Japan. Across the Tingib River at Patrana, Leyte, the first American detachment I met served a handful of guerrillas and me a hot turkey dinner.

After being in combat, it seemed as though close calls became commonplace. Every once in a while something happens to bring a person back to reality. That may be what occurred to **Raymond J. Hunt** *of Glenview, Illinois.*

W E HAD LANDED at Tacloban Airfield in Leyte in late 1944 after a ground support mission. It was rapidly turning dark and four of us pilots were in a jeep driving from the field to our squadron camp area. Suddenly we heard machine gun fire and bombs exploding. The Japs had come in behind the hills from Ormoc area, avoiding radar, and were strafing and bombing Tacloban Airfield.

We all dove out of the jeep, and as I lay in the ditch along the road through the trees, it seemed so funny to see the jeep still chugging along in the ruts of the road, all by itself!

What wasn't funny was that, when the "All Clear" sounded and we got up, we found that we were surrounded by piles of 500 lb. bombs—we had taken "shelter" in a bomb supply dump!

An air raid is a direct attack. There's nothing sneaky or surprising about it. The Japanese, however, had other ways of mounting an assault, as described by **L. W. Clark** *of Westminster, Texas.*

I WAS WITH THE 5TH AF, HQ, HQ Sqdr and we were on Leyte Island, at the Dulag Airstrip, 20 miles west of Tacloban Philippines. Front lines were west of Dulag.

For days, Filipinos had several funeral processions each day walking through Dulag. Each casket seemed very heavy. On December 6, 1944, 1800 hours, some GIs marveled at the large flight of aircraft coming in until a crack sounded.

Japs were dropping 10,000 paratroopers over Dulag. We were ordered to stay in our fox holes as the 88s and 90s shells would be bursting directly over us. About 500 Japs reached the ground alive.

The "forced" funeral processions were Japs in the caskets infiltrating to form a second front east of Dulag.

Tokyo Rose reported 5th AF HQ. wiped out. Our infantry marched all night in rain from Tacloban to reach us. The salvation army marched with them with hot coffee and donuts and the 5th AF HQ survived.

Japanese resistance was becoming intense in the air, on the ground and at sea. Perhaps nothing instills more fear than fighting an enemy you know intends to die, and is intent on taking you with him. That defines a Kamikaze attack, and that what **Joseph R. Clark** *of Bella Vista, Arkansas, witnessed.*

O N DECEMBER 7, 1944, I was serving aboard USS LST737 as a Quartermaster second class, we were returning to our forward base after landing troops and equipment at Ormoc Bay on the coast of Leyte.

With enemy aircraft in the area, we were at General Quarters, when from our stern, out of fluffy clouds came a Kamikaze heading straight at us with a P-38 right on his tail, its wing guns blazing.

My greatest concern was that I would be hit, not by the enemy, but by a bullet from the P-38.

The Kamikaze was smoking as it went over the bridge where I was keeping the ship's log. It's left wing struck the guy wire to the starboard yardarm, catapulting it onto our starboard foc'sle.

Three men were killed and seven were blown or jumped over the side. We dropped life rafts for them and learned later that they all made it to another Philippine Island among friendly natives.

Of course, not all air attacks were Kamikaze attacks. In fact, at least one seemed to be for the pure value of harassment, according to **Hugo Schnabel** *of Aberdeen, South Dakota.*

A FEW WEEKS after we landed at Mindinao, Philippines, everything was getting nice and quiet except for a Jap plane that used to come over 'most every night and keep us awake. We called him Washing Machine Charlie because of the sound of his engine.

The Army used ack-ack and search lights on him, but most of the time couldn't find the plane.

This went on quite a while until one night the Army moved a lot of search lights and ack-ack guns down the valley. A few nights later when Charlie came over they lit up the sky and once they had him in the lights, shot him down.

Although he was the enemy, somehow we all felt sad about it. We missed Charlie.

But the skies weren't safe for American fliers, either. Just ask **R. Tom Young** *of Louisville, Kentucky.*

I PARTICIPATED in the first B-29 daylight bombing mission over Japan, from a base in China. The target was the Yawata Steel Mills. We later received a Unit Citation for this mission of August 20-44.

As co-pilot of the plane flying on the left wing of our Commander's lead plane, I saw all the action. Enemy defense was intense. Flak was laid up in square patterns on our course and level. We had to fly thorough it.

Behind the flak fighters waited, in the event we got though. One plane ahead of us was rammed.

Flying straight and level, we dropped our bombs. The plane flying on our leader's right wing went down, hit by flak. The fighters damaged our lead B29 causing a bailout over the China Sea.

We returned to Base alone. Our gunners received credit for three fighters.

The drive to liberate the Philippines was well under way. Better still, the news from the European Theater of Operations was good and it was obvious that the Axis powers there would not last much longer. That's probably why **Joseph S. Regenfuss** *of Bloomington, Minnesota, was sent to the Philippines from New Guinea, instead of to Officers Candidate School.*

A FTER 11 MONTHS in New Guinea, working for a Communications Center and expecting to be sent to Australia to an Officer Candidate School, the school was closed, and I was shipped to the Philippines to take over a Signal Corps installation on Bataan Peninsula.

After that period of time in New Guinea and no fresh fruit, I was given an orange by a Navy man. I recall very vividly the odor, taste and wonderful sensation on my taste buds, having to consume it shucks and all.

To commemorate that 1944 experience, I still eat one orange a year, shucks and all, and think how wonderful it was, and how fortunate we are to have an excess of Vitamin C and all the rest.

Like the flavor of that orange, as New Year 1945 arrived, the Allies could finally taste victory.

Chapter 14
Beginning of the End

*As US forces gained ground in the Philippines, Mother Nature unexpectedly stepped in to deliver a blow against the war effort. Perhaps **Paul T. Kelley** chose to live in landlocked Tulsa, Oklahoma, because of his experiences.*

W E DEPARTED from Guam late one evening and after a mile or so out at sea, we noticed the winds began to blow. The ocean skies slowly turned black and large swells that were developing began to turn the Pacific Ocean white with froth.

The radio operator had already received storm warnings that a tropical storm was heading this way. So the ship's crew made ready for the on coming storm.

At evening show the pitching angle was so bad, and becoming so much worse, the captain of the ship order all troops to their compartments.

During this storm, I witness the death of a sailor. He was swept across the deck by high waves carrying him into the ocean. The death was investigated by a committee aboard the ship, and they found the death accidental.

God knows, I witnessed a few deaths during World War II, but this one just seems to stand out the most.

*The storm wracked the Pacific area, and any ship unlucky enough to be caught outside of a protected anchorage was in for a wild ride. Indian Harbour Beach, Florida's **Karl G. Heinz** was aboard one of those ships.*

O UR SHIP, the USS Sigsbee DD502 encountered a typhoon of tremendous proportion. No one knows the force of the sea and wind until he has sailed through a typhoon of winds in excess of 148 MPH.

The sea was at the height of 80 to 100 ft. Our can rolled and twisted until we thought she would be torn apart. One wave rolled us 48 degrees to starboard and lost all depth charges on starboard side. Numbers one and two 5-inch guns were damaged, the port anchor lost, the whale boat completely destroyed, the bulkhead to wardroom smashed, and we lost electrical steering and gyro.

Sound was deafening like a jet warming up. After 4 days of fury, the sea calmed. One says to himself, how small man is on this earth, and how delicious a cup of black Java would taste because it would not stay in the cup.

A ship without power in typhoon-wracked seas was at severe risk. **Melvin S. Breyfogle** *of Estherville, Iowa, almost found out what that was like.*

I WAS ABOARD the USS Laws DD 558, in mid-December 1944, operating in the South China Sea, Luzon. The Laws developed a bad vibration, and divers determined there was a cracked strut on the port screw. That left only the starboard screw for power.

We were entering typhoon Cobra with a short supply of fuel oil. We did manage to take on some oil, refueling in heavy seas and poor control on one screw was a great undertaking. Our Captain Woods had to be a great seaman to bring this destroyer through this ordeal.

The typhoon claimed three other ships before the fleet was out of it. The walls of water pitched the Laws and made her roll sixty five degrees at times. The stacks took water down to the fire boxes. This 17 year old was very impressed with this power of nature and of course in wartime.

Perhaps one reason storms such as the 1944 typhoon are so terrifying is that there is absolutely no way to fight them. **John William Hoskins** *of Kilmichael, Mississippi, says he experienced . . .*

SEVEN HOURS OF TERROR in the great Pacific Typhoon on December 17, 1944. With each roll, the ship almost capsized. The worst part was we had a long time to think. It seemed we were hanging on and swimming for six weeks.

I served on the Destroyer USS Dewey from December 5, 1940 until March 30, 1945, having earned the rating of Chief Gunners Mate prior to separation. I was privileged to serve in 16 campaigns and 29 battles in the Pacific including operations at Bougainville, Midway, Coral Sea, Guadalcanal, Tulagi, Solomons, Aleutians, Gilberts, Marshalls and the Marianas.

I was aboard the Dewey in Pearl Harbor when the Japanese attacked. Second to the typhoon, the Japanese firepower in the Marshall Islands campaign scared me the most.

Before the weather subsides, the Navy will have lost three destroyers and three fleet carriers. In addition, four escort carriers and 11 destroyers will be damaged. **Thomas E. O'Grady** *of Saginaw, Michigan, details some other losses.*

I WAS A WATERTENDER on the aircraft carrier Cabot. We covered every invasion from the Marshall Islands until the end of the war. We were hit by two Japanese suicide planes and were under attack frequently.

My most frightening experience was during the typhoons. During one typhoon the planes on the flight deck were not lashed down properly and eight were damaged so severely they were thrown over the side.

For several days it was dark nearly all the time, we listed as much as 37 degrees. Several destroyers with us capsized due to running out of fuel. Most items such as shoes in our berthing compartment were found on the opposite side of the compartment after the storm subsided.

We had sandwiches for three days as it was too rough to cook regular meals. When we rolled and pitched, the waves were so high they left the lookouts in the gun tubs standing in water. "Frightening" is a mild term for our experience.

*Of course, even in this, there was a lesson to be learned, as **Richard H. Greivell** of Thomaston, Georgia, reveals.*

H EAVY SEAS, typhoons and months underway taught me to hook my arm around the bunk chain and use my blanket belt to strap myself in.

I shall always remember our first typhoon. The inclinometer showed 68-degree rolls and I could feel the ship as she valiantly tried to right herself. It was as though King Kong were trying to destroy us with his fists. Our ship, the USS Thorn (DD647), writhed, shook and trembled from stem to stern, keel to masthead as it twisted, bent, rolled and pounded at the same time.

When this matriarch of all winds passed, three destroyers were gone.

Sudden Georgia storms still make me wince. It would be years after the war ended before I could sleep without wrapping my arm around the bedpost.

***Kep Stankey** of Yankton, South Dakota, also rode out the gale.*

I WAS ABOARD the USS Coupens (CVL-25) from "43" through "45". We were operating in the South China Sea, when a typhoon hit us. We had 150-foot waves and over 100-feet of ocean going over the flight deck. We lost all aircraft on flight deck, and the 40mm and 20mm guns were torn off. All life rafts were gone. As I remember, the one person we lost was an air group commander (over the side).

At times we were listing over 35 degrees. The specs for this type of ship to capsize at 20 degrees.

All I can say, is "one helluva ride".

*A "helluva" ride, indeed. There was another group, however, who also experienced a wild ride in heavy seas. **Gabriel Marge** of Augusta, Georgia, was there when US forces landed on Luzon, Philippines.*

A FTER MAKING the initial landing at Lingayan Gulf in Luzon, Philippines with the 37th Div. on January 9, 1945, our unit, the 112th Signal Radio Intelligence Co. was assigned to help unload ships until our radio gear was unloaded.

Heavy surf came up suddenly and we formed a human chain to assist the infantrymen ashore from the LCI. The comments made to us as we pulled men from the heavy surf and the looks of gratitude and thanks earned us the Bronze Arrowhead.

Sometimes thinking of some duty as safer than others is easy. That's the thought that **Mrs. William Lippert** *of West Amherst, New York, had. It was tragically wrong.*

DECEMBER 1944 was filled with ominous war news. Casualty lists were lengthening. Life "at home" was bleak. With Christmas near, holiday shopping seemed in order. Hurrying past a close friends' neighborhood store, I admired the windows where lights twinkled together with a huge pine wreath centered with a blue service star and red bow. Their son, Raymond, was serving aboard a supply ship in the Pacific.

"Safer than most", I thought, recalling him proud in his dress whites, on his only leave. Thus comforted, I hurried on.

Upon my return, I was startled to see the store darkened. Now the wreath held a gold star and a black bow. Rain had begun and streamed down the glass as if in tears.

Notice that the supply ship, MT. HOOD, had blown up was terse and final. The war had become personal. Christmas would never be quite the same.

William W. Kanour *of Naples, Florida, witnessed the* Hood *disaster.*

I WAS STATIONED on Pityliu Island (Admiralty Group) north of New Guinea, a sergeant with the 43rd Coast Artillery Bn. (155 mm guns). The Navy requested we stay to protect Seadler Harbour and the large base on Manus Island, Los Negros, and Pityilu.

On a relatively quiet morning I decided to write a "V" mail letter home. I had just started writing when the building began to shake, the chair move, and small objects fall to the floor. I ran outside and scanned the sky, and looked toward Manus. Finally, I looked toward the harbor and saw splashes in the water. Smoke was rising high in the sky and spreading over the water. The noise from the explosion was terrific.

I went to our radio shack and learned the USS Mt. Hood (an ammunition ship) had blown up in the harbor. We immediately pressed all of our trucks into service as rescue, and ambulance service.

The harbor was full of small craft and ships before the explosion. After the smoke cleared the harbor looked empty. I will always remember this event and the damage which was not caused by combat action.

Joe G. Acee *of Sulligent, Alabama, was also there when the* Hood *exploded.*

I WAS IN THE SOUTHWEST PACIFIC, a patient in a Naval hospital on Manus Island. It was a warm and humid morning as they usually are in the tropics. Suddenly without warning, as I gazed out toward the sea, a cloud of black smoke shot straight up resembling a huge jet-like funnel. Following a mighty roar and then a strange odor that was oppressive and almost overwhelming.

The next thing I knew debris and fragments were falling from the sky like hail. This took place in 1944 about mid-morning. Later that morning they began bringing ashore casualties from the USS Mt. Hood AE-11, an ammunition ship.

A young Naval Lt. Wallace with 13 enlisted men from the vessel were ashore. They yelled, "Look! OUR SHIP! IT HAS EXPLODED!"

The Naval officer and his shipmates ashore with him were the only survivors.

For the families of the men aboard the Hood, *it would be a bleak Christmas. For others, like* **Harry Galpirino** *of Buffalo, New York, it marked the beginning of experiences that would affect him for life.*

B Y CHRISTMAS 1944, I was barely out of my teens. The hospital ship USS Marigold brought my organization, the 49th General Hospital, to Tacloban, Leyte Philippine Islands from Milne Bay, New Guinea and we prepared to disembark the next day.

Being the 4th day of Summer in that portion of the world, I attended both religious services top side. About dusk the public address system shouted excitedly, "Now hear this", the Japanese with a satanic sardonic sense of humor chose that most sacred day for an air raid. After 2-3 hours they suddenly flew away without even wasting a bomb on our hospital ship.

During the time I stood at my appointed embarkation station, I did say some long forgotten prayers, maybe the Lord heard my prayers along with others in my buddies. At least I think so.

A lot of prayers were being said in those days. On January 9, 1945, US forces moved from Leyte to Luzon, in what was called Operation Mike I. US forces will experience heavy Kamikaze attacks, including attacks by small suicide boats rigged to ram and explode against the sides of US war ships. The Japanese war resources are running short and this will mark the final surface engagement of the Pacific campaign. By February, most Kamikaze activity in the Philippines will end as well, because most of the planes have been destroyed. **Harry Kalustian** *of Fresno, California, probably wishes the Japanese had run out just a little sooner.*

J ANUARY 1, 1945 our convoy left New Guinea for the invasion of Philippines, Lengay on Gulf, Luzon. By January 6 we were in the China Seas. That morning, Japanese Kamikaze planes attacked our convoy.

I was on the deck USS John Peirce. Our Navy gun crews had never seen action, but a few of us troops stayed on deck, in case the ship went down.

The Kamikaze came right at our ship. Our gunners firing 40mm guns cut the wing off, and it missed our ship. As it passed, I could see the pilot. He was bleeding from the mouth. The plane hit the ship next to ours. I'll never forget that sight as long as I live.

*Nearby, **James W. Montgomery** of Wichita, Kansas, was also wishing the Japanese had run out of Kamikazes just a little sooner.*

AFTER LANDING TROOPS at Lingayen Gulf in the Philippines in January 1945, my ship, and a large convoy, was steaming south past Manila to a dispersal point at Leyte. As Chief Radioman my battle station was with the Captain high on the flying bridge. A Japanese Kamikaze dove through heavy anti-aircraft fire and struck the aft quarterdeck of the ship immediately in front of us.

Several men jumped or were blown over the side into the water. Because it was too late and too dangerous to change course to avoid hitting the men in the water we released life rafts and rings.

Stress of the occasion caused the Captain to become extremely pale. When I asked him "what to do" he answered, "Have the Executive Officer assume command and call the Doctor."

The men in the water were picked up later by an escort destroyer. Our Captain was taken to his quarters where he recovered rapidly.

The captain of Montgomery's ship wasn't the only one feeling stress in early 1945. As US troops press the offensive, there were vicious attacks launched on Leyte by Japanese. Losses are heavy on both sides.

Overall, the fighting on Leyte has cost nearly 70,000 Japanese dead and 15,500 dead and wounded Americans. The 6th Army, which carried the fight for Leyte, is moved to Luzon and replaced by the 8th Army.

*There are an estimated 260,000 Japanese troops on the island and by January 11, when the 25th Division and an armored group land at Lingayen, they meet heavy resistance for the first time. US forces are concentrating on a southern beachhead with the intent of taking Manila. At the same time, guerrilla activities are increasing and the fighting was intensifying as **Florencio Esteban** of Baguio City, Philippines, relates.*

DURING THE LIBERATION CAMPAIGN of Northern Luzon, I was at prone position in an observation post. I had one Enlisted Man with me. As I was pointing out to my enlisted man the movements of Japanese soldiers, a mountain gun fired at us. I saw the debris flying in all directions and I was covered with debris.

As I started to fall back, I noticed that my body was splattered with blood and human flesh. I imagined that I received the direct hit and that I was dead but merely dreaming. It turned out that the enlisted man who was with me received the direct hit. His legs were smashed to pieces, but I am still around to tell the story.

*Nor was it any safer off shore, as **Jerry Newton** of Beaumont, Texas, relates.*

I WAS WITH CO A, 16th Signal Operation Battalion aboard an LST en route to Leyte Island from Hollandia in December 1944. To our starboard was a large troopship.

One early afternoon when well on our way, I glanced up to the northwestern sky and saw a small airplane bearing down on the troopship at great speed. Suddenly there was a scurry of activity aboard our transport as a gunner rushed to man a machine gun which came alive spraying bullets at the plane.

Our gunner was unable to bring it down and it slammed into the poopdeck of the troopship convulsing the whole structure in flames. I was never able to learn any details of this Kamikaze attack and often wonder how those aboard that ship fared.

*The Japanese defenders in and around the Philippines were tenacious, as **Blas B. Afos** of Surallag, South Cotabato, Philippines, describes.*

IT WAS IN THE LAST WEEK of March 1945, when almost all the remnants of the Imperial Japanese Forces in Manila were annihilated except the cream of their army bottled in Intramuros, Manila. Intramuros is a Walled City surrounded by strong cement walls. The two gates were strongly guarded by long range cannon. The US infantry soldiers could not easily enter. It was so dangerous.

So a Japanese army man, a naturalized American citizen well versed in Nippongo, broadcast through the radio to let the civilians get out. The Japanese did not like to allow them to get out. They used these civilians as their defense. After a few hours the US Army began to bomb their fortifications. The bombing gradually increased. Before noon after that same day the US Army entered the Walled City and engaged in street fighting routing all the enemy. Finally the Japs surrendered even to the last man.

Though many civilians were injured, few were killed.

Francis J. Callaghan *of LaGrange, Illinois, had personal reasons for wanting Manila liberated.*

I FOUND my mother's cousin, her husband and three little girls imprisoned by the Japanese. They spent three years in Baguio, then interned to Manila.

Manila was still burning when my outfit, the 530th Light Pontoon Engineers, approached the city. We were unable to build a pontoon bridge across the Pasig River in the daylight, so I looked until I found Bilibid prison.

The father and little girls were locked behind bars. The mother was in the hospital. After a short reunion, I returned to my outfit to finish the bridge.

That night, a lone Jap bomber dropped a bomb near the prison. An American tank commander who had befriended the family, was one of the six killed. Ironically, the family and other GI prisoners, who had remained in the prison due to snipers survived.

As Americans and Filipinos gained ground, life in some areas returned to normal—or what served for normal during the time. **Richard H. Miller** *of Amherst, Virginia, remembers.*

THERE WAS A REAL CONTRAST to be found in the Philippines. In the town of Tacloban on Leyte Island, the guns firing in the hills above the city, raw sewage in dirty little ditches drained into the Leyte Gulf while the people calmly shopped in the market for food.

The relative quiet and ease of the people living in Zamboanga, Mindanao was a drastic contrast to life in Manila, with the destruction of ships in Manila Bay, the waterfront a shambles, destroyed docks comparable to the scenes around Ford Island in Pearl Harbor, and the senseless destruction in Old Manila. This included the church and monastery which once contained some of the most beautiful hand-carved ebony furniture in the choir loft that anyone could image.

The Americans had returned and **Dante J. Mercurio** *of Marlboro, New Jersey, describes the reaction of the people.*

THAT WHICH I REVERE MOST to this day is trudging through several Philippine villages during the early part of 1945, with the entire population lining the unpaved and dusty streets, waving jubilantly to us, revealing in their expressive faces the joy for their deliverance from the hated Japanese occupier.

The scene which remains most inescapable in my mind—and was repeated in village after village—includes the children, some being held in their mother's arms, others running along our line of march like joyous yelping pups, all shouting "Veetoree" with their hands raised and their tiny fingers showing the V sign.

I was only 24 at the time and not fully cognizant of the utter debauchery these people had suffered for three years under Japanese occupation. My naiveté was stirred sufficiently to believe that it was "I" they were welcoming as their deliverer.

A soldier about to engage the enemy can have no stronger or more galvanizing assurance that his mission is surely worth the effort. All this from an almost primitive, unsophisticated people demonstrating their joy through their children.

Richard (Dick) Peulen *of Bayport, Minnesota, reminds us that even when the fighting stopped, the Grim Reaper was always nearby.*

EACH SEASON as we prepare for Memorial Day and the special services planned to honor our fallen comrades from all wars, a very strong picture comes to mind of soldiers lying face down, bobbing in the water, or lying disfigured on many battle fields.

But there are other gallant military people to be remembered who died, not during battles but by accidents and medical problems that occurred during occupation of lands that were secured.

A vivid memory is of a young soldier who died during our return to the Philippines on the Island of Luzon. During that maneuver we had some free time and a large group headed for a river to swim. The trucks were overloaded and driven with reckless abandon.

The soldier was thrown from the front fender and later died from his injuries. His gravesite was a lonely Philippine rice paddy. The scene was very moving as we thought, "There but for the grace of God go I."

Chapter 15
Uniformed War Effort

As the battle for the Pacific was being fought, a heavy concerted effort was also taking place to place troops in Europe. Tens of thousands joined up while thousands more were drafted.

For millions of Americans, the 1940s was the first time they had ever been any distance from home, the first time they had met anyone from a distant part of the country, let alone a foreign land, and the first time they had ever worn a uniform.

There is no particular chronology here, but rather a collection of experiences, emotions, and incidents that tells much about the life and times. ***Roy G. Doolen*** *of Kinmundy, Illinois, sets the tone.*

I AM HUMBLED by the courage, efficiency and adaptability of kids 18- to 20-years-old. The war was fought by many of these young people just out of high school, with guidance from a few older professionals.

I helped train some of these young people and mold them into an efficient, reliable fighting force and still marvel at their courage and heroism under adverse conditions, also their ability to adapt to any situation. They learned the various specialized jobs very quickly, showing remarkable efficiency and personal initiative.

This observation is from my service with the 102 Cav. Group, from Omaha Beach, Normandy, to the meeting with the Russians near Pilsen, Czechoslovakia.

Another who trained young people was ***Roy W. Peters*** *of West Bend, Wisconsin.*

IN 1943 I WAS ON the faculty of the Infantry Training School at Ft. Benning, Georgia when a senior officer, Lt. Gen. McNair visited the post. All faculty members were ordered to assemble at the post theater to hear what he had to say. One of his first remarks was that he was proud to say that all our Army regiments were now commanded by regular Army officers.

The faculty was composed of 90-percent Reserve Officers. Needless to say, we were not impressed. The silence was deafening.

*When war first broke out, the US was poorly prepared. **William B.
Eichelberger** of Venice, Florida, relates how units were assembled.*

THERE WAS ALWAYS intense activity associated with training and
collecting personnel and unit materials to Activate Replacement Battalions for the USMC. Starting with an orange crate and a telephone,
units would be formed from the NCO cadre and officers assigned. Housing was in tents, with temporary mess halls and latrines.

Rosters were compiled from Military Specialties Numbers. As the unit
expanded, so did the training routine. Areas of the base were made to
simulate battle areas with emphasis on danger and realistic training.

As the battalion reached full strength, a troop train was ordered and
last Liberty granted. A final Shipping Roster was prepared, records were
gathered and the unit was given a final check and marched to the loading area for assignment to the appropriate cars. With a whistle the train
pulled out taking another 250 man Replacement Battalion to the action.

*Before being sent away on various assignments, freshly trained recruits
were normally reviewed. Often it was a high ranking officer who reviewed
the troops. Sometimes, as **Clement G. Fortin** of Rockwell, North Carolina, recounts, it was someone well known.*

AT TENT CITY, Camp LeJeune, North Carolina, 1,200 men ready for
overseas were ordered to fall in with weapons and full packs at 1230
hours. FDR was coming to review and wish us well!

We marched to a drill field and were halted at attention facing the microphone the commander-in-chief would use. Alternately the commands
came to stand at attention or parade rest, and my pack became heavier
and heavier as the afternoon progressed.

At 1630, a motorcade stopped before us, an arm from the rear window
of the lead car beckoned our major and from the third car, a woman got
out with Fala, the Roosevelt dog. After the dog urinated, the woman
waved, got back in the car and the motorcade departed.

The major went to the microphone and announced to us that the President wanted each of us to "get a Jap" for him!

*Of course, being trained and knowing exactly what you are doing are
two different things. Consider the experience of **Charles F. Troidl** of
Cheektowaga, New York.*

IN FEBRUARY 1944, we were aboard the USS PC1086 escorting as
convoy from New York with several other PCs and a leader DE. The
second day out, we picked up a contact and were ordered to follow
through.

We fired our bow rockets, then laid a pattern of depth charges, after
which we saw an old ice box, some collectible items and debris on the surface. We discovered that an old wreck had come close to the surface.

It was a hazard to shipping and we were ordered to destroy the remains, which we did with our guns and charges.

The ocean was full of stunned fish, one of which was the biggest red snapper I ever saw. The skipper had us bring it aboard. We did—and the crew ate well.

Whether on land, on the sea, or in the air, part of the motive for training enveloped camaraderie and team work. **Donald L. Meyer** *of Boone, Iowa, knew enough not to abandon his mates.*

I T HAPPENED while flying patrol in a TBF Gruman torpedo bomber, over the Atlantic, with a F4F Wildcat fighter escort. The faster plane would fly port and starboard, returning to one wing then the other.

One time he pulled to our right wing and I saw his engine quit and his plane went into a dive. As radioman I hit the Emergency IFF button and contacted our pilot and we followed the plane as he decided to ditch rather than bale out. Our pilot made a good water landing and got into his small life raft.

The Wildcat sank about 200 miles east of Norfolk. We returned to 10,000 ft. to give rescue a fix as to where the larger life raft should be dropped. The PBY came to pick up the survivor but the North Atlantic was so rough, a boat had to rescue and tow the PBY.

Our TBF returned to the VC 15 Squadron at Fentress Air Station. Two days later our wing man, returned to the ready room, with his head bandaged, from a cut received in the water landing, ready to fly. He thanked us for staying with him and helping in the rescue.

As group after group of young men marched off to war, were they truly prepared? **Samuel R. Harvey** *of St. Cloud, Minnesota, was one.*

I WAS A GAWKY, 138 lb., 18-year-old kid from Arkansas in the Navy in 1943. When we arrived at Midway Island on a Liberty ship from Pearl Harbor, I thought I knew it all.

But I did some growing up on Midway, on the edge of a horrible war. I became a third class ordnanceman in charge of four young fellows like myself and four big ammo magazines filled with all kinds of bombs and shells. We loaded these in and on aircraft to use against the Japanese.

This was the most desolate and lonely place in the world. Only the gooney birds felt at home.

Being proficient and being trained are not the same thing, according to **Don Andrews** *of Valley, Nebraska.*

I WAS SO EAGER to fly as a Naval Aviation Cadet. I had been fully trained in Pre-Flight and knew every aspect of Aerodynamics, so when I got to Ottumwa, Iowa, for Primary, I knew I could answer any question an instructor might ask.

How wrong I was! When I went out to the flight line, saluted and reported, the flight instructor said: "Cadet, what makes this thing fly?" Being very sure of myself, I went through the theory of aerodynamics, i.e., lift, drag, thrust, etc.

He looked at me like I was an idiot and said: "You dumb SOB—it's that noise up front! If that quits, you don't fly no more!"

Once a person is proficient, one should make sure one sticks to one's area of expertise. At least, that's the hint that **Franklin A. Bryan** *of Fort Wayne, Indiana, offers.*

I WAS THE BATTALION SURGEON for the 983rd Field Artillery Battalion serving in the South West Pacific Theater. Our first combat action was at Maffin Bay, New Guinea. I was standing next to the fire control officer of B Battery while it was aiming at a Japanese target. I raised my arm to adjust my helmet. The gunner interpreted my action as the signal to fire.

Inadvertently, I the only non-combatant officer in the battalion, was responsible for our first combat artillery round being fired. The target, I was later informed, was a Jap Army hospital.

According to **Dick Stedler** *of Tonawanda, New York, becoming proficient took a while.*

D URING BASIC TRAINING at Fort Niagara, New York, I was in a platoon being introduced to close-order drill. After a brisk workout, the Sergeant chose a well-known athlete, noted for his clownish antics, to run the drills. "Platooon, at-tens-sshun!" was his first command. Then, with a mischievous grin, he shouted: "Toooo, the rrr—eeearrr, march!"

No one moved. Embarrassed the blundering private smiled again, but sheepishly. Meanwhile, his buddies responded with a rollicking roar and even the serious-minded Sergeant laughed.

Neither the raw recruits or Sergeant had heard this command to a platoon in stationary formation before, and most likely never would again.

Glen I. Boston *of Franklin, Illinois, says that there may have been a lack of proficiency one day aboard his ship.*

O N NOVEMBER 14, 1943, the destroyer William D. Porter nearly succeeded in torpedoing the battleship USS Iowa during an Atlantic crossing.

President Franklin D. Roosevelt was aboard the Iowa along with his Joint Chiefs of Staff. They were heading for a secret conference with British Prime Minister Winston Churchill, Chiang Kai-Shek and Josef Stalin.

The Porter was making a simulated torpedo attack during defensive exercises and accidentally fired a live torpedo at the Iowa.

After a quick warning from the Porter, the Iowa made a high speed turn and escaped. The Porter was then sent back to Bermuda and the entire ship's crew placed under arrest.

The Porter was later sunk by a Japanese plane off Okinawa in June 1945, but no lives were lost.

I was a torpedoman aboard the Porter.

Bernard J. Marron *of Sheridan, Wyoming, tells another tale of proficiency lacking.*

A N INCIDENT that occurred at the Naval Air Station, Norfolk, Virginia in June of 1944. A friend and I wanted to get a hop to Washington D.C. Directly inside the gate was a perfect line of Wildcat aircraft. As we approached the control tower a plane suddenly moved out of formation and onto the runway, taking off almost vertically.

A plane was ordered up to keep it in sight. Twenty minutes later a speaker announced "Plane coming in", "Out of Control", "Clear the runway"!

The plane hit the runway, bouncing high, after several attempts turned on its side near the end of the runway. Shore patrol and fire truck units followed to pull out the culprit, an Aviation MM 2/c who is said to have never flown before.

Of course, once GIs became proficient in their job, their reputation was sure to grow. That's what happened to **Ed Bonds** *of Hesperia, California.*

G EN. WHITEHEAD, commander of the 5th Air Force, was inspecting our Norden bombsight shop. Shop personnel have been instructed to "carry on."

The General approached my workbench and said, "Your captain says you fix little things; little things like this damned cigarette lighter?"

"Yes, sir!" Cameras, lighters, knives, glass frames, all kinds of little things needing screws and springs and so on, I fixed them. The captain knew.

"Can you fix it now?"

"Yes, sir!" A quick check showed me the lighter needed a new indent spring, a common problem. The catch is, I needed three hands.

"Here, let me hold that," and Gen. Whitehead held the case. Now the screw, new spring and flywheel I can easily manage. Zip, pop! It works.

"Thanks, sergeant. We sure fixed that fast." Me and the general—we!

Proficiency to many minds meant victory. Perhaps that's why, when one of your own displays skill and expertise, it's easy to feel proud, as is the case with **Rocco Cozzi** *of Rahway, New Jersey.*

W E ALL FELT GREAT the day that Second Lieutenants Joseph Shaffer and Elza Shahan of the 334th Fighter Squadron shot down the first German plane credited to the US Army Air Force in World War II. It happened on August 14, 1942 near Reykjavik, Iceland.

I was a medic with the 33rd Fighter Squadron at the time and I helped take care of the dispensary where we treated all the pilots and other members of the group. Lieutenants Shaffer and Shahan were flying P-39's at the time and the German plane they got was a four-motored Focke-Wulf Kurrier bomber.

It sure was a great day for our squadron and we all celebrated the event. I am proud to say I served with the 33rd Fighter Squadron in Iceland.

It's a long stretch from milking cows or delivering papers to the skills developed by **Elgin G. Enabnit Jr.** *of Fairfield, Connecticut.*

F OR A FARM BOY brought up in Minnesota, and having only traveled as far as Iowa and Wisconsin, going to Missouri for basic training was an exciting event. But that was just the beginning, as I found myself aboard the Queen Elizabeth with about 20,000 other Americans and no convoy. We went north of Ireland into the Glasgow harbor and were taken ashore by boats on June 6, 1944. What excitement when we heard of D-Day in France.

We built numerous Bailey bridges across France for 3rd Army tanks and trucks. Some 88mm shells interfered with construction, but the forts at Metz were a real challenge. Our company commander designed a mobile bridge by welding two trailers on one end and mounting the other end on a tank.

Imagine what the Germans thought when they saw this bridge coming over the hill!

For some, proficiency entailed the art of warfare. For others, like **Leola R. LeBar** *of Norfolk, Nebraska, another skill superseded killing.*

T HE ROYAL VICTORIA HOSPITAL Netley Hauts, Southampton, England Channel was taken over by our USA government. As the receiving of the wounded began, we took it to heart when our retired USN Medical Commander in charge of Unit Ma 56, said, "To all hospital personnel: When a patient enters these hospital doors, be it friend or fighting enemy, WAR STOPS AND MEDICINE BEGINS."

And it did.

Mix the optimism, youth, and adventurous nature of young people with the military's penchant for travel, and many, like **Bob Bittck Sr.** *of Tulsa, Oklahoma, turned tourist when the opportunity beckoned.*

E VEN THOUGH I spent eight months in Europe, my most memorable memory was leaving Camp Campbell, Kentucky, on Christmas day, 1944, in a snow storm, headed for the Battle of the Bulge in Germany. There was a transportation delay, and our unit was held at Camp Kilmer, NJ for six weeks.

My eldest brother was living in New York City, and worked for RCA radio. I got to visit and see Roseland Ball Room, Jack Dempsey Bar and Grill, Grand Central Station, Pennsylvania Hotel, Empire State Building, and the Statue of Liberty. I saw Mary Martin and John Boles in a stage play, Fred Waring's "Lucky Strike" radio show, and danced to name "Big Bands" at the USO, or at The Stage Door Canteen.

New York City was a wonderful service man's city during World War 2.

*The holidays were hard for someone stateside. For someone in a foreign port, like **Richard E. Taylor** of Wenatchee, Washington, it was especially memorable.*

I T IS NOT necessarily the memories of combat at sea, though they would become forever lodged in my mind and effect me for the rest of my life.

My ship was in a foreign port on Christmas 1942. Everything was strange, the climate hot, language indiscernible. Then from some outdoor market, a scratchy but recognizable voice issued forth. It was the one-of-a-kind voice of Bing Crosby. His rich baritone was singing White Christmas.

I was in Boot Camp when it first had been popular. He sang of things I longed for—family, a Christmas setting in a crisp, clean atmosphere. Such a contrast to my surroundings with the future so uncertain. I immediately left for the ship. The gangway watch was surprised to see me back so early. Once alone down in the cramped compartment, I sat down on my bunk and wept.

*If misery loves company, **Oliver J. Jones** of Garden City, New York, was hardly alone.*

I T WAS NOVEMBER 1942 in San Diego as we boarded the 10 thousand ton Dutch Motorship, Bloemfontein, for a voyage I will never forget. A mixed group of Marine replacements for the South Pacific, 2,300 strong. Only two meals a day consumed standing up as we moved through a mess hall no bigger than today's average home garage. Only two dispensers for drinking water as a result, trench mouth ran rampant. Everyone received the standard navy cure, daily swabbing with Purple Jensen, we called it the purple crud smile.

Wooden lavatories were built hanging over port and starboard sides, no paper needed in rough winter. Crossing the Equator on December 23, I remember old timers and new recruits singing Christmas carols under the Southern Cross.

Arriving in Noumea, New Caledonia we went our separate ways. Myself to Guadalcanal, others to serve elsewhere and some never to return. No Marine who made that trip will ever forget it.

*Almost nothing stayed static. Consider the itinerary of **Merle T. Franz** of Yelm, Washington.*

I RECALL crossing the English channel in a crowded ship, sleeping on a mess table before landing ashore at Omaha Beach.

First night in France was spent in a cow pasture between American and German troops, "top brass error" needless to say, they moved us out in a hurry.

My Engineer Regiment was rushed to Belgium during the Battle of the Bulge, later in Antwerp, repairing bombed warehouses, we often had to hang from roofs for dear life while buzz bombs, rockets cut off over us, absolutely, no place to run. After a tour in the Philippines, and Alaska, I was then stationed in Seattle where my most vivid memory occurred.

General MacArthur stopped there after being relieved of duty, I was one of several chosen to guard him in his hotel room. While shaking hands he thanked us for the care given him. I'll never forget his warm smile and firm handshake.

*Of course, playing tourist had its own hazards, as **David S. Kloss** of Somerdale, New Jersey, discovered.*

CARNEY AND I received orders in New York City to report to Treasure Island, California. Green, who was finishing his leave, wished to take his car to California, but needed gas stamps. We were able to obtain same and left from NYC via NJ, Route 30, PA Turnpike to Canton Ohio for a "pit stop."

Peoria was our planned stop for shower, sleep and a change of clothes. We stopped at a hotel and approached the desk in uniform wearing ribbons. The clerk informed us that there were no rooms. We stood in line at the dining room. Upon approaching the door we were asked if we were guests of the hotel. "No, sorry, you can not use the dining room." Went to the desk to ask why. "Today is VE Day".

We had to buy gas from police to be able to continue on.

*Nor do most tourists see the country from a machine of war, as did **Carl M. DiMedio** of Bronx, New York.*

IT WAS SEPTEMBER 9, 1944 the first time I saw the white cliffs of Dover. I was flying over the English Channel at 5,000 feet aboard my B-24 Liberator. We were returning to our home base at old Buckenham Airfield in Attleborough, Norwich, England and had just completed our first bombing mission over Germany.

The white cliffs of Dover are a truly majestic sight.

*Some GIs, like **Paul K. Paisley** of Newton Falls, Ohio, got to see the world, like the recruiting posters advertised.*

I RECALL what Reporter Clay Gowran wrote in the Chicago Sunday Tribune, 4 June 1944, about the 459th Fighter Squadron (AKA) Twin Dragons. The heading was "FIGHTER PILOTS DRAM 123 JAPS IN THE BAG IN 58 DAYS." Some of our pilots made ace the first day out.

When I was in the service, I went all the way around the world. East coast to the west coast. Across the Pacific to Australia. Up the Indian

Ocean to India for 27 months. After the war was over we shipped out of Calcutta through the Indian Ocean to the Red Sea and the Mediterranean. Across the North Atlantic to New York.

The best part of the trip was when we arrived in New York aboard the USS General J.R. Brooke. Several boats came out to meet us. The band was playing "Happy Days are Here Again".

I was very proud to be a part of the 459th, they did a lot to help win the war.

To be sent to foreign lands was often a great adventure, but, too, it was also a learning experience, as **Jim Jackson** *of Prunedale, California, discovered.*

S HE WAS A YOUNG MOTHER in London. I had met the young lady in a pub and walked her home after the closing hour. She was staying with her sister since her brother-in-law was in service.

I accepted an invitation for a cup of tea. The kitchen was small and seemed even smaller because the table was one of the famous ANDERSON SHELTERS. A steel top and bottom separated by 4 inch angle iron legs. Three sides were of heavy iron wire mesh. During the "Blitz" the Anderson Shelter became a standard piece of furniture in homes without room for a garden bomb shelter.

Suddenly the air raid sirens started to wail and, without saying a word, the young mother disappeared up the stairs. She returned almost immediately with two small, sleepy children and an arm load of bedding. After setting the little ones in the shelter she returned to her chair and we resumed our conversation.

We talked until the "all clear" was sounded and I was able to leave. Her fear and her worry never entered our conversation, but I have never been able to forget the terror that I saw in her eyes.

Others saw military service as a tradition, such as **John Robert Denny** *of Tallahassee, Florida.*

I WAS A TEENAGER and had just turned 13 a few weeks before the hostilities erupted. Teenage years in high school were times of shortages, rationing, deaths of friends. Upon finishing high school in 1944, I started infantry training at Camp Blanding; training curtailed by the Battle of the Bulge; overseas immediately; rode a 40 and 8; remembered that my father, 27 years before, was in France fighting another war; received my M-1 rifle on Easter Sunday 1945; assigned to combat engineers; strafed by German jet planes; witnessed hundreds of dead at Dachau; found burnt potatoes still on the stove in Hitler's kitchen at Berchtesgaden; watched mass surrender of German army; arrived in Austria before V-E Day; served in Russian zone behind "Iron Curtain" (still a teenager); joyfully returned home joining my father and others as members of the American Legion.

Still others strove to do their duty, as they saw it. **Lloyd Stott** *of LeRoy, New York, knows one officer who performed.*

I T WAS MY FIRST CHRISTMAS away from home and I was temporarily stationed at Santa Anita race track. Our company of Air Corps men were to sort mail at the Los Angeles post office for the Christmas rush.

We bunked in former stables, a change from our regular barracks. Our lieutenant, fresh out of OCS, was in charge of his first command.

He wanted a good report so to entice us to do good work, he held a meeting and promised us a party and a three-day pass on December 24.

Sure enough, the'day before Christmas we awoke to find one bay of the stables decorated and tables of food and punch. Somehow, he had wrangled a small gift for each of us.

It wasn't home, but it was better than what many others had that year.

War time or not, Christmas away from home is hard to take. **Edward E. Ryczek** *of Milwaukee, Wisconsin, remembers one special holiday.*

I T WAS CHRISTMAS EVE, 1942, at the U. S. Naval Training Station, nestled in the Bitterroot Mountains of northern Idaho. My new friend, Len Spitzer, and I were seated on chairs set up in a drill hall, along with hundreds of other cold, lonely, homesick sailors attending Midnight Mass.

The altar was an orange crate set on a table and a priest was telling us about Peace on Earth. Through half-closed misty eyes, my mind wandered back to the resplendent altar of my home church where my loving wife would be attending. I could almost hear the sound of the mighty organ heralding the birth of the Christ Child.

Now the Mass was over. There was no music; just the sound of the wind and of boots sloshing though mud and snow making their way to the barracks.

I wished a "Happy Hanukkah" to Len before I turned in.

Many military leaders of the time were new to the game. **Milton Haskell** *of Beaver Dam, Wisconsin, offers a philosophical view of the leadership.*

I T'S LIKE THIS. The Top Brass always did their strategy work hind end to and the enemy never knew what to expect and it worked.

To the bombings and threat of invasion, GIs in England soon learned of another Nazi threat, as **Willard F. (Bill) Evans** *of Tucker, Georgia, tells.*

I WAS IN UXBRIDGE, ENGLAND where, using a crudely made time and sound chart, I would call out to all within hearing as I tried to determine where each V-1 bomb passing overhead was actually landing. We were all caught up in the war, doing our thing, with little thought otherwise.

Frank C. Gengel of Bellevue, Nebraska, offers a vivid description of a buzz bomb attack.

I EXPERIENCED my first sighting of the V-I Buzz Bomb when I was 19 and stationed at HQ EBS, Watford, Herts., UK. One day at work we heard the sound of a strange aircraft going overhead. Suddenly the sound stopped and we rushed to the window in time to see a mini-sized plane gliding away from us. Then came a terrific explosion that rattled the windows and shook the entire building.

Shortly thereafter the "Stars and Stripes" described the new German weapon and we then knew what we had seen.

As the weeks wore on the sightings of the V-I became more frequent and there was always the fear that the engine might stop while overhead. The damage to the local area was devastating. I will always admire the English people for their courage and perseverance during those terrible times.

*Friendships created during the war would last a lifetime, and nothing hurt worse than to be separated from your unit. Men like **Douglas W. Frederick** of Superior, Nebraska, felt they should be with their comrades, even when the danger was great.*

I T WAS PAINFUL when I heard of the bombing of the USS Ben Franklin, CV-13, known as "Big Ben". The ship was bombed on March 19, 1945 in the Sea of Japan. The fire and explosions killed 894 men but the ship survived to make it back to port, "the ship that wouldn't die."

The Marine Corps had two squadrons on board as well as their own war planes, F4Us, called the Corsair. Major "Pappy" Boyington's squadron was the 214 aboard and the "Sky Raiders", VMF-452 with pilots and crews.

My first assignment was to the airbase at Mojave California. The pilots were in advance training for carrier duty. The squadron moved to El Centro, California for rocket fan bomb practice. The pilots were trained on the Ranger for proficiency in landing F4Us on carrier decks.

The Marine training group didn't go aboard the CV-13. Instead, the rear echelon was broken up and transferred. I was sent to Camp Pendleton to a tent camp out in the boondocks and given mess duty.

That was a real come down having a specialty and out of an air conditioned office. I would go to work at the mess hall at 04:00 and since the Lt. couldn't find me I was listed as a deserter for a spell. I could see that I would have an exasperating career in the Marine Corps so I took my discharge certificate in March 27th 1946 I left for home in Wyoming.

I often think of the buddies and acquaintances that didn't make it and at a young age found a grave in the ocean.

*Even for those stationed outside the actual war zone, like **Joseph R. Connally** of Geneva, Illinois, there were still fears to deal with.*

I WAS STATIONED at Natal, Brazil, no where near the war zone, but still a long way from home. There was very little to do on base except play cards, drink and dream about going home.

Going to town wasn't much better. The only places we were allowed to go were government regulated. Everything else was off-limits.

One of the highlights of the day was going to the base movies. One night the film was an animated cartoon on how we were going to win the war in the Pacific. It was based on an Igor Stavinski prediction that to conquer Japan would take 20 years.

That night I didn't sleep, thinking about how I would be middle-aged before the war was over.

Men and women by the thousands joined the service or worked in the defense industry. But according to **Mrs. Elman Swanson** *of Bedford Park, Illinois, it wasn't necessary even to be human to be part of the war effort.*

I T WAS HARD saying good-bye and taking movies of the 75 boys and girls, plus one dog, GOLIATH—Golly for short—who heeded the call from Uncle Sam from the Village of Bedford Park, Illinois.

Golly was trained as an Army attack dog and went into active duty on May 4, 1944 and terminated before the war was over when his soldier partner was killed in action. Because of his attack training, his owners, the Downs family, contacted Orphans of the Storm for his placement in a new home.

He wound up at a monastery in Wisconsin where he could roam. He was the only Protestant on the grounds, and the only one who would be served meat on Fridays.

The Downs family had two stars in their service flag one for their Merchant Marine son, Jimmy, and one for "Golly", in the K-9 Corps.

Dogs may or may not get homesick, but it is certain that GIs do. For many, like **D.B. Almandares** *of Tampa, Florida, it was a traumatic time.*

I WAS 18 AND AT Camp Blanding, Florida on New Year's Eve 1942 and would be inducted into the service the next morning. Tears flowed down my cheek as the bells rang, the horns blew and the merry-makers welcomed in the year 1943. I was saddened not because I was going into the service, but because I had never been away from home before, not even for a night.

I was classified 1-A and inducted the next day and sent to Ft. Bliss, Texas a few days later. What a lost poor soul was I, still wet behind the ears!

After training I was sent to the Pacific and participated in many battles and later in the occupation of Japan. Though I am no longer young, I would do it again.

*In some case, enlisting was a family matter. **D. Allen Davis** of Lemoyne, Pennsylvania, joined with his brother.*

EARLY IN 1944, my identical twin brother shocked the family at the evening meal with the news that he had enlisted in the Navy, on that day. My physician father looked at me and said, "You do the same thing tomorrow."

We were seniors in high school and enlisted on the delay after graduation program. Five days after graduation we were in boot camp. My parents wanted us to be together no matter what happened. We were discharged almost three years later. Together all this time.

Shortly after we enlisted, I received word that I had passed the Officer's Candidate test given to high school seniors. It was no longer valid, since I was already in the Navy.

I have no regrets. We are Grandfathers now, and we each had a daughter serve in the US Coast Guard.

*Family was important in the '40s, perhaps more so than today. **Lucille Oehlerich** of Keystone, Iowa, learned something visiting her cousin.*

I MADE A TRIP to see a cousin of mine who was hospitalized in an Army Hospital at Topeka, Kansas. He was serving in the 34th Infantry in Africa, and was injured when a live bomb exploded, and was brought back to the states in a body cast up to his chin.

I saw all kinds of injured service men in the hospital, and one wondered, would they all get better and what kind of scars the war would leave them.

Dick, my cousin, did recover and received a medical discharge, after a long time of suffering and pain, he was left with a crippled leg, he took up watch repairing, service connected, and enjoyed what he did, and got a job in a jewelry store repairing watches.

*Whether overseas, or just down the road, loneliness was always an enemy. **George F. Lamb** of Pittsburgh, Pennsylvania, says Christmas was the worst.*

I REMEMBER one Christmas, it was 1942, I was stationed in Manitowac, Wisconsin on a guard detail. I had liberty Dec. 25th. "Holiday Inn" was playing at the local theater. I went to see it, I enjoyed the show and when it ended I went out to the street. There had been a heavy snowfall, a winter wonderland. The snow was falling, great big flakes, slowly falling, the air was full of them.

I was 19 years old, my first Christmas away from home. Dec. 24th was my birthday. I will say this, I didn't cry, but it was close.

Now, after 47 years, this is my most memorable Christmas.

*Some seemed unlikely candidates for the military, yet did very well, as is the case of **Herbert G. Raab** of Fayetteville, Pennsylvania.*

A T FIRST it was extremely difficult to adjust to the sudden withdrawal from an 11-year career as a public school teacher to an entirely new career of strict militarism. Eventually, however, I was able to acquire many of the new skills of a combat engineer. In fact, I shifted from a high school math teacher to a battalion sergeant major with the 88th Inf. Div., 313th C. Engineer Bn. in North Africa in approximately 18 months.

*Of course, for many, like **Joe Nathan Anderson** of Marysville, California, there wasn't a lot of choice.*

I CAME HOME from work in 1943 and there was a long envelope waiting for me. Inside: Greetings from the President of the United States of America . . .

I was told to report to Camp Blanding in Jacksonville, Florida for examination. I passed and was given an "ACCEPTED" tag August 10, 1943.

Then it was boot camp, leave for nine days, more training, then we, the sailors of Company 1231, boarded a troop ship for the South Pacific. We stayed over there until 1945.

*In the case of **Raoul N. Aucoin** of Baton Rouge, Louisiana, participating in the service was one of the high points of his life.*

I WAS 32 YEARS OLD and had not had any military training before. On October 8, 1943, I was presented with the "Honor Man Certificate" from my boot camp company, 43-353.

When I got that certificate, I felt I had done my best and someone had recognized it. It was a very good feeling.

*For others, like **John T. Krans** of Galesburg, Illinois, it was something less than a dream come true.*

A T 37, I WAS EXEMPT from the draft because of my employment with a daily paper, the Waukegan, Illinois News Sun. But when I took employment with a weekly paper in another draft board's jurisdiction, my status was challenged and I was called up July 19, 1943. Though my employer appealed, it was to no avail. I served in the southwest Pacific, earned a combat infantryman's badge with five battle stars . . . and was later found unfit for combat.

*Of course, as GIs before and since, it was important to keep a sense of humor, no matter how grim things might get. Sometimes that humor was just a bit morbid, as in Deltaville, Virginia, resident **Marion C. Hall Jr.'s** case.*

I WAS WORKING for the Food and Drug Administration in Washington, D.C. when I was drafted.

The day we took our physicals and shots remains vivid in my mind. There were five medics giving shots—three on the right, two on the left.

It was very amusing to see men built like football players walk a few steps and then pass out.

Sometimes there was no other word for humor than gruesome. **John F. Drennan** *of Dallas, Texas, offers a horrid example.*

W E WERE VERY CLOSE to the front lines watching a performance presented by Special Services. The entertainer was Frank McHugh, a comedian.

Two infantrymen, carrying a pasteboard box wrapped like a gift, walked right up to the performer and presented it to him. When he opened it, he set it down on a chair and said, "Good-bye," and walked off.

Within the box was the head, complete with helmet, of a dead German soldier.

For some, the philosophy of humor was simple. If it happened to officers, it was funny. That seems to be the case with **Robert F. Johnson** *of Green Bay, Wisconsin.*

A T ONE TIME I was working a pistol range as we were armed with 45 service automatics. The Army saw fit to send some reserve officers to fire 45s on our range.

We fired our 45s with arms extended at that time, but these officers wrapped their arms around their bodies with the piece right up to their eyes.

I called a cease fire and called their attention to what they were about to do. The Col. in charge of them said let them go, so I called to commence firing. The first rounds they fired, the slide came back and hit them between the eyes and we had some beautiful black eyes and broken glasses.

I lost a lot of respect for Officers after that day.

When millions of people are interacting, a lot of strange—even eerie— things can happen. Consider this tale from **Norma A. Phinney** *of Floodwood, Minnesota.*

M Y BROTHER was 16 and I was 14 years old when he decided one day to take his rifle and go deer hunting in our back forty. He was gone a long time and when it started to get dark my mother began to worry so she sent two people out looking for him.

While they were searching for him, I was sitting in the kitchen facing the back door, when suddenly my brother came through the door with rifle in hand. What a relief for all.

During WWII this same brother was in combat in Europe. My parents were frantic upon receiving a telegram from the War Dept. telling them their son was missing in action. They telegramed me at the Naval Hospital in Mare Island, California.

It upset me so much that same night I dreamed that I was again in that same kitchen facing the back door when all of a sudden this same brother came through the door wearing his uniform and carrying his rifle.

The next morning I sent a telegram to my parents saying not to worry as I was sure this was an omen and that he would be coming home again.

Well, he did come home eventually. He wasn't missing at all, as he had been captured and held prisoner along with thousands of other troops during the Battle of the Bulge.

Mary B. McClusky *of Port Charlotte, Florida, is another one who had dreams.*

THE MORNING of New Year's Day, 1945 at the Opa-Locka Naval Air Station, Miami, Florida, after 0800 muster that morning in the parachute loft, I told everyone of a dream that night—seeing several parachutes blossoming to earth from a plane. Everyone had a good laugh!

At 1100—a call to the loft sent our truck out to pick up several parachutes used in emergency jumps. (the swamp weasel picked up the airmen).

A TB squadron flew an oxygen hop with oxygen masks ordered at 8000 feet for the climb to 14,000 feet. In emergency, a bail-out was ordered which involved the pilot, gunner, and radioman. Hearing it over an open transmitter, another TB crew bailed out. A total of six parachute jumps— all into the swamp. (My dream.)

The rest of the squadron circled the crash and kept watch over the men until rescue arrived. This account was written out fully and signed by the radioman involved—whose parachute I packed.

*For a country at war, the ultimate nightmare, perhaps, is to lose your leader. **Nathan Lit** of Philadelphia, Pennsylvania, remembers that day.*

IT HAPPENED on a sunny day in April when we chairborne commandos were ordered out for a training session. We were marching to a training ground when our company was called to a halt at the main intersection of the camp to allow a line of military vehicles to pass.

While waiting, a door opened in a nearby building and out burst my friend Norma who worked in the Public Relations Office. Seeing me, she yelled, "Nate, guess what happened!" And then she blurted out, "President Roosevelt just died!"

Everyone nearby heard her and everything came to a dead stop. Silence descended on the area. Nothing moved. No one made a sound. Everyone looked at each other in dismay.

After what seemed like an eternity, people and vehicles began to move again. But that day, and moment, stuck in my head forever.

The president was just one of many who would die during the war. ***Franklin A. Bryan*** *of Fort Wayne, Indiana, remembers too well the memory of . . .*

STANDING NEXT to those dark metal caskets at the funeral home in Hallowell, Maine. Our Legion Post #6, took care of the Honor Guard duties for our area, each time one of our wonderful friends or citizens came home for their final resting place during and after the war.

These duties were shared by many Legion members from my Post. I feel those hours may have been a final time for most or all of us veterans of past wars to think back and reflect on ourselves also. I know I did.

I can't say I did much in the Army Air Corps from May 27, 1943 when I enlisted with a friend, Bruce Campell. We both were called to active duty, when we turned 18 years that summer, August 13 (Friday) 1943. I came home alive, Bruce came home in a metal box for burial in Hallowell.

Chapter 16

Impressions

Many who responded to The American Legion's request for their most vivid memories sent letters that did not deal with history, but rather perceptions of people, places, events, and the spirit of the nation at that time. They do not follow a historical pathway, nor do they fit into specific actions, battles, or points in history. They are simply . . . impressions.

Irene Rachko Pearson *of Clifton, New Jersey remembers the pride.*

OUR TOTAL COMMITMENT of patriotism amongst GIs, our families, and employees who worked on government contracts was unsurpassable.

GIs are the best people in the world. We lived in an era that forced us to face how we lived our lives, served our country, and measured our true worth as well as the next guy or gal. We GIs, men and women, felt a closeness to each other that could never compare to any other commitment under any other circumstances.

Most of us were close in age and the respect we had for each other and our superior officers was just too marvel to observe. After our personal hygiene and immaculate barracks, our uniforms took our next priority before we faced our dedicated daily routines. We took great pride in our work, our appearance, our branch of service and what we stood for under our great American red, white, and blue.

I still get that deep patriotic thrill and feeling when our national anthem is played and our beautiful flag is waving amidst us in parades and displayed on our American holidays, especially on Memorial Day, 4th of July and Flag Day.

But just what is patriotism? Do you have to be born here to have it? Not according to **Thomas Savarese** *of Port Elizabeth, New Jersey.*

I CAN STILL HEAR my father, an Italian immigrant, saying, "Be quiet. The President, he talk now!"

Roosevelt's fireside chats and declaration of war brought out more than flag waving. It gathered a host of stay-at-homes into a Civilian Defense Corps.

Pop was designated Block Warden and he volunteered his ice truck for emergencies.

When the air raid alarm sounded, Pop would rush out onto our street, helmet and flashlight in hand, yelling to the neighbors to ". . . closa da lights, pulla shades down! The enemy, she comes maybe!"

This little job made him feel important. It gave him what is known as self-esteem.

Pop loaned three sons to Uncle Sam. All returned home safely, but later one would give up his life in a place called Korea, but Pop died before this tragedy.

I'll never forget him.

*It's easy to remember the sacrifices on the battlefield, but others sacrificed too, as **Eleanor Kodish** of Lock Haven, Pennsylvania, relates.*

TWO MEMORIES STAND OUT as they were the only times I saw my Dad, a tough, little undemonstrative Welshman, cry!

The first was the day we said good-bye to my brother, Joe, at the bus station when he reported for Naval duty. Afterwards Dad said, "I pray that Joe never has to set in some muddy trench the way I did in 1917". He started to cry and cried all the way home, great sobs racking his body.

The second time was the day Joe came home at the end of the war. We watched him strutting proudly down the lane, looking wonderful in his Navy uniform, white hat at a jaunty angle, duffel bag flung over his shoulder! Dad embraced him and started to cry. This time he cried for happiness and thanksgiving that his only son had been spared and had returned home safe and sound.

***Virginia Meyer** of Mount Gilead, Ohio, has the memories of a small child.*

I REMEMBER rationing, air raid drills, and endless paper drives, and oh yes, the 25 cent savings stamps we bought towards war bonds, or were they 10 cents? One vivid memory has always stuck in my mind and that is V-J Day!

We lived on a farm on a dirt road with few neighbors but somehow we children got the word that this was a day to celebrate. We gathered pots and pans and wooden spoons and other clangable objects, and marched up and down that lonely dirt road banging and clanging and cheering. There were about 6 of us ages 7 through 13. I am sure no one heard us but the crickets, but we had fun and we knew what we were celebrating.

World War II made us patriots all and when we were victorious, we cheered even in the remotest parts of our land.

*Another youngster touched by the war years was **Marjorie Barnes Finley** of Arcadia, Nebraska.*

MY FATHER AND I would watch the dogs being trained for assault and rescue at Fort Robinson, near Chadron, Nebraska. There was also a prison camp for captured Germans nearby at Crawford.

Churches fed and entertained the soldiers—men and women of the Army, the Army Air Force, paratroopers and Naval air cadets—on the weekends and The American Legion Post became a USO center. Convoys were on the highways and citizens learned to identify aircraft.

Ration stamps were used to buy sugar and gasoline and C-rations were eaten on maneuvers. Esprit de corps was high and everyone was buying war bonds.

Kenneth B. Young *of Ft. Wayne, Indiana, believes he learned something from the war years.*

W HO WOULD HAVE THOUGHT that a mid-western, almost farm boy, would, at age 19, be on the Queen Elizabeth, crossing the North Atlantic Ocean, and stepping off on the firm soil of Scotland on his 20th birthday?

Or spend the next three years of his life learning the ways and some of the languages of the European countries?

Another lesson to be learned, was living with comrades from places like, New York City, New Jersey, Texas and the southern States. Sometimes it was difficult to get used to the colloquialism of the southern boys. The experience of living with men from different cultures and ethnic backgrounds, was the most rewarding of my life.

While there is nothing earth shaking about my experience in World War II, I believe it is worth telling.

David C. Vaas *of Ashland, Ohio, remembers the nation's industry.*

I WAS IMPRESSED with the way our country produced so much material for our soldiers, sailors and pilots. They were provided with the best and our citizens pitched in to provide, not only for our United States servicemen, but also for our allies.

Carl A. Minor *of Maysville, Missouri, was overwhelmed by the mass of material America generated.*

I WAS ASTOUNDED by the huge amount of supplies and equipment that our country was able to provide in the war effort. The volume and the quality was overwhelming when applied to the enemy.

Visualize, if you will, a Navy convoy off the coast of Manila in the South China Sea. There were ships in columns and rows stretching beyond the horizon in all directions. Ships with many people and much cargo.

Our personnel were equal to that of our enemy and we rose to the occasion. I believe that we prevailed because of the arms available and because of superior leadership.

I was proud to be a part of it.

Another proud of the country's industrial might is **Richard J. Alarie Sr.** *of Putnam, Connecticut.*

THE WAY AMERICA rose to the occasion and united its resources into a "Goliath". We became giants in our determination to exterminate the disease of injustice.

Admiral Yamamoto phrased it best when he said, "We have awakened a giant." These quotes from the enemy, no less!

My brothers were in the Air Corps—Leon (meteorologist) and Phil (bomber pilot). I was in Uncle Sam's artillery in Germany. Just before going overseas, I went home on furlough to visit my folks.

I was greeted by a small banner in the front door window. It displayed three blue stars on white background bordered in red. It was their way of showing support for their three sons. They showed double emotions—very proud and very apprehensive. Their steadfast faith, however, saw them through.

Let us remember those who never came back. Their sacrifice is perpetual. Our remembrance should also be perpetual.

For many, lending a hand to forward the industrialization into war material production was their way of contributing to the war effort. **Opal R. Marts** *of Park Rapids, Minnesota, joined the army of women in the workforce.*

WORK WORK WORK! After one week of welding school I was sent to the armored tank line and then the amphibian duck line was started. There I learned it was better to do a good weld the first time and not have to grind it out.

The first duck we women welded went right to the bottom of the test tank. It spurted water like a fountain. Did we ever feel insecure! However later we found out that the foreman had forgotten to shut the stop cocks! Were they trying to sharpen us up?

After the Anzio-Sicily invasion I saw a news-reel where the ducks were coming out from the ships, going through the water and driving onto the beaches. Wow! I got chills!

By-golly, it was worth it. We worked 10 hours a day 7 days a week for a year or more. My husband took a picture in 1986 and found my little weld mark under the wench box, which I welded, for posterity.

Joy Patterson Bowers *of Littleton, Colorado, was another who went to work.*

I WANTED TO HELP with the war. Our freedom was on the line. After attending college for one and one-half-years and waiting for four days until I was 18 and eligible for a job, I went to work for Consolidated Vultee Aircraft Corp. in Ft. Worth, Texas. This was the world's largest airplane double assembly line in the largest air conditioned building, stretching nearly a mile. Inside, more than 30,000 workers toiled around the clock. A new B-24 Liberator bomber came off the assembly line every four hours.

I walked down the assembly line to and from work daily.

Once as I was coming out, pictures were being shown of American prisoners of war. In one, a man with his hands tied around a pole, was being beaten on his back with barbed wire and blood was running down.

A man a few feet from me recognized the prisoner as his son.

The horror that unknown man must have felt is indescribable, but given the spirit of the country, it's almost certain someone was there to comfort him. The warmth and friendship of the nation made a lasting impression on **John X. Supinski Jr.** *of Rockville, Maryland.*

W ITHOUT HESITATION it was the enthusiasm, the favorable and warm response and support that all Americans expressed and shared, and quickly too, as soon as the United States declared war against Germany. It was a moving experience and remains today a lasting memory that moved the writer to enlist like thousands of others.

Military personnel were greeted always in a friendly manner; with a smile and there were the prayers for a speedy end of the war and the safe return of all our boys and girls called to duty and who served with commendable dedication and love for Country; who stood tall to final victory.

We are a United Nation, and our basic cause "to live in a free democracy" will always be a most precious guarded lighted symbol which no one shall darken. We are the United States of America.

One small example of that warmth and friendship is offered by **Minnie R. Ragland** *of Cocoa Beach, Florida.*

I T HAPPENED in Buffalo, New York on December 22, 1943. Military orders had ended togetherness for my husband and me. He was off to fly "The Hump."

From the cab at the station, I stepped into a desperate sea of humanity clamoring to board the incoming train. The minute it stopped the screaming throng wildly stampeded the protesting trainman.

Down the track, a curious Pullman conductor leaned out. I dashed toward him and in tearful terror pleaded to get on. His look softened and he reached for my hand. Once aboard, he unlocked the ladies' room and hurried me inside.

"Stay until I come for you."

I mopped my tears, the train moved and I breathed easier. Eventually my kindly conductor returned, ushered me to a seat and wrote out a ticket for an upper berth.

How I wanted to hug him. I would be home for Christmas!

And another lady marked by the kindness of an era was **T. Hays** *of Portland, Oregon.*

I WAS 18, had a three-month old baby, nearly broke and stranded in New York. It was late night and I found myself on the same block as the Waldorf Astoria. My baby kept crying for milk, but the only place open was the Waldorf.

I asked the doorman for some milk for the baby and he handed the bottle to a waiter who quickly returned with a warm bottle of milk. I took out my change to pay him, but he refused the money, so I thanked them and left.

It was years later before I became aware of the fame of the Waldorf, but if any former employees who worked at the hotel during the war years are still around, thank you.

*Kindness was not confined to only U.S. soil, as **John W. Bednarcyk** of Simsbury, Connecticut, discovered.*

HAVING SERVED in the South Pacific area for 39 months, my memory goes back to the time while on a furlough in Sydney, Australia. I went to a Sunday Mass in the beautiful St. Mary's Cathedral. As I sat shaking and shivering, as this was the winter season in Sydney, about 65 degrees, as my blood had thinned out, my jacket wasn't warm enough to ward off the chill.

I suddenly felt a coat put around my shoulders. I turned around to see who my benefactor was. A bearded elderly gentleman who later, after mass, I found out was a sheep rancher. I gave him a great big hug and thanked him.

I often think of him and say to myself, may God bless him wherever he may be.

*For **Allen Stuart** of Baudette, Minnesota, it wasn't just the GIs, but the common effort that touched him.*

MY MEMORY includes the unsung heroes on the "home front" with their many sacrifices with the rationing coupons, shortages, collecting and saving of war materials, their drives for war bonds and stamps, the involvement of school children, donations including blood, the volunteers for just about every thing to help the war effort, the many factories that worked around the clock in shifts. It became common that women entered the work force, (remember Rosie the Riveter?), the USO and canteens in all the major cities, the overall hospitality of the people toward servicemen and perhaps the pride to see the blue star in the windows of homes that indicated a family member was giving `prime time' in the armed forces.

Last but not least was to see the gold star in the window of a home that indicated a family member gave a life for this country. I hope this will always remain vivid in my memory.

*One of the sacrifices of that era was seeing off a family member, as **Dorothy J. Oakman** of Lake View, Iowa, recounts her memory.*

I REMEMBER the day in 1944 when my brother-in-law, Ralph Fraizer was inducted. We lived in Johnston, Iowa, about a mile from Camp

Dodge, the induction center north of Des Moines. On the day Ralph was called up, he had to go into Des Moines to ride the troop train out to the camp. The train passed right by his home and ours (we lived next door to each other), and there we were—Ralph's wife, his mother-in-law, and at least three sisters-in-law—standing in the road by the track, sobbing and waving good-bye!

Looking back, it's a comic scene, but we weren't laughing that day. Ralph was sent overseas to New Caledonia, Iwo Jima and Okinawa, and he was even "wounded" over there when he had to have hernia surgery; but he returned safely to his family and still enjoys life as a retired businessman.

*Life changed for everyone in those days, as **Jim V. Acosta** of Hightstown, New Jersey describes.*

WHILE MY BROTHER was fighting with the 3rd Armored Division in the Battle of the Bulge, my mother worked assembling binoculars in a factory, my sister making walkie-talkies (and other electronics).

I was just a small boy. Teachers would excuse us and we'd push a large two-wheel cart through the neighborhood collecting old newspapers, tin foil, etc., for the war effort. When the cart was full with hundreds of pounds worth, we'd empty it and start over again. It was extremely hard work for boys, but we did it.

When the war ended, my brother came home—safe and sound without a scratch.

It happened about 45 years ago and I remember it as if it happened yesterday. Five years after that war ended, my family saw me leave for another war. And after that war ended, I would be involved in yet another war.

*The sacrifices at home made a deep impression on young **Gary C. Howe** of Steeleville, Illinois.*

MY FATHER was drafted into the Navy in 1944 at 31. We lived in Indian Head, Maryland near Washington D C.

In mid-August 1945, two things happened that would forever be part of my earliest memories. A huge flight of airplanes roared over our government housing project all in perfect formation in celebration of V-J Day. While they were going over my mother shouted to me that the grocery store had received a shipment of bananas. They had been scarce to nonexistent for the duration of the war and this little boy really loved bananas.

*While the world breathed a collective sigh of relief that the killing and maiming had come to an end, a 4½-year-old remembers airplanes and bananas. **Saul Sokel** of Boca Raton, Florida, reflects some of the bitterness many veterans feel.*

A S A COMPANY AID MAN, attached to General Patton's 2nd Armored Division, the stench of our dead buddies will remain in my nostrils forever.

Do you know what a direct hit by a shell does for a guy by a mine or a grenade? The one's who stink the most are the guys with internal wounds. Dead for weeks some bloat up in the sun, but they all stink. The stink gets in your clothes and mouth. It remains forever. If every civilian in the world could smell that stink, we'd eliminate wars. So Mr. Congressman—Mr. Senator, don't create a stink when a Vet asks for more compensation. "Life is cheap—don't you be."

*Bitterness extends to the aftermath, as **Clarence Luedemann** of Indianapolis, Indiana, seems to indicate.*

A FTER SEEING the almost unbelievable bravery and dedication of the young American boys that walked across open fields while many of them were killed or injured by enemy fire and they just kept advancing. It was a thing to behold. They did a beautiful job and put the enemy in his place.

Now enter the "educated idiots," who sat down at the bargaining table, made stupid decisions, and sent money and machinery to the losers.

Today the only money going up in value is that of Germany and Japan. The German mark was 27-cents at wars end and is now 57-cents.

How is your American dollar doing?

It looks like we won the first part of the war, and lost the second part.

*It was an era of war heroes. Some wore medals. Others were simply heroic by nature as **Concetta Doucette** of South Windsor, Connecticut, tells us.*

C HRISTMAS 1944 . . . My father wore no uniform, but he was a veteran of pain. He changed my life forever because his mind was in his heart. I had a sub-teen's understanding then; nothing more than surface observation of him. Yet I knew that some current of unspoken language would show me a path to making withered petals shimmer with beauty.

An outstanding example of Papa's silent teachings seeping into my bones happened the day a legless sailor was carried up the stoop into our home. Although he was a stranger, we crowned him king for the day.

It was snowflake touching snowflake, blending—then to separate journeys, different missions, but holding memories of that sharing.

Today, I know that the hero who speaks in his heart does not need a uniform.

*According to **William N. Caldwell** of Phoenix, Arizona, there was an unmatched spirit in the nation at that time.*

I T IS NOT SO MUCH any one event but rather the spirit of the country, united in a single purpose, 130 million strong, whose common goal was nothing less than victory over tyranny at whatever the cost. Men and women wore their country's uniform with pride and nobody dared burn the flag.

Young boys and girls collected scrap iron for the war effort, while their older brothers and sisters made sure it was delivered in proper form to the enemy. Millions of homes displayed a service flag in the front window, and some of them were gold in memory of those who had fallen in the cause.

Women who had been housewives traded their aprons for a welder's mask, and Rosie the Riveter was born.

Then there was the music: "Praise the Lord and Pass the Ammunition", The White Cliffs of Dover, and dozens more that still elicit a twinge of nostalgia for those who lived through those times.

And the joy—the unmitigated joy when it was all over! We had won! Not only "we" but the whole world had won. As a paratrooper in the South Pacific I had been a part of that something greater than myself, or of any one event, and as Walter Gilmore so aptly put it, we did indeed have our rendezvous with destiny.

We fulfilled it.

Another example of the spirit of the times comes from **Dick Stedler** *of Tonawanda, New York.*

I WAS SITTING in the Army camp recreation room listening to Dizzy Dean, the legendary pitcher who became an ungrammatical baseball broadcaster after his pitching career ended, as he described a Cardinal game in St. Louis.

A sudden shower caused a delay in the game, but the government banned mentioning weather conditions in newspapers or on radio in those days before TV.

Dean simply told his audience, "This game's being held up and it looks like it's going to be held up for quite a spell. I ain't allowed to tell you why, but if you stick your heads out the window, you'll soon find out."

It was quick, on-the-spot thinking like Dizzy's that helped us win the war.

Music was important to the nation during the war years. The war also shaped children's play. **Cletus W. Perrotti** *of Mazeppa, Minnesota, was touched by both.*

WHO CAN FORGET the songs composed as a result of war? The songs, "Let's remember Pearl Harbor" plus "Praise the Lord and Pass the Ammunition" and "Coming in on a Wing and a Prayer" were very popular. I was a 14 year old boy when Pearl Harbor was bombed.

My 2 younger sisters and I played war games by pretending we were parachuting from United States airplanes crippled by enemy anti-aircraft fire. We jumped from the top of a grain bin into a shallow pile of grain on floor of bin. The pile of grain cushioned our fall so we did not break arms or legs.

We children were having great fun until Mother, brandishing a wooden broomstick, told us to stop dangerous war games and do some work on the farm.

The music of an era may say more about that era than any history. **Thomas Villarial** *of Forest Heights, Maryland, touches on that and more.*

THE SONGS that tugged at the emotions. Seeing people waiting in lines (many blocks long) for hard-to-get-items like coffee, sugar, booze, and cigarettes. The excitement of downtown Milwaukee on Friday and Saturday nights watching the servicemen flirt with the girls. The night clubs and dance halls always crowded. Everyone danced to live music, mellow music.

I remember the scrap drive block parties; polka music, dancing, pots and pans, everyone gave something. Money was needed for the war effort. There were the War Bond drives, school kids purchased 10-cent war stamps, movie theaters passed the can for coins, junk dealers gave 10-cents for 100 pounds of metal or paper.

Slogans: "I'd walk a mile for a Camel", "Loose Lips Sink Ships", "LS/MFT [Lucky Strike/Means Fine Tobacco]". Planes overhead, military parades, "E" for Efficiency, gold stars in the windows, hellos, good-byes, happiness, sadness, all lasting memories of World War II.

Another touched by music but on a more personal level was **Mel Zipes** *of Wappingers Falls, New York.*

I WAS 16, about three years after the Japs bombed Pearl Harbor. It must have been around '43 or '44 when the draft started calling up middle-aged married men. We lived on the ground floor of a tenement at the time and our next door neighbor's husband, who had become a new father a few months earlier, was somewhere overseas in the Army. He would eventually return safely to resume his role as husband and father.

The weather was warm and his wife was minding the baby outside in the back under our adjacent windows. It was very quiet, which is unusual for a tenement. Suddenly, with no musical accompaniment, she started to sing softly.

"Gonna take a sentimental journey. Gonna set my heart at ease..."

Her voice was crystal clear and penetrating. Even in my immature teenage years, I recognized the plaintiveness behind that singing.

There was another music that could be heard during the war years. **Robert H. Anderson** *of Los Angeles, California, experienced it.*

IT WAS A LONELY NIGHT in the middle of London in the middle of a war. Suddenly, through the cold fog, came the melancholy strains of distant bagpipes. The pipes belonged to battle-weary troops returning from North Africa. It was their way of letting the world know they had survived and were ready to go wherever ordered.

On the way back to my bomber base, I could not forget that eerie music.

Perhaps the greatest contribution The American Legion ever made on a national level was its battle for a GI Bill. Perhaps that's why **Shelby V. Langford** *of Hemet, California, joined the organization.*

I WAS ONE of the lucky GI's who benefited from serving in World War II . I am grateful for the experience and educational benefits.

The greatest of all was to serve with the average GIs who gained my admiration and respect. I never met one GI who shirked his duty. They accepted their missions with little or no training and a lot of bitching and griping and then turn out a good job. I treasure the memory of these soldiers I served with.

Another man who felt the training was worthwhile is **Lloyd A. Jacobson** *of Swan Valley, Idaho.*

I JOINED the Air Force on January 3, 1942, as an Idaho farm boy. After traveling through 15 states and some training, we were loaded aboard the Queen Mary, where we spent the next forty days. We landed in Sidney, Australia, where I had the opportunity to see most of the country before being sent to Port Moresby, New Guinea, to spend the next two years as an airplane engine mechanic.

I served the next seven months on Owi Island, and was then shipped back to the States where I was given the chance to attend mechanics school in Detroit, Michigan. (This, I enjoyed immensely, and it provided certification for the work I had been doing for two years.)

I have no regrets for my time in the Air Force; to me it was a learning experience, and I feel blessed by living during this time in history.

William D. Kiley *of Arcadia, Florida, seems to offer an itinerary of a WWII veteran's life.*

I WAS A YOUNG BOY of 17. Never had been out to the state of Wisconsin. Leaving Mother and Dad and sisters and brothers, trying to put on a brave front so no one would worry too much. And then the realization that I will be leaving to assume the duties of a man and to see the huge vastness of our world, how big the oceans were. The training on how to kill, then the true test, will I be able to do the job?

The Pacific Islands so green and lush, turned to blackened foliage and splintered trees. We did the job. Some lived and some died, many were injured, some for life. Our lives will never be unscarred again.

Then to school, getting married, having children, working hard, time to retire. Each night I pray, Please God, watch over our people that didn't make it. Thank you People, and God bless you.

Frank J. Keller of Tonawanda, New York, speaks of war's scars.

I CAN REMEMBER the magnificent sight of sailing beneath the San Francisco Bay Bridge in 1944. I remember three weeks aboard an unescorted troop ship as it sailed through the vastness of the Pacific destination unknown.

Our first glimpse of New Guinea with its lush green foliage bathed in eerie wisps of white clouds presenting an enchanted world. Undercover of darkness in fox holes, I witnessed the pyrotechnics of a fire fight. After surviving our first of many intense aerial bombardments administered by the Japanese, I witnessed our men bewildered by fear, suddenly take a new interest in their creator. There is only one thing worse than the blood and guts of war—the experience of a homesick boy at Christmas time.

I remember battle scarred veterans crying profusely upon hearing of the death of President Franklin D Roosevelt.

There is something both sweet and melancholy about the memories **Lewis M. Santefort** *of South Holland, Illinois, shares.*

I RECALL having the measles in New Caledonia and waiting for reassignment, Guadalcanal with miserable 130 degree heat, Cebu in the Philippines with mistreated and hungry Filipinos ever present, and after nearly two years, the final waiting to go home from Leyte.

My most vivid memory of World War II is one night when 650 servicemen were aboard US Marine Tiger and headed in convoy toward Australia. It was hot and humid approaching the Equator. Every inch of space on the hatches was taken by young men trying to get relief from hot stifling quarters.

As we lay on our backs looking at more stars than imaginable, the air was heavy with feeling as lonely young men quietly talked and wondered what the future held for them. Home and loved ones, and even the Good Lord, seemed as far away as the stars.

For some, there was another aspect of World War II to consider. Men like **Clifford H. Ogle** *of Tampa, Florida, had, unfortunately, seen it before.*

I N OCTOBER 1943, I was a sergeant in the Postal Battalion in New York, working sometimes on the pier in South Brooklyn. One night I stood on the pier and watched a single file of infantry march onto a transport for overseas and was deeply saddened.

Some 26 years earlier, on June 12, 1917, I marched off a New York pier onto a transport with Co. G, 16th Inf., 1st Division and 99 of Company G failed to come back.

As I write this letter, it was 72 years ago today—September 12, 1918—that I received my third wound in the St. Mihiel assault.

We didn't finish the job in 1918, resulting in World War II and the violent deaths of 40 million humans.

Chapter 17
Soldiers In Skirts

As American fighting men queued up to the recruiting offices across the country, another group, too, was raising their hands and "joining up." **Helen Weiss Siegel** *of Amory, Massachusetts, was one of the first.*

A S A VERY EARLY VOLUNTEER enlistee in the newly formed Woman's Army Auxiliary Corps, I was sent to the first WAAC Training Center, Fort Des Moines, Iowa.

The manufacturers of clothing for this new women's organization were very slow in deliveries—therefore that first cold snowy winter found us wearing enlisted men's overcoats for warmth.

To this day I can still see us falling out for reveille cold winter mornings wearing the long GI overcoats with sleeves so long for most of us they reached our foreheads saluting long before our hands. You could barely see the toes of our servicemen's galoshes due to length of coats.

Although we didn't present a stylish picture, were nevertheless warm, thanks to Army ingenuity, and a good Supply Sergeant.

While there had always been nurses and other traditionally "female" jobs in the armed services, it was not until World War II that any serious effort went into recruiting females. **Laurel W. Phillips** *of Perrysburg, Ohio, was one who joined.*

I T WASN'T AS POPULAR then for a woman to enlist, but I was proud to have enlisted in the Women's Army Corp. After basic and medical training at Ft. Oglethorpe, Georgia, I was assigned to Fletcher Army Hospital, Cambridge, Ohio.

I remember the guys lying side by side on hard beds lining the walls of seemingly endless wards. Some were in body casts reaching nearly from head to toe. They complained very little but some patients had frequent nightmares about cruel treatment and beatings suffered while in German and Japanese prison camps. Others understood and all prayed to forgive and forget.

The day came for some to leave for home. A group of us girls were waiting at the ward door to say good-bye. They stopped, gave a snappy little salute and in unison said, "Thanks, soldiers!"

Yes, that was the day I was very proud to be a WAC!

*In spite of the fact that females in uniform were considered "non-traditional," many, like **Ruth Lee** of Phillips, Wisconsin, were determined to join.*

I HAD TRIED to enlist in the WAC on a few occasions, but I was turned down because I was too thin. Finally, in November of 1944, I made up my mind I was going to get in. I was still underweight, but the doctor finally passed me and I was sworn in. I was very proud to have been accepted.

*Honor, pride, a feeling of obligation—whatever their reasons women, like their male counterparts, signed up for the war effort. Women like **Mrs. Olga P. Rogers** of Watertown, New York.*

I TOOK THE OATH to become a woman Marine in Watertown, New York on January 5, 1944. After a physical in Rochester and testing in Buffalo, I was sworn in on January 12, the only one sworn in that day.

As I stood with my right hand raised and repeated the oath, I felt myself truly becoming a part of the war effort. When the officer utter the words, "Now you're a Marine," he couldn't have realized exactly how I felt.

*Another was **Viola L. LaBelle** of Worcester, Massachusetts.*

I T WAS VERY PERSONAL and non-combative, the moment I took the Oath of Allegiance, July 15, 1943 and was sworn into the United States Coast Guard WR. Ensign Mary E. Scarff, SPAR recruiting officer in Boston, came to Worcester to administer my pledge, making me the first woman in this area to become a SPAR.

I would do it all over again.

*But why would someone like **Mary L. Mika** of Florissant, Missouri, basically flaunt public opinion and enlist?*

N O OTHER EXPERIENCE in my life has ever given me the feeling of self-esteem, complete understanding of personal being and value, a reason for existence, to feel such a love for one's fellowman beyond a call to duty, than standing there in the USO lounge, 2nd floor Union Station, St. Louis, Missouri at 6:45 PM, 14 November 1944.

Duffel bag as big as I, knowing what I was doing would change my life forever.

At twenty years of age it did give me memories I have cherished all my life and wouldn't trade for a million dollars.

*For some, like **Marie Keno Sieminski** of Grand Rapids, Michigan, enlistment offered an opportunity, albeit unplanned, to meet some very famous people.*

I WAS STATIONED in Algiers, North Africa, in the Judge Advocate's Office. This very hot day the two of us had the duty of delivering confidential material to Allied Forces Headquarters.

We could not requisition a jeep, but did get a ride there, but decided to hitchhike back. After a while, a staff car came around the corner and stopped. The rear window rolled down and the smiling face of Gen. Dwight D. Eisenhower appeared.

He apologized as he was in a hurry and we were going in opposite directions. As he drove away, we saluted and waved and eventually did catch a ride back.

Of course, our allies had their own females involved in the war effort, as **Norman Graber** *of Encinitas, California, relates.*

THIS TOOK PLACE in England just before we went to France. Our unit was sent to Warminster where there was a woman's anti-aircraft company nearby. While stationed there we were able to attend some of their Saturday night dances.

One evening an air-raid siren sounded as German bombers were passing over to bomb one of the nearby larger cities. The ATS girls ran out, helmets on, and proceeded to fire their Ack-Ack guns at the bombers. When the danger passed, they returned, a bit bedraggled, but proud of their action. The funny part hit us as we realized that all that time we "brave" GIs, who really had nothing to do, were hiding under the tables while these ATS girls were outside protecting the area.

For many women, enlisting was their chance to participate, and like the reasons many young men signed up, it was a chance to meet people, see new place, and experience new things. That's what happened to **Margaret H. Graber** *of Springfield, Illinois.*

ABOUT 3 WEEKS before the New Year, the merchants of New Orleans, LA would send to the Algiers Naval Base, Algiers, LA an envelope with 25 FREE tickets for the WAVES to enjoy the Sugar Bowl Football Game on January 1st.

The 3 years I was stationed at the Algiers Naval Base, I was lucky enough to draw a winning ticket each year. But on January 1 in 1944 Georgia Tech and Oklahoma played their football game but to secure a ride and a good seat, I had to root for Georgia Tech because this WAVE said if I went with her and didn't root for Georgia Tech and they didn't win, I would have to walk back to the base! (She was a graduate of Georgia Tech.) And of course, Georgia Tech won but I don't remember the score. Later, I would sit in the same row that Captain Eddie Rickenbacker was sitting and he did introduce himself to each of us WAVES.

In truth, many well-known men admired the women in uniform, including the President of the United States. That admiration was mutual, according to **Jean W. Pugh** *of Terre Haute, Indiana.*

I WAS IN THE WAACS and stationed at Ft. Oglethorpe, Georgia in 1943. I saw FDR that spring as he toured the southern Army posts and on May 12, 1943, I was one of several thousand that stood behind the first WAAC anniversary cake as the news photographers took photos.

*Many, like **Mary E. Manning Robison** of Tempe, Arizona, simply felt it was their duty. But in this case, joining up held an unexpected bonus.*

I DIDN'T HAVE any brothers, so I volunteered as a Navy WAVE in 1943. After boot camp and yeoman school, I was stationed at Norfolk, Virginia where I worked in the Provost Marshal's office.

Ray C. Robison was a provost guard in that same office. We met, dated, and became engaged, but were going to wait until after the war to marry. His orders for overseas and love changed our minds and on July 14, 1945, we had a military wedding Mass with all our Navy friends present.

The war was over the next month. The Indiana Sailor and the Iowa WAVE will celebrate their own 50th anniversary soon.

*Still, joining could not have been an easy decision to make for many young women. But most, like **Jeanne Steele Kean** of Bridgeville, Pennsylvania, would lose their doubts later.*

A T THE VERY BEGINNING of my enlistment in the USCG, we were en route to Boot Camp on a Hospital train carrying wounded Servicemen. The trip took longer because we frequently pulled off on sidings to give the injured men a rest from the jarring ride.

We had to go through the hospital cars to get to the dining car and seeing these young men so crippled and sick broke our hearts. We were not permitted to stop or talk to them but even though they were so ill, they looked forward to our trips and whistled and hollered as any healthy young men would do.

The war had been a distant tragedy until this journey and now we knew how devastating the fighting actually was. It brought the War home to 12 impressionable girls and erased any doubts we had about joining the Coast Guard.

*For many, the valor, pain, and suffering of American GIs would leave a lasting impression. **Estelle H. Soergel** of Lake Park, Minnesota, remembers vividly.*

I WAS A MEDICAL CORPS x-ray technician WAC stationed at Tilton General Hospital, Ft. Dix, New Jersey. Ft. Dix was the separation center for the east coast and the wounded were brought to our hospital. I witnessed the tragedy of the broken bodies—and sometimes minds—of many of the brave men who fought in World War II.

To me, it was a privilege to do anything I could for those valiant men emotionally, along with my x-ray work. I spent a lot of my free time visiting the wards and chatting with these young men and it was a thrill when I got a smile or a chuckle from one of them in response.

Vivian T. Talbott *of Humboldt, South Dakota, also remembers the harsh reality behind all that suffering, and also the heartache of prejudice this country held for so long against women veterans.*

A S AN ARMY CRYPTOGRAPHER, I received the message, the first group of injured soldiers were arriving at Camp Shanks, New York for treatment and discharge. They came, weary, minus an eye, an arm, and a leg or more. Their devotion to America was apparent.

I prayed my fiancé would be spared such a fate. He was.

Red Cross personnel arrived, had pictures taken with the men, made headlines and departed. The medics asked all off-duty WAC's to minister to these men. We did.

Soon, I became a disabled woman veteran myself and began the long journey proving veteran status, disability, and finally hospitalization. All denied by the Veteran's Administration. Undaunted, I persevered, received hospitalization, medication, and compensation.

Will a grateful nation reward veterans and future veterans by refusing hospitalization, medication and compensation—or consider them budget factors—used and forgotten, "unhonored and unsung?"

Invariably, those who worked with women, whether in uniform or in jobs traditionally considered "male," would eventually hold a considerably different opinion than that which was normal for the times. ***Dwight C. Brown*** *of Arlington, Virginia, was one of them.*

M Y EXPERIENCES do not include capturing a "Hun" overseas, but a yet more satisfying one of training and supervising the Army Quartermaster's top "all female" warehouse crew.

A limited service classification rendered as a result of a hearing impairment sustained at Officer Candidate School allowed me to graduate but it also destined me to a "home front" assignment as Training Officer at the Jeffersonville, Indiana Quartermaster Depot. If I had any doubt about the ability of the "once-called" weaker sex to do a man's job, even in war time, such soon vanished. The patriotism of a just war that prompted our troops to give their all, was also portrayed by the devotion, dedication and outstanding military support rendered by my "Lady Crew"—an unforgettable memory of my four years in service, more vivid that I have accumulated since.

For those women in the military, life was not always easy, nor was it necessary to go into combat to experience the horror of war, as ***Marian Renninger*** *of Fullerton, California, describes.*

I JOINED the USN WAVES at age 18 and went to Hunter College in New York for my basic training, then to Naval Air Station, Grosse Isle, Michigan. The base was for the Navy Cadets Training School. I worked for the Public Works Dept. as a yeoman apprentice.

On a warm summer morning, I was standing at my office window looking out over the flying field when all of a sudden a plane took off from the runway and right before my eyes it exploded in mid air. All I saw was a big ball of fire. This accident left a great impact on me for many years.

Even today, when I fly, I still remember that sight and shock. I don't care much for flying. Still, I am very proud that I was fortunate to serve my country and flag 50 years ago. God bless America and its veterans.

Nor were the jobs given to the women easy, as **Virginia Ford Malon** *of Oklahoma City, Oklahoma, can attest.*

I WAS A WAC stationed at Love Field, Texas after I completed communications training as a skilled teletypist at Ft. Oglethorpe, Georgia.

One day a B-29 bomber circled the base several times preparing to make a landing when it suddenly crashed and burst into flames. The airmen trying to flee through the escape hatch were trapped and died. Their names were released to me to send the messages that would notify their next of kin.

Through my tears and though badly shaken, I managed to get the messages completed.

Still, there were lighter moments, as **Betty R. Whiteside** *of Potwin, Kansas, relates.*

I WAS STATIONED in Palm Beach, Florida in the Coast Guard (SPARS) going to Cooks and Bakers School. One morning, the fire alarm rang. It was 3 o'clock.

We all marched out to the parade ground, stood at the parade rest and waited and waited. Finally, a whisper came down the line. "We're waiting on Lt. 'B'. She's putting on her girdle."

Lt. 'B' was a good officer, but was a stickler for being in proper dress.

Nor were the adventures of the ladies limited to stateside, as **Iva Faye Burden Duckett** *of Holt, Michigan, recounts.*

WE ENCOUNTERED the "buzz" bombs starting the first night I got into USTAAF (I was a clerk-typist), Teddington, England, a suburb of London.

The bombs were pilotless and were constant. It was compulsory that we go to the shelter (a cement block building with a cement floor). I got so tired of running in and out of our Quonset hut that I took my "biscuits" (a three piece mattress) and slept out there rather than run in and out all night. On the floor, I might add.

Finally, it was decided that because morale was getting bad because of lack of sleep that we didn't have to go to the shelter at night. I worked up enough nerve to move back into the hut and got so I could sleep right through the alerts.

*Overseas duties for women did harbor at least one morale problem, according to **Billy Prior** of Palo Alto, California.*

WE WERE WACS camped in a camouflaged apple orchard in Normandy. During the night the penetrating cold gnawed me awake. Because the Nazis often came behind our lines we weren't allowed to go to the latrine without a male MP. But I was darned if I was going to call an MP to take me to the toilet.

I lay quietly on my back hoping the sharp pain in my bladder would ease. I agonized. Finally, I couldn't stand it any longer and summoned an MP.

We walked the path in silence. At the entrance of the tent housing the latrine he stood waiting with his M1 rifle. I went in and sat down on the wooden plank over a hole in the ground. Outside the silence was merciless—the MP could hear everything I was doing!

*The risks involved in putting on a uniform for both men and women were very real. **Lily G. Joules** of Rochester, New York, considered it "spice" in her life.*

WHAT DO I REMEMBER and cherish? Not the V-1 rocket klunking overhead, the sudden frightening silence of its descent and imminent explosion. Nor the huge V-2s launched from Norway. Nor the unexploded land mines and ticking time bombs deeply buried. Nor incendiaries during a raid landing near piles of shells and ammo. Nor our wet Nissan huts, a lower level than the River Humber flowing beside us.

Four years an O.F.C in an Artillery Regiment, provided tedium and excitement—the day another O.F.C. daughter of wealth, exercised a racehorse in the field, home of our 5.5 ack-ack guns, radar and other equipment. Horse returned, refreshed, rider limping in hours later!

But outstanding is the constant battle with a raucous old Billy goat, his single objective when we raced to the distant toilet-hut, being to impale our rear ends on his sharp horns. Without success, but the contest added spice to searching the skies, air-raids and gun-laying.

*Of course, there's a flip side to being a woman in uniform. **Anibel Mello** of West Warwick, Rhode Island, has faced a peculiar problem many women might appreciate.*

I WAS TRANSFERRED from Camp Blanding, Florida to Camp Hara hand, Louisiana in 1943. This big 1st Sgt. was to pick me up when I got off the train in New Orleans. The boys back at the base where the sergeant was stationed knew that I was a male, but the 1st Sgt. had in mind he was going to pick up a female WAC.

I got off the train and waited around a while with my barracks bag. About 10 minutes later, I see this jeep pull up with this big sergeant all polished to kill. He went into the station and asked the telegraph operator if a WAC had gotten off the train.

The guy said no, just a soldier.

He came out where I was and asked me if I saw a WAC get off the train and I said no.

"Well," he says to me, "I was supposed to pick up this Anibel Mello girl."

I looked at him and said, "Well, you got the girl. Let's get going."

He didn't like the way I answered him, but when we got back to camp, did his buddies give him the royal treatment! From then on, they called him Anibel.

*Excitement, adventure, duty, whatever the reason, women like **Lillian P. Kudla** of Chicago, Illinois, joined up. And those who were touched by them will never forget.*

I WAS WATCHING my first regimental review while training in boot camp at the US Naval Training Station at Bronx, New York. It was a beautiful and awesome sight.

Flags flew, the band played, sailors and WAVEs in Navy and white marched in perfect time as one regiment after another passed the reviewing stand.

As new WAVE recruits, we watched wide-eyed and I was so emotionally moved that I broke down and cried.

Some of those marching were overcome by stress and fatigue. When they passed out, stretcher bearers would come on the run, but the marching went on.

Six weeks later I graduated and proudly took part in the front line of the Regimental Review with Co. 36.

Chapter 18

Encounters

Thinking of the war years as a constant, unending parade of combat, death, wounds, and heroism would be easy. In fact, while all of these things took place, the war years for many were a time of experience, encounters, and attitudes. What follows are not war stories, but experiences from the war.

One could safely say that America was star-struck in the 40s, and many of Hollywood's legends eventually would find themselves in uniform. **Joy McLeieer** *of Boynton Beach, Florida, was so busy when she met one of her screen idols, she didn't even know it.*

DECEMBER 7, 1941, I was working in the CO's office at Langley Field, Virginia. A few days later I left to visit my family in Philadelphia. This was a six-hour trip up the Del-Mar-Va Peninsula in a slow, uncomfortable train which had no food service at all. Knowing this, and also aware that the train would be crowded with Navy men from Norfolk Navy Yard, I always prepared a suitcase full of sandwiches and cookies that I could pass around.

On this trip, an attractive Navy lieutenant shared my seat. He looked familiar, but I couldn't place him, and was too shy to ask him any personal questions. Instead, he drew me out, and we chatted about my own family and my boy friends, etc., becoming quite chummy. He was amazed when I opened my suitcase and served a lunch to him and others around us, and most appreciative. His charm and humor made the long trip pass quickly.

I still wondered where I might have seen him before, but didn't even ask his name. When we pulled into the terminal, a crowd—reporters, photographers, and passing individuals—suddenly surrounded us before we were out of the train and began to shout, "Hey, Lieutenant Fairbanks! Can we have your autograph?"

So one of my own screen idols gave me a hug, and disappeared into the mass of fans. But I had served lunch to a very popular movie star—Douglas Fairbanks, Jr.

Tony A. Kozach *of Taunton, Massachusetts, met one of his childhood heroes during the war.*

I WAS 5 YEARS OLD, when on May 21st, 1927 Charles A Lindbergh landed in Paris, after a solo flight from New York, in "The Spirit of St. Louis."

In early 1944, I was a crew member (R/O) on aircraft flying out of the island of New Guinea. On one memorable flight "Colonel" Charles A Lindbergh, was at the controls when we touched down at Garbett Field in Townsville, Australia.

Bru Mysak of Jackson Heights, New York, lives up to the legendary Marine traditions concerning Marines and girls.

ONCE ON LIBERTY in Hollywood, my buddy and I were invited to the home of Howard Hawkes at Carroll Drive in Beverly Hills, who at the time was engaged to Evelyn Keyes, a movie star. The phone rang, I answered, told her this is a moment of destiny, introducing myself as Sergeant Mysak USMC, guest of her fiancé.

I told her that her voice enraptured me, a beauty beyond compare, a bliss of delight. I said, "You must come over, as we need you as our mascot to go into battle."

Howard took the phone out of my hand and said, "No, it's 2 AM, don't come over." He turned to me and said, "Look, tomorrow night a cocktail party is on the agenda. I will personally introduce you to Hedy La Marr."

But I was due at the base the next morning at six AM first call. I chose duty and missed out on Hedy. Who says war isn't frustrating and doesn't hurt.

*For **Paul Austin** of Grafton, Virginia, a girl caused all sorts of headaches.*

A GIRL from Australia sent a letter, with a newspaper clipping to my family. It stated our ship had been sunk and there were no survivors. But the truth was, there were no casualties.

We were torpedoed in the Persian Gulf, in the Gulf of Oman and we went ashore at Sohar. The reason we didn't have any casualties was because of a German Submarine Captain. He called us early one morning on a bull horn (woke everyone up) and told our Captain he would give us twenty minutes to clear the ship he said he had bigger guns, than we did plus torpedoes. Which was true, we were a Navy gun crew on a Merchant Marine ship.

The German Captain said he had to sink our ship but did not want to kill any men. Our Captain gave the order to lower all life boats and abandon ships.

*GIs and girls—somehow, it goes together like ice cream and cake. Unlike the movies, however, the GI didn't always get the girl, as **Louis Burkett** of Parrish, Alabama, painfully recalls.*

I AWOKE in a hospital in India to see the most beautiful nurse I had ever seen. I fell in love with her, and she with me. For seven months we had a wonderful time. She kept me going when things got rough.

We went swimming one day. A big wave pulled her under. I meant to save her at all costs. I got hold of her, but she was pulling us both under. I did what I had to do, I slapped her and carried her back to shore and brought her to.

She said, "You slapped me."

I said, "I had to, you were drowning us both."

She went to change clothing and didn't come back. I went to see about her. All I found was a piece of paper that said, "You hit me." I never saw her again, but, where ever you are Mary Sue, I'll never forget you.

*When the girlfriend of Souderton, Pennsylvania's **Jasper "Jeep" Camarata** didn't hear from him, she took action.*

W HILE I WAS IN A HOSPITAL overseas, a GI asked if I was Pvt. Camarata, then handed me the Stars and Stripes.

There was photo of my girl. She hadn't been receiving my mail so got in touch with the Stars and Stripes. To top it off it was published on my birthday.

I married that gal and she is still my bride after 44 years together.

Keeping up morale is in the military's interest. It tries very hard to develop what is called esprit de corps. *Most airborne troops have it in quantity. **James O. Bergdoll** of Madison, Indiana, tells of his father's and grandfather's devotion to their units.*

T HIS EXPERIENCE is not my own, but that of my Father and my Grandfather, who have both since passed away. These two men never spoke of the death and destruction that was brought on by war, but talked of the good times, their friends and comrades in arms.

My father, Charles W. Bergdoll, Sr., was a proud member of the 82nd Airborne Division, the "Devil's in green baggy pants". Dad was out late in the night and fell into a bombshell breaking his arm. After going to the Aid Station and getting his arm set in a cast he was given a cot and told that he could stay for a few days to recuperate. I'm sure the thought of sleeping on a cot in the warmth of the aid station was most enticing, but Dad also knew that his unit was to move out the next day. If he stayed behind he was sure he would be transferred to another unit away from his buddies he had come to trust and rely on. Dad's respect and trust for his friends and love for the 82nd would not have that, so he went back to his unit, broken arm and cast, ready to move out when morning came.

My Grandpa, David Bartlett was also a very proud man, he belonged to "Patton's" 4th Armored Division. Grandpa Bartlett was heading for Bastogne when a land mine put him out of action. It was some years later that Granddad's story unfolds. After the war he got a job in the Fisher Body Factory in Marion, Indiana. He was a millwright and while working on a job, struck up a conversation with a pipe-fitter who was working two stories up on a set of scaffolding. The talk turned to the last war and Grandpa told this man that he was knocked out at Bastogne while coming to help the 101st.

Well, this man came down from his scaffolding as fast as Patton crossed France; grabbed Grandpa's hand—shaking it—saying he always wanted to meet someone from the 4th because he had been with the 101st at Bastogne, was wounded and never met anyone (until this day) who saved his division! Three great stories, by two great men, fighting for ONE GREAT NATION!

Sometimes one GI's esprit de corps inspires another, as is the case with **Nan Wilkinson Heacock** *of Bradyville, Tennessee.*

A N INCIDENT that happened in the PX at Kennedy General Hospital, Memphis, in 1945, when I was serving there as a WAC.

A patient in a body cast, including one arm and shoulder, was wheeled in by a group of ambulatory buddies. They had Cokes and whatever and the stretcher patient asked for a pack of cigarettes. The chap who got them for him asked, "Shall I open 'em?"

The patient grabbed the pack and tore it open with his teeth. "What the hell you think I am? A God damned cripple?"

Men like that don't lose wars.

R.O. Hecht *of Highland, Illinois, witnessed an incident that was above and beyond the call of duty.*

M Y UNIT, the 22nd Base Post Office, was en route to Manila onboard the APA Gen. A E Anderson. We sailed alone from San Francisco to Hollandia, New Guinea. Here we joined a convoy.

En route a Navy DE came close enough to be able to read its ID number. A member of our unit, Lou Belken from Brooklyn, recognized the vessel as the one on which his brother was serving. Lou headed for the bridge and got to the right people and our ship began signaling via blinker light.

Verification was established that the brother was on the DE. Here in the middle of a war the Navy made the arrangements for these two brothers to meet in Manila on a certain date, time and place.

To think that the Navy would take out under the conditions of war to do this personal favor for these brothers really registered with me and I shall always remember that!

Leave it to siblings to get a little sly, as **Teresa O'Connell Ennis** *of Bronx, New York, describes.*

T HERE IS ONE CHRISTMAS that I'll never forget. My brothers and I were in the Army and the Air Force. Larry was over in CBI, Joe, a pilot, was at some unknown staging area waiting for his overseas orders, and I was stationed at the Hampton Roads Port of Embarkation.

On Christmas Eve I received a call from Joe, wishing me a Merry

Christmas. When I asked how he was doing, all he said was, "Hm, we have some free time so we're having a drink and playing 'Trivia', and I'm stuck on a quotation. I can't remember who said, "I know not what course ... as for me, give me liberty or give me death.""

I knew and he knew I would know where he was despite the telephone call being censored. One of the staging areas for our Port was Camp Patrick Henry, 15 miles away. That evening I got a ride out there to the Officers' Club. Sure enough, there was Joe at the bar. We hadn't seen each other in three years. We really celebrated Christmas!

Six months later he was missing in action, but three months later, Joe turned up alive in Italy.

***Benjamin J. Lomaestro** of Troy, New York, also met his brother in the Pacific.*

I T HAPPENED while serving in the US Coast Guard Amphibious Forces on April 3, 1945, during the battle of Okinawa. In the midst of Kamikaze attacks, our LST 830 was unloading ammunition. An LCI arrived about 200 feet away from our landing. The LCI was unloading soldiers from a Troop Transport nearby. To my surprise, off the LCI came my brother Mike, who I had not seen in four years! Mike was serving with the US National Guard's 27th Infantry Division, and was supposed to be in the New Herbides Islands, on stand-by orders for the attack of Okinawa.

It was quite a reunion to say the least!

*Friendship was important and without it, life was very lonely. Just ask **Kenneth F. Hanst Jr.** of Naples, Florida.*

W OUNDED in early November 1944, I was hospitalized in Liege, Belgium. Friendships were difficult to establish in the "shock" ward but blossomed despite the circumstances.

Unfortunately, I was flown to England on Thanksgiving eve, thus being deprived of friends to share that holiday with. A month in England gave time to make friends with those bunked close enough to communicate with. Not easy, but necessary and then on Christmas Eve, a move to a holding hospital to await transportation home.

One week later, I was put aboard ship—on New Year's Eve! Another holiday isolated from my latest group of friends. When we entered New York harbor, everyone who could do so, went on deck to greet the Statue of Liberty. We bed patients had to believe their assurances that we were indeed home!

Eventually, my litter was placed down on the pier, a Red Cross volunteer put a doughnut and carton of REAL milk on my chest and I knew I had made it. I'm an amputee from WWII, wounded while serving as a Rifle Co. CO.

William A. Wolf of Ocean City, Maryland, made a practice of picking up wounded.

D URING THE BATTLE OF THE BULGE, the American Army obtained many men from the rear Echelon to serve in whatever areas they were needed. With my training as an Army Medical Corpsman, I was assigned to a hospital train. We traveled to different counties and towns to pick up critically wounded American soldiers, then to take them to Cherbourg for their embarkation to the states for medical treatment.

During many of the trips, we witnessed people plowing their fields to plant winter wheat, or whatever, however, on several occasions, we saw some of those farmers one minute, and then a horrible explosion, and whenever the smoke cleared, there was neither farmer, plow or oxen to be found. These people suffered the ravages of war as much as some of the military personnel. That makes me wonder why this was never publicized.

For many, like J. Byron Newton of Powder Springs, Georgia, one person would guide them from the very beginning.

T HE MAN who affected my life more than any person, other than my Father was Cameraman Sgt. Carl Smock, (1st CCU). He was outgoing, arrogant, yet gentle. Assigned in training to photograph inspections, Smock's flash failed to fire as the first General we ever saw climbed out of a foxhole.

Shoving his cigar to one side, Smock almost commanded, "General, SIR, my flash didn't fire, how `bout jumping' back down in that hole for me?"

And the General did, smiling, and Smock thanked him.

Shocked I whispered to Smock, "That guy is a General, you can't talk to him like that!"

He replied, "Look J.B., that guy puts his pants on one leg at a time, just like we do. Don't ever forget that!"

So to this day I remember. My life changed so that I became a very successful business person, able to take charge, but still be understanding.

Thanks, Carl.

Peter J. Hernon Sr. of St. Louis, Missouri, had a similar experience.

I HAD EATEN my first mess hall Thanksgiving dinner. Stacking my tray I stepped out into a Scott Field night. The mess hall lights illuminated the Mess Sergeant, a soldier I never forgot. From campaign hat to shiny boots he was "Spit and Polish Army" his numerous campaign ribbons and hash marks proclaimed "Old, Blooded and Dedicated Army".

This sergeant, who wore the Meuse-Argonne and Purple Heart ribbons reminiscent of my legless uncle, offered me a small bag.

"Chocolates", he said; his other hand offered a cigar and a hand shake. Then he said, "Happy Thanksgiving soldier."

I figured if this Master Sergeant with all his clout, combat history and blooded experience would personally try to make me feel less homesick, the army must truly care for its own. That day I found and really joined the army of the United States.

Fate sometimes deals a strange hand, as **William Pachenker** *of Brooklyn, New York, discovered.*

I WAS STATIONED in London, England in 1944 with the Strategic Air Command, attached to the Signal Corp. My buddy and I took leave for the day, and were enjoying ourselves at the USO club.

As we were walking down the steps to return to base, a soldier from the 8th Division was coming up the stairs. I couldn't believe my eyes, as we bumped, it was my brother. We hadn't seen each other since we entered the service.

The 8 or 4 hours I had left of my leave were enjoyable ones. We laughed, embraced, had dinner, took pictures. Mom was happy to get photos and a nice long letter. We left with a happy feeling. When the war was over, I thank GOD we came home safe, sound and in one piece.

There were many who shared the war with their siblings. **Erwin A. Graewin** *of Norwalk, Wisconsin, saw his brother in Italy.*

"MERRY CHRISTMAS! I can see Mt. Vesuvius, too," my brother wrote me at Christmas time. I had landed at Salerno Beach on September 10, 1943 and after things had settled down had written my brother, who was in North Africa at that time, that I was close to Mt. Vesuvius.

Now that I knew we both could see this famous mountain, we knew that only a few miles separated us. I obtained a pass and walked to Naples, asking every soldier I met if they knew where the 3106 Base Ordnance was located.

None could help me out until finally a soldier patrolling the streets in a jeep stopped. I explained why I was in Naples and he said, "Jump in. There's a new outfit near here."

A short time later, I met my brother.

For the families back home, it was a time of worry, but **Ken Brownlow** *of Spring Hill, Florida, was unexpectedly able to relieve the anxiety of one family.*

IN MARCH 1944, the main topic of conversation was the three waves of B-24 Liberators that had recently bombed us, mistaking our Venafro area with the German held Cassino. They had missed us, but had caused many casualties to our attached French Colonial troops.

We moved northward to Casale, where, while sleeping on the floor of a house one night, felt a draft coming from beneath a cabinet, the only piece of furniture in the room. When we moved it, we uncovered a doorway and a section of wall with a calendar advertising Calabrisi Grocery Store, Binghampton, New York, my hometown.

Why would this calendar be here in this tiny Italian mountain town?

Two buddies who'd witnessed this returned later with two teenage English-speaking boys—Dominic and Angelo Calabrisi. They were born in Binghampton, but now were living with their grandparents with no communication from home for months.

A short time later, I was able to notify their parents that the boys were safe and the war had bypassed them.

Sometimes, brothers are not related, but rather brothers-in-arms. That is the spectral outfit that **Kenneth G. Bradstreet** *of Emporia, Kansas, encountered.*

W HEN THE 12TH ARMORED DIVISION was moving south closing the Colmar Pocket we were on the right flank of the French First Moroccan Mounted Division. It was a moonlit night and we were halted with our tanks along a road awaiting orders. As we watched, a line of shadows appeared, men on horseback hunched against the cold, long rifles slung across their shoulders and curved swords at their waists. Some had crates of poultry and other livestock tied behind their saddles and leading goats on tethers.

An odd feeling came over us as these apparitions filed silently past. I often imagined these ghostly cavalrymen charging German tanks waving their curved swords. We learned later we had been watching the last combat active cavalry in World War II—the First Moroccan Mounted Division.

Edward F. Gay *of Harrisburg, Pennsylvania, is convinced he met someone who was, or at least should have been, famous.*

A S A HEAVY MACHINE GUNNER in Company H 488th Infantry, 103rd Division, I was at our bunker outside of Schillersdorf (Alsace Lorraine) late winter of 1945, when I saw coming toward me, out of No Man's Land, the biggest bicycle and on it the biggest man I have ever seen in my life!

I stopped him for ID and he was a French Civilian. When he got off his bike I couldn't believe the size of this man. I said, "You have got to be the biggest man in the world".

He was 8'6". He told me he used to be, but an American beat him out by 2 inches causing him to lose his job at Barnum & Bailey Circus. His bicycle seat was even with my eyebrows 5'10".

We spoke for a few minutes and he told me of all the problems he encounters: low doorways, short beds, small chairs, etc. His name was George Kieffer (now deceased). His picture is in the 103rd Division album with a GI standing on 2 ammo crates to face him. So I believe I hold some kind of record for letting the biggest person through the front lines.

*It is said that World War II helped shrink the world. Even for those in it, like **Robert O. Maier** of Oak Harbor, Washington, the point was driven home.*

SERGEANT WILDMAN looked at me and in a pronounced German accent said, "Vare did I zee you before?"

We first met at a roadblock near Mertzwiller. A jeep approached our roadblock and I stopped it with a loaded bazooka pointed at it and asked, "Where are you going?"

The passenger replied in his very German Accent, "I'm Sahjent Vildman, the Vire Chief. Ve are checking communication lines."

This was in December of 1944 and we had been told about Germans getting through our lines in American Uniforms. So, we kept them waiting at our roadblock for a couple of hours until the Battalion commander, a Lieutenant Colonel, showed up and identified him.

About 2 months later I got reassigned to the 3rd Battalion wire section where I met my friend, Sergeant Wildman for the second time.

***Raymond J. Meehan** of Lewisburg, Pennsylvania, remembers that there were prisoners of war on U.S. soil.*

HAVING BEEN A PART of the 7986th POW Bni at Camp Grady, Arkansas, with three kinds of POWs. They were Mussolini's Italian Army, Rommel's African Corps and the Japanese.

Their educational levels, living habits, and work habits were varied, to say the least. It ranged from 5th Grade (Italian) to Ph.D. for the Germans.

Recreation in the compound ranged from soccer for the Italians, to symphony orchestra for Germans. The Japanese were the quiet type.

I treasure my four souvenirs from the POWs. Namely, one aeroplane (from melted GI mess kits) USA, 1 music box, 1 picture frame, and a charcoal portrait of myself by (Reigel) for two cartons of cigarettes.

I also taught them English at $2.00 an hour before they left for Germany.

*Allies often made a major impression on American GIs, like **Edwin S. Dojka** of Niagara Falls, New York.*

ON DECEMBER 1, 1944, while serving as a PFC with the 406th Infantry regiment, 102nd Inf. Division, I was severely wounded during an attack on Linnich, Germany.

Part of my journey through the Army hospital system took me to the 40th General in Paris where I was moved by ambulance to a RR Station to continue on my way to England. While riding through the streets of Paris, the driver stopped his ambulance, jumped out, ran to the rear, swung open the doors and said to the four of us as we lay on our stretchers, "This is the Arc de Triomphe".

I turned my head and strained backwards to get a glimpse of the huge, impressive monument. He allowed us 5-10 seconds for viewing then quickly closed the doors and took off for the RR station. This was the only part of Paris I saw, just a bit of it.

James H. Brown of Benton Harbor, Michigan, experienced hospitality down under.

I T WAS JUNE 1943 aboard the converted carrier USS Barnes. We were loaded with planes for MacArthur when we left Alemeda, zigzagging across the Pacific, hearing the general quarters alarm daily until, 35 days later, we arrived at Hamilton Wharf, Brisbane, Australia.

We were given liberty in a port where the bars opened at 1700 and beer was rationed. We'd heard of an excellent restaurant, but were warned to arrive early because it filled up fast.

By 1630, a line, including a Navy captain, three commanders, other officers and assorted civilians, had formed that was longer than the building. At 1700 a woman appeared. She looked around, then motioned to us and said very loudly that white hats (enlisted men) never went first, but they would today.

She escorted us inside, sat us at the best table, had a waiter get us a beer, recommended the menu specialty and told us to stay as long as we wished.

Then she ushered the rest in.

The beer was great, the steak delicious and watching those officers wait and follow was something I'll never forget.

Too often, the world tends to view war in an impersonal manner. For those touched by it, like the people Jack E. Robertson of Houston, Texas, tells about, it was a time of deep personal pain.

P ATRIOTISM, AND COMPULSION, were big reasons for my fighting in Germany in 1945. For some time, though, I had an illusion that I had no real purpose for being there. Patriotism didn't seem to be enough.

One night we had to find places to dig fox-holes. Since we couldn't see very well we had to dig by feeling around the ground.

The next morning I saw what was to be my most vivid memory of WWII. All around me soldiers had completely destroyed what had been a vegetable garden, by digging fox-holes.

Walking toward a wine fence I noticed an old man and woman looking at the devastated garden. With tears streaming down their cheeks, the hurt and frustration of a lot of work gone for naught was showing in their faces. From that moment forward, I knew exactly what my purpose was for being in Germany, fighting a war.

Pain, frustration, loss mix with hospitality, friendship. All this and more were experienced by GIs around the world. It would be hard to for-

get the scenes witnessed by **James Darwin Stephens** *of Georgetown, Kentucky.*

W E WITNESSED the liberation of the Polish Officers POW Camp at Murnau, Germany, 28 April 1945. Here imprisoned were 23 general and 4973 other officers of the remnant defenders of Modlin and Warsaw, who finally surrendered to the Nazi hordes in October 1939.

As a young reserve officer and bank teller, I sat at the bank booth in September-October 1939 and heard the radio voices of Lowell Thomas, Boake Carter and H.V. Kaltenborn, all describing the plight of Poland and the Polish Army. The name of Major General Juliusz Rommel (spelled the same as the German "Desert Fox" General Erwin Rommel except an accented "o"), was mentioned several times; the last Polish commander to hoist the white flag of surrender, and the highest ranking Polish officer held captive by Germany throughout the war.

On 28 April 1945 one of the most surprising coincidences occurred. Suddenly, I realized I was liberating General Rommel and the entire remaining Polish Army officer corps, about whom I had heard so much on the radio five and one-half years before. Becoming quickly acquainted with General Rommel, he gave me his photograph and a rare panel of Polish POW Camp stamps, the only such set in existence.

John E. Paton *of Brandon, Florida, says that if you give a GI an inch, he'll take a mile.*

I WAS ON A ONE DAY PASS in London and had a date with a lady friend. As we were walking up the street air raid sirens began blasting away because of a flying bomb—a V-2—in the sky. Suddenly the light on the bomb went out and it started down directly toward us.

We ran a short distance, then decided to drop to the street. The bomb exploded less than half a block in front of us, followed by massive flames and cries for help. I was hit in the back of the head by flying debris, but my lady friend was uninjured.

After giving assistance, I got her safely home and myself back to base. You see, London was off limits and restricted at that time.

Yet, perhaps more than anything, it was the children that veterans remember the most. **K.W. Vanda** *of Endicott, New York, met a few.*

I N ENGLAND on Christmas Day, 1943, the 326th Squadron invited a group of English war orphans to the base for dinner and a party. My job was to escort a 4 year old boy to the mess hall and entertain at dinner.

The little guy quietly sobbed all during the meal. Try as I would, I couldn't console him. His heart was breaking and so was mine. A chaperone finally came to his rescue (and mine). He joined the other children at the Christmas tree.

Had I put too much food on his plate? (Probably). Did they dash too much gravy over it all? (Definitely). Maybe it was my American accent or the smell of my uniform (a mixture of mothballs, tobacco and aviation gasoline). What did I know about 4 year old orphans? Did he think he was being given away and I was to take him home? I'll never know, but it's a Christmas I'll never forget.

Children and war: a tragic, unforgettable combination. Yet, at the same time, an innocent charm transcends ethnic backgrounds and even war, as **J.A. Wilson** *of McAlester, Oklahoma, relates.*

A FTER WE HAD MOVED way north in Italy, and the fighting had subsided, Bob Eldridge and I drew R&R for a day in Rome. We arrived at the Square along with a number of two-and-a-half ton trucks from other outfits in for a day in Rome. As we began walking toward the business district, a small Italian lad ran up, got between us, and in great eagerness said, "Hey, Joe, you give me tip and I show you what you want."

I looked down at him and said no, we'll just walk around. He looked at my buddy who told him the same thing.

There was a few steps of silence, then the young fellow came at us again, with even more enthusiasm. "Hey Joe, you wanna eat? I know good place to eat. Spaghetti, American steak, meat-a balls . . . " he said in very broken English, but I told him no, we didn't want to eat.

His head hung down for a few more steps before he came back at us with his full enthusiasm. "Hey Joe, you wanna dance? I know place got bootful women, vino, American beer . . . Joe, you wanna drink or dance?"

Again we told him no, and he was slightly disappointed and hung his head down for several more steps. All of a sudden, he came at us again. "Hey Joe, you want woman? I know place that got dou senoritas. Una virgin. Joe, you want woman?"

We were laughing as we told him no. He stood between us, facing us and grabbed our hands to stop us. Then, in his best broken English, "What the hell a' you comma town for, Joe?"

Well, he had us there and it was a good lesson. Ever since then, I have tried to plan better so that I would better know "What the hell I comma town for."

K.W. Vanda *of Endicott, New York, also recalls he learned never to sell short the pride of a child.*

W ITH A DAY OFF from flying, a friend and I bicycled to Rusden, England in 1944. A summer carnival in town gave us a touch of home. Children were lined up at the "Bumper Car" concession. Remembering our own childhood delight at the wheel of those cars, we arranged to rent the whole concession for an hour (a modest sum) and treat the kids to a surprise gift of free rides.

We were embarrassed when the operator pointed us out as the sponsors. The children and adults turned to stare, but no one moved to take the free ride offer. Two mothers came forward to voice their displeasure. "We were uncouth show-offs trying to be heroes to the youngsters by throwing our money around," voiced one.

The other barked, "The children had saved their pennies all year for this day and didn't want our arrogant charity."

With our ears burning, we rode away.

*Yet it is true, war affects the young more than anyone, as **Ulysse Alix** of Milford, New Hampshire, tells.*

OUR UNIT was ordered into the town of Erching in the Saar region. In mid-morning when we reached the crossroads, the Germans opened fire on us and on tanks in and around the town.

As I neared the crossroads, I saw two small children coming from a house. The little girl, eight or nine years old, was holding an orange in her hand; the boy, about 10 or 11, held an egg in each hand. Since the shelling made it dangerous for everyone, I bent down, put the girl's free hand over the orange, patted her head and motioned her back to the house. I also closed the boy's hand over each egg and sent him back home.

With tears flowing down her cheeks, the woman waited in the doorway for her children. I gave her a thumbs-up and a wink, and I last observed her blowing a kiss to me. I shall never forget this incident, and I have often wondered whatever became of these people.

*Perhaps if everyone could experience what **John Dolan** of Whiting, Maine, experienced, there would be no more war.*

WHAT LIVES in my memory is not the horrors, nor the leave in Paris, nor the happy return home, but the memory of the children, the most innocent victims of the war.

I remember many European children, most of them barefoot and in rags, looking cold and hungry, carrying an improvised pail made of a discarded food can to catch scraps which they picked out of the garbage near the army kitchens. These salvaged bits would be the only meal they would enjoy that day.

Bill Mauldin realistically portrayed their misery in a drawing entitled "The Prince and the Pauper", in which a small girl coming to a camp to beg food scraps meets a GI who is returning from the chow line.

I have Mauldin's cartoon framed and hanging in my breakfast nook and whenever I sit down to eat, I thank God that my children were spared this fate. It is a memory I can never forget.

*As **Bill McHarry** of Anderson, Indiana, relates his tale, remember the privations the Allied troops were going through at the beginning of the Ardennes, the Battle of the Bulge.*

I T WAS CHRISTMAS EVE, 1944, and we were pulled back behind the lines for a warm dinner. We were at Amelrhied, Germany, in the Ruher Valley in the Ardenner, 4 km from the Siegfried Line. I was a lineman and forward observer for the 771th F-A Battalion, HQ and Service Battery.

The kitchen truck was there and I got in line, opened my mess kit up and they stocked it high, all the good stuff mixed together. After K-Rations all week, who cared! Hot turkey, dressing and all.

I carried it over at a place to sit and enjoyed it, using my steel helmet for a seat. I said, "Where do I start?" I looked down to dig into it, but as I looked up, there were 3 sets of little bare cold feet and I looked on up to their little faces.

I said "My God!" as I stared at their little arms, sunken eyes, skinny bodies, barely clothing enough to cover them. My first hot meal. I could speak German so I told them, "Der beiet por do, Kinlern essen", "This is for you children, Eat."

They put their little fingers into it and ate. I cried to think that there were so many, that it was not the children's fault what Hitler had done. After they ate, I went back through the chow line and said, "Hey Sarge, how about seconds?"

"OK Mac, Jump in" and I did.

After the third trip, the other guys saw what I was doing and shared their food also. In what was left over the Mess Sergeant told one boy to go to the village and tell all the kids to come and he would feed them till it was gone. After that the Stars and Stripes Magazine said, "Don't bury it, feed the little hungry children."

I felt that God had given me a message, so that I could help do something besides just fight a war. I never let a child or person go without since that experience.

1st Sgt. Warren Sugars and John Flemin, an 11-year-old French boy adopted as a mascot at a U.S. Army base post office in North Africa.

Chapter 19
Across the Atlantic

The quick mobilization of America's armed forces was made possible, in part, because the country still had a major maritime fleet. Yet Mother Nature can be as devastating as the enemy as **Joseph A. Rosen** *of Sparkill, New York, remembers.*

FOUR DAYS after the declaration of the war with Japan, I was on the troop ship Chateau Thierry, headed for Iceland. The North Atlantic Ocean was angry, with 70 foot waves washing all heavy equipment from the decks into the ocean. Ninety per cent of the troops on board became seasick. Those who were well had to bail out water from the lower compartments. We landed in Iceland, December 23, two days before Christmas. Needless to write, this lonely island was not the place to celebrate Christmas.

The Atlantic is notorious for its bad weather, and it sounds as though **Irwin Windt** *of Liberty, New York, had his share of it.*

I WAS SHIPPED overseas aboard a Liberty ship. As we crossed the North Atlantic in December, 15-foot waves pounded constantly against the hull and the bow would raise skyward, then plummet directly down, creating explosive vibrations and leading me to believe that the ship would surely break apart at the seams. I had a strong feeling that we would never reach our destination.

Then, as we were crossing the English Channel, with so many disabled ships in view, we prayed that another mine would not seal our fate.

The risk from German wolf packs was every bit as dangerous as the volatile North Atlantic weather. **Thomas Sullivan** *of Raytown, Missouri, could be considered something of an expert on the subject.*

I WAS A PRIVATE in the Marines. Our detachment was aboard a small transport in the North Atlantic making passage for Iceland. In the early morning hours on February 7, 1943, our transport was torpedoed and sunk by a German submarine.

Some of us abandoned ship by lifeboat in the rough sea and wintry air. When dawn finally came, there was no sign of our convoy or rescue vessels until, at last, a ship was sighted. As it altered course, we were able to see its colors. The Star Spangled Banner—proud, bright, magnificent—flew above the dark waves against leaden skies. Rescue and safety were at hand.

*Merchant ships and support vessels had to be constantly vigilant for the telltale signs of the deadly subs. Sometimes they got lucky and spotted the subs first, as did **Charles J. Caulfield** of Clearwater, Florida.*

A BOARD the SS Chester O. Swain oil tanker in 1942 on the Atlantic Ocean, I was a member of the armed guard. There were eight of us, all seamen second class.

A periscope was spotted and we took our position and I acted as gun captain. We had drawn a bead on the submarine and I was about to give the order to fire one when I spotted a blimp heading our way.

I saw the bomb drop right on the submarine. About 15 minutes later the bow of the submarine rose out of the water at a 45-degree angle. She hesitated, then began to slide backward in the same wake she came up in. A naval officer talked with the gun crew, and he was satisfied it was a kill.

*It's easy to think of wolf packs prowling only the sea lanes between New York and London, but as **Harry D. Deputy Jr.** of San Bernadino, California, describes, they were everywhere.*

O N JULY 7, 1943, we were in the Atlantic off the coast of Brazil when three torpedoes fired by the German submarine U-185 slammed into our numbers two and three holds. We abandoned our ship, the SS James Robertson and later that day hoisted our sail and headed southwest.

The next morning I looked out at that vast, empty ocean and thought to myself, "What a hell of a way to spend a birthday!"

But then I realized that I might be the only BM 2/C in the U.S. Navy that ever spent his 23rd birthday in a lifeboat in the Atlantic Ocean.

We arrived in Cascavel, Brazil on July 9. On the 10th, we climbed aboard donkeys and rode to a highway—little more than two ruts in the jungle—and boarded a 1935 vintage bus that arrived in Fortaleza, Brazil that afternoon.

In September, an incident occurred that would also change the way U-boat attacks were carried out. On September 12, the German U-156 attacks and sinks the Laconia *off the Cape of Good Hope.* Laconia *is an ocean liner transporting the wives and children of servicemen and a number of Italian POWs.*

The U-boat commander, Kaptain Leutnant Hartenstein, surfaces to help the survivors. In the process, he sends an uncoded radio broadcast in clear language to Allied authorities, requesting help for the people in the water.

Instead of a rescue mission, a U.S. airplane is dispatched and U-156 is attacked. After this incident, German command issued strict orders that henceforth U-boat commanders would no longer make any effort to rescue survivors of the ships they sink.

The Atlantic now has become even more dangerous, and the Allies tried various methods to protect the shipping that was so vital to English survival.

The incident contrasts well with the experience of **Harold E. Pruett** *of Gainesville, Florida.*

I WAS GUN CAPTAIN when general quarters sounded to man all stations. The report from the bridge was that a ship had been torpedoed. My experience aboard an oil tanker sailing the deadly east coast early in the war gave me the jump on the officer, Ensign Nathan L. Smith.

I had spotted a life boat with many men aboard and lookouts spotted the submarine as well. Then the order to fire on a submarine came from Ensign Smith, but it was the same position as the life boat. I refused to fire on a life boat, and we took the men aboard.

I was placed under ship's arrest. We reached Durban, So. Africa where the survivors were taken to the port directors office. According to the report from the port directors office, the merchant seaman said that I was a hero. The gun crew was promoted to first class seamen. I was promoted to second class boatswain mate. I was also to receive a medal, a medal I never received.

Considering the devastating effects the war had already had on loss of life and materials for Britain, it seemed they would welcome the United States's entry into the war. Yet, when the US finally declared war on the Axis powers, the British parliament had a long, heated debate about whether or not to allow US troops to be stationed on English soil. It was not until January 27, 1942, that Britain agreed to allow American ground forces to be based in England.

Of course, it's possible that the British reluctance was not entirely without grounds. At least, that's the inference that might be made after hearing what **Michael Luciano** *of Westport, Connecticut, recalls of his tour in jolly old England.*

W E CALLED IT Pub Duty. We couldn't seem to empty the barrels of beer and ale fast enough (and hardly managed to retain much of their content!).

Oddly enough, none of us got into trouble or gained weight. Perhaps that's because we kept running all night. We never did figure out how many pints a GI could put away in an evening.

We crossed to Omaha Beach July 4, 1944 for a more serious go of it.

Another who looks back fondly at England is **Oreal H. Halland** *of Thief River Falls, Minnesota.*

I N THE FALL of 1943 we were landing the greatest air force in England. We were billeted near the estate of the Duke of Norfolk and because it was the Christmas season, we were invited for some Christmas cheer at the castle.

We were late in arriving at the Great Hall. The honored guest, Princess Elizabeth II, was late also.

We were almost at the end of the line of a hundred 8th AAF GIs. Standing in line was a bore. You could hear the Princess asking, "Where are you from, Sergeant?"

We all hoped she'd skip us, but no luck. She stopped directly in front of me and asked, "Where are you from, Sergeant?"

I had the presence of mind to say, "From Minnesota, Mame." She said, "Oh, that's near California, isn't it?"

I smiled and said, "Yes, Mame." I didn't want to contradict royalty.

Britain had already been at war for almost two years when Americans first landed on British soil. In those days, there was a wide difference in wages and customs, and sometimes, according to **Francis X. Buckley** *of Malden, Massachusetts, this led to misunderstandings.*

I WAS STATIONED in England from 1942 to 1945 and came to understand the English people's attitudes toward "us Yanks." One of the often heard remarks was that "Yanks are overpaid, oversexed and over here!"

I was in a pub not often frequented by Yanks when four American paratroopers entered. Boisterous and loud, they sat at a table and yelled to the waitress for a round of drinks. When served, one of them paid for the drinks and received a 10-shilling note and some coins from a pound note.

The paratrooper looked at the wrinkled note and demanded a clean new one. The waitress told him that he knew what he could do with it. The change was correct.

He rolled the note up and threw it into the fireplace.

Two English sailors at another table saw this and one said, "Blimey, these Yanks have more money than brains." The money burnt represented two weeks' wages for the English.

The paratroopers overheard the remark and invited the sailor outside. Surprisingly, the sailor accepted the challenge, though he was shorter and the paratrooper outweighed him by 25 lbs.

I went outside to make sure fair play prevailed. The sailor must have been a boxer, because his machine gun left soon bested his opponent. When the rest of the paratroopers entered the fight, I appealed for fair play. One trooper called me a "Limey lover" and knocked me out with one punch.

But the debate in the British parliament didn't focus on the ethnic and income differences between the British and the Americans. Instead, the main problem centered around who would be in charge of various major forces.

At the same time, the United States was facing a diplomatic dilemma of its own. France, a traditional ally, was now controlled by the French Vichy government, established after the Nazis invaded France. Negotiations will take place with the Free French, the French Resistance, before Roosevelt commits fully.

The former commander in chief of the French navy, Adm. Jean Francois Darlan, had been appointed to the Vichy government, the government of occupation after France had been defeated by the Germans, and eventually placed in charge of the French armed forces in French North Africa.

Darlan was caught in Algiers when Operation Torch, the Allied invasion of North Africa, began. Gen. Dwight D. Eisenhower and Gen. Mark Clark saw that Darlan's cooperation would be useful as the Allies proceeded with their invasion of North Africa, though the British strongly objected to negotiations with him or any Vichy government official.

*Darlan had pledged cooperation, but never became a factor in the invasion because he was assassinated on Christmas Eve, 1942. Still, **Nathan Hale Snider** of Mandeville, Louisiana, describes how Darlan's indecision affected him.*

FRANCE HAD FALLEN: General Petain, German approved, controlled at Vichy. Admiral Darlan commanded French Fleet at Toulon wavering on disposition and Free French General DeGaulle in London prodded Churchill who needled Roosevelt in Washington.

In Martinique and Guadeloupe, French carrier Bern, cruiser Joan'de Arc and three destroyers were part of Darlan's indecision.

In San Juan, USS Matagorda received orders: "Make all preparations including arming small boats preparatory joining support unit proceeding liberate French Caribbean units located . . . unless resolved favorably Allied Cause prior . . . "

Preparations made, we got underway for rendezvous with other units. En route, Darlan's decision was favorably made.

Orders changed: We took protective station off DOMINICA overseeing evacuation 2500 French by transport en route joining Free French from islands. Sight unforgettable! Duty complete, picked up submarine "contact" and trailed for days!

Upon return to Port found ships set for "liberation" had become Free French—and were docked in our berth!

*The holidays were near and **J.M. Evans** of Falls Church, Virginia, relates a sad tale.*

WE WERE IN NORTH AFRICA and had completed training for combat and a troop ship crossing in an all-male environment.

We were going by amphibious jeep from Morocco to Tunisia, for the invasion of Sicily. In Algeria we had stopped for the night. With Hal, a big bear of a man, we walked to see the deep ravine that splits the city of Constantine. It was quiet; we had our separate thoughts about the immediate future.

Far from home, in geography and time, we suddenly heard voices of little French children at play—sounds of a forgotten normalcy, one to which we were not sure we could return, and for which millions of Americans were committed.

We never met those children, but their little voices carried an indescribably deep emotional impact.

Joseph R. May of Malad City, Idaho, remembers . . .

THE MORNING of the invasion of North Africa.
The 781st M.P. had landed at Suez, Egypt on June 13, 1943, along with approximately 6000 American GI Engineers and Quarter Master Corps. We were attached to the British 8th Army under the command of General Montgomery.

Our job was to repair and rebuild the airfields and shipping docks preparatory for the Invasion. After going through many bombings by the Nazi and Italians, when the air raid sirens went off that morning, we all hit our fox holes and waited. After one flight of bombers went over we were brave enough to look out and up and see that beautiful, wonderful American flag on those bombers and fighters. It was the most wonderful sight that will never leave my memory.

Abraham Littman of Tamarac, Florida, thanks the guys in the sky.

WHEN MY OUTFIT landed in North Africa in early 1943 and our anti-aircraft battery was assigned to guardian air field against enemy attack.

One night we got a call over our field telephone that a report came in that German paratroopers were landing in our area. I was the only one on guard duty that night and in case of anything, I was supposed to alert the men who were asleep.

There was no moon out and it was pitch dark and all of a sudden I saw something move toward me. I felt the hair on the back of my head stand up. I thought it was the enemy. I clicked off the safety on my rifle and then the figure stopped. I called out and a voice said, "This is MacDonald of Battery B." He said he came over to use our phone to call Headquarters because their phone was out.

I will never forget that night.

Perhaps Edwin L. Heinle of Lewiston, Idaho, was one of the people who worked on the aircraft.

DURING THE INVASION of North Africa, I was one of the 1865 men in the 12th Air Force's task force. A support group to help take, stabilize an air field out of Casablanca. We, the third ship to enter the

Casablanca Harbor, tied up to the dock. When the first ship disembarked troops, all of us on deck, "hell" broke loose. The French Forces started to fire on us.

After firing ceased, we disembarked, marched through Casablanca, toward what was to be our destination. Fifteen miles out, stopped, ate K-Rations. Word came, going wrong way, marched back in a pouring rain to Casablanca. Pitched pup tents in a park, crawled in, ate K-Rations, went to bed.

Wakened at mid-night, hauled in French trucks to original destination. Spread shelter-half on cement barracks floor, went to sleep about 2:00 A.M. No wake call in morning, got up about 10:00 A.M., stiff as a board. Ate cold C-Rations for breakfast, how exciting.

Men, ships, and supplies poured into England. Even this is not without risk. **M.D. Thompson** *of Sarasota, Florida, had an ugly surprise one day.*

I WAS ON WATCH amidships on the port side of the USS Skill (AM115). At 11:40 a.m. I was awaiting my relief so I could go to lunch. One relief man came up, but he went to the starboard side to relieve his buddy there.

The next thing I knew, I was in the water hanging on to a piece of wood. I found out later that we had probably been torpedoed on the starboard side. It broke the ship in two. I was thrown overboard with minor injuries, but many of my shipmates were badly burned. Out of approximately 108 men in that crew, only 31 survived. Neither the relief man or his buddy survived. Their friendship had cost both their lives and saved mine.

Phillip Levin of Bay Harbor Islands, Florida, knows from experience the hazards of the sea, even close to port.

I WAS FIRST SERGEANT-MAJOR aboard HMS Queen Mary, which transported more than 12,000 troops every trip without escort.

We were within sight of the Irish coast. There was a submarine alert and British cruisers and destroyers arrived to guide us into port.

The cruiser Curacao crossed the path of the 82,000 ton, 1,025 ft. Queen Mary and was literally cut in two. More than 300 British sailors were lost.

The Queen had a 40 ft. hole in her bow, but continued on to her scheduled port. There were no injuries on our ship.

Temporary repairs were made at anchor in Scotland and the QM was once again ready to transport war brides and rotation personnel back to the states and Canada. A new bow was fitted on in Boston, then it was off to New York to take on another 12,000 troops.

Not only will it take some time to establish bases, but also American troops and flyers are not experienced. The USAAF will not perform its first independent bombing mission until August 17, when US bombers target

Rouen in occupied France. The first attacks made by US planes will be against targets in Holland, flown on July 4, 1942. By the end of 1942, they will have flown 1,547 sorties and will lose 32 aircraft.

However, none of these raids is over Germany, and each enjoys the air cover of fighter aircraft.

On the ground on August 19, a major raid is staged against Dieppe with a combination of British and Canadian commandos, along with a small number of Free French and Americans. The operation is a disaster. Few of the targets are destroyed and out of 6,000 troops, some 3,600 are lost, compared to German losses of about 600. But valuable experience is gained and preparations for Operation Torch, the invasion of North Africa, proceed.

*This will be the first major test of American troops in Europe. **Robert Gainor** of Port Richey, Florida, served aboard one of the many ships that would transport men and material for the African invasion.*

I BOARDED the train for the trip north from Norfolk to Portland, ME, to report aboard USS Rhind (DD404), the morning of October 23, 1942. After securing my gear in the forward mess deck, and listening to the instructions of the Chief Boats, I was introduced to my GQ Station, loader on the 20MM on the port boat deck.

Next day Rhind got underway for North Africa. Screening Massachusetts en route, what a thrill it was to view so many ships all part of one of the greatest armadas ever assembled.

Rhind arrived off the Moroccan coast on the night of November 7. On the 8th she shelled Vichy shore batteries, and through the 12th she supported the troops ashore and screened larger ships in the Fedhala-Casablanca area. From my GQ station topside it was quite a sight to see and hear the 14 in. shells being fired from the Jean Barte toward Massachusetts before being silenced by the larger 16 in. batteries.

Back at Hampton Roads, November 20, Rhind resumed escort duty and into the new year, 1943, guarded convoys to North Africa. Christmas Day, 1942, found me enjoying my Dinner aboard RHIND in Casablanca. My experience ends on a quiet bridge watch at sea in the early hours of February 20, 1943. It is my birthday, I am eighteen today.

*Aboard the ships, GIs wait nervously for the word to go. When the word was given, **Morris Aaser** of McVille, North Dakota, was among those who were supposed to hit the beach.*

THREE HUNDRED of us were on the destroyer Malcolm. We were to hit the booms at 4 a.m. It was supposed to be a peaceful landing, so we had no ammunition in our pieces.

French shore batteries manned by the Germans opened fire on us, scoring several hits on the ship, which started to sink. When I stepped off the Malcolm onto another ship, water was about 8-inches from the top.

Eight soldiers were killed and eighteen others wounded, those killed were buried at sea.

Shortly before we were to hit the booms an English officer wished us luck and gave us each one swallow of rum.

We had trained for eight months in Northern Ireland. My job was to take over the crows nest on a big French merchant vessel. Luckily we didn't make it in, or I don't think I would be writing this letter.

__Harry L. Callahan__ of East Meredith, New York, said that as he was cleaning out the attic, he came across a box that belonged to his grandmother who passed away several years ago. In the box was the following poem about her son, Harry's uncle.

I T WAS September 10, 1941
He went away, our youngest son.
He little knew where he'd have to go
It was all right for God had willed it so.
In England then he pitched his tent
Wondering where next his buddy and he would be sent.
At St. Paul's Cathedral he worshipped one day
But soon after that, he was on his way.
November 2, 1942,
He went ashore with hundreds of others too
At Oran he landed, I remember it well
Perhaps some day the story he'll tell.
The rain, more came and the mud was deep
No one knew just where he'd sleep.
At last some straw in a stable he found
But that was better than the cold wet ground.
The invasion, to Sicily next he'd go
Would it be hard and rough and slow?
To Italy then, he wasn't too keen
For in all of his travels, no friend had he seen.
When would it be as it had been before,
Again we'd meet at Henderson's store.

To Harry's nameless uncle and thousands of others like him, Henderson's store probably seemed a world away. Another poet wrote of his own impressions of the deserts of Northern Africa. His name is __Isaac R. Bahored__ of Flushing, Michigan.

W E LANDED in the dead of night tens of thousands of miles from home
We cursed and swore and wondered more just why we chose to roam
There is no more valiant soldier than the US fighting man
But it doesn't help your chances when your lungs are full of sand
The whistling wind is hot as hell from out of the desert wide.

It's something you must get used to and learn to take in stride.
Sun, its rays and vitamins are good for you they say
But if I had my choice of vitamins then I'd get a box and pay
Taught we were of maidens fair and so bewitching to the eye
Whoever told these stories told a bunch of g.d. lies
Whores, syphilis, pimps, and vodka and magic to entice
Amidst beggars on the sidewalk half naked picking lice
We've been around and seen for ourselves and are not what anybody
    thinks
Our truthful answer to our friends this country rhymes with Sphinx
Dogs and cats and children, mosquitoes and flies
Nothing much is thought of it if a man stretches out and dies
The market place is colorful, even through a sordid scene
All matter of exchanges and merchandise at you gleam
Carpets richly blended, with high and low priced tags
While the sellers of these treasures sit in sack cloth and in rags
Chickens, ducks, and vegetables, fruits and spices rare
Are the things they make a living from while rice is their fare
Stolen goods are plentiful, sold way out of sight
Necessity is the creator to those in piteous plight
Fish and dates and tea and clothes, sheep's entrails and the rest
Anything that will help them live, in this hideous acid test
Toilets know no water, sewers there are none, streets and offal
That stinks in the mid-day sun, body sores and blindness, limbs twisted,
What a sight, to see these helpless people asleep, on the sidewalks cold at
    night
The shylocks on Bazaar street who will sell silver, rubies, rugs,
We know we're a bunch of suckers as we spend our dough like mugs.
The women and the donkeys share in all the labors
While their lazy, useless men folk go calling on their neighbors.
You walk around from morn to night
And many sight to see,
But the funniest on you gaze upon
Is the men who squat to pee.
Graft and corruption, dysentery and smells
Are constantly beside you
No matter where one dwells.
Men and women old at twenty
In their struggle to fight and live,
Weakened and stripped of everything
By those who could not give.
We talk of development and culture
Of art and Science too.
Why can't we give a lending hand
To those it's truly due?

I hope that when this war is over
And peace once more it reigns,
That we shall use our power
And teach the world to use its brains.

From the poet's description, North Africa was not a place most would want to visit, much less fight a war there. The Allies would land in French North Africa and form a 200-mile front around Casablanca.

The landings take place at Algiers, in Casablanca and Oran. Only the Algiers landings go well. For **Lewis W. Kime** *of Matawan, New Jersey, North Africa was a place where young men learned fear.*

WE LANDED in North Africa in the middle of the night. We were camped near the beach, when we were caught in an air raid. The planes were after the ships in the harbor, but I was sure they were after me.

I wasn't scared until I noticed my buddy in the fox hole with me reading his Bible.

Hugh L. Hall *of Asheville, North Carolina, remembers the menu, or lack of it.*

IN JUNE 1943, I arrived in Oran, Algeria, North Africa, spent about six weeks there, then left by cattle cars for Bizerte, Tunisia, where I spent five days and nights with nothing but C and K rations to eat. Arriving at nightfall, we went to the mess hall and were presented with two huge Spam sandwiches. They tasted to me like the best thing I had ever eaten before or since.

Africa would serve as a training ground for U.S. GIs and a staging area from which to launch bombing raids, but some of the things they learned, as **Barnes S. Webb** *of Madison, Tennessee, points out, were very hard.*

I TRAVELED from England to the North African invasion, with 97th Bomb Group—340th Squadron, as crew chief on B-17 Bombers.

Many Aircraft and nine member crews were lost and/or shot-up by ground flack and German fighter planes, while flying daylight bombing missions over enemy territory, our airbases were bombed and strafed nightly.

To get aircraft repaired and ready for next day's bombing missions, I and ground crew had to work hard and fast under extremely bad working conditions, with most daily temperatures reaching 130 degrees F. and sand blowing in all directions.

We lived in foxholes, dug in our spare time under pup tents.

Another hardship was seeing our flying crew buddies lost or come back from missions killed and shot-up. Once I washed the remains out of tail gun position with a gasoline hose, and another time the belly ball-turret position, due to German explosive artillery.

A year later, Webb and his bomb group would move to Italy and repeat their duties. The 9th Air Force would bomb Naples on December 4, the first US bombing raid against an Italian target. It will not be until January 27, 1943, that US bombers will participate in a raid over German targets.

Robert M. Ryan *of Williamsville, New York, also witnessed the North African invasion, but in a different capacity.*

O UR FIRST NIGHT was spent in a sprawling Oran winery, where our medical BN was billeted following the D-Day landing. All was eerily dark and ominously still, until, soon we were alerted to a strange sporadic squealing and a flip-flopping noise.

Prompt investigation showed the source: big fat rats!

They were out like a light, stoned from stale "working" grape fermentation oozing out of a big barrel overhead.

Billeting with soused rats was just maneuvers compared later to Hill-609, and then came, the "Flying Rats". Buzzards encircling the Tunisian hills, to harass our wounded, dying, heroic buddies, whose memories we'll always cherish.

Ryan goes on to describe how the medical detachment would be urgently needed as the ground war took its toll.

T HE MENTION of North Africa revives haunting thoughts from desolate Algeria in 1942.

After evening chow, Chaplain Waters said to me, "Get the jeep—we've a burial."

We drove some distance in silence, then saw our destination, a burned out light French tank—turret open.

The chaplain spread a camouflage cape on the ground as I gingerly began the grisly removal of a gelatinous mass, a lone faceless gunner, baked to a charcoal-like crumble. No head, just a ball shaped diminutive mass, arm and leg bones exposed.

I eased the cindered remains down, closed the bag and headed for burial detail. For I.D. purposes, I copied unit information on the tank. On my cot when we returned, someone put a bottle of Vin-Rouge.

To unshock me the chaplain said, "If you're hungry, make a sandwich."

I am relieved to know the unknown cremated soldier eventually received full and proper honors from grateful homeland and resigned family and even now, 50 years later, I'm glad we cheated the buzzards.

John T. Scally *of Park Forest, Illinois may or may not have ever needed to be "unshocked," but he remembers North Africa and . . .*

C HRISTMAS EVE 1942. It was my first one ever, away from home. I was a member of the 1st Armored Division encamped south of Oran. It rained for three weeks, and we lay in pup tents in a sea of mud. Nothing moved.

About 4 p.m. the rain stopped, a chill wind sprung up, and after an early "chow", someone found a scruffy pine tree and decorated it with C-ration cans, tangerines, and other colorful junk. We had built fires and now were grouped around them singing Christmas carols. We all missed home very much.

Suddenly, our captain burst from his tent with an order to "kill those fires, and fall out, we're on alert." Admiral Darlan, the French governor had been assassinated.

So on Christmas Eve, with five others I manned a machine gun outpost in deep mud. I was tired, cold, and hungry, and thought of other Christmases as I looked at the stars, now so clear that night. I wondered would I ever see another Christmas Eve like the ones I remembered at home. It was a very lonely time in my life.

Combat and wounds in Tunisia and Germany would come later, but that first Christmas away from home in 1942 that remains etched forever in memory.

Christmas! **William Wilson** *of Livingston Manor, New York, remembers one vividly.*

"I T CAME upon a midnight clear . . . "
The words echoed as a bright moon illuminated the English countryside. Voices and the sounds of plodding feet could be heard as the men made their way to the airbase chapel and base theater. A Catholic chaplain from the hills of Pennsylvania was starting Mass inside while three English youngsters stood before the Christmas crib, their faces wreathed in smiles despite the tragedies of war they had endured.

Two soldiers of Jewish faith played the organ and violin, as they would for Protestant services later that day.

The congregation knelt in prayer—a soldier whose family was devout Irish from Boston, a youngster from a Nebraska farm next to him, and close by, a man who always deeply impressed all of us with his friendship and kindness, a Baptist who read the Bible daily.

There was a young college graduate from New Mexico. He had everything to live for. He was engaged to a beautiful girl and his father owned several large department stores. Yet, death would come for him on what would be called a "milk run"—a mission to drop food to the Dutch.

That night, we thrilled to the words, "Peace on earth, to men of good will."

Of course, the war didn't stop for Christmas, and neither did a GI sense of humor, according to **Worth O. Hamilton** *of Monroe, North Carolina.*

O N CHRISTMAS EVE, I was stationed at Seething Air Drome in England. It was a cold and snowy night and a B-24 Liberator had run off the hard stand and become stuck in the mud.

We worked by flashlight in the blackout for a long time. Sometime in all that turmoil, someone called our engineering officer, Maj. Laws and informed him that Corporal Griffin had just ran into the plane's vertical stabilizer with his jeep.

Maj. Laws reply: "Private who?"

Shortly after New Year 1943, Gen. Mark Clark's 5th Army becomes operational in Tunisia, where British and American troops face the new German Tiger tanks for the first time. The Allies have nothing that can match the new generation of German armor. The fighting is very heavy and the green, under-equipped Americans are thrown back time and again.

On February 14 a horrific attack takes place, and by February 17, nearly two-thirds of the US 1st Armored Division are destroyed by Rommel and von Arnim's Panzers near Sbeitla.

German armor continues to press its attacks through Kasserine Pass and Sbiba, Tunisia.

As US forces at Tebessa come under heavy attack, they are able to hold until February 22, when during the night General Oran's artillery group, which has marched 800 miles from Oran in four days, arrives to support them.

With the help of Oran's artillery, US forces are able to advance.

By mid-March, Rommel will leave Africa for good and the Allies, by late in the month, will face another major battle, this time at El Guettar, Tunisia. As fighting intensifies, more replacements arrive. Even before the troops arrive, they would discover that the passage itself is hazardous, as **Joseph D. Mancuso** *of Washington, Pennsylvania, describes.*

W E WERE IN THE MED in convoy, with about 30 amphibious ships and 4 destroyers as escorts. We left Oran, Algiers on our way to Bizerte, Tunisia. When we got to the "straits" of Sicily and Africa, we had to get in 2 single files.

As we were going into the channel called "Torpedo Junction", we were attacked by 25 German torpedo bombers and Stukas. They got 2 of our ships.

We kept putting up a barrage and it got pretty fierce. Our captain called for a cease fire because we were shooting at the other ships in the convoy.

Just then a German plane came between the convoy, almost at the waters edge. Our guns were trained right on it. My 20mm was ready and my gunner started firing. Everything was confusion, but we got him. I was all excited.

I could see the pilot trying to pull the canopy back and then he hit the water and that was it. He sank in a minute. Everybody cheered, but the skipper was mad because he had called for a cease fire. But we were all tensed up.

Next day they put a German plane with swastika on the smoke stack. We were a real proud ship!

Unlike the Japanese in the Pacific, when the situation became hopeless the German troops would often surrender. ***Joeseph E. Nichols*** *of North Creek, New York, tells of one capture.*

WE HAD BEEN FIGHTING Rommel's troops in Battle of El-Guettar, North Africa. I was a combat infantryman S/Sgt. with 16th Infantry, 1st Division, I & R Platoon.

The CO sent me with four men to recon a hill to our right. We climbed the backside to the top. I was lead scout and heard a noise behind a boulder. I swung my Tommy-gun around to cut loose, thinking it was a Nazi, and came face to face with a gray-uniform.

He hollered, "Don't shoot, I'm from Brooklyn."

He was a captain of Mussolini's elite San Morocco Marines. He'd been drafted when visiting and war broke out.

He was my second POW and I'll never forget his look.

In the political situation the United States faced in Europe, many commands were shared with the British. ***Helen Ersley*** *of Okeechobee, Florida, recalls what this was like.*

THE JOINT British and American planning HQ was located in a remote area of Algiers at a place called Ecole Normale, Bouzareah. This was a self-contained installation, with contingents of British, Scottish and American officers, soldiers, WAAFS and WAACS making up the logistics of Operation Husky.

Even those brought in for the day were served British mess and high tea with treacle pudding.

The SQMS in charge of "Q Maint." (G4) had his Friday gas mask on. Once a week, all personnel wore this extra equipment to familiarize themselves with its function, if poison gas were used against this facility.

In spite of this solemn atmosphere, everyone was in an upbeat mood, for this was the day of their first chorus practice during lunch hour. Some were clever officers had recognized the importance of good morale. Chorus practice became more important than treacle pudding.

Even as casualties mounted in North Africa, replacements were arriving seemingly daily. ***Richard L. Anderson*** *of Baltimore, Maryland, makes an interesting observation.*

I WAS A CADET aboard the troop ship USS Argentina and we were docked in the Port of Oran, North Africa. The troops we had transported from the United States disembarked to the stirring music of an Army band. These were Americans, whole in body, entering the battle zone.

For our return voyage to the United States we took aboard casualties and Italian prisoners. The casualties consisted of amputees, blind, shell shock, etc. Most of the wounded were the result of castrator mines. We had a section of one deck with padded cells for victims of shell shock.

These, too, were Americans, but broken in body, leaving the battle zone.

Ironically, while we were at sea many of the wounded and prisoners gathered on deck singing and playing accordions or guitars. Yet it was not many days earlier they were deadly enemies.

As the wounded made their way home, replacements continued to flow in. **Kenneth C. Weidemoyer** *of Perkasie, Pennsylvania, was one of them.*

THERE WERE 5,000 TROOPS aboard the converted British cruise ship when we departed New York for Casablanca, Africa in April 1943. We were told we could outrun any German submarines.

I don't recall what the captain said when we asked him what happened if the sub were in front of us.

Nearly everybody slept with their life jackets on, but I don't remember sleeping for any of those five days.

It is likely that even when they reach dry land, there will be more sleepless nights.

The US II Corps in Tunisia, now led by Gen. Omar Bradley, on April 22 attacks Hill 609 in "Mousetrap Valley," trying to advance to Mateur, but it will not be until May 1 that Hill 609 is taken.

However, that is the turning point in Tunisia, and by the 7th, Bizerte and Tunis are captured. Three days later, there is a wholesale surrender of Axis troops and on May 10 Gen. Jurgen von Arnim, who replaced Rommel in North Africa, surrenders in Tunisia.

Chapter 20
Sicily and the Race to Rome

As the war progressed both in the Pacific and in the European Theater of Operations, known as the ETO, word began to reach the general public of events that were war-related, but unexpected.

One of the first happened April 12, 1942, when the Germans announce the discovery of mass graves in Katyn Forest of 4,100 Polish officers murdered by Soviets.

This will be the first of a long list of atrocities that will come to light, generated from all sides. Within six months, from September 24 to August 2, the RAF and US will bomb Hamburg, and for the first time create a firestorm that will kill 50,000 civilians and make 800,000 homeless. The details will be slanted by both Allies and Axis powers to create war-effort propaganda campaigns.

The Allies, who had a number of options available to them, were planning to invade Sicily next. In a somewhat gruesome but effective ploy, the British submarine Seraph releases a corpse near the Spanish port of Huelva, hoping that it will be found and that papers planted on it will misdirect the Germans into thinking Allies plan on attacking Greece instead of Sicily.

The body is found and the scheme is moderately successful. After much preparation and political dealings, General Eisenhower is made Supreme Commander. The operation, with 1,200 transports and 2,000 landing craft, begins to land US and British forces near the area of Malta in Sicily on July 9, 1943. The assault is known as Operation Husky.

An additional 3,700 aircraft will support the operation, which is delayed somewhat by bad weather. About 150,000 troops land the first three days and eventually will number 480,000 against German/Italian forces of about 240,000.

The first Allied attacks are airborne landings, but elements of General Gavin's 82nd Airborne are widely scattered and a third of the British airborne troops are dumped into the sea and drown when their gliders are released too early. One participant of the airborne invasion was Venice, Florida's **Vincent E. Wolf.**

I PARTICIPATED in the first-ever parachute invasion into Sicily on July 9, 1943. We were dropped miles from our drop zone and had to fight individually or as small groups until we were able to assemble enough paratroopers to attempt to meet our mission objective.

The next day we watched our own Navy shoot down C-47s from the 504th Parachute Infantry Regiment. It was a sight never to be forgotten.

In spite of the high mortality rates, we captured the island of Sicily in 31 days.

The high incidence of casualties meant that a lot of people back home would be worried. **David Bennett** *of Cohasset, Minnesota, falls into that group.*

I WAS SEVEN YEARS OLD when my brother, a paratrooper in the 82nd Airborne, made the drop in Sicily. Three days later he was wounded.

He was in a foxhole and just before he was wounded, he managed somehow to get his hands on a German Luger pistol. His friend had to take some German prisoners back to HQ for interrogation, but he didn't want to take his M1 and borrowed my brother's Luger.

My brother never saw his friend, the German or the Luger again. Two days later, a Messerschmidt made a strafing run and my brother caught shrapnel in his arm and leg.

I can remember my mom the night she got word. I recall listening to "Jeannie With the Light Brown Hair" and my mother crying.

"Don't cry," I told her. "It will be OK," and later we heard he was in the military hospital and everything would be OK.

Sadly, for some, like **Delores Franzen** *of Melbourne, Kentucky, everything was not all right.*

I WAS 14 YEARS OLD on Labor Day, 1943. It was about 6 p.m. when the phone rang and my little sister answered. They told her, "We regret to inform you . . . " and she said, I'll let you talk to my dad.

Again they said, "We regret to inform you that your son, Pvt. Raymond B. Gunkel, was killed in action on August 10 in Sicily. You have our deepest sympathy."

That's exactly how we received the terrible news.

My brother was in the service exactly nine months, from November 10 to August 10. After six weeks of training at Camp Wheeler, Georgia, he was sent directly overseas without so much as a furlough. Raymond was only 22 years old.

Though the Sicilian campaign would not last long, the scars from the losses would last a long time.

Once the airborne troops had arrived, the invasion began in earnest.

The main landings take place on July 10. Gen. George Patton's troops of the 7th Army begin landing in Sicily in Gulf of Gela between Licata and Scoglitti. They meet light opposition and take Gela, Licata, and Vittoria. LSTs and LCTs are introduced, allowing armor to be landed, but while the British forces are able to advance almost unopposed on Sicily, US forces meet resistance in Gela.

But the Italian troops defending Sicily were poorly equipped and suffered from poor morale. In quick succession, US forces take Agrigento, Porto Empedocle, Caltanisetta, Sicily, cut off and secure the Palermo-Enna Road, capture Menfi, Corleone, Castelvetrano, and finally Palermo, where some 50,000 Italian troops find themselves cut off.

By July 23, US forces occupy Trapani, Marsala, and Termini Imerese, and the next day take Cefalu and Nicosia, Sicily.

The Italian government has lost its stomach for war. On the 25th of July, Mussolini is summoned to the Italian king's presence, relieved of command and arrested as he leaves the meeting.

By August 17, Patton has reached Messina where he had hoped to trap German and Italian troops. He is disappointed to find that over 100,000 troops and a vast quantity of armor and supplies have been evacuated across the Messina Straits.

The escape of the German and Italian troops and the supplies means that once the Allies move to Italy itself, they will face that much more resistance.

To many troops, it now appears that Sicily might turn into a long campaign. For a time, it looks as though the Allies might receive an early

American troops patrol the smoky ruins of Messina in August 1943.

Christmas present when, in spite of the successful evacuation, the Italians let the Allies know they want out of the war. Two days later, representatives of the Italian government meet in Lisbon to talk with the Allies of surrender.

A little more than two weeks later, on September 3, 1943, Italian General Catellano signs surrender of Italy, but announcement is delayed until September 8 to prevent a German take-over.

On September 9, the Allies land at Salerno under Gen. Mark Clark, while Rangers land at Maiori and Vietri with orders to secure passes on the way to Naples.

The Salerno landing will not prove easy, according to **Fred C. Murphy** *of Upland, California.*

I WAS A CREWMEMBER aboard a Liberty ship during the invasion of Salerno, Italy. The men hitting the beaches suffered heavy casualties, many dying before reaching dry land.

The bodies in the water floated in and out with the tide past my ship for two or three days before LCVPs could take the time to drop their ramps, pull them aboard with boat hooks and take them to the beach for Graves Registration to identify and bury.

My ship was seriously damaged during the invasion when a 500 lb. bomb exploded beneath us. We were drawing about 20 feet of water which put us about 30 feet off the bottom of the bay.

After unloading all of our cargo, we limped back to North Africa at four knots to make repairs. It took two months to repair the ship enough to allow us to make it back to states.

George Dawson *of Wantagh, New York, had a scare even before setting foot on Italian soil.*

O UR SHIP was headed for the Mediterranean in 1943 as part of a large, slow (8 knot) convoy. Ours was a Liberty ship had been converted to carry troops instead of cargo.

One day we developed engine trouble and sat dead in the water. The rest of the convoy passed us by. No escort vessel could be spared for the sake of protecting a single ship in these U-boat infested waters.

We sweated all day with all hands and passengers wearing life jackets and helmets. Finally the engine was repaired and we set out to catch the convoy, eventually catching up with the slow-moving group just as the sun was going down. Two words were on everyone's lips: Thank God!

Considering how some of the Italian campaign plans went awry, perhaps **Harold W. Passow** *of Hazelhurst, Wisconsin, is lucky his ship broke down.*

I WAS ABOARD a Kaiser Liberty ship with the rest of our Air Force crew and infantry personnel on our way to Bari, Italy. Those of us that were 21 or older were given absentee ballots to vote for president. I remember how proud I was of this privilege and cast my vote for Roosevelt, who was running for a fourth term.

Before we reached the European coastline, our ship developed propeller shaft problems. While it was being repaired a destroyer circled near us as the rest of the convoy continued on. Eventually even the destroyer left.

We heard on the radio of ships being sunk just south of us near the coast of Africa and this really made us sweat. After about two days we were underway again and caught up to the convoy just as it approached the Rock of Gibraltar.

Wilson J. Labour *of Berwick, Pennsylvania, is another seagoing survivor of the Italian campaign.*

THE ATTACK OCCURRED in the shadows of evening, the Luftwaffe's favorite hour. Our destroyer was working a rear screen for a British flat-top, part of a battle group heading for the invasion of Italy.

CIC picked up two radar blips, one portside and the other crossing over starboard. Once identified as German torpedo bombers, our AA opened fire and the ship's maneuvering speed was increased.

The Nazi torpedo launched starboard passed harmlessly astern, but the portside bomber's aim, which took advantage of our avoidance maneuvers, was more deadly.

The thunderclap blast tore the afterdeck structure and stern apart. Depth charges were hurled skyward, then two depth charges exploded beneath us, adding to our helpless disablement. Still, the deadly accuracy of our gunners destroyed the two aircraft.

Luckily, the explosions missed the aft powder magazine and enough bulkheads held fast so that, after our SOS was answered, we were rescued by two destroyers and towed to Port Algiers.

Ships are not the only target. Progress at Salerno is again disrupted when, on September 13, US forces are driven out of Persano as the Germans attempt to drive a wedge between British and US troops at Salerno. The delay hurts Allied morale, and it suffers even more when it is learned that on the day before, a German unit in a daring raid has managed to rescue Mussolini. On the 15th, Mussolini will again declare his authority.
Stanley C. Motush *of New Lisbon, Wisconsin, tells what may have turned the tide at Salerno.*

I WENT ASHORE at Salerno, Italy as a member of the 45th Division Artillery in the wave to support the 36th Division, who were taking a beating.

A few days later, while I was at Artillery Headquarters, I witnessed Gen. Clark discussing the possibility of a retreat and evacuation.

Offshore, a naval officer received permission to open fire with its guns, which in itself, was picturesque. We fired our own artillery at point blank range and then watched the gun crews swabbing the barrels with oil while the guns were still white hot and witnessed the results of this on the guns the next day.

As we advanced, I saw the German tanks destroyed all along the way. All thought of retreat or evacuation were "discharged."

*On the 16th, Salerno is taken. Though the Italian city is under US control, this did not mean it was safe. Consider the experience of **Helen L. Callentine** of Jefferson City, Missouri.*

COMMAND SAID they did not want us debarking from a troop ship via rope ladder. They said that would be suicide. So I was one of 101 Army nurses and several American Red Cross personnel who were transferred to the British hospital ship Newfoundland for safety.

At 0500 hours on September 24, 1943, a bomb plummeted through the red cross atop the ship. The explosion killed all the British doctors and most of the nurses.

My lifeboat was blasted away, so it was down the rope ladder, grasping the rope and not the wooden rungs. The nearby British hospital ship St. Andrew rescued us.

I am thankful for the reassurance and efficiency of the British seamen, the gift of the American Red Cross ditty bag containing comb and toothbrush, the sharing from the Army nurses at Bizerte, the LCI transportation (where we slept beneath the gun turrets) and to the 16th Evacuation Hospital two weeks after the Salerno invasion.

The Germans in Italy are pulling back in the face of Allied advances except in the pass areas around Naples. But from September 27 to September 30, the residents of Naples revolt against their German occupiers. The civilians suffer heavy losses until Allies draw near the city.

On September 29, Geeral. Eisenhower and Marshall Badoglio sign the Italian Armistice and on October 1, Naples is taken by the Allies.

In quick succession, the towns of Benevento, Caserta, Capua, Volturno, Liberi, and Alvignano are captured. But on October 12, the Allied advances in Italy are abruptly stopped at Reinhard Line.

*According to **Bill R. Harper** of Cookville, Texas, the Germans weren't the only ones that presented problems for his armored unit.*

MY PLATOON of tank destroyers were waterproofed for the Volturno River crossing. After the tanks were waterproofed we drove some 12 miles over rough country to get to the river. We arrived at our staging area, in late afternoon, to find that all our waterproofing had been damaged to the point of giving no protection.

By radio our captain was advised of our problem. It was decided to remove the damaged waterproofing and ford the river. We scouted the river for a place to cross and made the crossing early the next morning.

I told Parkhurst, the driver of the first tank, to give it everything it had and don't let up. Being somewhat of a "cowboy" but a very good driver he made it across. We followed with the remaining 3 tanks for a good crossing.

This gave us the honor of being the first armor to cross the river.

Harper's success isn't enjoyed by other units. In the air, disaster strikes the US Army 8th Air Force when a bombing raid against the Schweinfurt, Germany, ball-bearing factory results in 60 of the 291 planes being shot down.

The week before, 88 aircraft had been lost. Up to this point, US bomber pilots had been convinced—mainly based on earlier successful unescorted raids over other European targets—that fighter escorts were unnecessary. After Schweinfurt, the USAAF abandons long-range unescorted daylight bombing runs.

This was not the only problem faced by the USAAF.

Back in the U.S., President Roosevelt has been facing continuous problems as coal miners, steel workers, and other unions strike, taking advantage of the "war effort." Roosevelt asks Congress for powers to break strikes and to make it illegal to strike at vital war industries. It will not be until January 11, 1944, that Roosevelt, after railroad workers threaten go on strike, appeals Congress for a new national service law to prevent damaging strikes and to mobilize the adult work force. On January 14, the railroad accepts terms by the President and avoids potential strike.

*Meanwhile, reinforcements were pouring into Italy. One was **James E. McAllister** of Kalamazoo, Michigan.*

O N OCTOBER 1, 1943, when we landed south of Naples, we climbed over the side of the ship hand over hand with full packs and barracks bags into a landing craft below. When full of soldiers and equipment, it took off toward shore at full speed and when it reached the beachhead, the front gate fell open making a ramp for us to wade out into water up to our waist.

Once we reached shore, we moved to a nearby road and formed quickly into two columns and with full packs, began marching double-time until some trucks came by to pick us up.

By now it was dark and we were transported without lights through dark streets to the place where we set up the 17th General hospital. Here I would experience 35 air raids and the eruption of Mt. Vesuvius.

*Inexperience was a common trait in this second full year of the war, which **Robert M. "Rip" Collins** of West Palm Beach, Florida, admits.*

I WAS SHIPPING OUT for the first time. It was Thanksgiving night, 1943 and I was aboard the SS Antitian, an oil tanker, as a member of the Navy Armed Guard.

As we left New York harbor and headed toward the North Atlantic, I was standing next to the chief gunner's mate on the bridge, watching the Statue of Liberty slowly disappear on the horizon.

I heard what I thought was thunder and said, "That's the first time I've ever heard thunder in November."

The chief replied, "You dumb ass boot, those are depth charges."

But even green GIs knew what they were fighting for, including **Harold E. Jesso Jr.** *of Gloucester, Massachusetts.*

A T EIGHTEEN I was a full fledged veteran, having completed six convoy crossings. I remember not the submarine attacks or the planes screeching by.

I remember on our second crossing, noticing that our flag was missing, it was not flying from our mast. Even though it was tattered and torn, it should be there. I felt safe and secure under it and still a part of America. Without it we were just another ship sailing the Atlantic.

I reported it to the signalman on the bridge. He told me that it was still there. He explained that too many flags were destroyed on our crossings so they had wrapped our flag with twine and hoisted it folded to the top mast. A strong yank on the halyard would snap the twine and our flag would bellow in the breeze.

My flag will always fly high and proud, until it covers me as my shroud.

As the Italian campaign continues, the Germans develop a jet aircraft. In November 1943, the Me262 is demonstrated for Hitler, but thanks to technical problems, it will not become fully operational until June 1944.

Meanwhile, in Italy, Monte Camino is attacked by US II Corps and British X Corps as offensive begins once more on December 2. Monte Camino is captured the next day.

During the night, an incident takes place at Bari, Italy, that will have long-reaching effects on some of the ground troops stationed there.

A German aircraft bombs the harbor at Bari and destroys an ammunition ship, which explodes. It is not admitted until much later—1992, in fact!—that amidst the munitions were canisters of mustard gas.

By December 7, the Italian peaks of Mignano Pass are controlled by Allies and the US forces move against Monte Sammucro and San Pietro where resistance is heavy. **Russell J. Darkes** *of Lebanon, Pennsylvania, tells of his experience there.*

I T WAS EARLY DECEMBER 1943, three months after the Salerno invasion. The 1st Battalion, 143 Inf. of the 36th Division was given the mission to capture Mt. Sammucro, better known as Hill 1205 as a part of the overall plan in the push to Cassino. In a daylight attack, with C Co. to the left, A Co. on the right, and B Co. in reserve, we accomplished our mission. Or so we thought.

Late in the afternoon, C Co. commander, Capt. Horton received orders

to continue the attack down the forward slope of Mt. Sammucro and capture the village of San Pietro. He called all platoon leaders to assemble at
the crest of the mountain to issue the attack orders before dark. It was to
be a night attack.

Suddenly, there was a sharp crack followed by a light thud. After several seconds of trying to determine what had happened, Lt. Simmons and
I noticed that Capt. Horton, along with two other lieutenants, were lying
very still, bleeding profusely from head wounds. All three were killed instantly by a single bullet fired by a German sniper from the A Co. area.

Lt. Goad, second in command, informed the battalion commander of
what had happened, who ordered us to send a rifle platoon to attack
through the Co. A area. By now, A Co. was pretty well pinned down because Germans had infiltrated their position.

Lt. Russ was given that mission while I moved my platoon several hundred yards down the mountain to the rear of A Co. and had my men fix
bayonets. This was one of the few times that we attacked with bayonets.

I cautioned my men to shoot only when necessary and to shoot only
Germans, and not Co. A men. When they saw us coming with fixed bayonets, their hands went into the air and they pleaded, "Komerad,
komerad."

Within 20 minutes we were at the crest of the mountain in A Co. area
and had captured 17 Germans without firing a shot. No doubt one of them
had fired the fatal shot that killed three of our fine Co. C officers, but Mt.
Sammucro was finally secured.

*The Allies are intent on taking a strategic point called Monte Cassino.
On January 9, 1944, US II Corps attack Cervaro and Monte Trocchio near
Cassino. Within a week, Monte Trocchio is captured, which opens the way
to Rapido Valley and Cassino. On January 20, US forces begin attacks
across Rapido Valley against Monte Cassino.*

*Meanwhile, on January 22, 1944, a new series of Allied landings in
Italy are made at a place called Anzio. At first, resistance is very light. Of
the 36,000 men who wade ashore initially, only 13 are killed. The port city
of Anzio is captured intact. Though the initial landing does seem to go
easy, it is not without incident, as* **Le Roy Allman** *of Garden City, Kansas, can attest.*

O UR WORK had started January 15, 1944. We had waterproofed our
weapons carrier in Naples, but on January 23, we were stunned
when our carrier flooded in three feet of water just off the end of the LST
ramp at the Anzio beachhead.

A tank hooked onto our vehicle and yanked us ashore where we had
the job of staking out an airfield on the as-yet unsecured beachhead. As
we reached shore, English anti-aircraft guns pumped away as a German
dive bomber laid down a stick of bombs.

They started at the water and walked their way toward the gun. One bomb came so close it tipped over the weapon and knocked the gunner unconscious.

It seemed like an eternity before we got the weapons carrier started and reached our camping area. The first thing I did was dig a foxhole I could slide into from my bed within three seconds.

In spite of the apparent success of the landing, General Lucas, who is in charge of the US VI Corps in the Anzio assault, is hesitant to push forward.

It is a major error. Lucas's hesitation allows the Germans to bring up reinforcements. On January 30 Lucas finally tries to move out. The results are disastrous. One US Ranger unit has all but six men killed. **B.J. Daurio** *of Bronx, New York, witnessed what was to follow.*

ANZIO WAS A bloody battle kept from the American people. We came up from Naples in convoys of six LSTs loaded with trucks, ammo, gasoline and tanks. The worst three nights were January 23, 24 and 26. The Germans sank a British destroyer, a hospital ship, damaged another hospital ship and beached a Liberty ship. They came in at dusk and dropped bombs, torpedoes and glide bombs.

On January 29, 110 Dornier 217s, Ju88s and ME210s dropped radio controlled glide bombs. We were alongside the British anti-aircraft cruiser Spartan, the So Galant and Painted Black. All were sunk along with a Liberty ship that is not yet listed on the registry. The Germans had 71,000 men on the beach. The Americans had 61,000.

In the first five days, casualties exceed 4,000 and we captured 4,838 prisoners. We took them back to Naples on our return trip.

I was glad to be part of it aboard Coast Guard LST 326.

The information on the Anzio landings was not kept from everyone. **Barbara S. Solker** *of Bath, Pennsylvania, was one who knew.*

I WAS FOUR YEARS OLD when my mother received the phone call that her brother was killed in Anzio. We did not yet have a phone, so the call was received at a neighbor's.

I remember my mother's uncontrollable tears as she ran home for another handkerchief every once in a while during the lengthy phone conversation from another family member revealing the circumstances of his death. I don't remember my uncle, but I remember very well my mother's apprehensions concerning his well being preceding his death.

On the grounds that he was the only male member in a family of six children as well as their main source of support, he could perhaps have avoided the draft. He chose not to do so.

He is fondly remembered by his sisters as a devoted and caring son, brother and American.

Just as air raids and shelling became commonplace, so did death. No one was immune, including those in the skies above Anzio.

Although US fliers took to the air to counter the massive German air strikes with bombing raids of their own, they paid a price. **Joseph A. Watters** *of Friesland, Wisconsin, recalls in graphic detail what those days were like.*

A LL DAY LONG, wave after wave of bombers rained bombs on the advancing Germans who were trying to destroy the Anzio beachhead. The big planes never hesitated and paid a heavy price as the Germans blackened the sky with fire from their dreaded 88s.

We watched in horror from our foxholes as crippled aircraft exploded above billowing parachutes and brave American airmen fell to their deaths as flaming gasoline sprayed into the air. Just a single drop of that burning gas hitting a 'chute caused a flash of flame, a puff of smoke and the 'chute vanished, plummeting the unfortunate airman to certain death.

The sight of those boys plunging to their doom was appalling and sickening. It will remain in my mind forever.

Nor were the fliers the only combatants affected. **Steven G. Muller** *of East Northport, New York, tells the story of the Spartan.*

T HE HMS SPARTAN, the light cruiser aptly named by the Ministry of Defense of the Royal Navy, was under the command of Capt. R.V. McLaughlin. It served with honor during the Sicilian and Italian invasions and was part of Operation Shingle, the British Anzio-Nettuno landings.

I was ships cook aboard the US Landing Craft Tanks (LCT) 24 and had been under fire in Africa, Sicily and now at Anzio. Amphibious sailors are accustomed to combat and this landing was just another notch in our gun handles.

LCT's are 105-feet long, with a combined firepower of two 20mm anti-aircraft cannon.

A British cruiser of Spartan's class was 485-feet long and armed with eight 5-inch cannons, 12 two-pound anti-aircraft guns, twelve 20mm cannon and six torpedo tubes. Its turbines produced 62,000 hp and it could reach speeds of up to 33 knots.

On the evening of January 24, 1944, just at twilight, the Anzio beachhead was on the receiving end of a sensational air raid. Three waves of German fighter bombers—15, then 43, and finally 52 aircraft—hit the harbor area. Every ship in the harbor and every gun on the beach was firing at the attacking planes.

At the height of the attack, the HMS Spartan pulled up astern of us. Her imposing size made those of us on LCT 24 feel safe and protected.

The air raids continued under cover of darkness. Star shells and tracers filled the sky. The Spartan's guns barked again and again, and each time a broadside was fired, she was silhouetted against the blackened sky.

Several ships, including the British hospital ship St. David, were hit and sunk and within 24-hours, four destroyers had been put out of action and landing craft of all types had been sunk. Though allied forces were taking a heavy toll on the enemy aircraft, the attacks continued.

Suddenly, an earth-shattering explosion occurred off our stern. The Spartan had taken a 500 lb. bomb directly down her smokestack. A second explosion followed as the very guts of the ship were torn out and she rolled over to die. Many brave men died in a few short minutes, but Cpt. McLaughlin survived.

I was topside at 0500 and my mind could not accept what my eyes saw. The Spartan was bottom up, her screws reaching to the sky as though to ward off another attack. She remained upside down for several hours, then finally let out a roar as the last of the air trapped inside her hull escaped. Then she slid to the bottom of Mare Nostrum, gone forever.

The dictionary defines Spartan as one of great courage and fortitude. In the year one thousand, nine hundred, forty four, I witnessed the death of a Spartan.

To the green GI, Anzio must have seemed like a slice of hell. **Victor E. Wade** *of Cromwell, Connecticut, was fresh out of boot camp.*

AFTER 17 WEEKS of training, at the age of 18, I found myself an infantry replacement landing from a Navy LCI in the port of Anzio. The town had already been secured and I was assigned to the 3rd Div.

The first night I dug in an open field not too far from the beach and witnessed the most spectacular air raid over the harbor. As our anti-aircraft fired, German bombers attacked the ships. Searchlights and tracers came from all positions on the beachhead and bombs fell all around the ships and the harbor area. One anti-aircraft position was nearby, firing its four 50-cal. machine guns.

The sounds, sights and smells were unbelievable. A sergeant came over and said, "Welcome to Anzio."

Beaumont, Texas, resident **Grace Cornell Newton** *was just down from Anzio at a second landing area called Nettuno.*

WE HAD BEEN SET UP near Nettuno, five miles from the beachhead, since January 27, 1944. The landing craft that brought me and the other Army Nursing Corps personnel of the 93rd Evac. Hospital had been forced to wait out an air raid offshore in the Tyrennian Sea. The raid was one of many that daily and nightly plagued the US 5th Army's foothold on the Anzio beachhead.

Raids and bombings continued, taking their grim toll. Yet, though flak rained all around us, we managed to escape serious injury until March 29 when, at 2200 hours, a phosphorous bomb was dropped on our hospital.

A shower of shell fragments and ignited pieces of phosphorous fell all about. The blast turned night into day and a blazing sky showed through gaping tears in the canvas, setting the tents afire.

Miraculously, only four men were killed and four others critically wounded.

The siege-like battle of Anzio raged on. **Lambert W. Fyhrie** *of Duluth, Minnesota, was one of the casualties.*

I AWOKE in the recovery tent on the beach at Anzio. It was 0300. A surgical team of strangers had saved my life. How could I thank them?

Then I heard the loud "KRUMP!" of German heavy artillery firing at the ships. Some of the rounds fell short and landed in the hospital area, riddling the recovery tent with shrapnel.

I was moved to a British hospital ship and transported to Naples. On the way, I thought about things—the war, the 3rd Infantry Division, six campaigns, North Africa, Sicily, Italy, death, buddies, loved ones back home—and a strange depression settled over me. I was feeling sorry for myself and couldn't shake it.

My eyes were moist as they carried me from the ship.

Suddenly a smiling Salvation Army girl greeted me with a cheerful, "Hi, soldier!" and kissed my cheek, then laid a large bag of candy, fruit, cookies, playing cards and other items on my chest. Her timing was perfect.

The Anzio situation has an affect on other operations in Italy. US forces have taken points 593 and 445 near Cassino, Italy, but can get no help because Allied forces at Anzio are being forced back. Finally, on February 12, the exhausted US II Corps is replaced by New Zealand troops near Cassino.

Throughout the drive for Cassino, the monastery at the top of Monte Cassino has remained untouched. Until they were relieved, GIs had reported taking no fire from the historic edifice.

Once relieved, however, the monastery is bombed on February 15, a strategic mistake because the wreckage of the buildings provide better cover for Germans, who had not held the monasteries until after the bombings as **Harold W. Paine** *of Mason City, Iowa, found out.*

O UR UNIT, the 935 Field Artillery Battalion, was situated in an olive orchard near Monte Cassino within full view of the abbey. I lived in a cave for approximately two months and can still see the donkey trains up at night carrying supplies, then returning in the morning with the injured or dead.

When the huge armadas of aircraft flew over and dropped their bombs, the Germans would just go down another level. This was also the place and time when I saw Ernie Pyle, our beloved journalist, sitting by his tent with portable typewriter, getting out his ideas and reflections on the events of the day.

This was a tough, cold campaign, a test of perseverance and endurance.

On February 28, the Germans launch another concentrated assault against Anzio, this time aimed primarily at US 3rd Division on either side of the Cisterna-Anzio road, but the four attacking divisions fail to break through.

The 3rd Division is hit again March 3, this time at the Ponte Rocco and again holds the Germans off.

Morale of US troops improves when they learn that on March 6, US bombers have made their first raids over Berlin with 660 aircraft.

Although 69 are lost, the raid is repeated March 8. Again, of 580 aircraft, 10% are lost in spite of 800 fighter support aircraft.

Two more concerted Allied attacks against the town Cassino take place before the fighting dies down in Italy as forces regroup. Neither the Anzio beachhead nor the Cassino stronghold will witness action until May.

However, as the fighting temporarily died away, Mother Nature once again stepped in. **James E. McAllister** *of Kalamazoo, Michigan, again tells about it.*

O N MARCH 15, 1944, most people were thinking about income tax, but I was in Naples, Italy, where German planes were continually coming over for hours, dropping everything they had, anywhere they happened to be at the time. Some of these bombs hit our 17th General Hospital, causing our tents to sway, my teeth to chatter and my knees to knock.

It also took my breath away.

The hospital had a red cross on top, but I guess the Germans didn't care where they dropped their bombs, anymore, as long as they could unload them and head back to base. This would be their last big raid. We would not see them again until April.

Everything was blacked out, even the fluorescent watches in our pockets.

But on March 18, after the German bombing stopped, Mount Vesuvius let loose her loudest eruption in 70 years. It began with thunder and lightning shooting out of the massive mountain's cone. Then the volcano began throwing lava and rock thousands of feet into the air.

Some of the rocks were as big as hens eggs and they rained to earth, stripping limbs off trees. Clouds of smoke and dust rose 20,000 feet into the air and ashes fell in towns a hundred miles away.

Three great streams of hot lava poured down the mountainside, destroying everything in its path, including the town of Sebasiano. Cercia was right in the path of the flow and had to have help of the US Army to evacuate.

Naples was spared because of a high ridge running away from it and because the wind was blowing southward.

It is unlikely the troops stationed in and around the various fronts in

Italy were bored. In the meantime, all coded communication coming from Britain ceases in April as the Allied planners prepare for Operation Overlord.

On May 23, the Anzio beachhead again becomes active when US VI Corps attacks Cisterna and Terracina. Casualties are heavy, but the next day Terracina is occupied by US troops—though at Anzio, Germans still hold Cisterna.

However, on May 25, patrols from US II Corps and Anzio's VI Corps link up and together take Cisterna and Cori.

*Then another strategic mistake takes place. Gen. Mark Clark, who has replaced General Lucas, is intent on the glory of capturing Rome. If US forces were to continue to advance toward Velletri and Valmontone, a large segment of German troops would be cut off. In spite of this, Clark serves as an inspiration to those who serve under him, like **Roy G. Lee** of Indianapolis, Indiana.*

I T WAS JUST ANOTHER MORNING in 1944 on the Anzio beachhead. Not much had happened during the night and three or four of us were squatted down eating breakfast when Gen. Mark Clark, commander of the 5th Army at Anzio, approached us.

He started past, then suddenly turned around and said, "As you were. How are you men getting along?"

We said, "Just fine, sir."

"Are you getting enough to eat?"

"Yes, sir!" we answered.

He said, "Stay with it a little longer and we'll get you out of this damned place." That afternoon, every gun on the beach started firing. The next day, we were on our way to Rome, Florence and other parts of Italy.

*The breakout from Anzio and the race to Rome was greeted with enthusiasm by troops like **Fitzgerald F. Harder** of Arkansas City, Kansas.*

I WAS A MEMBER of an anti-tank crew in the 15th Inf., 3rd Div. We were all fired up with enthusiasm and thought it would be no time at all before we would take the seat of civilization in Italy. After months of fighting in Sicily and then up from the boot heel of Italy, we were assigned to make the landing at Anzio on January 22, 1944.

It was here that I truly realized the horrors of war. The talk was no longer what we were destined for, but survival. In the early morning hours of June 3, we began the break-out from the beachhead. My battalion started its attack and totaled a Mark IV and a Flakwagon, taking several prisoners while the rest retreated to Palestrina.

We finally realized what we had hoped for since the Casablanca landing: We were on our way to the city limits of Roma!

In spite of his popularity, Clark's decision let the Germans prepare a strong resistance at Arce and Ceprano, which allows German forces to withdraw behind Caesar Line. The line will be ruptured on May 31 when US forces capture Velletri.

*At the same time, testimony from Richwood, Ohio's **Beryl L. Phipps** proves that the risks were far from over.*

O N JANUARY 18, 1944, we were practicing amphibious DUKW invasions near Salerno, Italy, preparing for the invasion of southern France. We were 15 miles off the coast when we backed the DUKW off the LST. Nearly all of them sank.

I saved the lives of seven men and earned the Soldiers Medal under the command of Lt. Gen. Mark W. Clark.

On June 1, 1944, two things happened. In Italy, the race for Rome began.

In England, the French Resistance was warned of the impending Operation Overlord, known by most as simply D-Day.

The original date of the landing was June 4, but bad weather prevented it.

*However, on June 4 in Italy, the US 88th Division entered Rome. The Germans have preserved the antiquity of the city, and considering it an "open city" have already abandoned it. **Howard K. Fay Jr.** of Westborough, Massachusetts, witnessed the liberation of the ancient landmark.*

W E ENTERED the eternal city of Rome, June 5, 1944.
I was a 19-year-old rifleman in Minnesota's 34th Infantry Division pursuing the retreating German troops. At daybreak the triumphant march through Rome began. Enemy resistance was almost non-existent. The German High Command was sparing the city from destruction.

One million happy Romans lined the streets extending a joyous welcome. Cheering throngs showered us with flowers and fresh fruit. Italian and American flags appeared. Centuries old streets, buildings, fountains, monuments and priceless works of art were in my line of sight. By nightfall the liberation of Rome was completed.

History had been made. We had conquered Rome from the south. The first of the World War II Axis capitals had fallen and I had been a participant in a "Roman Holiday".

*Another youngster to enter the town that day was **Leo B. Lawrence** of Pipersville, Pennsylvania.*

W E WERE ADVANCING on Rome. I was 18-years-old and about to participate in a once in a lifetime adventure. I had studied Roman history and the Roman Empire and had learned how Rome at one time had ruled most of Europe and Africa. Now I was about to become one of the conquerors of Rome, taking it from the south, which no army had done before.

As we advanced, I thought about the ruins of the city I never dreamed I would see. It was hard to believe that I was a part of this hundreds of years later.

The big moment came when I saw the sign for "ROMA" on Highway 6 as we entered the city. I'm told Gen. Mark Clark took that sign and it is now in the Citadel in South Carolina.

*But even the road to Rome was not entirely smooth, according to **J.K. Holmes** of Oneida, New York.*

I N THE RACE to Rome, my outfit, the 88th/351st were out in front when word came up to let someone else lead. Our battalion commander disagreed and with Rome in sight, pushed us faster.

Our own air force must have thought we were retreating Germans and strafed us. We were lucky. I found a drainage pipe large enough for me and the radio on my back. As we got closer, there was sniper fire and my captain relieved me of my rifle. I was thankful because that radio was getting heavier every minute.

Everyone was happy, believing we were first in Rome. We deserved it. Later we heard some recon troops were ahead of us. I think they must have been lost and very lucky. Pictures in history books show a joyous time for the troops in Rome, but not for the 351st.

After too little sleep and some hurried food, we headed north. It wasn't until many months later that I finally got to see Rome.

Yes, Rome was taken, but the battle in Italy and throughout Europe was far from over.

Chapter 21
D-Day

It's hard to imagine the thoughts that must have passed through the minds of the Allied commanders as June 6, 1944 approached. Germany had 58 divisions in place in Western Europe and 10 of these were the dreaded Panzers, capable of launching their awesome armored forces with incredible efficiency.

Moreover, the Allies could land only a meager six divisions during the initial invasion. The Germans had four full years to entrench themselves, fortify their positions, mine strategic areas, and study the terrain. On the surface, an all-out invasion from English shores against German forces in Normandy seemed suicidal.

It also seems utterly incredible that such a massive and ambitious invasion as Operation Overlord could remain secret from the Nazis, and the Allied Command worried mightily about potential leaks.

However, sooner or later the leaders had to be told, including those who would handle the casualties, like **Emery P. Kertesz Jr.** *of Ottsville, Pennsylvania.*

I WAS STATIONED in North Mimms, England with the 1st General Hospital under the command of Col. Arnold A. Albright M.D. I was a Technician 4th Grade serving as a recording secretary to Major Vincent M. Whelan, M.D., Chief Radiologist.

Sometime in May 1944, Col. Albright was summoned to Headquarters in London. After his return he assembled the entire unit and explained that when we would observe US and allied aircraft aloft with black and white markings on the fuselage and wings, "D" Day will have arrived.

When this finally happened on June 6, it was to say the least, an awesome sight. Hundred upon hundreds of aircraft above heading for France. As the day went on some aircraft were returning for resupply. It is still very vivid in my memory.

Warren R. Lloyd *of Altamonte Springs, Florida, remembers the briefing.*

"**M**EN you are going to France."

These words rang out loud and clear early Saturday morning May 27, 1944 in a huge tent in the southern part of England. We (about 200 soldiers) of Company B—359th Infantry Regiment assigned to the US 4th Infantry Division were assembled while an officer on a raised platform next to a multi-colored map briefed us about our part in the upcoming D-Day landings in Normandy.

The officer indicated that H-Hour would be at 6 AM and we would go ashore 180 minutes later or 9 AM. He pointed out the 14" sea wall, the higher ground, the first objective, the causeway, the password, French invasion money, more live ammo, and restriction to the area, etc.

Finally he indicated that church services would be held in another smaller tent the next morning in the same area. I did attend and the tent was overflowing with soldiers. We all had the same thoughts in mind— be closer to the good Lord for comfort, protection, and courage to keep going for the reality of war was very near—nine days to be exact.

*However, maneuvers that were mere practice for the invasion sometimes proved lethal, as **Leo Gross** of Pound, Wisconsin, found out.*

IN THE SPRING of 1944, our equipment was loaded and we boarded a LST at, I believe the port of Weymouth, England. Sometime after midnight we saw flashes in the sky and heard guns booming.

I asked our Staff Sergeant what all the shooting is about if this is only a dry run. He told me it is to be more realistic. We soon were ordered to go below and stand behind the heavy equipment and follow it out when we landed at the beach.

Operators already had the motors running on the equipment and tanks assembled, and the noise was terrific. Darkness was absolute, communication impossible as we stood tightly packed, waiting. After what seemed like hours, and several shakes and shudders, the huge doors began to open in the semi-darkness, and we began to file out to walk on the beach through what seemed a deserted village.

We were told our heavy equipment was lost, so we could not complete our mission of building a landing strip as ordered, but did get a small plane to land before the day was over.

I did not know until the fall of 1987 that 749 soldiers lost their lives, (more than 4 times as many as the 179 that were lost at Utah Beach on D-Day), in this operation.

*It was, in fact, an open secret that the Allies intended to invade the European continent. The big questions were where and when, and these two facts were successfully concealed from the Germans, or at least from Hitler, who was reported as having slept through the beginning of the historic D-Day. Yet, it was obvious something big was afoot. **Melvin Smith** of Scottsdale, Arizona, was one of many helping to prepare for D-Day.*

I REMEMBER the long and tedious preparation by the 9th Air force C-47 troop carrier and glider personnel weeks before June 6, 1944. There was constant training and preparation by these troop carrier pilots. It was unforgettable to see these young, fearless glider pilots prepare for on-target landings.

Paratroopers were trained to drop from the C-47s and the glider planes. The training was intensive and exacting. As time went on, we knew the apprehension these pilots and airmen faced and of the dangers ahead.

*The construction of gliders to carry the airborne troopers to their D-Day landing was a massive job. **David F. Lindsay** of Sierra Vista, Arizona, was another who was involved.*

O N JUNE 5, 1944, I had assistant engineering officer in the 97th Service Squadron at Newbury, England. We had just completed building 2,400 CG-4A gliders with the help of 2,000 airmen at Greenum Commons, England and were standing around in the rain waiting for the word to invade or not.

Generals Eisenhower and Montgomery were there together about 11 p.m. trying to decide if the word was go or no-go. Thousands of paratroopers, C-47 and glider pilots stood around all night waiting. At 12:20 a.m., Ike gave the word to go. Twenty four hundred glider pilots and 1,200 C-47 pilots ran to their takeoff positions. The invasion of France began when the first paratrooper dropped over France at 1:40 a.m. June 6, 1944.

*Allied command was deeply worried about the weather. It was crucial that the weather be serviceable for aircraft operations or the invasion was doomed. For this reason, the original invasion date, June 5, 1944, was delayed 24 hours to allow for a window of opportunity in the weather. As the lead airborne forces anxiously awaited the word to go, naval forces prepared their men and equipment. **Murray Durst** of Randolph, New Jersey, was at his station when the abort order came.*

I WAS A RADIOMAN attached to Admiral Hall's staff and assigned to the British minesweeper HMS Kellett for the invasion of Normandy.

The minesweeper flotilla put to sea June 5. Our destination was unknown. About halfway across the English Channel I was on watch and received an action message from SHAEF to the commander of the mine flotilla broadcast in plain language.

It read: "Post Mike One" which evidently meant postpone the invasion for one day. We turned around and returned to England only to put to sea again June 6.

*For those with duties prior to and during the invasion, like **Terry J. Sahler** of Athens, Georgia, the night before D-Day seemed to last forever.*

I WAS AN "OLD SALT" of 19 at the time. My ship, the USS Nuthatch AM60 was the flagship for six seagoing minesweepers. Our job was to sweep the sea lanes for the invasion armada. We worked all night in the dark. The only lights we could see were from the anti-aircraft tracer fire along the French shoreline.

My battle station was the ack-ack gun atop the quarter deck. As dawn came, I had a good view of a sight I will never forget. As far as the eye could see, there were ships of all sizes and shapes and the skies were full of planes going to drop their load, then returning to be reloaded in a constant stream. It was the longest day of my life and I shall never forget it.

The airborne units would be the first into the fight. **Charles Moore** *of Ft. Wayne, Indiana, saw them off.*

THE NIGHT before D-Day, the 82nd Airborne were stationed at our base. That night, they boarded our C-47s and Ike and Churchill wished them good luck. All the C-47s met over our base, when they were all in position, before they left for France, they all turned on their landing lights. There were 200 or 250 planes.

It was a wonderful sight and a final salute.

Of course, viewpoint is everything. For some, D-Day was a great adventure. For others, like young **Frank H. Caruk** *of Palatine, Illinois, it might have been something else altogether.*

I HAD ENLISTED in the US Army at age 16 before Pearl Harbor and had just completed basic training when Pearl Harbor was bombed. Time and service went on in the states and then overseas, until finally landing at Liverpool.

I have fond memories of the Welsh, Scots and the English, but what stands out was our last dinner before boarding the crafts for the D-Day invasion. I don't know about other units, but we were served steak and fresh vegetables.

Those with the sardonic sense of humor termed it "fattening the pig before the kill" or "the last meal before the execution," and that occasion still stands out. It was a great meal!

Allied command knew that if the weather deteriorated, the invading forces would be like lambs to the slaughter. Weather would remain a continual worry even in the final moments before troops began landing on the beachheads. Planners of the invasion relied heavily upon weather reports from spotter pilots and from pilots and crews of bombers returning from their missions.

One of the crewmen aboard those incoming bombers was **Worden F. Bishop** *of Spokane, Washington.*

I REMEMBER the early morning briefing June 6. The walls of the briefing room literally vibrated from the cheers and applause from the crew members when the briefing officer said, "Your target today is the coastal defenses in support of ground troops landing on the beaches of Cherbourg Peninsula for the invasion of Europe."

After months of periodic "softening up" missions to the continent, this was the mission these B-26 crew members had been waiting for and wanted to be a part of.

From my waist gunner's position I had a birds-eye view of the greatest spectacle ever assembled. Landing craft were arriving at the beach, battleships were firing broadsides at enemy positions and ships were stretched across the Channel for miles.

Another crewman aboard a bomber was Edmond, Oklahoma, resident **Robert L. "Bob" Perry.**

I WAS NAVIGATOR aboard a B-17 assigned to the 527th Squadron of the 327th Bomb Group-Heavy of the 8th Air Force.

I was awakened early for a briefing. After being told the target, bomb load and course in and out, we were told our ground troops were to invade "festung Europa" on that very day. Our target was Arromanches, part of the invasion area.

As we left English air space and headed south over the English Channel, we saw the thousands of ships that made up the invasion fleet—more ships than we had ever seen before. It appeared that our armies could literally walk from England to France, like an irresistible force that could not fail.

According to **Mary Hannah Hitchcock Hughes** *of Lake Worth, Florida, the sight from the English side was equally inspiring.*

I WAS STATIONED with the 9th Air Force, Ascot, England, located in a direct line south of our airstrips en route to Europe.

On June 6, I left our signal room to go outside and observed the most mind-boggling, spectacular, long-awaited sight in our history. The waves of planes in formation going out to war covered the sky as far as we could see. I did not move nor talk and hardly breathed.

A pain arose in my chest and stayed a long time. I knew later it was entwined with a special pride for our men and our country on the first day of a long-awaited action and preparation for a horrendous war. And it would certainly mean our eventual victory.

Myron Zownir *of Long Island City, New York, was also on the ground that morning, but his duties were quite different.*

A LMOST EVERY DAY until the invasion of Normandy was a maximum effort for me to keep my B-17 Flying Fortress, "Heavenly Comrade" in battle-ready condition. As the assistant crew chief, I made it my job to always perform the preflight warm-up of the engines with my crew chief.

On June 6th, I performed my duties with a 'super' maximum effort, because my plane went over the channel at least three times. Throughout the war, I was very fortunate that none of my planes were shot down or my crews lost. At least 6 crews finished their required missions and were sent home, very happy and appreciative of the ground crew. At first it was 25 missions, then 35.

When the war was over, I had the feeling that my maximum effort really contributed to our victory.

For most GIs, the invasion was a secret. Imagine the surprise of men like **Rexall L. Meier** *of Wisconsin Rapids, Wisconsin, when they looked to the sky that morning.*

W E WERE AT GREAT BARRINGTON, Oxfordshire, England working at building and maintaining airfields. On June 6, we were standing reveille and as the roll call was being taken, we heard the drone of aircraft in the distance. The drone got louder and eventually reached a level at which roll call could no longer be heard.

As we looked skyward, we found the drone was that of hundreds of aircraft, darkening the sky like a huge storm cloud. There were C-47s, P-47s, P-38s, P-51s, B-17s and several types of American and British aircraft towing huge wooden gliders. No one had to be told this was D-Day.

Still, even as the massive assault force moved out, secrecy remained vital. One word, one slip and the entire operation could end in disaster. D-Day may have been the moment that **William A. Turner Sr.** *of Valdosta, Georgia, had the scare of his life.*

I WAS LEAD RADIO OPERATOR on a B-24 with two generals aboard. My direct orders: "Don't break radio silence."

Allied identification code was given at 24:00 hours, making it possible for the code to fall into enemy hands prior to our mission. Complete surprise was top priority.

Then I received the unthinkable: Just prior to departing the British coast, a call with proper identification from supposedly the Allied Command to "hold down your key for position fix."

I pleaded for help from my superiors aboard.

"You have your orders. We have ours."

What to do? I could be held for treason either way.

I prayed as I requested additional identification and my trembling hand opened the key. The deed, right or wrong, was done.

I found the truth when I returned to base where a very hot Major met us as we shut off our engines. "Sergeant Turner, follow me. You will be held for court martial now."

It seems that my log book and finally a call to High Command proved that timing was the final key and I didn't give the war away.

In all, 47 Allied divisions had been gathered together to form the Normandy invasion. The Germans had anticipated the attack to take place just south of Boulogne. In an effort to cripple the Germans' mobility and communication, Eisenhower had instructed all resistance fighters to mount an all-out effort to destroy bridges and communications links just prior to the landing. Road blocks and rail-line sabotage took place across the intricate French transportation system, and the efforts of the resistance combined with bombing missions succeeded in destroying all but one major bridge across the Seine River.

Although the diversionary forces landed near Boulogne were successful in slowing the German response to the true invasion area, Operation Overlord did not come off quite the way the Allies had originally planned. For instance, the first drop of airborne troops near Cherbourg that preceded the invasion was disastrous.

*Elements of the 101st and the 82nd Airborne were widely scattered across the Cotentin Peninsula. This, coupled with fierce anti-aircraft fire, could have spelled doom for the operation and for **Richard L. Warren** of Warrenton, Missouri.*

I WAS WITH the 376th Battalion, Battery C, 82nd Airborne. We were loaded into C-47s in England and the flight across was uneventful until we reached the drop zone. Everyone jumped from the plane OK, but after we regrouped on the ground we realized that anti-aircraft fire had hit the main switch that would drop our 75mm howitzer. All we had was 12 rounds of ammo and the gunsight. The plane had to make a special flight on D-Day + 1 to drop the rest of our gun.

Robert Nelson *of Cincinnati, Ohio, was flying one of those aircraft.*

D URING OUR PARATROOP DROP in France on D-Day, June 6, 1944, I was a flight leader in the 29th Troop Carrier Squadron. We had engine trouble and had to transfer to the stand-by plane. It was 11 PM, June 5, 1944. The rest of the squadron had gone. We were a three plane invasion force. Sicily and Italy were breezes compared to this.

We picked up ground fire as we passed the Channel Islands. We approached Normandy at 800 feet, looking for the DZ signals. There were none. We went too far and had to make a wide 360 degree turn back over the DZ.

Tracers were coming at us from all directions. Our mission was to drop our paratroopers at the DZ and we did.

We were hit. I was hit!

After several agonizing minutes, we determined that we had no critical aircraft damage. We proceeded back to England and I spent the next 17 months in the hospital.

Sidney M. Ulan *of Wallingford, Pennsylvania, was piloting another of those aircraft.*

A S A PILOT (Captain) in the 99th Squadron 441st Troop Carrier Group, my most vivid memory of World War II is the Normandy Invasion—D Day.

Shortly before midnight, June 5, we took off from England loaded with paratroopers of the 101st Airborne Division. Our drop zone was just north of the town of Caretan in Normandy.

As we crossed the invasion coast, all hell seemed to break loose. The sky was filled with red and green tracers, and search lights beamed up at the planes just ahead of me. I could also feel the vibration of flak coming up and shaking the plane. It seemed almost impossible to fly through that wall of fire without getting shot down, but I had no choice. There was no turning back.

After dropping our paratroopers, I hit the deck to avoid the flak and ground fire, and flying at treetop level finally ended up just above the Channel, skimming the water, then pulling up to reform our formation.

The baptism of fire was over, and I breathed a sigh of relief.

With the enormous number of aircraft in the skies, accidents were almost certain to happen, and one did, according to **John J. Fahey** *of Broadview Heights, Ohio.*

T HERE IS AN INDELIBLE IMPRINT on my mind resulting from an incident on D-Day. As I returned from my first bombing mission as a radio operator gunner on a B-24, and while flying over the English Channel, I was looking out the window at the group off our wing. Suddenly, within that group a mid-air collision occurred.

Hundreds of pieces of the two airplanes that crashed together were in my view. To the best of my knowledge no bodies were ever found.

What a useless waste! No enemy action, 20 men dead, two airplanes destroyed, and many families devastated to say nothing of the emotional impact on the group as a whole, and particularly the bunkmates of the downed fliers.

In short, within seconds losses that cannot be measured and absolutely no help to the war effort. I'll never forget it.

It's hard to imagine the thoughts that must have passed through the minds of the men in those early hours of the invasion. **Arley L. Goodenkauf** *of Table Rock, Nebraska, shares his thoughts at that time.*

I REMEMBER that two hour flight from Membury, England to a deserted field in Normandy. The hours before takeoff were so hectic that it was only when we were airborne that I had time to fully realize that the long awaited invasion of Hitler's Europe was here and that these paratroopers would be some of the first Americans into combat.

While crossing the Channel, I stood in the door and tried not to entertain the thought that within a few hours I might be dead. The French coast appeared below and simultaneously, anti-aircraft fire—almost like fireworks and far enough away to be pretty. The green light finally came on and I followed the last man out the door. It was exactly 0100 hours, June 6, 1944.

Weather had been only marginal from the very beginning and the Allied Command had debated whether or not to delay the invasion once more. However, the huge number of ships, planes, and troops that had been amassed in and around England could no longer be concealed, and all the Allied commanders felt that further delays would jeopardize the operation.

By sunrise, June 6, Allied forces were committed and the Germans were beginning to organize their defenses. As the first contingents of the invasion hit the beaches along a 100-mile swath of the French shoreline, German defense ranged from light to heavy.

The beaches include Omaha, Utah, Gold, Sword, and Juno. Two pockets of extremely tough fighting were the Omaha and Utah Beach areas. The outcome of the fighting at Utah Beach, where the Allies miscalculated the landing sites, was in doubt until D-Day plus one.

*The huge number of ships involved in Operation Overlord must have seemed like shooting fish in a barrel to German artillery gunners. In addition, in spite of minesweeping efforts, the waters off Normandy were heavily mined, making passage doubly dangerous, as **Edward F. Gorch** of Maspeth, New York, found out.*

I WAS ABOARD the USS Bancroft Gherardi DD637 the morning of June 6, 1944. Our mission was to run parallel to Omaha Beach firing our five-inch guns at targets of opportunity while our forces landed.

Before we even made our first run, a sister ship, the destroyer Emmons struck two mines and sank. The command ship, the battleship Texas, sent in PT boats to pick up survivors.

We made our next run successfully, but two ships behind us, a destroyer escort, also struck some mines and sank. While we were preparing for our third run, the ship before us was hit by shore batteries and sunk.

We made our third run amid heavy supporting gunfire from the Texas and the heavy cruisers stationed farther out. Finally, we were detached to return to Plymouth, England to replenish our ammunition, which was completely exhausted.

I didn't know until after the war that three more ships were sunk, nor did we know that Okinawa was in our ship's future.

Ralph H. Ayers *of Cedartown, Georgia, is another who had a close call.*

AFTER TWO AND A HALF YEARS at Charleston Naval Hospital I shipped out to New York, thence via convoy overseas. Was assigned duty aboard Liberty Ship Wheelock (supplies and troops) for Normandy invasion.

The "abandon ship" alarm was sounded during an air raid at Omaha Beach. I was a medical corpsman in sick bay with about a dozen corpsman in sick bay and about a dozen bed patients. I saw to it they all had on lifejackets and directed any who could to assist others to topside.

I said to myself, "If this is it, so be it! God help me to do my duty topside." But none reached topside.

Word was passed that the alarm was in error, but it was real enough for us at the time.

I completed my Navy service at USNAS Bermuda, returned to work at Post Office and married the girl who prepared my orders to leave Charleston.

Though the invasion was a surprise, the Germans were not long in opening fire. **Robert Needleman** *of Chicago, Illinois, was ferrying troops ashore that morning.*

O UR SHIP was high and dry as we commenced to unload US Army Medical Corps and their vehicles.

Upon completion of unloading, I was up on the bow. I looked to the port side and noticed a large splash in the water, a minute later, another splash, closer to the ship, another minute and a shell screamed overhead, we were ordered to abandon ship.

We took cover in a trench up the beach, after several hours we returned to the ship, however, the tide was in and we were lucky to have a US Army DUCK take us back.

We were hit 3 times, once below the water line, which was repaired by our shipfitter before the tide came in, once in an empty storage room, and again in the officers wardroom. No casualties.

We were glad to get back to England for some pink lemonade.

Probably a lot of men would like to return to England that morning for some nice, peaceful lemonade—for instance, **Richard S. Bills** *of St. Benedict, Pennsylvania.*

A BOARD LCT (a) 2488, we crossed the English Channel with three medium-sized tanks. English-made LCTs, Rocket Ships, and gunboats were manned by amphibious sailors from the Gunfire Support Craft group based at Camp Roseneath, near Helensburg, Scotland.

About 6:30 all hell broke loose. A gunboat in front of us hit a mine and sank almost immediately. We got hung up on a sandbar about 60-yards from the beach.

Lt. Grace gave the order for the tanks to evacuate. All three made it to the beach as we watched on our way back to the rendezvous area.

Being a sailor, I considered myself lucky. All I could think about was the tough job ahead for the infantry, tank crews, and airborne troops.

I'm proud to have been a participant and pray to God there will be no more.

After the initial landings, the landing craft not only brought men and equipment to the beach, but they also took the wounded back, according to **George P. Yule** *of Lakeside, California.*

I HAD JUST PUT a stricken soldier in quarters, returned to the half-track and while I mounted, it hit a teller mine. The force from the explosion disabled the craft. Unfortunately I fell on the steel deck injuring my knee. The explosion blew a hole in the landing craft floor where I quartered the soldier. I heard him crying for help. I opened the door discovering that half of his lower body was mangled with both legs broken in about five places.

I carried him out, gave him morphine, put him on a stretcher and turned him over to the Navy.

Later, I was awarded the Silver Star and the Bronze Star by Brig. General Taylor, who is known to have said, "We're dying here, let's go inland to die."

From the indications that **Derwood Caldwell** *of Spring, Texas, saw, the GIs that day knew what they were wading into.*

I WAS THERE during the invasion of Omaha Beach, Normandy, France on the ship LCI 541. We took aboard the 29th Infantry Division a week before the invasion and hit the beach around 6:30 am the morning of June 6, 1944.

When we got back to Weymouth, England a few days later I went below into the Number One troop compartment. On the bulkhead was drawn the picture of cemetery headstones and out of the headstones ghosts were rising. It had clouds and a moon in the sky.

Underneath the drawing of the cemetery was written—"In memory of the many deaths we have died waiting for D-Day."

It was signed by a 29th Infantry Division soldier from Baltimore, Maryland.

I will never forget this picture as long as I live and have often wondered if the artist made it through the invasion.

Leonard Brock *of Phoenix, Arizona, in a few short verses, gives an idea of what it's like to wade ashore.*

LET the thunder roll,
Smoke and flame, will show th' way.
I am the Beach at Omaha,
And this is Judgment Day.
The gates of hell, are open wide.
For all who come to play,
The stakes are high,
The game is death,
No winners here today.

I am the Beach at Omaha,
And only time will tell.
Of the Fifty Yards of Glory,
At the very Gate of Hell.

Earl M. Macholl of Marietta, New York, learned to redefine trouble that June morning.

H EADING for the Omaha Beach, June 6, 1944, we heard that the earlier waves were having a little trouble. We were coming alone, passing floating Americans dead a mile or so from the beach.

Off to the right, the battleship Texas was firing its freighter-big guns. To the left was a mine sweeper overhead marking the end of clear area.

By now our boat is zigzagging because we are drawing fire. The coxswain lowered the ramp partially and told us to leave the boat as fast as we could when we beached. By now the minesweeper was getting hit hard. We almost caught a shell on the ramp. We were still 150 yds from shore, when we ran aground.

A third of the men disappeared into the hole. The boat revised, we left them, moved to the left and crunch, we were 75 from shore and the water was chest deep.

Shortly I was on the beach and could see the shot up LSTs and the long line of dead GIs. By then I had the idea that if this was a little trouble, I would hate like hell to see a lot of trouble.

George W. Aldridge Jr. of Chevy Chase, Maryland, also hit the beach that morning.

I WAS STRUCK by the courage of the thousands of Americans that I saw on June 6th and 7th 1944. On my 20th birthday, June 1, 1944, we loaded aboard LST 375 at Portland Hard in the south of England and cruised the choppy English Channel for five long, seasick days.

Then came the once postponed D-day landings. From the LST to a Rhino ferry and then on to several aborted landing attempts at Omaha Beach caused by congestion and intense gunfire. Finally onto the beach that was littered with equipment and fighting, wounded and dead comrades.

The crossing of the beach was a battle won only by the sacrifices, courageous acts, skill and determination of those gallant men. After World War II, I went to war three more times in Korea and Vietnam. But never did I witness a feat like the taking of Normandy's Omaha Beach in June of '44.

Joseph Carubia of Montgomery, New York, like so many that day, was brand new to combat.

A T THE BEGINNING of my World War II career, I was a replacement radio operator into the combat experienced 33rd F.A. BN, 1st Inf. Div., I was chosen by my C.O. to be included in an advanced party to land on

D-Day in Normandy to help direct artillery fire in support of the infantry.

It didn't take long after I waded onto Omaha Beach, despite my fear, nausea, being wet and seeing death at every turn, for me to become battle hardened.

What followed was 11 months of combat: Northern France, Belgium, into Germany across the Siegfried line, the Battle of the Bulge and the crossing of the Rhine.

The end found me somewhere in Czechoslovakia on May 8, 1945, VE Day.

My knees were sore that day, not from over exercise but from being on them thanking God for seeing me through this ordeal in the service of our country.

Loren M. Greiner *of Emmetsburg, Iowa, found himself a good place to witness history.*

I CAN STILL ENVISION a scene I witnessed as I sat on the back slope of a bluff overlooking Omaha Beach the first night of the invasion.

Directly below me was Omaha Red. This was not our planned point of landing, but we were there. I sat that evening in a carved-out hole on the back slope of a terrace excavated with a rusty old construction shovel sitting near by, used by someone in the past.

But this terrace had a purpose. A few feet from me that evening a causal misstep created a casualty. A mine field had been discovered. Below us, in a clump of brush, we had discovered a string of booby traps. By luck, some were faulty from rust.

I was shivering cold, without a blanket.

This was the setting for one of the greatest evening shows of fireworks I ever hope to see. Shortly after dark, there appeared three low flying, strange sounding planes that proceeded offshore from over the bluff. They flew directly over the huge assembly of ships I had been watching all day.

Full alert came to life. It all happened so quickly, as these three planes flew in a low circle out over the water, above this sea of ships. From all directions, an intense life or death show of fireworks spontaneously erupted. Tracer bullets arched skyward from every direction, as the planes continued to fly in a great circle. It was a sight to remember.

A flare-up in the distance indicated a strike on a ship.

But, in this show of deadly fireworks, high in this dark evening sky, there was a message. The message to rescue, and make free, people in need had begun. "We were there". That was the message these pilots were forced to take back to their commanders in the East.

And indeed they did.

A reported interview with one of the pilots, after this "Game" was over, confirmed this mission. An invasion had begun.

In a landing craft, preparing to land that morning, there were, from beyond the bluff, low angle shells bracketing the landing course before us.

This activity delayed our landing.

But, the culmination of my "Longest Day" looking over Normandy Beach, was this gigantic display of deadly fireworks.

Andrew W. Sevec Sr. *of Clarksville, Pennsylvania, witnessed the event that would eventually lead to the liberation of Paris.*

I SAW THE BOMBING of St. Lo. At the time I was platoon Staff Sergeant, with Company A of the 300 combat engineers in Normandy, and all the front lines were being stopped by a German Tank outfit, located in land around St. Lo.

It was a clear day with a wind blowing towards the Germans, shortly after dawn the first wave of planes came over from the British Isles and dropped smoke bombs ahead of our lines to establish a line for the bombs, next came wave after wave of bombers too numerous to count (thousands I do believe) and continued all day long. It was really a sight to behold, one I never will forget. It also was a fateful day as General McNair was accidentally killed in the bombing.

Results: Germans were wiped out completely and the way to Paris now open.

Edward E. Ruggles *of Anita, Iowa, was moved to verse by what he witnessed.*

IN THE EARLY MORNING FOG on Omaha Beach, we saw sunken ships around us—a breakwater it seems. We boarded an LCT and after landing we walked up the beach, inland a couple of miles we set up tents. We could hear the cannon fire near St. Lo, maybe 15 miles inland.

One evening formations of Liberators came roaring over at treetop height. We heard the bombs drop and learned there were hundreds of bombers involved.

After that there was silence.
In France the calm trees stand
Silent unruffled.
As they stood along the hedgerows
A score of years ago.
Far off the rumble of a
Receding storm
That leaves piled along the rows
The trash of war.
As the waves recede at sea
From the drift along the shore
So the thunder fades
The shrapnel rain, and cordite clouds
Have gone.
In the silent fields
The taint of death remains

Reinforcements land at Omaha Beach, June 6, 1944

Steward S. Brosius *of Strasburg, Pennsylvania, may have had some doubt who the enemy really was.*

I WAS THE STATIONED DRIVER to a "bird" Colonel with the XV Corps. I went everywhere he did; from the St. Lo breakthrough to the South of Paris in 30 days (Aug. '44). Late one day we drove into the new bivouac at dusk. I quickly dug my trench so I could easily roll into it while in my sleeping bag if attacked.

Somewhat later, "bed-check-Charlie" (ME 109), started strafing the area. Shaking profusely, I rolled towards my trench; I felt a thud, and rolled over it. I turned and with my blackout flashlight, saw that the Company derelict had beaten me to it! He didn't dig any and jumped into the nearest "freebie" available.

I uttered about 100 unprintable words plus I gave him a good healthy kick. We remained friends, but I never bivouacked near that "lazy scoundrel" again.

No one who has never lived through it can ever understand what it feels like to have strangers trying to kill you. **Henry F. Heller Jr.** *of Fond du Lac, Wisconsin, knows that feeling.*

A FTER LANDING on Utah Beach our Co. "B" 634th Tank Destroyer Bn. was located in a wooded area at Carentan. One afternoon, a German Reconnaissance plane came over our area. Everyone ran out in a clearing to watch it. That night we were bombarded with German Artillery.

It was my turn for guard duty at midnight. I ran to the main gate for duty, there was a large foxhole to stand in, the person I was to relieve stayed all night, no one came to relieve us. The German guns could be seen firing. We counted 5 rounds to "A" then "B" and then "C" Co. each time they raised their guns. By 5 am the shells were landing in front of us and throwing dirt into our foxhole.

Suddenly the shelling stopped. We were now full-fledged veterans.

The landing units didn't just hit the beach, then mill around. Each had its own assignment, including the rangers aboard **David D. Beattie Sr.'s** *ship. Here's what the resident of Oak Hill, Florida, saw.*

I T WAS DARK when we moved into position 1,000 yards offshore. We had some rangers on board who were to go after a big gun emplacement. They left the ship under cover of darkness.

Red tracers and anti-aircraft fire was lighting up the sky around us. We started firing at shore batteries and they returned our fire. I saw a puff of smoke from the USS Cory. She had hit a mine. She broke apart and started sinking.

We went to her aid and picked up about 250 survivors. We had to go over the side into the water after them. Most were wounded and suffering from burns. The water was cold and they were unable to climb the cargo nets we had over the sides.

We were still returning fire and shelling the guns on the beach during this time. We had more than 40 near misses from enemy guns.

For **Joseph A. Dahlia** *of Chicago, Illinois, D-Day was not at all what he had expected.*

D URING THE INVASION of Normandy 6th of June 1944, I was wounded and taken prisoner by the Germans. They transported me to a German aid station, set up at a Catholic Monastery. A German doctor operated on me and saved my life.

The next day when I was awake, still under the effects of ether, I heard a voice over and over again. I opened my eyes and saw a monk going from bed to bed with a basket of fruit. He said, "Fresh fruit from the garden."

I thought I was in heaven for a moment. But looking around the room I saw 6 beds and a German guard at a table.

Next to my bed was a glider pilot, across the room was a paratrooper from 101st, a soldier from the 29th Infantry and a P-51 pilot and others.

The Monk came everyday with apples, pears, grapes etc. This lasted two days until they moved us to a prison hospital in Renneo, France.

We were liberated on August 4, 1944.

*Getting ashore was one of Fayetteville, Pennsylvania, resident **Dale L. Shoop's** biggest problems.*

I SERVED with 1st Infantry Division AP01, 1st Battalion, 1st Platoon, 1st Squad (Demolition Squad) and I was on the landing craft in the English Channel on D-Day in the first wave of troops.

I couldn't swim so when we departed the landing craft, I was tied by rope around my waist and tied to my platoon sergeant and was towed in by him to shore.

The English Channel was considered the roughest piece of water at that time. I couldn't swim then and still cannot swim!

***Wayne A. Reese** of Overland Park, Kansas, knew a guy who couldn't sleep.*

WE HAD COME on Utah Beach after the first troops of the invasion had cleared enough real estate to land an Armored Division. We spent all day trying to find out where equipment and people belonged. It was a jammed up mess and our first experience of what a war would be like—organized confusion.

Late that afternoon, we staked out some space on a small hill for sleeping in bedrolls. A sergeant came by and suggested we dig some fox-holes, in the same breath saying we wouldn't be here very long.

We took this to mean, to hell with digging, get some sleep. A lieutenant spotted our good sleeping place and asked that we hold a spot for him, he would be right back. He came back just as it was getting dark, carrying an Army cot and a white mosquito net. He unfolded the cot, drove a stake at the foot, one at the head, and draped the net over the cot.

Propped up on our bedrolls we were beginning to see gun flashes to the south. The lieutenant was on the cot, under the white netting and appeared to be asleep when the first shell came in.

Another landed closer and I looked over and saw a white blur running for cover. With the mosquito net draped over him, the guy was bailing out. He looked like a ghost on Utah Beach on a dark night with gun flashes lighting up the area.

After seeing the Ghost on Utah, and much later in the war seeing the Ghost of Wallendorf, how can one forget?

***William G. Schuler** of Souderton, Pennsylvania, also found a little humor amidst the terror.*

I WAS IN THE 382 AIR SERVICE SQUADRON on Normandy at Air Strip A-1. My vivid memory was the sudden, frightening Alarm, "Gas", in the middle of the night.

The all clear sounded, but then a second gas alarm was went off. It was especially frightening for I chose to sleep in the supply tent rather than the fox hole, where my gas mask was located.

In my fright, I ran barefooted past two guards calling, "halt."

We never did hear "officially" what happened. We did hear that a gas drum was dropped while unloading a truck.

The alarm covered a great distance and some showed up at the medic tent fearing they were "gassed", for they couldn't breath—only to find they hadn't removed the water proofing from the gas mask canister.

But then, there is very little funny to be found in the D-Day invasion. The price was incredibly high. **Mrs. Walter Shepherd** *of Noel, Missouri, knows from experience.*

O N A SATURDAY MORNING in March when a man from our small town drove into our yard and approached our door with a telegram for my folks informing them my youngest brother had been "killed in action." Our terrible grief and shock as he had only been overseas 6 months. My older and only other brother was in Germany on the front lines and had been for over a year. The war didn't end for my family on D Day in 1945 and will never end.

Imagining the immensity of the landings is difficult. The landings did not all take place on June 6, as **Gus Solomon** *of Bronx, New York, points out.*

O N JUNE 7TH, "D" Day + one, my outfit, the 294th Combat Engineers, embarked on a ship named "The Susan B. Anthony." We left early in the morning and arrived at Normandy Beach in the afternoon. Between those times, we were hit by a mine. We did not know the damage done, but the order came, "Remove you gear."

We did and placed our rifles on top of it, after what seemed a lifetime an LST pulled in and we climbed down the nets and got on. As we pulled away the Susan B. Anthony went down.

The LST dropped us off in water over our heads, we walked until we hit the beach. We picked up rations in wooden cases and used the wood from the cases to make forks to eat with. (All our regular utensils had been left on the ship.)

We headed inland between two white tapes, on the outside of the tape, under water, were mines. A German plane got in back of us coming down to strafe us. We took off into the mined water.

The plane was shot down from batteries on the beach. We had just gotten out of the mined water and back into the tape column, when another plane came down in back of us again. This one also was shot down. (Read after the war that Germany left two planes at Normandy, all the others were sent elsewhere.)

Even in these bleak days, The American Legion's presence was felt, says **Robert L. Fulmer** *of Spring Mount, Pennsylvania.*

I T WAS JUNE 8, 1944; our second day in Normandy, France. I was an ammunition carrier in the 81mm mortar platoon of "D" Company,

9th Infantry Regiment, 2nd Infantry Division. We were not yet on the front line.

We were sent out just up from the beach where we landed the day before to reconnoiter the area for any Germans still hiding out. What I saw were fields of wild poppies that brought back memories to me.

My father was a member of The American Legion and I was a member of the Sons of the American Legion. I remembered the Memorial Day services the Post conducted in our community and the poem, "In Flanders Fields" and the poppies we wore on Memorial Day, in remembrance of those who made the supreme sacrifice.

Wearing the poppy on Memorial Day now has a deeper meaning to me than before.

Though they knew they could die, still they stepped forward. **Paul Aaroe** *of Belvidere, New Jersey, was another of that group.*

O N JUNE 6, 1944, my outfit, HQ 184th Ordnance BN, left Southampton for Normandy, arriving off shore later that day. Due to some foul up in orders (not uncommon in military operations) our small boat lay off shore until June 10 when we finally landed on Utah Beach.

During one of these days, as I was talking with our senior officer, Capt. Jack Gellman, I called his attention to a splash in the water as a probable fish jumping. When another like splash came on the other side of the ship, I realized what was happening.

I told Gellman we were being zeroed in by a German shore gun and to get the boat captain to back off or we would be blown out of the English Channel very soon.

Jack told this to the young naval ensign in charge of our boat but he refused to move without orders from headquarters.

Realizing the imminent peril, Jack told the ensign that in such emergency, the Army practice is to act on our own. This advise was followed, the boat moved back a half mile and the gun gave up trying to hit us.

After assembling on Utah Beach, our little headquarters participated in the Normandy battle, and battles known as Northern France, Ardennes (Battle of the Bulge), Rhineland and Central Europe, meeting the Russians near Leipsig.

Losses were heavy and even before the battle was over, replacements— **Bill M. Currell** *of Saginaw, Michigan was one—were sent in. Being a replacement can be very lonely.*

I T WAS NOT THE MUD and snow nor the rages of battle as bad as they were. It was the loneliness of the initial joining of my new division.

After I landed in England in the summer of 1944, I was reassigned from anti-aircraft into infantry. At that time there was a drastic need for infantrymen. I remember it well. After a brief training period I landed at Omaha Beach as an infantryman replacement. About five of us were assigned to the same Company of the 80th Infantry Division. Here we were, just kids far from home and now on line . . . everything totally alien. The attitude of the old-timers was distant and remote. At that moment I felt utterly alone and isolated.

Little did we realize in a very short time we would be the veterans and those who followed us as replacements would harbor the same anxieties.

Not only were some GIs not familiar with combat, but many were not even in combat positions. At Normandy, that didn't really matter, according to **William R. Heffren** *of Shively, Kentucky.*

I WAS A SERGEANT and company clerk. We were separated from the fighting troops. Meanwhile our clerks crossed the English Channel and went in on Omaha Beach.

My first glimpse of the shore line and beach were frightening. There were numerous sunken ships, tanks and guns sticking up half out of the water, plus bodies floating in the surf.

With no directions we walked down a dirt road about a quarter of a mile and set up our pup tents. Only then we realized that we had very little ammunition. That night each guard had one clip of ammunition.

The next morning some of our fighting troops came ashore, walked down the same road we had, stepped on a land mine and several soldiers were permanently injured.

After that day and night I never expected to return home again.

Meanwhile, the airborne units that had been dropped earlier were still trying to do their jobs. One of them was **Bud C. Olson** *of Choteau, Montana.*

THE BATTLE for the crossing of the Mederet River in Normandy took place on June 9, 1944.

I was a S/Sgt. of Headquarters Company, 3rd Battalion, 325 Glider Infantry, 82nd Airborne Division. The 3rd Battalion was ordered to lead the attack and establish a bridgehead across the Mederet River.

We had to attack across a causeway that was 400 yards long. It was heavily defended by German troops using small arms, automatic weapons and artillery fire against us. Dead and wounded troopers littered the causeway from one end to the other. Our Division commander, Gen. Ridgway, kept urging the remaining troops forward.

Under heavy enemy fire, we finally succeeded in eliminating the 88 gun emplacements on the far side of the river. The bridgehead was established and a severe counter-attack was repelled.

That night I was ordered to cross the causeway again to locate and lead the 90th Division across. The causeway was still under heavy enemy fire.

I think I am one of the few survivors who had to cross the Mederet River three times that day. It was an experience I will never forget.

*To a man, those who were there will never forget Normandy, and that includes **Maurice E. Berkey Jr.** of Salem, Indiana.*

U PON LEAVING UTAH BEACH our vehicle stalled. Soon the MPs found us and led us through the dark to our area. The following evening, I drew guard duty. As soon as I started walking my post, an ugly white dog with a large head came through the hedge row. I picked up a rock and threw at him. I missed but he went yelping back through the hedge row to a trailer next door where Gen. Patton questioned the dog's reason for his outburst.

Next having never seen tracer bullets, I called the Officer of the Day who explained this to me. Later, it seemed as though there came a field of moving lanterns. This puzzled both of us until we discovered glow worms in plentitude on the hedges.

There were worse days and better days that followed.

Better days and worse, indeed.

It takes some time for the beachheads to link up. On June 7 at Normandy, now called the Western Front, the four beach units attempt to link up. Gold and Juno accomplish this, but the others are at least a day behind their objectives.

In spite of this, the US 4th Division (VII Corps) begins advance toward Cherbourg the next day. Also on the 8th, Omaha and Gold Beaches are now linked, but it will not be until the 10th that the hard-won Utah and Omaha Beaches finally join.

By June 12, the third wave of divisions is largely ashore in Normandy, giving Allied troops a strength of 326,000 men.

The next day, the first V1 Flying Bomb hits England. Ten are fired but only four successfully cross the Channel and only one of them lands in London, killing six civilians.

The airborne landings have accomplished one thing: They have drawn the attention of the dreaded German Panzers away from the beaches long enough for the landings to take place.

The Western Front is becoming defined as US forces secure and clear Montebourg and Valognes. However, from June 19 to June 22, gales ravage the coast. The raging seas destroy some of the Allies' recent inventions, the temporary ports called Mulberries. Without sheltered secure mooring places many landing craft sink, especially the DUKWs.

*Still, the troops pour ashore and fight their way inland. Though he makes no mention of the gales, **Michael P. Kramer's** father writes home during this period. Kramer is from Bath, Pennsylvania.*

"I STILL CAN'T QUITE REALIZE that I am a part of all that I have read about, heard about or have seen in the movies. I actually see some of those things happening, Formations of planes, A.A. defenses, barrage balloons, convoy's etc.

It sends a tingle up and down my spine when I hear what is happening to the Germans, and knowing that we still have a lot more in store for them. I only hope that it will mean a speedy victory for us, so we can all return home again."

Love to you both

"Mike", Sr.

These words were written by Paul R. Kramer, my father, (now deceased), who served in World War II. This quote is from a letter that he sent to my mother and myself on 22 June, 1944, just two days after he landed on Omaha Beach, France.

He was subsequently assigned as a platoon leader in Co. L, 119th Infantry Regiment, 30th Infantry Division on 14 July, 1944. He was wounded in action on 26 July 1944 while participating in "Operation Cobra," which began the day before. This was the successful offensive by the First Army to "Breakout" of the Normandy hedgerow country.

Allied forces were stuck in the treacherous hedgerows. It might be fair to say that Merrick, New York, resident **Tom Carr's** *youth showed plainly.*

DURING THE NORMANDY CAMPAIGN sometime in June of 1944 a sniper was firing at us while we were in the cover of the French hedgerows. I told my comrades that I would stand up on our hedgerow and wave in the direction of the sniper while they would watch to see if they could detect a gunpowder flash.

Sure enough the sniper fired, the flash was seen and they fired back and the sniping stopped. When we advanced to the tree where the sniper fired from, we saw a woman who we presumed to be a French German sympathizer wearing a white blouse splattered with blood, lying dead at the base of a tree.

When the CO heard about the incident, he sent for me and told me that the next time I did a dumb thing such as I did, he would have me court martialed for stupidity in action.

Though deadly, Carr's recollection seems lighthearted compared to that of **George Spiskok** *of Pricedale, Pennsylvania.*

WHEN I JOINED, I was told by the examining doctor that I'd be put in limited service in the States. I ended up in the in 4th Inf. Division. Trained for invasion in Florida and England. While in English Channel saw one of our ships on fire, set by Germans PT boat. We lost hundreds of men.

Invasion went off as scheduled. France's hedgerows lost us lot of men and officers. I was a 33 year old PFC and eventually was assigned to HQ Co. where I was used as sniper bait by officers.

New officers had me carry their brief cases from one hedgerow to other. They told me to walk through hedgerow openings and check the other side—nice open spaces and trees with snipers.

When the first officer called me back, I was handing him his case, and sniper shot him dead. The second officer went through the same procedure. When I handed him the case, his heart was blown open. I carried a third case with the same result.

By this time we were in Germany, with no hedgerows, and no briefcases.

*Word of the D-Day invasion did not take long to reach home, and the results were predictable. For a teenager like **Myron V. Goff** of Livonia, Michigan, the graphic scenes created a lasting memory.*

I REMEMBER seeing the film footage of the Normandy D-Day landing on June 6, 1944. I was 13-years-old at the time and still remember the newsboy shouting in the early morning. "D-Day started," and "Invasion Started," over and over.

But seeing the film of the landing and two soldiers being shot down will forever stay etched in my memory.

*For those already in the service, D-Day made a terrific impact, according to **Frank Pellino** of Ridgefield, New Jersey.*

ONE JUNE EVENING I was in an overseas movie theater with a group of three or four hundred service men and women watching this movie. There were Navy, Air-Force and Infantry on this isolated Aleutian island and most of us had already served many months overseas.

Abruptly our movie was interrupted with the announcement, "The Supreme Allied Command has just announced that the invasion of Europe has begun."

The answering roar was something that I will never forget. It was so spontaneous and strongly vocal that I felt at that moment the roof of that theater was being lifted. It was a moment of a lifetime!

*Ignoring the fact that the war was being fought in other places besides Normandy was easy. To **Jack S. Dutton** of Normandy, Missouri, the coming Normandy invasion may have taken a back seat to what happened just two days earlier.*

JUNE 4TH, 1944 when the bow of a German U-boat came out of the water just a few hundred yards behind the Escort Carrier Guadalcanal. My battle station was a 5" gun on the fantail. We wanted to fire but the order was not given as Captain Daniel V. Gallery wanted to capture this one. The Destroyer Escorts Chatelain, Pillsbury, Flaerty, Pope and Jenks proceeded to fire close misses to avoid sinking the U-Boat.

The Germans were abandoning their sub which was running in a tight circle. A boarding party from the Pillsbury boarded the sub and confiscated the code equipment. Later, two other boarding parties prepared the sub for towing to Bermuda. After the war, the U-505 was placed in the Museum of Science and Industry in Chicago when last year was designated as a National Monument.

I was there.

As weeks passed, the Allied push did not let up. **Louis G. Schoofs** *of Harlingen, Texas, is reminded of Normandy in July.*

THE 4TH OF JULY, 1944 in Normandy! Whenever I hear the words of our National Anthem "the rockets red glare and bombs bursting in air"—I am carried back to that night.

We celebrated our nation's birthday with a concentrated shelling by ALL of our artillery at high noon. After a day of intense action, the Germans came to pay us back with a heavy aerial bombardment that night. Never have I heard or seen such a thunderous crashing din—exploding bombs, intense anti-aircraft fire, shrapnel tearing through the apple trees like a heavy hail storm. Then one German bomber, very low overhead struck by anti-aircraft fire exploded and rained down on us in pieces—including bodies of the crew.

It's also true there was some confusion in and around the invasion, and it lasted quite a while. **Woodrow W. Yoakum** *of Hobbs, New Mexico, had a harrowing experience.*

ON AUGUST 1, 1944, our Unit (951st F.A. BN.) moved from Le Bourg to Percy, France. We were well ahead of our Infantry, and Percy was still in enemy hands.

We began firing our 155 MM Howitzers at the enemy and were answered with mortar fire on our position. We soon had two or three men injured, who were evacuated back to a hospital.

Our infantry soon came up from our rear and were amazed to see us in front with heavy artillery. They quickly set up their mortars behind our artillery and began firing at the Germans. Our CO and two other officers were pinned down in a bar ditch by machine gun fire while on reconnaissance. We had already moved our Howitzer to the road, to fire direct on enemy tanks or other vehicles, should it become necessary.

I managed to take cover for awhile in a wood shed, until the smoke cleared away. Our troops soon pushed the Germans back, and once again we took our rightful place, as a heavy artillery unit.

Gus Solomon *of Bronx, New York, adds his tale of one careless move.*

MY OUTFIT landed in England, boarded a train and embarked in beautiful town named Sherborn. It was night, the fog was so thick we had to walk holding onto the soldier in front. We received our training of building Bailey Bridges and laying mine fields. Co. "C" had a platoon put down a mine field. They picked it up at 11 o'clock as they had to go back for lunch, in picking it up, someone must have left a detonator in a mine. The mines are put in a case. The detonators were kept separately. They are then put on a two ton truck. The mines exploded. The blast shattered windows 5 miles away. The truck was brought back to camp in a Jeep. Eighteen men were blown away, six were hospitalized in shock. This was something that upset Co. "C", they were never the same.

So, it was on through Normandy and into France. **Luke Anthony** *of Fort Recovery, Ohio, offers a last humorous reflection.*

OUR CONVOY was moving from Normandy towards Paris, and we were somewhat nervous about German planes. We had no combat experience, (we were a Depot Group). Everyone was watching the clouds—except Leo, the lanky, shiftless cut-up of the outfit.

Leo, for his sins, had been set to polishing our jeep's twin 50's—over and over again until they shone. He was sick of all the Army's guns—and discipline!

Sure enough, one morning, here comes a plane (Ours or theirs?) low over the road. Tension was building fast, until Leo's agonized voice was heard over all the noise and confusion.

"Any s.o.b shoots those guns hasta clean 'em!"

Mostly laughs took over—and the plane passed on.

And so began the final battles for Europe.

Chapter 22
Battle for Europe

The advance from Normandy is painfully slow. However, events back in the States were coming to a conclusion that would affect literally millions of veterans.

The American Legion had, since shortly after the war began, been spearheading a campaign to create a set of GI benefits that would be available to American troops once they returned home.

Two major items of this benefit package were special home loans for veterans and GI educational benefits. Finally, after much lobbying, the bill was narrowly passed by Congress and on June 20, 1944, while American forces were trying to penetrate the outer defenses of Cherbourg on the Western Front and the Battle of Philippine Sea was being fought in the Pacific, President Roosevelt signed the GI Bill.

By June 27, 1944, Cherbourg is finally taken, but Allies find that it is heavily booby trapped. Three days later, the last German forces in Cotentin are either wiped out or surrender.

Since D-Day, Allies have landed 630,000 men and lost 62,000 dead and wounded. Replacements would have to be found for those killed or wounded and one of these would be **Donald Sprowls** *of Salem, South Carolina.*

O N MY WAY to combat as a rifle replacement via forty and eights and army trucks, I was quite nervous. Our last stop before being assigned our company was what I believe to have been Battalion headquarters for the 359th Infantry, 90th Division.

There, we replacements were assigned our company and were told to go out to the paling fence in back of the building and to pick out a rifle and two bandoleers of ammunition.

As I said, I was quite nervous. Immediately upon coming upon hundreds of M-1 rifles, I spotted a rifle facing me with the name HAZEL carved in large letters in the stock. This would be and became my rifle. My mother's name was Hazel.

You have no idea how much this relieved me of my anxiety.

Anxiety in this time and place was common. Often, GIs would break the tension with a little humor, as reported by **Lawrence H. McCauley** *of Columbus, Ohio.*

I T WAS NEAR 11 P.M. (double daylight savings time) when the German strafing came in at tree-level. Five or six of us dove under a 2½ ton 6X6 truck for cover.

After a couple of passes, the aircraft moved on and following a few moments of silence, Cpl. Jim White from West Virginia broke the stillness with a takeoff from the gas mask drills when we would bend to the ground, pull a corner of the mask from our face on the order: "All Clear! Test for Gas!"

That particular night near St. Lo, we were not wearing gas masks, but Cpl. White did his takeoff of the drill by raising his head and whispering to those with him under the truck: "ALL CLEAR! TEST FOR SH.."

Needless to say, that command caused an outburst of laughter as we went back to our business.

We learned a few minutes later that we had suffered just one casualty from the strafing.

Luck plays a big part in any combat GI's life, according to **George L. Myers** *of Cedarburg, Wisconsin.*

I T TOOK PLACE during a containing action we were performing in France. While holding some 60,000 German troops in the Ports of Lorient and St. Nazaire pockets, I escaped what could have been a serious injury.

I was serving with a Forward Observer Unit of Battery "B", 301st Field Artillery Battalion, 94th Infantry Division when one of our shells fell short of its target. Just as I started to remove my field glasses from my eyes, a piece of shrapnel which had been somewhat spent hit the top of the glasses putting several gouges in them.

Had the glasses been lowered any further I would have been struck in the face. Luckily I received no more than several small bruises on my face.

More than luck would be necessary to retake Europe. St. Lo was proving a stubborn obstacle for the Allies, but by July 12 U.S. forces are within two miles of St. Lo, where Hill 192 is taken. Five days later in the fighting for St. Lo the German Desert Fox, Gen. Rommel, will be badly wounded near the town. By July 18, St. Lo is almost completely under U.S. control.

But then British General Montgomery makes a major error by calling up massive bombing attacks in an attempt to break out of Normandy. Dust, smoke, and rubble coupled with only four usable bridges cause serious backup as the units try to move forward.

Though France was still largely under control of Petain's Vichy government, the US announced that same week that it would recognize Charles de Gaulle's government.

In addition to the Western Front, heavy fighting is taking place again in Italy, especially around the area of Cecina and Volterra. On July 12, Allied bombers hit the Po bridges.

It is vital for forces both in Italy and on the Western Front to make progress. The Allies hope to create a pincer movement from the south and the west to force the Germans back.

Meanwhile, some of Hitler's own people are growing disillusioned and on July 20, 1944, a bomb in a satchel explodes in a conference room where Hitler is attending a meeting. Through a quirk of fate, Hitler escapes with only minor injuries.

*In July, Gen. George Patton is assigned to command the 3rd Army in Europe. **Al Gerstan** of Garden Grove, California, was on his staff.*

THE PILOT BOAT was guiding the Queen Mary into Prestwick when Gen. Patton suddenly appeared before our small advance detachment of 3rd Army HQ personnel.

He addressed us in his uniquely shrill voice: "Gentlemen, welcome to the U.K. I'm George Patton, your new commander of the 3rd Army. Your baggage will be taken on a special train and we will meet in the club car where refreshments have been laid on.

"In the morning we will go to work at Peover Hall, our new headquarters, where you will wear many hats until the main body arrives.

"My presence and assignment here are secret, so don't talk or write about me. Thank you and good night."

We all stood silent for a moment, staring at each other, mouths agape, wondering what the future held.

I was already wearing a number of "hats." I was an infantry captain among generals and special staff officers and sergeants.

I was "troop commander" and at Peover Hall was acting HQ commandant and acting provost marshal for HQ. Eventually, three full colonels relieved me of these assignments, to my everlasting gratitude.

*On August 1, 1944, Patton's 3rd Army became operational. The Allies are beginning to make good progress through western Europe. By August 5, the Allies are on the outskirts of Brest, where **David Kitchen** of Poplar Bluff, Missouri, has an experience he's not likely to forget.*

I WAS A RIFLEMAN in the 2nd Infantry Division and we were approaching Brest, our platoon on an old dirt road that had been worn down by centuries of travel. German soldiers had set up a machine gun overlooking our positions but if we sat down on the roadside they couldn't see us.

Some of us were told to run down the road past an open space. I ran past it and sat down, out of sight of enemy troops.

Joe Kwaitoski, my best friend, followed me and sat down 3 feet away. If I had taken one more step I would have been the one killed by the antipersonnel mine that ended Joe's life.

The Germans in both Italy and western Europe had proved masters at booby trapping areas they abandoned. **Eugene Eising** *of Miami Beach, Florida, remembers one incident.*

I WAS ON DETACHED DUTY in Purple Heart Valley above the River Arno. Land mines were all over the place and we had to walk within the white ribbons that marked the cleared areas. As I was sleeping in my tent one night, a blast threw me up in the air and I landed on my back on the ground. I lay there for a while, then started to feel if my arms and legs were still attached or if I was bleeding. Everything seemed OK.

The next morning it was decided that a sheep or small animal had wandered into our area and set off a land mine the sappers had missed.

Mines and booby traps were not confined to just Italy. **William A. Hendrix** *of St. Joseph, Michigan, recalls an incident during a mine sweep.*

WAR CARRIES WITH IT its grim and serious side, but there was an occasion that, at the time, was humorous.

It happened as we were riding the tanks and stopping at a bridge until it was cleared and checked for mines. As our squad waited on the tank, a Kraut civilian wearing his green hat with a green feather was slowly and cautiously proceeding by our tank on a bicycle.

He had gone past about 50 feet or so when the tank commander pulled out his .45 and shot into the air. The Kraut actually leaned over on his bike and rolled onto the ground as if he had been shot.

At the time we had a pretty good laugh and I still have to chuckle when I think of it.

Turn around is fair play. **Gus Solomon** *of Bronx, New York, had a scare of his own one day.*

OUR SQUAD was on a road in France sweeping it for mines. Every man gets to be a point man. Point man is about 50 or 60 yards in front of the men. He is supposed to warn the men of any trouble. The road made a sharp turn so I lost sight of the men.

As I made that turn I saw the largest German tank coming down the road right at me. It scared the hell out of me. A GI stuck his head out of the turret and said, "Don't worry, we captured it."

In Europe, the cities of Vannes, Le Mans, Alencon, and Argentan all fall before the end of the month. By mid-August, Paris is almost entirely liberated and General Patch's 7th Army has landed in southern France between Toulon and Cannes and is pushing ahead. **Gene H. Fasig** *of Camp Hill, Pennsylvania, remembers the welcome.*

WORLD WAR II took a heavy toll on the 28th Infantry Division. As a Medic during its five campaigns, I witnessed much suffering and death.

My most vivid memory, however, has nothing to do with the din of battle. On August 29, 1944, the 28th was selected to make the victory march through the streets of Paris. Battle weary we marched onto the Champs Elysees and headed toward the Arc de Triomphe. Nothing prepared us for the sights and sounds of thousands of wildly cheering French people.

To this day, 45 years later, when I am alone and my mind wonders to things past, I still hear the band, see the crowds, and hear the marching feet. I get a lump in my throat and the memory makes me proud to have been a participant in so great an event, but prouder still to have been an American soldier.

Stubborn German resistance in the city of Paris, in spite of the fact that French freedom fighters had begun openly fighting even before the Allies entered the city, may be why **Robert W. Levy's** *unit was held up. Here's what the Las Vegas, Nevada, resident says about it.*

I N SEPTEMBER 1944, the 1465 Eng. Dep. Co. landed on Utah Beach amid the shattered remains of LSTs, barbed wire, general debris and the litter on the shore. We stayed just past the beach for several weeks before we were able to get to Paris' outskirts.

Yet, by late August, the Germans in northern France had been broken and were either retreating or surrendering. However, the Russians, fighting what's known as the Eastern Front, make a horrifying discovery. They have evidence that Germans have killed 1.5 million people at Majdanek prison camp. This is the first of many discoveries and may have served to intensify the fighting.

But now, supply problems of all sorts are beginning to plague the Allied advance. Not all the problems were caused by shortages, as **Burns R. Dickens** *of Mt. Pleasant, South Carolina, points out.*

W HILE WORKING communications in a pipe line company that pumped 85 octane and 100 octane at 600 barrels an hour we came upon a geyser of gasoline shooting 50 feet across the Red Ball highway.

While Foltz called stations to stop pumping and send an oil field truck Springer stopped traffic one way and I flagged down the convoy coming the other way. The first truck had a boy who had taken basic with me. He said they had 200 vehicles with medicine that had to go. Fearing flash fire and explosions I asked for 10 minutes to try to stop the leak.

Taking a wrench I waded 50 feet to the pipe line coupling and tightened it to a running leak but could not stop it. Telling the drivers to cut motors and coast until clear, they started rolling. The oil field truck arrived and took charge.

Nor were all the supply problems in Europe proper. **Wayne Childs** *of Edina, Minnesota, had supply problems created by human nature.*

I WAS SERVING as a Military Policeman in the dock and Harbor of US in Port of Spain Trinidad, British West Indies.

I was born and raised in Dickinson, North Dakota and our Heart and Queen Rivers seldom had enough water to float a rowboat, when suddenly the Army has me on a dock where Allied Ships of 7,500 tons to 21,000 tons anchored at our dock to unload.

Any ship over 21,000 tons had to anchor in the harbor and be unloaded by lighters, but our dock was able to handle 90% of the ships coming in. Every ship coming in flew a yellow quarantine flag. Trinidad had Army, Navy, Air Force, Coast Guard, and Marines so there was concern about any infectious disease. Only after the Medical Authorities had cleared the ship's personnel, could the yellow quarantine flag be lowered. Until the quarantine flag was lowered, only the captain of the ship could leave.

One day the captain and several of his crew came down the gang plank. I stopped them and reminded the captain that only he could come off the ship until the quarantine flag was lowered.

He said, "Don't pay any attention the that damn thing, it does not mean a thing."

I said OK, then pulled it down.

He said, "Oh, you can't do that, it is against the rules."

US armored forces are having supply problems. **Herbert R. Wolf** *of Lancaster, Pennsylvania, helped out.*

WHEN GENERAL PATTON'S TANKS were running out of fuel during his courageous dash through France, within hours truck after truck loaded with five gallon Gerry cans arrived on our base along with a C-130 fuel tanker.

Next thing we are loading 140 Gerry cans on the C-47's; tying them down with rope and taking off.

Talk about a "NO SMOKING" flight!

Our destination was a marked-off grass pasture; land, unload and leave. How General Patton was able to get the cans from the field is another story.

In spite of supply headaches, the 3rd Army crosses the Moselle River in early September. **Ohland F. Morton** *of Eufala, Oklahoma, became intimately familiar with the area.*

WE WERE CROSSING the Moselle River my first day of combat. We had to cross at night to set up a first line of defense. We held onto a one-inch rope, holding our rifles over our heads. The water was shoulder deep and swift. Moving to our hill, we dug in around 1 a.m. and about 4 a.m. the Germans came through our line and set up between us and the river in total darkness.

At daylight, we had to take back the river. We lost a few men. They lost several.

Then 90 of us rode the backs of 15 tanks and made about a four mile circle, surrounding large numbers of Germans and their equipment. We dismounted and cleaned out thickets and ravines of Germans.

We'd lived through our first day of combat. We dug in.

Edward Rychnovsky *of Neillsville, Wisconsin, was at the Moselle.*

WHEN F. CO. crossed the Moselle River, our orders were to reconnoiter some forts on the high ground 27-yards from the river.

We arrived at the forts about midday, drawing only sniper fire from our flanks. If the forts could talk, they could tell quite a story. In addition to their battles fought in the early part of the 18th century, this was also a World War I battlefield.

My lifelong dream would be fulfilled if time would give some recognition to the more than 500 Americans who fell there on the 8th, 9th and 10th of September 1944, in an attempt to establish a bridgehead across the Moselle River at Dornot. The awesome price they paid is realized and they have not been forgotten.

Another soldier at the Moselle was **Victor H. Nelson** *of Richland, Washington.*

I WAS IN A BILLETING PARTY and was crossing a pontoon bridge across the Moselle River just outside the city of Metz, when the Fort of Joan de Arc, which had been bypassed by the 95th Division, started firing on us.

A shell just missed my jeep and exploded in the water a scant 5 yards to my left. The lead vehicle stopped at the bank, so my driver and I had

Crossing the Moselle River, September 1944
(Photo provided by Edward Rychnovsky.)

to leave the jeep and run for cover. When the shelling stopped, my driver was so scared, I went back to get the jeep.

Later, in an early morning attack on Kaiser-Lautern, I was accompanying the Battalion Commander to locate a battalion CP. I approached a concrete pillbox and remarked to the colonel that this would make a good CP. To my chagrin, the door was still locked.

Later in the afternoon, five Germans were removed.

The Moselle means something a little different to each person who was there. **William A. Uricchio** *of Southwick, Massachusetts, has some very unusual memories of the area and times.*

W HILE SCOUTING for Co. G, the 94th Division, part of Patton's 3rd Army, we found ourselves trying to clean up the Moselle Saar River Triangle. A new 60 day wonder, took over our platoon and we advanced until we reached the banks of a small river.

It was cold and clogged with ice flows. Our new Lieutenant told us wade in and take up positions on the opposite bank. As we advanced, MAC (Bar-man) watched my tail and I watched his, if it wasn't for MAC I'd be dead, from looking down a rifle barrel the size of an "eighty-eight".

We captured a number of "Supermen." On one, I discovered a quart of Schnapps. We were told to dig in for the night. Well, needless to say, the next morning, I was the only GI with a 3-inch fox hole and a six-foot head.

Though advancing, **William G. Henderson** *of St. Peters, Missouri, and other GIs would soon learn they faced a tough, skilled opponent.*

I WAS in the 114th Infantry Div. 44 Co. F. It was 102 days after D-Day when we landed at Normandy and walked across France into Germany. We saw some fighting along the way, but nothing like what went on at the point where we finally dug in.

We dug our foxholes deep!

We were to take a farmhouse called the Brandellfuzerhoff. We had three companies, one to our right, the other to our left flank. Our group in the middle was to attack at 6 a.m. There was snow on the ground and more in the air.

In spite of all the air support and artillery, when we attacked we lost almost the whole company. We'd gone up against an SS Panzer tank. They counter-attacked, all in white suits, white tanks and there were land mines. We had no chance. The men were all blown to hell.

Myself and the first sergeant were all that were left.

That night, some men came back that had hidden in ditches and put their white long johns over the outside of their clothes.

The replacement GIs that flowed into Europe were still not blooded, and for many, their first true encounter with war was traumatic. **Kermit C. Hollen** *of Philippi, West Virginia, graphically describes his reactions.*

W HEN I RECEIVED my schooling in the '30s, we were taught that the United States was the greatest nation on earth. We still are.

I was a tank gunner in the 8th Armor Div. and trained for 18 months, so we became almost as brothers. When we entered combat in Europe, I will never forget the first time I saw one of our buddies lying dead upon the ground.

Though we are the greatest nation on earth, it was a shock when I first realized that we die, too. War has a terrible price. The Revolutionary War was the down payment. All the rest is the interest on the price of liberty and freedom.

*That first night of combat. No one ever forgets, including **Scottie Ooton** of Effingham, Illinois.*

M Y FIRST NIGHT in combat, I was scared. I was with the 84th Div. fighting in the Siegfried Line and shells were bursting all around. The sky was lit with tracer bullets bright enough to read a newspaper.

A "rat" got in my foxhole and scared me even more. Afraid of drawing enemy fire, I covered my hole and struck matches until I located and killed the . . . MOUSE!

When dawn came, silhouetted against the bleak November sky were several pillboxes. From behind them came the rumbling sound of the German '88s' and the nerve chilling sound of the screaming meemies. Exploding shells were digging huge craters near me and in the beet field were some of our infantrymen that paid the supreme price.

That first night was sheer hell.

*No matter what your job is, the first time it becomes obvious someone is shooting at you, your life changes. Just ask **Kenneth E. Fogle** of Frederick, Maryland.*

I WAS A LOADER in a tank crew. My baptism by fire took place as we were staring up German nostrils with small arms clicking off the tank and mortar exploding all around.

The tank was hell inside as we choked on our own firing smoke. I could not load fast enough and screamed at the tank commander to keep his pants on. Maybe this was insubordination to an officer, but not while fighting for our lives!

Finally, mission accomplished and back at the rendezvous, I was happy to enjoy some R&R in a pup tent and sleeping bag on pine branches laid atop the snow.

*Of course, those silly accidents that a person would ignore in normal life take on new perspective in combat. Just ask **Elmer W. Sass** of Nevada, Missouri.*

I WAS with the 121st Infantry, 8th Div. Co. F, while going through Germany, we stopped at a vacant house to rest my squad leader and I went down in the cellar. He laid down to rest and covered himself up with a blanket. I decided to clean my rifle, I took it all apart and laid the parts on the blanket.

Somebody yelled "the Germans are coming" and my buddy through back his blanket and my rifle parts flew all over the place. I never did find one pin that held the pieces together. I finally found an 8 penny nail, cut it the right length and it worked. The Germans retreated when our machine guns opened up.

Depending on the situation, darkness could be a friend or a foe. Perhaps in the case of **Elmer Bovee** *of Addison, New York, it was his ally.*

IT WAS ABOUT 2 AM, when one scared 19 year old captured a bunch of Germans in front of our C P., the 119th Infantry Regt.

My Sgt. Howard Benton had said, "Guard this post with your life."

It was pitch dark, I could barely see their outlines. When I halted them, I used my German, "Hailten!" They stopped so abruptly, the back ones banged into the ones in front.

Then after calling for the Corporal of the Guard, Sgt. Benton, etc. Nothing—so I concluded they should put up their hands. Again, in my best German, I called out "Handen zie Ruf."

At this they dropped whatever, guns, etc. They made one helleva racket, Bang, clang, thud.

The noise alerted someone—we collected their arms, put them in a field nearby in a pile. Then I left, since he said something like, "I'll take care of this now."

For a comrade of **James W. Gresham** *of Princeton, Kentucky, darkness was disaster.*

WE WERE IN FOXHOLES and Germans were shooting all around us, killing many. One guy in Co. C could never remember the password. He just said, "Surf's coming," and everyone in Co. C knew it was OK.

One night he entered another company's area and not knowing who he was, they shot and killed him.

George E. McDonough *of Brownsville, Pennsylvania, remembers a time when he simply made a decision that was accidentally correct.*

WE WERE PULLING BACK from Haganau because the Germans had broken through our lines. I was a truck driver with Service Co., 242nd Inf., 42nd Div. It was dark and I had loaded my truck with 375 cans of gasoline.

Cpt. Joe Shoemaker said, "Mac, I'll ride with you."

As we pulled out of the courtyard, there were some German tanks up the street. We crossed over where the railroad tracks used to be and found the road jammed with troops and vehicles.

I told Captain Joe that if I was going to die, I wanted to see where I was and turned on my headlights. Everyone else did the same thing and the German tanks turned tail and ran. The captain told me not to admit that I turned my lights on first because there would be no medal, but there might be a court martial.

*Youth, inexperience, artillery and darkness—these are the ingredients of terror. In addition, the draft had a tendency to place people—many of them green—somewhat indiscriminately. Perhaps that explains the dilemma **James Gray** of Hallandale, Florida, found himself in.*

I N MY CO. (Engineers), I was a "shortie". The rest were in the 6 foot range. Our Captain cruised the area in his jeep. Once he found a fallen tree about 45' long, came back to where we were, told the Sgt. it would be ideal for bridges building. We went out and shouldered the log—when it was shouldered, my fingers were holding "up" my end. Noticing this the Capt. told the Sgt., . . . "put that man back in the ditch, he's not up to the task."

*Circumstances sometimes dictate the outcome of actions that normally wouldn't be applied to inexperienced troops. Consider Lawrence, Kansas, resident **Vic ImMasche's** tale.*

O UR SQUAD of replacements was patrolling several miles along the Loire River when French Forces of the Interior smuggled a note to us stating that 400 Boche had pulled out the day before. The note invited us to cross the river, but the 12-section bridge had been blown and the only way across was by a French manned rowboat.

The three of us, Marty Kopit, Joe Jeff Davis and myself, all privates went across. Our arrival was met by spontaneous celebrations and we were deluged with cider, wine, cognac and champagne. Obviously every household had hidden a bottle away with the vow that it would be opened when the Americans came.

We were carried on their shoulders to the town square where the mayor insisted that the French women who had consorted with the Boche during the occupation be present. He made an impas-

Vic ImMasche is mobbed in Fontevrault, France, September 1942. (Photo provided by Vic ImMasche.)

sioned speech, pointing out these women had betrayed their homeland. Their heads were shaved and they were forced to witness the liberation.

None of the three of us were fluent in French, but we understood the crowd's reaction and cheers. Late that afternoon, we were rowed back across the Loire to rejoin our unit.

That's how three privates crossed the Loire River on September 1, 1944, and liberated the town of Fontevrault, France, without a shot being fired.

As the Allies advance, not only towns are liberated. **Frank J. Chybrzynski Jr.** *of Natrona Heights, Pennsylvania, shares his experience.*

S ERGEANT JOSEPH "PAPA" NIEMIC of Omaha, Nebraska and myself, a Sergeant Technician, were both in communications with HJQ Co. 2nd BN 343rd Regiment 86th Black Hawk Infantry Division. We were told to take a message to "F" Company by jeep. We had radio silence and our telephone lines were cut.

We left for Company F traveling only about two miles, when a man ran out in the middle of the road yelling, "Help Me" in Polish. He said there were Polish people held captive on top of the hill.

Papa Niemic and I debated but both of us were Polish, so we detoured and went to the top of the hill. There was a barracks with two jeeps, two trucks and about 5 motorcycles. I saw about four German guards, so I raised my M-1 Rifle and shot five rounds over their heads.

They got in a jeep and ran away, possibly believing we had a full company behind us. The people, old folks and kids, streamed out of the barracks kissing our hands and thanking us in Polish and telling us to go kill the Germans.

But we left in a hurry to deliver the message to Company F in our battalion. This took only about 10 minutes, but we kept this a secret from everyone but ourselves.

I just pray we did no harm to Company F or to the war effort.

As the Americans advanced, many POW camps were liberated. **James R. Upham** *of Grand Blanc, Michigan, had an odd experience at one.*

M Y UNIT was in the Rhur Packet when I came upon a prisoner of war camp. Though orders were to by pass there camps, I could only think of how they must want to be a found.

With six other men following, we ran across the field thinking machine-guns could be set up in a cross fire. Getting to the gate the prisoners had overpowered their guards and were breaking open the gate.

The first one was in the air force. After hugging me, he asked me if I had anything to eat. I had a K-ration Bar. He went on to say he was glad we had found him for he was afraid they would shoot him for bombing their cities. I smiled to myself for being in the infantry. What did he think they had fun trying to do to me.

Every war has had its casualties as a result of friendly fire. Luckily for **Al Turno** *of Inverness, Florida, he and an unknown comrade managed to avoid what could have been a deadly situation.*

I WAS A LINEMAN with "B" Battery, 156 Fld. Art. Bn., 44th Inf. Div. One night I was in the observation post when we got word our telephone line was out. I went out to find the trouble, thinking the wire was broken somewhere between the observation post and the infantry switchboard.

I picked up the wire and started following it, at the same time feeling for any break. I didn't know at the time that another lineman had been sent out from the switchboard end. We were walking toward each other in pitch darkness.

When I was about 20 feet away from the other lineman, I felt a tug on the wire. I laid low and waited for the next move. Finally he challenged me and asked for the password. I was so scared I couldn't think of it.

Luckily we started to talk and discovered we were both from New York and asked each other questions that only a New Yorker could answer.

We met, shook hands and never saw each other again.

Communications was vital to the war effort. Often, creating communication links was a risky business, according to **Joseph E. Dunbar** *of Midland, Michigan.*

ONE DAY I and my associates were sent to the front line companies in Alsace Lorraine to emplace a switchboard in a dugout for further use as a regimental headquarters switchboard as we advanced.

We had dug the hole for the dugout and discovered a railroad about 200 yards away. Walking over to the tracks we found enough ties to cover our dugout.

That night the Germans laid down a rocket barrage upon us, as we were hand-laying a telephone line. As the rocket launchers fired, we could see the silhouettes of the German soldiers from their muzzle blasts. They had been on the other side of the tracks that previous afternoon and could have done us in as we gathered ties for our dugout roof.

The men and women in World War II literally witnessed history. As fighting intensified, **Adam S. Mickiewicz** *of Meriden, Connecticut, saw history twice. Once in person, and then in the paper.*

I WAS with the 258th Field Artillery Service Battery in September 1944 and we had just moved from Heerlin, Holland into a little town called Schaesburg. My job was to pick up supplies for the battalion.

I was alone this day, driving back from the supply dump in Maastricht. As I left Heerlin, I was about halfway down a stretch of road about a quarter of a mile long offering no cover when I heard our antiaircraft guns open up to my left.

I got to an embankment on my left and pulled over for cover.

A German Me-109 came over the hill, blazing from nose to tail. I could see the pilot sitting at the controls in what was just the frame of the aircraft as he went over me. I managed to get a photo of him before he crashed on the other side of the highway. I turned the film over to be developed by the signal corps, but never got it back. Weeks later, I saw my picture in "Stars and Stripes."

Unfortunately, enemy aircraft weren't always crippled and doomed, as **George E. Simpson** *of San Angelo, Texas, points out.*

L OW FLYING PLANES appeared overhead. Another armorer said, "It's just some Limeys giving us a buzz job." But Limeys don't fly this far south or in the daytime.

I spotted three of them coming toward me, their cannons winking. Missiles exploded right and left of me. I yelled, "Limeys, hell, those are 190's."

I ran into the narrow room with double brick walls and dropped to the floor without my helmet. I looked up and it was on a hook about six feet above me. I decided not to reach for it, then began wondering what end I'd cover if I had it.

Sometimes troops found their progress suddenly halted, as was the case with **Joseph E. Kapec** *of Spring Hill, Florida.*

A S AN ARMORED INFANTRYMAN of the 3rd Armored Div. we entered the attack in various ways, depending on our task force commander. During our armored thrusts in France we would often ride the tanks squad per tank. When we penetrated into Germany we didn't use that tactic, until the order was received. Off we went.

Our armored thrust went full speed ahead then we hit a German defense line, they were dug in and as each tank approached them, they traversed and fired their machine guns, we were the last tank and when the tank turret traversed some of our squad fell off and were captured. I held on, lost my helmet and I could hear the Germans shouting at each other.

Those few moments are etched in my memory forever.

Marvin C. Drum *of Jackson, Missouri, talks somewhat matter-of-factly about making the best of a bad situation.*

O N OCTOBER 29, 1944, I was in Asten, Holland when my tank destroyer was hit five times by enemy fire and burst into flames. Though dazed, I was able to crawl about 1,000 yards to join another crew from my battalion, but not before we destroyed two German tiger tanks and damaged another.

Within two months, I had my second tank destroyed. I didn't know winters could be so cold and bloody. The only thing that kept my feet from freezing was heating my socks over the vent on the motor and changing them as often as I could.

Remember that many of these GIs were very young. To some, the war was an adventure. **Sherrill W. Hayes** *of Nashville, Tennessee, had to deal with that attitude a bit.*

M Y PLATOON and I had to abandon a blazing house that had been set on fire by a German tank firing onto its roof. It was nighttime and the blaze began to light up the whole area.

I immediately started pulling off my field pack and getting rid of any extra weight, and instructed everybody to do the same. We jumped from a second story window on the dark side of the house and cross through some thick hedges into another house.

The German counterattack stopped suddenly, the tank turned away and when daylight came, we found the enemy had abandoned the village.

The platoon was sort of "put out" with me because we lost all our German "loot" when we left the burning house. I informed them they still had their lives.

The Germans had created a formidable line of "dragon's teeth," the Siegfried Line. It was supposedly an impenetrable wall of fire. In October 1944, the Allies broached it and **Charlie W. Mills** *of Louisville, Kentucky, was there.*

M Y UNIT, the Co. B of the 172nd Engineer Combat Bn. was in a holding pattern on a line from Horbach through Achen, Germany in October 1944. From reconnaissance reports, we knew we were near the Siegfried Line and several of us wanted to see it.

We went up on a ridge called Snow Woods overlooking Vaals, Holland. There appeared before us what looked like a line of dragon's teeth. We were really frightened at the sight of this monster. Our battalion commander, Lt. Col. Black, was booby trapped at this location and did not recover.

The Siegfried Line proved to be a dragon that had to be destroyed at all cost.

Chapter 23

Air War

The skies over Europe were definitely not safe and in 1942, the Axis had a very definite air superiority. When US forces entered the fray, American pilots and crews were totally inexperienced and Allied Command decided to limit their activities somewhat until they had accumulated some combat flying time.

The first missions in Europe were flown over airfield targets in Holland on July 4, 1942, and the first American-only bombing flights were against Rouen on August 17. In that raid, 1,547 sorties were made at a loss of 32 aircraft.

By December, still somewhat green, US bombers made the first attacks in Italy against Naples and heavy raids took place later in the month against Tunis and Bizerta in North Africa.

*Life in the sky had its own hazards, and not all came from the enemy, says **Glenn A. Profitt** of Punta Gorda, Florida.*

OUR BOMB RUN in our B-17, Superstitious Aloysius, was over. We'd flown through heavy Nazi flak after the German fighters had worked us over, leaving one engine feathered. Worse, the last of our 12 demolition bombs was hung by one lug. We were over northern Italy when the 500 lb. bomb failed to release, though the arming wire had been pulled from the nose fuse. We were still at high altitude and on oxygen in 20-degree below zero air.

As bombardier, I had to remove the fuse and free the bomb before we could land our crippled Flying Fortress. If I touched the detonation pin, the bomb would blow us all to Kingdom Come.

The bomb bay was too cramped to wear a parachute. The portable oxygen tank hampered my movements, but with the help of two crew members, I was able to remove the armed fuse, free the hung bomb and save the warplane and crew.

By the end of 1942, US pilots were confident they could fly against any and all targets unescorted. The over-confidence was reinforced in the first raid over Germany against Wilhelmshaven on January 27 when only three aircraft are shot down while the Germans lose 22.

However, US planes attack the aircraft factories at Bremen with 117 B-17s on April 17 and lose 16 aircraft.

From July 24 to August 2, 1943, grim history is made when RAF and US aircraft bomb Hamburg so heavily a firestorm is created. Some 50,000 civilians die and another 800,000 are left homeless.

Life—and death—in the sky was measured by missions, and the magic number was set at 30 in June 1942. It would later rise to 50. Just the simple act of crewing a bomber aircraft is hazardous as **K.W. Vanda** *of Endicott, New York, vividly describes.*

FRIGID AIR BLASTED through the open hatches of the B-17. The frost covered machine gun refused to complete its charging cycle and the hot spots in my heated suit indicated it was shorting out. Icicles hung from my oxygen mask and only manual crunching kept the vents open.

At 28,000 feet, the German sky was festooned with ugly black bursts of flak. With a loud grunt, the bomber would lift suddenly, indicating a near miss.

A severed wing from a B-17 came twisting by, engulfed in flames, props still turning. As it continued its grotesque spiral downward, I eyed my parachute on the floor and mentally rehearsed shucking off my flak vest, retrieving the chute and making a fast exit.

What in the world was I doing here?

The following comes from the diary that **John W. Butler** *of Oxford, Massachusetts, kept during the war. He was in the 389th Bomb Group and finished up in the 93rd Bombardment Group, 328th Squadron.*

COMBAT IS PRETTY GOOD, if you make it back, especially the money. But the raids are very tiresome as the oxygen and the cold temperature really tire you out.

A lot of my good friends have gone down. At first it bothers you, but now I don't mind it so much. To think I used to be afraid of the dark and wouldn't even ride a roller-coaster. But I can say truthfully that I'd rather face fighters than flak. You can shoot back at the fighters, but flak you have to just ride through it and hope for the best.

Another I sweat out is my heated suit.

This damn war is getting tough. You have to beg to go on a mission. Our pilot took another crew into Sweden, so we are just spares now and hoping to stay together. The fellows are fighting over the cap I leave behind when I go on a raid. When you don't make it back they divide up anything they wouldn't send home to your next of kin.

Target: Foggia (Italy)
Mission place: Banghazi, Libya
Pilot: T.W. Atkinson
Ship: U-Bar
Bomb load: 9-500 lb.

Position: Top turret

Date: August 1, 1943

Took off at 9:15 a.m. to bomb the marshaling yards.—little flak and no fighters. It was nice and warm in the top turret. Our first mission. Felt kind of funny and I was kind of tired as it was a long run. All the guys were happy at getting their first mission. They gave us a shot of whisky when we landed back at our base.

Mission two: (Same target)

Took of at 10:05 a.m. and bombed the supply depot. Landed at our base at 19:35. Flak was pretty good and those flak gunners were really on ball. I saw five fighters but they didn't attack. The planes behind us caught hell. Red Carey, our right waiste gunner, opened his chute by mistake while leaning out his waist window. He hit his trigger and shot some rounds into our tail plane.

Third mission:

Base Hardwick, England

Took off at 3:30 p.m. and headed into France. We ran into quite a lot of flak and it was pretty damn good. We hit our target which was an airfield, and we really were on the beam.

On the way back it was pretty dark and some fool started firing at a flak burst. Then someone mistook a B-24 for a bandit and set his number-two engine on fire, then they all started to fire at the poor devil. Four chutes got out.

I really sweated it out as tracers were going all over hell. It was also the first night landing in the ETO landed back at our base at 9:15 p.m. There was an air raid taking place when we arrived and the sky was really lit up with search lights. There was an FW-190 that followed us back but they didn't bother us.

Mission four: September 24, 1943

Base: Tunis, Tunisia

Target: Pisa, Italy

Bomb load: 16-250 lb..

Took of at 10:25. There was no flak or fighters. It was really a milk run. The day was nice and warm and we knocked hell out of our target. It was also Tommy Atkinson last mission with his crew. He flew the next mission with T.U. Collins crew and was forced down in Sweden.

Mission Five: November 3, 1943

Base: Hardwick, England

Target: Wilhelmshaven, Germany

Took of at 10:15 a.m. to bomb the docks and submarine pens. There was 600 planes on this raid. It was the biggest U.S. day raid on Germany. We had P-47s as escorts. Boy, did they look good!

Before we came to the target we had to feather number four engine on account of a oil leak. Four FW-190 attacked our formation and the right waiste gunner fired some rounds.

They then barrel rolled right through our formation.

Saw a B-17 go into a spin and explode. No chutes.

We had to fall back, so our sister ship fell back with us to help us in case of a fighter attack. Flak was pretty good and there was plenty of it. They had our range but not our deflection.

It was minus 40-degrees and pretty damn cold. The weather was very clear.

The fighters looked very pretty as they left their vapor trails in the sky.

I received the air medal, so I am pretty happy over it. as I certainly sweated it out long enough. Combat wouldn't be too bad if you could get a mission a week. That way you get in the habit and it would be just routine.

Mission six:

Target: Muenster, Germany

Bomb load: 10 incendiary cluster of 500 lb..

Took of at 10:40 a.m. to bomb a very important target and the Jerries did their damnedest to keep us from hitting it. Visibility was good and the weather was 37 below.

We had P-47 and P-38 for escorts, and they sure did their job well. Our job was to burn the town and transportation system.

We ran into heavy flak three or four places along the way and there was plenty of it. Our supercharger on number three engine stopped so we had to drop back.

Three Me109s came up and Haggerty, the right waiste gunner, fired a short burst at them. They threw their bellies up and dove. Than an Me110 came in at 9 o'clock and I gave him a short burst.

He lobbed a rocket into the formation ahead of us, so I gave him another burst of about 20 rounds and he started to smoke. He peeled off and came in at 7 o'clock where I got in another short burst. A P-38 jumped his tail and he had started down when I lost sight of them.

Mission seven: December 1, 1943

Target: Solingen, Germany

Took off at 8:30 a.m. to bomb an important target in the Ruhr district, which we call happy valley because of the heavy flak there.

The weather was minus 37 and I really froze.

We had to fly 15 minutes into France before we picked up the escorts. We had P-47s, P-38s and M-9 Spitfires. I was very glad to see them because we were then attacked by Jerry and he really pressed his attack. It lasted at least for 45 minutes and I really sweated it out! There was also plenty of flak.

We were supposed to drop our bombs on a flare, but they couldn't see the target, so we had to go around to the secondary target. Plenty of flak there, too, but it was 10/10 cloud cover so it was inaccurate on our formation.

Ship on our wing had his wing shot off.

Carey, our right gunner, shot a JU88 down. Four Me109s, of the famous Yellow Nose Squadron, came diving down so close you could see their chute harnesses. Carey fired at them but no luck. I fired over 90 rounds at a Me110 and a Me109 and a JU88 but I really didn't have a good shot at them.

I saw one bandit attack a B-24 and it was in trouble. Three chutes came out. Then five more bandits came down and they shot off the left wing off another bomber. It went into a spin and burst into flames.

One plane was Iron Ass, from our squadron, and the other was Southwind from the 328th Sqdr. Harry Byermen was on Iron Ass. Jerry really tried his damnedest, but our fighters were too good. It was our pilot, T.U. Collins, 25th mission. He was very happy.

Mission eight: December 5, 1943

Target: Cognac, France

Took off this morning at 7:50 to bomb an airfield in France.

It was quite a long way to the target area, which we reached with no mishaps. We were escorted by P-47s and P-38s. The weather over the target was 10/10 cloud cover, so we couldn't drop our bombs. You are not allow to drop your bombs just anyplace over occupied territory, except of course over a direct military target, as we want to do as little damage as possible to the French people.

I had just called the navigator over the interphone and said that it would be nice if we could run into some flak so we could get credit for a mission, when all of a sudden I had all the flak I wanted.

A ship in the 389th received a direct hit. He blew into a million pieces. The whole wing came off in one piece and it dropped by itself turning lazy circles. It was all on fire and it reminded me of a cartwheel from the Fourth of July. Two chutes got out.

Temperature was minus 30.

Ninth mission: December 11, 1943

Position: Tail turret

Target: Emden, Germany

Took off this morning at 8:30 to bomb the city of Emden, which is a pretty important shipping center. It was 39 degrees below zero. My heated suit worked very good back in the tail. Being a tail gunner is nice as you have armor around you and all the bad stuff has gone by.

We ran into a lot of flak at the target and it was pretty accurate. I heard a loud noise in the tail and got out of the turret to see where we were hit. The flak put a large hole in the vertical stabilizer.

Then some bandits came in at six o'clock and in my hurry to get back in the turret, I pulled my heat connection off on my right boot, so my gloves and boots were not working. I checked all my circuits and even my fuses. I was beginning to become real cold when I happened to check my right boot and put the plug back in.

A JU88 came in on the tail, but he was gone before I could get a shot off. I fired around 30 rounds at one Me109, but no results.

Flak hit us in the waiste. The tunnel gunner had just passed out from lack of oxygen. He fell forward on top of the camera hatch and the flak came through the side of the plane and pass the spot he had been, the lucky stiff.

The Red Cross had hot cocoa waiting for us. It sure tasted good.

Harry Fargo, flying tail gunner on N-for-Nan, froze his hands and feet and they had to land at another field so they could carry him to a hospital. Q-for-Queenie made a crash landing on our home base but no one was hurt.

My guns worked OK.

Mission 10: December 16, 1943

Target: Bremen, Germany

Took off at 8:40 a.m. to bomb the city of Bremen. It was a very important target, as the world's biggest submarines are built their.

The flak over the target was very good and Jerry wasted a lot of money trying to shoot us down.

My right glove burned out, so I had to get out of the turret to get a new pair. Just as I was getting back in, I heard our right gunner firing, so I started firing at some yellow noses (Me109s). I counted seven and fired about 100, but couldn't see any hits.

Jerry would attack in pairs on a diving approach from five to seven o'clock.

Lt. Russ flew our plane today on his first mission and had the hell shot out of it. Two of his gunners went to the hospital, plus he had to land at another field. I also received my first oak leave cluster to my air medal.

Mission 11: December 22, 1943

Target: Osnabruck, Germany

Took off at 11:15 a.m. to bomb the marshaling yards. The weather was very cold and I really felt it. It was minus 41 and we were at 25,000 feet. We lost one supercharger as we crossed the enemy coast. We had P-38s and P-47 for escorts.

Only saw a few bursts of flak, but the enemy fighters pressed their attacks. There were a few planes lost, plus quite a few shot up.

Some Me110 fired rockets into the formation behind us. One of the rockets hit one of our planes and put a large hole in the vertical stabilizer.

Also a B-24 had about 10 feet of his wing shot off, by fighters. She went into a spin, pulled out of it, then into a steep dive. There was no chutes.

A B-24 was hit by fighters, went into a inside loop and started down in a dive. She broke into three pieces when she exploded. No chutes.

I fired around 80 rounds at a Me-109 painted silver. No results.

Mission 12: December 24, 1943

Target: Hesdin, France

Took off at 11:40 a.m. to bomb some rocket gun emplacement. We flew at 12,000 feet, the day was very clear and visibility was very good. It really was a nice raid as we didn't have any flak or fighters.

We had P-47s and P-51s for escorts, but we didn't need them at all.

Mission 13: December 30, 1943

Target: Ludwigshaven, Germany

Took of at 8:40 a.m. to bomb the city of Ludwigshaven. The weather was nice and clear and the visibility was very good. The temperature was only minus 36.

When we came in over the French coast, the navigator noticed smoke up in the nose, but we didn't pay any attention to it. We were then at 22,000 feet.

The smoke started to come back into the waiste and we had the engineer going crazy trying to find the base of the fire. It gives you a funny feeling to know you have a fire on board but can't find it. I thought I would spend the new year in France!

We were 110 miles inside enemy territory when we had to abort. A lone plane is really a nice target for the Jerry pilots. They love to meet up with you as you make an easy victim.

As we turned around we met up with a B-17 that was aborting, too, so we flew formation back with them. When we crossed the coast of France we ran into some flak. Two bandits followed us for a way, but they didn't attack.

Mission 14: January 4, 1944

Target: Kiel, Germany

Took off at 8:50 a.m. to bomb the city of Kiel. Kiel had a 180 (anti-aircraft gun placement) around the city. They remind you of a neon sign. They go off four at a time.

The temperature was minus 47 and the slipstream was cold as hell. My oxygen mask kept freezing up.

The vapor trails are very pretty, but they help the Germans spot our formation. I'll bet Jerry was really upset as he used a lot of ammunition trying to bring us down. Three planes behind us were knocked down.

We lost a supercharger over the target, so we were tail-end-charlie again. As we had to dropped back, we had P-38s and P-51s for escorts. The Mustangs are very good fighters. It was good to see them around.

We were hit in the vertical stabilizer.

Mission: 15: January 9, 1944

Target: Ludwigshaven

Took off at 8:40 a.m. to bomb ice chemical works. It is like DuPont in the United States. The temperature was minus 37.

We ran into flak quite a number of times. Around the target area it was really hot. We had P-51s and P-47s for escorts and they sure look good. The clouds were very thick and you couldn't see the ground. When we were about 200 miles in from the French coast, the cloud cover was gone and we could see the ground very clearly.

We passed over quite a few big cities. Every once in a while, some German flak gunners would send up a few bursts to let us know they still had ammunition. We were now without fighter cover. As we passed over two German airdromes, you could see the German fighters taking off in pairs from the fields. We were in for a very hot welcome.

These fighters were very good. They were called the Abbyville Kids and they shot down seven B-24s from our group. They shot down both planes that were flying on our wing. They really are very hot pilots and they don't scare very easy!

I noticed four Me109s at about 1,200 yards at seven o'clock. I had my guns set on them to see what they would do. They were just milling around when one peeled off and came into attack. I held my fire until he was about 500 yards, then I opened up. I fired about 70 rounds. He was then into about 200 hundred yards and started to burn. He peeled off toward eight o-clock. As he threw his belly up, I let loose about 30 rounds, he bailed out and the plane started down and then it exploded.

My right waist gunner shot down a FW 190 and the pilot bailed as the plane exploded.

I received my second oak leaf cluster to the air medal. I was also credited with one plane destroyed, so I received another oak leaf cluster.

Mission 16: January 11, 1944

Target: Brunswick, Germany

Took off at 9:10 a.m. to bomb the aircraft works. As we crossed the Dutch coast we ran into quite a heavy concentration of flak. The mission was scrubbed due to bad weather ahead, but we received credit for a mission as we ran into some flak.

Temperature was minus 37 degrees.

Mission 17: January 21,1944

Target: Bois Carre, France

Took off at 12:10 p.m. to bomb rocket guns installation on the French coast. The weather over the target was cloudy so we couldn't bomb, so we just cruised around to see if would clear.

We came over Abbeyville and they threw up a quite a lot of flak, but it was way below us, so it didn't bother us.

One plane received a direct hit. There was nothing left of it. Those German flak gunners are getting pretty good. They were also shooting rockets up at us from the ground. They left quite a smoke trail behind them. Some planes were knocked down by fighters, so the mission didn't turn out to be a milk run, as all the kids thought it would be.

Mission 18: January 29, 1944

Target: Frankfurt, Germany

Took off at 8:30 a.m. to bomb the industrial city. We hit flak two or three times on the way to the target. Over the target the flak was really heavy. We bombed through 10-10 clouds.

We had P-36s, P-47s and Spitfires for escorts. I saw a P-38 shoot down a FW190. The FW190 started a dive with the P-38 right on his tail.

Flames started out of his plane as he exited. I also saw a P-38 shot down and a German fighter pilot floating down in his parachute.

Twenty-nine planes were missing.

Mission 19:

Took off at 9:13 a.m. to bomb some factories. There was quite a lot of flak on the way to the target, but over the target the flak wasn't too bad. We had P-38s, P-51s, P-47s and Spitfires, only saw one enemy fighter that made a pass at a B-17. Some P-47s showed up and the German ran for home. The last time we hit this target we lost 58 planes.

Mission 20: January 31, 1944

Target: Siracourt, France

Took off at 11:55 a.m. to bomb construction works in France. It was a very nice day and we could see our target real good. There was no flak or fighters, plus we had good fighter protection, so it was a milk run as a whole. One plane was lost through mechanical failure.

Mission 21: February 4, 1944

Target: Frankfurt, Germany

Took off at 9:15 a.m. to bomb the city of Frankfurt. At 21,000 feet, the temperature was minus 44, which is very cold.

Before we passed the enemy coast my heated boots went out, so I went up on the flight deck and borrowed the radioman's, since on the flight deck they have heat. I then went back to my waiste gun position.

We ran into heavy flak twice on the way to the target. Over the target it was pretty damn good. You should have seen Carey and I throwing the tin foil out. It is suppose the spoil the German radar equipment.

We dropped our bombs and started for home. My heated suit went out for good. I had the ball-turret gunner come back in the waiste to take my place and I then went up on the flight deck to try and keep warm. Our bombardier lost his oxygen supply so he came up on the flight deck also. My feet were frozen.

The radio man had fired a red flare as we came into land and the meat wagon follow us down the runway. We stopped, they took us off and we all went to the hospital. There was around 20 fellows in the hospital with frostbite.

This was the worst mission I was on to have so many things go wrong.

Mission 22: February 5, 1944

The CO called me at 6.30 a.m. to fly as a spare gunner. By the time I made briefing room and out to the plane, it was near takeoff time. I didn't have any breakfast because everything was in a hurry.

They had a oxygen leak in the tail turret. So they had to replace the regular system. We then had to take off 20 minutes late we then headed for the rally point, where we were finally able to pick up our own group.

The weather was nice and clear as we were only at 16,000 feet, so you could see the target pretty good. Temperature was only minus 13. My heated suit worked real good.

We had good fighter protection with P-38s and P-47s. I saw one P-38 go down in flames but the pilot hit the silk. The plane broke in two and I watch it hit the ground. We came to the primary target some ships dropped their bombs there. We went on to the secondary, where we dropped ours.

I could see quite a few fires burning.

A B-24 from the 509th Sqdr. was shot down by fighters. Four chutes got out. We received a large hole from flak.

It was good mission as a whole.

Mission 23: February 8, 1944

Target: Siracourt, France

Position: Nose turret

Took off at 7:15 a.m. to bomb a construction works. We flew at 15,000 feet. These construction works, we later learn were for the buzz bombs. The temperature was minus 30.

I didn't get in the turret until we were at 14,000 ft. You need help get into and out of the nose turret because they have to close the turret door behind you. When you want to get out, you have to call them on the interphone to let you out. Well, I threw my heated and heavy gloves up on the ammunition box, and then climbed into the turret. The navigator then closed the door for me.

The four little windows were open and the guns were elevated, so the wind was blowing in quite fast. It was very cold. I got my oxygen mask connected, then tried to close the windows, but my hands were frozen. I couldn't reach my gloves because my guns were elevated. The main line was off and it had to be turned on from the outside. I plugged in my heated suit, but I had no gloves on and my hands were beet red. I had no feeling in them.

I finally got my throat mike on yelled over the interphone to get me the hell out of this turret. The navigator opened the door and pulled me out. I went up to the flight deck for heat.

When my hands began to thaw out, I really suffered. We shot a red flare as we came in for a landing and the pilot called for a meat wagon, which met us at the end of the runway and took me to the hospital.

Mission 24: February 11, 1944

Target: Siracourt, France

Took off at 7:15 a.m. to bomb the construction works again. It was 14 below at 14,000 feet. We met quite a lot of flak at the target and those flak gunners were right on the beam. You could hear the flak bursting quite close.

Turner's plane received a direct hit that cut it in half. The tail gunner fell out his turret and hit the wing of the plane behind.

Mission 25: February 12, 1944

Target: Siracourt, France

Took off at 7:30 a.m. to bomb the construction works. It was minus 22.

Flak was pretty good but none was close to us. When I left the French coast behind, I was very happy as this was my last mission and I never wanted to see the French coast again except on a postcard or on a newsreel. It was a good mission to finish up on. I was a pretty happy guy when I landed.

Like Butler, **Weldon F. Phelps** *of Palm Harbor, Florida, faced problems both from the Luftwaffe, and from mechanical failures.*

O N JULY 29, 1943, we flew a bombing mission over Kiel, Germany's submarine base. Flying in formation with no escort at 18,000 feet, we scored a direct hit on our target. Immediately following "bombs away," our B-17 Flying Fortress was struck repeatedly by flak and enemy fighters descended on our formation from all directions.

We frantically returned fire from every gun placement, cursing and praying that this wouldn't be our last mission. Suddenly, I realized that I didn't have the strength enough to pull the trigger. My sight was blurred and I thought perhaps that I had been shot, causing me to black out, yet I felt no pain. I could vaguely see the attacking fighters but was unable to respond.

In the excitement of battle, my oxygen supply had become disconnected. A crew member alertly connected an emergency oxygen tank to my air supply, saving my life.

Later, on my 15th mission, I would be shot down over Germany and become a POW interred at Stalag XVII-B for 22 months.

Though neither Butler or Phelps specifically mention it, on October 14, 1943, the 8th Air Force bombed a ball bearing factory in Schweinfurt. Some 291 planes flew the mission and 60 were shot down. This, coupled with 88 planes lost the week before, led the Air Force to abandon the idea of unescorted bombing missions.

Like most GIs, flight crews maintained a grim sense of humor as they wracked up mission after mission. For instance, consider the words of **Gus Solomon** *of Bronx, New York.*

I WAS TOP TURRET GUNNER in the 386th Bomb Group when we bombed the Amsterdam Schipol airfield with B-26 Marauders on December 13, 1943. In all my missions, I had never seen antiaircraft fire so intense or accurate.

Our bombardiers hit their targets, putting Schipol out of action for months. Our bomb group lost one bomber over target, but battle damage to our planes kept us grounded nearly a week.

In spite of the damage, the rest of the group returned the 125 miles over the North Sea to England, thanks to the skill of our pilots and the sturdiness of the aircraft. There were crash landings and single-engine flights.

One pilot flying on a single engine was losing altitude. His waist gunner asked how long it would take to reach England. The pilot replied, "Twenty minutes by Marauder, two weeks by dinghy."

Michael J. Donahue *of Midland, Michigan, also found a moment for a chuckle in the midst of war.*

I T WAS AFTER A BOMBING MISSION when the interrogation officer failed to recognize the part I played in shooting the canopy off of a German fighter, but chewed me out good for releasing a trailing wire antenna over Germany.

I cut the antenna, because when I tried to reel it back into my radio compartment it became stuck and a 100 ft of wire with a 10 pound weight on its end trailed behind the bomber.

Even though we had just dropped three tons of bombs, my concern now was about the damage the weight might cause when it fell to earth. I visualized it crashing through the stained glass window in an ancient cathedral, blowing up a bomb dump, or better yet, discouraging and interrupting a German Field Marshal in his endeavors to seduce a beautiful young maiden.

Although there is no record in the files of the 8th Air Force that any of these events actually took place, I would like to take credit for putting that oversexed German Field Marshal out of his misery.

After all these years I often wonder where that leaded weight finally ended up. Then in the mid-80s when I watched President Reagan and the German Chancellor walk through the SS military cemetery in Bitburg, Germany, just for a second I thought I saw hanging in the background of the TV screen, a rusted old trailing wire antenna weight with a twisted length of tarnished copper wire hanging peacefully from a huge tree limb in the cemetery.

Even in the midst of combat, **Delmar H. Wangsvick** *of Key West, Florida, took the time to chuckle over what could have been a deadly situation. Of course, it was no longer funny when your own people are trying to bomb you.*

A TTACKING A RAILROAD YARD in Brunswick, my group made up for lost time by taking a shortcut. FW190 fighters were waiting for that and hit us head on.

I was in the nose turret of Group Lead and fired my .50-cal. machine guns as they approached.

Our pilot caught his thumb in his ripcord, the parachute billowed out and filled the cockpit. The other pilot laughed.

Once over target, the group above us, which had another target, dropped their bombs through us. Our bombardier was flying the airplane with the bombsight.

The pilot took control, wracking up the right wing, then the left, making us less vulnerable. We had been briefed to take no evasive action against flak or enemy fighters as we made our run, but these were friendly bombs!

Once past the friendlies, the bombardier was again given control with 45-seconds of the bomb run remaining. We "sacked" the railroad yard as scheduled.

The fighters returned once we were away from the target and my group lost seven B-24s that day. The 8th Air Force lost 27.

There is an unmistakable, almost fatalistic tone to the memoirs of airmen. Consider the eerie, sad tale offered by **Lewis J. Gould** *of St. Charles, Michigan.*

I WAS STUNNED as I listened to my best friend tell me he was not coming back as he readied for take off on his third mission.

Bob and I lived only two blocks apart in a small town, we were high school and college buddies. I met my wife-to-be at his birthday party.

We enlisted in the Army Air Corps at different times, he as a pilot, I as a weather officer. Fate would have it that we were assigned to the same 14th Fighter Group in Italy.

August 5, 1944, our colonel who was to lead the mission, asked me, after briefing, to take him to his plane. As I returned up the steel mat, I stopped at Bob's plane to wish him luck. He took off his fraternity ring, handed it to me and said, "Send it home, I will not be back."

We lost one plane that day to enemy fire, Bob is buried at Avignon, Southern France.

In spite of the danger and risks, thousands of bombers took off week after week to deliver their deadly cargo. **Vincent L. Fox** *of Sebring, Florida, tells of the one mission everyone had waited for.*

THE RAF and the RCAF had flown their Lancasters and Mosquitoes over "big B" in night time raids many times, but Herman Goehring had promised Hitler that the crazy Americans flying in broad daylight would never penetrate the ring of defenses surrounding Berlin.

On March 4, 1944, more than 750 Flying Fortresses and Liberators were dispatched to bomb Berlin, but because of the notoriously bad weather over the continent and a phantom coded radio recall, all but a composite group of 95th and 100th Bomb Group B-17s under the command of then-Maj. H. Griffin Mumford, returned to their bases or bombed alternate targets.

Mumford's group continued on, flying through heavy clouds and intensive flak, surviving an attack by a squadron of 20 Luftwaffe Me109s, they successfully deposited their bombs.

In spite of a mysterious recall radio transmission and bad weather, Mumford's group reached their target. **Phillip J. Kanarkowski** *of West Newton, Pennsylvania, offers some of the details.*

B Y JANUARY 1944, a thousand planes a day were being dispatched on daily missions. Every major objective had been struck but one: Berlin.

When Gen. Doolittle assumed command, the feared and dreaded Berlin was assigned, March 4, 1944. Dense fog and overcast extended to 25,000 feet. A disputed radio recall was broadcast and group after group returned to base, but Maj. Mumford who led our group, the 95th Bomb Group, assumed the recall was an enemy ruse and ordered us on to Berlin.

We encountered the heaviest flak ever and many fighters over the target. Our plane took a direct hit and the waist gunner was hurled out of the plane and killed.

This almost suicidal effort by 30 aircraft made a mockery of Goehring's boast that Berlin would never be attacked.

Maj. Mumford received a promotion and the Silver Star. The crews received the Presidential Citation for our efforts.

What was it like over the skies of Berlin? Here's how **Lawrence J. Vallo** *of Jemez Pueblo, New Mexico, describes it.*

W E COULD SEE great billows of black smoke rising over Berlin as the bomb groups ahead of us unloaded their bombs. The smoke was so thick it was about to obscure our target, but our bombardier could still see it in his sight.

At "bombs away!" we made a sharp turn to our right to avoid the heavy flak as best we could. As my crew and I watched, one of our B-17 Fortresses appeared out of the smoke, like an eerie rising Phoenix. She climbed straight up and seemed to hang there on her props for an eternity, then gracefully did an inside loop and disappeared back into the smoke from which she'd come.

Though we could not see her tail markings, it was our fervent prayer that her crew was able to leave their stricken ship.

Flak, artillery designed to be used against aircraft, was the terror of flight crews. **Robert J. Schuh** *of Chilton, Wisconsin, explains why.*

I SPENT a tension-filled day as a tail gunner on a B-17 over Brux, Czechoslovakia. Our crew had taken off early in the morning from Northumpstead, England, on a route around Berlin! I followed at least ten B-17s as they plunged to earth, victims of German fighters.

The flak over Brux—an oil refinery target—was very intense. The plane on our left, received a direct hit and plummeted down, trailing smoke. I knew we had suffered damage and I could not contact any member of our crew on the intercom. I thought about bailing out. After what seemed an eternity, the waist gunner crawled back to me and asked if I was hit.

We landed at our base, almost out of gas. An inspection showed that a piece of flak had severed all the communication wires back to the tail, leaving a very apprehensive tail gunner wondering about the future.

Sadly, there was no future for some. **Clem H. Holtcamp** *of Denver, Colorado, had a very grim job.*

I WAS A MEDIC assigned to the 8th Air Force in England as an aid man on an ambulance.

Our group was flying B-24's, and during the Invasion of France our planes received a great amount of flack and bullets from enemy guns, crippling and burning them. One flight came back very badly shot up, one plane crashed as it was making a landing, burning the crew and all.

We drove the ambulance to the wreck to recover the burned bodies, then headed for a small town for burial. On our way with the four crew members we heard a moan coming from the back. Upon checking out the sound we found one crew member had the flesh of one foot completely burned off.

He later died on the way to a hospital.

Nor was flak or fighters the only risk, as **June G. Davis** *of Shelbyville, Kentucky, explains.*

OUR FIRST COMBAT MISSION, June 14, 1944, turned into mortal danger when armed bombs failed to exit upon release. Homeward bound, far beyond "drop point", a waist gunner reported bombs remaining in our B-24's bomb bay. Armament specialists, the bombardier, Lt. Raymond Leonard, and I hurried into the bomb bay.

Four 250-pounders, arming vanes whirling, lay across the catwalk and a malfunctioning bomb door. Five hundred revolutions of these vanes "arm" the bomb for detonation—when sufficient pressure applied.

How ironic, bombs we brought to punish Nazis remained aboard, endangering us. Like cobra fangs, those shiny, spinning vanes, deadly if mishandled. Landing with live bombs prohibited everywhere.

Carefully, we stabilized and secured those arming vanes, unscrewing the fuses and dropping them through the partly open bomb door. Four jettisoned bombs followed them into the Adriatic 10,000 feet below. On schedule, the reprieved plane and crew returned to base.

As fighting intensified in Europe, the missions became more and more deadly. Some, as **Kenneth L. Baker** *of Walnut Creek, California, tells it, were more memorable than others.*

I 'LL NEVER FORGET the bombing mission of December 23, 1944. The Battle of the Bulge in Europe had started about six days before, but the weather had been so bad that our 391st bomb group had not been able to operate. On this day I was the pilot of one of the 30 B-26 bombers that our group sent to support our ground forces.

The Germans were waiting for us and although we accomplished our mission, 16 of our planes were shot down by fighters and anti-aircraft artillery. Of the 14 that came back, four crash-landed. Our plane was one of the other 10. We had holes in our plane but none of our crew was injured, thank God.

The 23rd of December is a three dimensional number on my calendar.

Robert R. Lopiano *of Rochester, New York, had a pretty good Christmas present in 1943.*

I T WAS MY 25TH and last mission as a B-17 tail gunner for the 8th Air Force, December 24, 1943. I can recall tougher missions—Bremen, Paris, Stuttgart—but my last mission was a milk run by comparison.

It was made more memorable because, in addition to surviving the 25 mission limit, it was Christmas Eve. I couldn't think of a better Christmas gift.

After the pilot parked the plane on the hardstand, the ground crew who serviced our plane rushed up to shake my hand and congratulate me. They sweated out every mission we went on. What a great feeling!

At times, arguments have arisen that men who fly in bombers see war in a light too sterile, because they fly above destruction. **Joe C. Kenney** *of Lander, Wyoming, apparently saw.*

I PARTICIPATED in the first shuttle bombing mission from Italy to Russia, where three troublesome targets were hit during our 10 day operation from Poltava, USSR commencing 2nd June, 1944.

In spite of the awesomely spectacular and terrible experiences every combat man is subjected to, my thoughts always return to the plight of the citizens of Poltava who had suffered horribly under Nazi occupation. The German retreat brought return of Soviet Government and continued privations of war, women subjected to extremely heavy manual labor, short on food supplies and their city pretty much in rubble.

Even so the citizens had completely restored their Town Square, lawns carefully tended, flowers blooming, the park neat and the children were kept clean.

The strength of character displayed by these impoverished people remains a vivid part of my experiences during my 50 mission tour with the 99th Bomb Group.

GIs have always been resourceful. **Walt Cooperider** *of Lompoc, California, tells of one instance.*

A UNIQUE PLAN was devised to lead the supply drop to the defenders of Bastogne. With all the planes grounded due to the fog, our commander, Lt. Col. Joel L. Couch, had a plan. If he could get off with one plane with pathfinder troops, the remaining supply planes could then track in via the beacons and drop regardless of the weather.

The planes lined up on either side of the strip and turned on their navigation lights and through the red and green haze, he got his plane airborne. When he arrived at the DZ, he raised from treetop level to an altitude where the troopers could jump. When notified that the beacons were operating, he radioed to send the armada. The sky cleared as the aircraft arrived but without this bold plan it may have been many hours before the armada may have started.

Paratroopers are trained in airborne technique. Flight crews are not. According to **Robin E. Taber** *of Fairfield, California, for flight crew, putting theory into practice takes a little work.*

GELSENKIRCHEN, GERMANY, and our 6th load of bombs behind us, our intercom not functioning, my Bombardier tapped me on the shoulder and pointed to the escape hatch. My duty as navigator was to open the hatch and dive out.

Opening went OK, but I forgot to dive and jumped into the open hatchway.

The slip stream plastered my legs against the skin of the ship. My head and arm caught on the front lip of the hatchway; my parachute pack caught on the rear lip. Looking at 32,000 feet of space I wondered what would happen next?

The lads behind me, wanting to use this escape hatch, juggled me loose and I fell free.

Unwilling to face unfriendly fire I did not open my 'chute for some 20,000 feet. The clouds below me obscured the church steeples as well as the locals, armed with farm tools waiting to capture me when I landed.

Another who had to bail out was **Michael T. Walsh** *of Phillipsburg, New Jersey.*

IT WAS MY 13TH MISSION out of a base in England flying as a crew member on a B-17 Flying Fortress (engineer) into Germany. We had completed the bomb run when we were hit by a heavy concentration of flak and set on fire; the pilot ordered bailout.

We exited the plane through the bombay. We had been trained to free fall until away from plane and I free fell until I began to spin and the parachute opened.

I floated down and landed in a sugar beet field; before I could get up a civilian policeman held a Lugar pistol in my face. He ordered me to strip, looking for weapons, I put my clothes back on and was marched out to a truck. I was transported along with others to a prison camp; Stalag Luft Four until May 1945.

That was the grim reality of war in the skies of Europe. Many paid the price with their lives. There was an active underground, and downed airmen often tried to make contact. Sometimes they were successful. Sometimes, as in the case of **Edward De Coste** *of Clearwater, Florida, their efforts were in vain.*

I WAS A MEMBER of the 36th Bomb Sqdr., 482nd Bomb Grp. (OSS) on March 2, 1944. We were over occupied France and too low to bail out. S/Sgt. Norman Gellerman, our flight engineer, was killed in the crash, but seven of us survived, though suffering from serious injuries.

Leiutenants Kendall and Shevlini and radio operator Ross exited the ship on the left, unbeknownst to the rest of us. Leiutenants McDonald and Kelley and Sgt. Gosswick and myself got out through the back turret, which had snapped off in the crash.

Seconds later, the plane blew up.

It took four days before we made contact with the underground. They tried to get us back to England by submarine, but all contacts were caught and shot by Germans. We were captured in the foothills of the Pyrenees while trying to make our way to Spain. I was in civilian clothes and treated as a spy.

I was POW # 2961 at Stalagluft IV Gross Tychow, Pomerania on the Baltic. From February 6, 1945, to May 2, 1945, I was on a forced Death March of about 700 miles—84 days of starvation and abuse by the Germans.

Life for POWs, no matter what theater, was not good. **Hobart A. Jarvis** *of Barbourville, Kentucky, would likely agree with that statement.*

O UR B-17 was shot down by an Me262 jet fighter, forcing me to make my first and only parachute jump. Never had I experienced the loneliness, anxiety, nor the eerie silence of empty skies during my descent into Nazi Germany.

There, my success in escaping a bloodthirsty civilian mob was not shared by the co-pilot who was murdered by civilians. Nor did our engineer who, so severely beaten, was robbed of his mental faculties.

The lot of we POWs was a starvation diet in lice and flea infested confinements. Mine ended while on a march into Czechoslovakia that met battling German and Soviet troops. Liberated by the Russian victors, we rejoined the Americans at Chemnitz after bicycling across the mountains.

The joyous and emotional conclusion to this memory came with sighting the Statue of Liberty and shores of home from the ship's railing.

Paul E. Keagle *of Pasadena, Maryland, managed something few other people have accomplished: He returned from the dead.*

I HAD REPORTED in at the squadron headquarters and was walking through the barracks area toward my quarters when I noticed that people were quickly stepping off the path to let me by. I am not that imposing or important and I realized that they had looks of disbelief or even shock on their faces. Arriving I found that my posessions were gone—divided up. We had been written off for dead!

World War II was winding down, but for three of our crew it had already ended at Wesel, Germany when we were delivering supplies to the airborne crossing of the Rhine. We went down in a ball of fire near German field headquarters. After a period of captivity and some hopping around, we survivors were delivered back to our base. It was the sort of experience that proves not only are there no atheists in foxholes, but also in bombers.

Many others went through what **Richard Radlinger** *of Park Falls, Wisconsin, experienced.*

I HAD FLOWN 50 missions, but 12 were turn-backs and didn't count. The turn-backs were most dangerous because you were in trouble, always alone, sometimes only minutes from the target.

We came in very low, making us vulnerable to small arms fire, which is what happened in Yugoslavia. We returned with over 100 holes in the aircraft, two engines out and four control cables shot away.

In September 1944, we drew a different mission when 2nd Bomb carried 1,250 POWs from Popesti airdrome in Rumania. It was a volunteer mission with skeleton crews, planked bombays, no bombs, no ammo for the guns and no credit for the mission. We did, however, enjoy some fine beer and rye bread from the peasants in the area.

The POWs came from the Plesti oil refineries and I considered it an honor to be part of it.

Then, on October 17, 1944, with 2nd Bomb leading, seemingly floating on the dark puffs of flak, there was convulsive explosions as our aircraft collided with another bomber over Blekheimer synthetic refinery. It cut us in half.

The tail section of our plane floated down with the gunner inside of it. The rest of the plane went straight down, burying itself three feet in the ground.

There were shouts as gunners helped the ball gunner to waist opening. Somehow I was pulled loose by my chute and my left leg was severed inches from the knee, as if by a saw. I was awake, dangling from the chute, bleeding profusely. My left hand and right eye were bleeding also.

I recall dense clouds, then a smoke screen, the pain deadening. Ground rushing up, hard jolt, guards stopping the bleeding, then calling Ruski. They thought I was Russian. Bombs exploded, flak batteries emitted projectiles with furious concussions.

I was the sole survivor.

The aircraft was above the clouds and when it plunged through after being cut in half, reports from other aircraft said no chutes, so no survivors were reported.

I was taken to eastern Europe, hospitalized, then transported to Du Lag Luft, Frankfurt West, interrogated, hospitalized. English POWs from a nearby camp working as orderlies in the hospital kept us posted on the bombing raids over the refinery as this was the last of Germany's oil supply.

My life was again spared on December 27 when area was misbombed during the Battle of the Bulge.

I was repatriated at the Swiss border and transported by railroad to the south of France, then to America to the family farm on the Swedish ship Gripsholm.

Chapter 24
Hazardous Duty

In Italy, 91st Division of US II Corps is in heavy fighting near Livergnano while 8th Army takes Lorenzo in mid-October of 1944. At the same time, US forces, still trying to breach the Seigfried Line, enter the city of Aachen where nasty street fighting takes place. German defenders in Aachen will not surrender until the end of the month after the city is entirely cut off.

Things are not going well internally with Germany. Hitler is becoming more paranoid and on October 14 Rommel, one of his most brilliant generals, is given the choice of suicide, with immunity for his wife and family, or a humiliating public trial.

Rommel chooses suicide and the Germans announce he has died of combat wounds.

Though heavy fighting continues in Aachen, US forces link up outside and cut the town off.

*Allied Command is painfully aware that forces must be able to move from Italy into France or the war will continue, but US advances in Italy are being bogged down by the onset of winter. Still, morale is good, as **Harry Fritz** of Philadelphia, Pennsylvania, seems to indicate.*

A FTER HAVING SPENT 4½ months in a Repple Depple in Italy, I was finally assigned to the 100th Chemical 4.2 Mortor Bn. We moved into the front lines on November 5.

I was a little scared and very frustrated because I was assigned to haul ammunition up to the guns instead of being assigned to a gun squad. I finally talked the sargeant into letting me fire just one round. He agreed and I picked up a round, kissed it and said, "This is from me personally, Krauts".

As I yelled "on the way", I immediately felt 10-feet tall and imagined I was glowing in the dark. I felt that I had become a part of history.

Since that November 5, 1944, I am able to recall, and relive that moment in living color at any time, day or night.

*Nor is Italy a safe place to be stationed. A GI by the name of **Nelson Brambier Fox Sr.** from Caryville, Florida, had a pretty bad week in a place where most people think of as a vacation paradise.*

W E WERE IN THE ALPS when I was wounded. When my buddy, "Hap" Hazzard, saw I was shot in the chest, shoulder, hand, heart and kidney, he ran for help, but hit a mine and had his foot blown off.

Four litter carriers arrived, loaded me on a carrier and started up the mountain. When they stopped to rest, they laid my stretcher on a mine and all four were killed. I was wounded in the foot.

I lay on the mountainside until sunrise, when I was carried to a tent. Unable to to talk or move for three days, the doctors said I was dying, but I lived and was moved in a gut-wrenching jeep ride to a hospital. There Maj. Gen. Robert J. Frederick, commanding general of the First Special Force, visited me.

He looked me over and said, "You just can't kill an old horse calvaryman."

Elements in both Europe and the Pacific faced problems with communications. According to **Edward A. Wojtowicz** *of South St. Paul, Minnesota, finding yourself behind enemy lines is a little unnerving.*

A S A MEDIC with Headquarters Company 752 Tank Battalion in Italy during the waning days of the War, two Civilians approached me, one badly wounded with his lower jaw and teeth missing. After first aid, together with our doctor and ambulance driver, we set out for the nearest hospital in Bolzano. We assumed it was under British control. Imagine our shock and surprise at finding it occupied by the 26th German Panzer Division.

Seeing a lady bless herself was scary especially when some German Soldiers brought their rifles to a firing position. The hospital staff thought we were British, hanging onto us for protection and indiscriminate shootings. We broke loose and decided to bluff our way back.

At high speed with our siren blaring we departed praying. Each of us carried side-arms which was illegal but smart at this time. Some days later we re-entered Bolzano on our way up the Brenner Pass.

Winter has set in heavily in Europe by late November. On Thanksgiving Day, 1944, **Allan Metzler** *of Oakhurst, New Jersey, is in a place called Hurtgen Forest.*

O N THANKSGIVING DAY, I was a wire communication man in the Hurtgen Forest with HQ Co., 1st Bn., 13th Inf., 8th Div. There was supposed to be a small pocket of Germans nearby which our battalion was to clean up. We were sent into the area in the morning and were supposed to be back in time for Thanksgiving dinner.

I was with two other men and we were to take a radio down to one of the companies that was seeing action. When we arrived, the company had been stopped by a minefield.

The company commander was trying to decide what to do when the Germans opened up with tree-burst artillery. Needless to say, the "pocket" of Germans was larger than anticipated. After dark, the three of us started to pull back to the battalion area. Of our group, I was the only one not hit.

Lloyd G. Huggins *of Petersburg, Virginia, was in command of Company E of the 60th Infantry in the Hurtgen Forest. Before he describes the actions that took place in those eight days, he explains the mechanics of a unit.*

WHEN YOU HEAR or read of accounts of casualties in infantry units, consider that a regiment officially consists of three rifle companies, which in combat can rarely field more than 100 men each. A weapons company may, perhaps, be able to field a few more.

At most, a battalion entered the Hurtgen with no more than 450 men. For two regiments, that means about 2,700 men went into battle.

After eight days of fighting, 160-percent had been replaced. With this kind of mortality rate, an infantryman very quickly came to terms with his own mortality. I doubt that any good soldier on the front line in WWII thought he would really come out alive.

What forces could motivate men to live like animals, fight continually for months on end, and the whole time strive to do their best? Even the survivors cannot answer that question.

I never felt a killing hate for the German soldier. Mostly I felt elation when we did well, and a grudging admiration when we were bested. Once locked in combat, all thoughts turned to concern for the unit and for one's comrades. That is why, even 50 years later, combat veterans feel such a special bond for those who shared life and death experiences.

I salute the survivors of World War II and combat veterans everywhere. Be proud. Only you can know what war is really like. No mere words can describe the horror, pain, abject fear, waste and ultimate futility of attempting to solve the problems of the world by means of war.

History records that two regiments of the 9th Infantry Div. lost 4,500 men carving out a 3,000 yard hole from the dark woods of the Hurtgen Forest—a cost of more than a man per yard.

I was commander of Co. E, 60th Infantry Regiment and I lived through the eight-day nightmare of crashing artillery, falling trees and the unbelievable curtain of bullets from an enemy we never saw. Amazingly, there was no other thought than we would try our best to move forward despite 20 to 30 casualties a day.

With the dawn of each new day, the men of Co. E would stumble from their holes and unhesitanttly move forward.

On the eighth day, the 60 men of Co. E were ordered to seize some pill boxes on a dominating ridge across a lateral road. As we attacked, we met the enemy in the middle of the road as he was attacking us. We fell back and fired from our holes as though the devil were pursuing us. And he was! Only this time we saw his face.

I remember exhorting the men to not shoot high, but the next day I had to eat my words. In the ditch on the far side of the road and on the ridge above were 190 dead Germans, stacked like cords of wood. I estimated we had decimated an enemy battalion.

At the time, I was elated, for we had received some measure of revenge for eight days of hell. Today I feel only sorrow for the waste of so many young lives on both sides.

I've never forgotten. It's been half a century, but writing of these brave men brings tears of pride. There were so many casualties and so many replacements, I never got a chance to tell each of them how much I admired them.

I will never forget the Hurtgen. Even today, the aroma of pine almost nauseates me.

*An argument could be made for Allied complacency. After all, except for the Seigfried Line, the Germans had been beaten back time and again. Most figured it was only a matter of time. Complacency from men in command almost cost **Gus Solomon** of Bronx, New York.*

W E WERE IN THE HURTGEN FOREST and our lieutenant and sergeant wanted our squad to remove a roadblock. They said, "WE went through it. There are no mines."

The roadblock consisted of one very large tree and a lot of small ones. We went to the large one first. As we lifted it, there was a loud explosion.

The blast ripped a hole in the tree about two feet long and a foot deep just opposite from where I was holding it.

The week before word had come down to not fasten the chin straps on our helmets; to just let them dangle. Had I had mine fastened, my head would be in Germany now because the blast blew my helmet about three feet into the air.

*Fate deals strange hands sometimes. The casualty rate in the Hurtgen Forest was horrendous, yet **Paul Treatman** of Brooklyn, New York, witnessed the horror and carnage and emerged unscathed.*

M Y SURVIVAL in the murderous Battle of Hurtgen Forest was nothing less than miraculous. I was a medic with the First Infantry Division, which had just captured Aachen but soon met fierce resistance in the rain-drenched woods.

German mortar and artillery shells often burst in trees, scattering shrapnel over wide areas and taking deadly tolls of GIs. Hurtgen Forest, soaked with chilling drizzle, cloaked for days in steamy mist, where no ray of sunshine pierced the canopies of densely topped majestic firs to dapple the forest floor, incised in my memory a wet inferno where trees and bodies broke in tandem and freshets of blood enriched the oozing muck.

I emerged from the forest without a scratch.

Other hazards existed in November 1944, as **Edgar L. Kuhlow** *of Sheboygan Falls, Wisconsin, discovered.*

A S A PRISONER OF WAR of the Germans in November 1944, I was one of a large group of prisoners being transported by train in a box car from Limberg, Germany to Stalag II B . . . Hammerstein, which is near Neustettein.

We were so crowded that we could not all sit down at the same time . . . some had to stand. We took turns. Those sitting were lined up toboggan style. This kind of cut the blood circulation to our feet. Many of us arrived at Hammerstein with frozen feet. I was one of these.

We were on this train for four days and four nights, with very little food and water. Our toilet was a ten-gallon open tin can, that always slopped over. Some got sick.

Everyone was irritated, so instead of fighting the Germans, we were fighting with each other.

Thanksgiving was not particularly cheery for anyone in Europe in 1944, according to **David Saltman** *of Wantagh, New York.*

I SPENT Thanksgiving Day at the Siegfried Line in Germany. After sweating out the mud and the mines and the K-Rations, the kitchen brought hot food to the front line troops. I gulped it all down, piping hot in my mess kit, standing up in a German pillbox.

Later, I was coming back from the coal mine showers with a truck full of men in Geilenkirchen. The whistle of a German shell on the descent heading for our truck was unmistakable. Thank God it was a dud.

The Battle of the Ardennes in December 1944 was our hottest action. I drove in a jeep to a prominent road intersection and a doughboy frantically shouted that the road was under enemy observation. I jumped out and yelled at the driver to drive down the opposite side fast, and a 75 mm tank shell followed immediately.

Stanley Grabowski *of Rutland, Vermont, had an odd Christmas present.*

D ECEMBER 25, 1944 . . . our division the 5th Armored, was guarding an ammo dump. Two Nazi planes, Stukas, were coming over our area at tree level.

One went to the right, the other came straight over our tent. We had our 50 calibar machine gun on an eye level tripod. I fired at the plane as it approached. When it passed by, I turned around and kept firing until the plane went down.

That was my Christmas present for 1944.

Oddly enough, **Edward Lund** *of Menomonie, Wisconsin remembers the deadly beauty of battle.*

I WAS A MEMBER of the 320th Combat Engineer's Battalion of the 95th Division attached to General George Patton's 3rd Army. In November of 1944, we were making our drive into the city of Saarlautern, Germany.

We were being bombarded with mortar and artillery shells by the Germans and were ordered to dig in as we promptly did. As our support tanks moved up with their turret guns blazing, in the distance we could see the bombs come tumbling down from our planes and then a huge explosion. It was like a big 4th of July celebration.

The G I's started getting out of their foxholes, some lighting up cigarettes, others just milling around. It was quite a thrill, like the war was over, but no such luck.

*No, it was far from over, in fact, and the officers of the unit of **Robert J. Baker** of Webb City, Missouri, would have done better to remember that fact.*

B ATTALION COMMANDER GOODING, had briefed his three rifle company commanders concerning the pending attack. Having concluded the briefing, the Company Commanders left the farm house Command Post. As they exited the front door a single shell wounded all three Company Commanders.

Colonel Gooding initiated a conference call to the next in command advising their company commanders had been wounded, that there wasn't time for another formal briefing and proceeded to give a hasty briefing by way of the field telephone. The Colonel asked, "Any questions?" to which the reply was, "None, Sir". At the appointed time the Battalion attacked and secured its objective.

This illustrated to me, very vividly, that in war or peace no one is indispensable. There is always someone available who can fill your shoes and do your job.

For this and subsequent action, the 3rd Battalion, 313th Infantry, 79th Division, earned a Presidential Citation.

*Within the next six weeks citations were, unfortunately, going to become very common. The experiences told by **Murray Shapiro** of Chatsworth, California, was only an indication of things to come.*

M Y MEMORY goes back to the morning of December 16, 1944, when at about 4:30 in the morning another buck sergeant and I were taking up the relief for our two heavy machine guns facing the vaunted German Seigfried line.

Climbing up a snow-covered slope to the rear of our guns, we made out the vague form of 10 hunched-backed shapes in the very dim light of a fog-shrouded dawn. These were soon joined by 20 more.

Discarding the idea that, hopefully, these were "K" company's cooks carrying early breakfast to riflemen's fox holes, we turned and fled. As our two gunners circled a hedgerow behind us to warn the company, the other sergeant and I ran directly to our rear to warn a sleeping anti-tank gun platoon. Before the platoon could be awakened the Germans were upon us, throwing hand grenades and attacking with bayonets.

Sergeant McGinnis was killed. I escaped by ramming my body through the hedgerow and getting to regimental headquarters to help lead a rearguard the next day.

Thinking of combat as hazardous is easy, but as **Kermit T. Wilson** *of Guthrie, Oklahoma, discovered, a person can be miles away from the battle and still wind up fighting for his life.*

Murray Shapiro at the Red Cross Club in Paris, France. (Photo provided by Murray Shapiro.)

ONE FOGGY MORNING I was crushed beneath the track of a D-8 bulldozer. I remember asking God for help and heard someone say I was dying.

Seven days later I opened my eyes in the 136th Station Hospital in the south of England. A nurse was there with a pan of ice cubes. They had kept ice in my mouth for seven days to break a 107-degree fever.

No one knew what my injuries were, so there was a lot of excitement for a while.

I had a badly broken shoulder and arm, broken ribs, a collapsed lung and a head injury. Thanks to the great effort of Maj. Richardson, my doctor, and the nurses and those that found me, I am doing fine today and think of them often.

Fear is a normal state for GIs during these times and **George H. Shimkus** *of Webster Grove, Missouri, probably agrees.*

THIS TOOK PLACE while I was serving with the 3rd Armored "Spearhead" Division. My tour of duty was from 1941 to 1945 and carried me from Camp Polk to the River Elbe in Germany. As the war in the European Theater progresses the units of armor were making a drive to Paderborn, Germany. Tanks and equipment were in urgent need by the tank battalions.

As we proceeded towards Paderborn we noticed some tiger royal German tanks, fairly well intact out of action with lights still on in the turrets. This was in the vicinity where General Rose met disaster. A major and lieutenant were leading the convoy of the extra noisy tanks, etc. but when we approached a "Y" in the road our contact was lost with them.

A decision had to be made of which direction to proceed with the column of equipment. Being the leader of the convoy and Staff Sergeant, the decision was made on direction we were to take.

It wasn't too cold in the darkness of that night but at that particular time it made one shake, it wasn't from being cold, it was from being slightly frightened.

Then one warms up rather suddenly when you know the tank battalion got more equipment that was urgently needed to keep the attack progressing.

*Supplies and equipment were the name of the game. Hitler's forces were hurting. The Russians were bearing down from the north and the rest of the Allies were pushing in from Western Europe. While battles were taking place on land, men like **Mrs. Mildred D. Stolicker's** husband were in a different theater of war, but one every bit as deadly. Here's what the Holly, Michigan, resident's husband told her about the Murmansk Run.*

HAROLD ENDURED a 41-day ordeal delivering a war cargo to the Russian Port of Murmansk. For his efforts, he won a commendation from the Chief of Navy personnel: Harold Lester Stolicker of Grand Rapids, a gunner's mate, 3rd class.

He was one of 30 crewmen of the United States Merchant Marines commended. The crew went without sleep, strapped to their guns and despite high winds, snow, and icebergs, fought off an extraordinary number of submarines and bombers.

They were credited with shooting down two enemy planes and with protecting the ship, after it reached port, from additional bombing. Several crewmen were lost overboard during this run to Murmansk, Russia.

I did not know the whereabouts of my husband until I read an article in the Grand Rapids Press, Grand Rapids, Michigan.

*Many wives, mothers, and sweethearts would wonder the whereabouts of their loved ones in the coming months. Too often, their fate will be as that described by **Ross K. Rasmussen** of Hot Springs, Arkansas.*

OUR UNIT spent Thanksgiving in London. Some would not live to see Christmas. On Christmas Eve in the wintry Ardennes of Belgium, "K" Co., 290th Inf., 75th Div. was attacked.

We had no preliminary combat seasoning, but were rushed forward to help stop the German advance. After a long, difficult march, we recieved orders to attack immediately. We accepted our destiny as only the infantry can.

Our rifle squads, machine gun and mortar sections had only standard issue amounts of ammunition. Some rifle squad members had only one clip. After two rounds of artillery cover fire, we made our attack over an open field, slanting upward toward a German-held woods line.

The rifle platoon took the first casualties, followed by the machine gun squads. The mortar section fired everything they had, then waited in the cold, in the moonlight as over 50-percent of "K" Company was dissolved.

Duty. Honor. Country.

Ardennes would soon become known as the Battle of the Bulge. **Paul T. MacElwee** *of Shamokin, Pennsylvania, was there.*

A FIELD PHONE rang in our bunker on December 16, 1944, where I waited with the rest of my unit, Co. "C," 1st Bn., 422nd Reg., 106th Inf., known as the Golden Lions. I answered with the customary hello.

"Is Sgt. Clark there?" the voice asked.

Sgt. Clark, my squad leader was still in the sack and I didn't want to disturb him. "Not at the moment," I replied.

"Who is this?" thee voice demanded. I answered and he said, "This is Captain Kulzer." Kulzer was our company commander. "Do you hear any motorized activity out in front of you?"

"Yes, sir," I replied. "It began several hours ago."

"How far would you say it is?" I told him I estimated about 3,000 yards and he said, "The Germans are on the move. Keep your head down, we're going to send over some heavy stuff."

Within a few minutes, artillery shells began soaring overhead. The shelling stopped the mechanized activity for a short time, but then it picked up again and continued non-stop. I was there when the Battle of the Bulge started, but little did my comrades and I realize that within a week, we would be prisoners of war.

The Germans launch a major offensive in the Ardennes on December 16, 1944. They hope to retake Antwerp and split American and British forces. The region is rugged and heavily wooded, with few major roads. This makes road junctions strategic targets.

Until now, it has been used as a rest area for US troops and a staging area for green GIs. English-speaking Germans attempt to infiltrate the areas wearing captured uniforms and equipment.

This was probably part of the force that **William F. Loebl** *of Chanhassen, Minnesota, met in 1944.*

W HAT STICKS in my memory is the night I got into a hand-to-hand fight with a German paratrooper. On December 22, 1944, we were defending our 28th Infantry Division PW cage in the police station at Sibret, Belgium, South of Bastogne. PW interrogations the previous day told us that the 5th German Parachute Division objective was to cut the road leading into Bastogne.

At 3AM they attacked, yelling, "Hurrah, Hurrah." I was defending the southwest corner of the building and heard them coming along the wall. It was pitchblack and I waited until I could see a shadow in front of me. I fired my carbine at the shadow, he yelled, "Au, au!" and grabbed my gun with one hand and my shoulder with the other.

I pulled the trigger 4 or 5 times and the hands disappeared. Then I reported the situation to Division HQ.

Allied Command had sent the US 82nd and 101st Airborne to reinforce combatants at Ardennes on the December 17. By the 20th, it is obvious that the towns of St. Vith and Bastogne, two vital junctions, must be held in spite of major attacks by German forces. Bad weather is keeping Allied air support on the ground.

By December 21 Bastogne, which is defended by the 101st Airborne and other US forces, is almost totally surrounded. The next day the Germans demand that US forces in Bastogne surrender.

General McAuliffe's reply: "Nuts!"

The simple litany of his fallen comrades tells of the pride and pain felt by **Jack Smith** *of Dallas, Texas.*

CHRISTMAS OF '44 . . . as a paratrooper and machine gunner with the 101st Airborne Division near Foy and Bastogne, Belgium.

I remember Captain Cann reading a small Bible on Christmas day, also these men all killed in action:

1st Lt Lyle C Fenton	Pvt Glenn L Knerr
2nd Lt Sherman N Sutherland	Pfc Leonard E Lundquistu
2nd Lt Roger L Tinsley	Pvt 2 Patrick H Neill
Pvt Harvey A Cross	Pvt John R Osborne
Pvt Clarence E Ishler	Pvt Claire M Peterson
Pvt Thomas A Knapp	Cpl Hubert Reasor

and Pvt James R. Sowards Jr, my closest buddy and S/Sgt Darvin Lee who saved my life, and finally K.P. Smith who was with me all the way.

I've suffered heart disease and major depression, age 64, denied VA benefits, but after writing this I feel better because I will never forget the Christmas of 1944.

Bastogne! A rallying cry for those who wore the screaming eagle, like **John O. Thach** *of Westminster, Colorado.*

DURING THE BATTLE OF BASTOGNE, I was with Battery B, 377th Parachute Field Artillery, 101st Airborne Division. The 101st was surrounded at Bastogne from December 18, 1944 until December 27 when Patton's tanks broke through to them. I rejoined the outfit the evening of December 30, 1944. (I had been injured in Holland and hadn't gotten back to the outfit when they were called up to Bastogne). There was about a foot of snow on the ground and it was snowing. Artillery was booming continously for miles along the front lighting up the sky. What a way to celebrate New Year's Eve.

On January 12, 1945 we were advised that we were going on the attack out of Bastogne. The gun positions would not change, it was a matter of getting forward observer teams up with the infantry. I was assigned to a team headed by 2nd Lieutenant MacFarland. Also on the F.O. team was Criswell, Radio Operator and Ball, Jeep Driver.

We proceeded to the assembly point of the 502, we were briefed and the attack was to begin at 0700 the next morning, January 13. The weather was zero degrees and probably below as our canteens begin to freeze and we were sleeping on the ground or in a foxhole.

We took off on the attack, as I recall from the sun, we were attacking east. We hadn't proceeded very far down this trail when a burst of machine gun fire came over our heads—this burst of fire was from the German lines outpost —(after that burst the German machine gun crew no doubt took off for their lives as that was the only burst that we got) our attacking troops immediately scattered into the woods on either side of the trail, then a German 88 artillery barrage started. Criswell got a piece of shrapnel in his knee and I helped him to a foxhole, Ball and MacFarland were already in the foxhole. Lt MacFarland said "Sergeant, you better get in here". I said, "I'll be ok, I'll just hug the ground out here." After a few minutes the Germans lifted their barrage. Criswell made his way back to an aid station, he never returned to the outfit. We continued to advance. Ball and I found an old dishpan, attached a rope to it, which made a good sled to pull the radio on. We probably advanced two miles that day without any further resistance.

By this time our canteens were completely frozen and we had to melt snow to get a drink of water.

The next morning we continued to advance. We had P-46 Thunder-Bolts air support, they were supposed to be bombing and strafing ahead of us. We got to a stopping point and Ball said to me, "Thach I'm scared" I said "so am I Ball" about this time we heard this loud roar, the P-47's were right on top of us. Either the Air-Liaison Officer was off or the pilots thought we were Germans. They dropped two fifty pound bombs right on top of us. I had hit the ground immediately after hearing the roar coming towards us. I got up kind of in a daze there lay Ball with a hole where his guts were. Ball apparently had not hit the ground and a big piece of shrapnel hit him in the guts tearing them out, he was killed instantly. Lt. MacFarland was OK, he had probably hit the ground fast also. One soldier of the infantry platoon had one cheek of his ass sliced off, as though it were sliced off by a surgeon's scalpel, his eyes were blown out of his head, he also died instantly. I was standing there in a daze and the infantry platoon leader, a 1st Lt was crying, he looked at me and said, "why don't you do something", there wasn't much I could do.

Our forward observer team started with four men, we were now down to two. Lt MacFarland took Ball's personal effects off him. Wasn't much: a billfold, a pinknife, to send to his next of kin. I got on the radio to battalion and reported "Ball, Able Peter", Able Peter was the code for "Killed in Action".

To die in war is to die in hell, you are dirty, tired, cold, hungry and scared.

*There has always been a proud heritage that goes with belonging to an airborne unit. Equally proud are the men of the units who drove to relieve the besieged troops, men like **Stan Davis** of Kissimmee, Florida.*

I WAS A Tank Commander with C Co 21st Tank Battalion of the 10th Armored Division and was a part of Team Ohara of Combat Command B from 18 Dec 1944 to 16 Jan 1945.

We were in a defensive position east of Bastogne, December 23, on the Wiltz road just North of Marvie which is southeast of Bastogne and a key part of the final defensive perimeter. We had successfully held off early and late night attacks by strong enemy Infantry and Tank units. Marvie was defended by the 2nd Bn of the 327th Glider Regt of the 101st Div and was also under heavy attacks by enemy Infantry and Tanks (3) which now occupied the southern half of the town.

Around midnight my tank was ordered into the town to assist the 327th in preventing any further advancement and to drive out the attacking enemy tanks. We moved into a blocking position about 20-25 yards from a partial road block of a knocked out American Half Track.

The three enemy tanks attempted to push aside the Half Track and move on to Bastogne but we were able to knock out the first tank after an exchange of point blank fire (75mm) adding this enemy tank to the road block and our direct fire on the other two tanks forced them back south out of town when they challenged our position. We held this position for several days.

The German forces were never able to get any closer to Bastogne in this sector and our remaining tanks shifted from defensive to offensive operations the last two weeks of our action in the Bastogne Area.

By December 24, the German advance in the Ardennes has been halted by the end of the day, and on Christmas Day the Allies mount a counterattack against German Ardennes offensive. The movements of the US 4th Armored Division around Mortelange is designed to give relief to the defenders of Bastogne, who are still holding on. On December 26, Bastogne is relieved.

*The 101st and the 10th Armored weren't the only ones seeing action that week. **Earle W. Alexander** of Minneapolis, Minnesota, was busy, too.*

THERE WAS a Kraut Tiger Tank on the hill at the edge of a small village in Luxembourg, Christmas 1944.

As A Company, 104th Inf YD left the ravine near the river and hiked around the hill, a German machine gun suddenly fired and screaming rockets mowed us down. I dropped behind a bush and tried to get lower in the snowy ground, digging with my bayonette.

I'll never know why they didn't shoot us in the back when we retreated with wounded. But a few days later I got hit in the leg, fortunately. Many went "back" that got wounded in other areas.

Relief troops were immediately mobilized. **Samuel Erlick** *of Cherry Hill, New Jersey, remembers his interrupted holiday.*

A FTER GETTING only one week of scheduled 30 day rest at Metz, our combat platoon of the 104th Infantry Regiment, 26th Division, 3rd Army, received bandoliers of ammunition, piled into trucks and rushed in a bumper-to-bumper convoy to a snow covered area in Luxembourg.

There was heavy fog and overcast skies. No one explained why we had to leave the rest area, or why we were at this assembly area. Much later we learned that we were there to halt Von Rundstedt's Ardennes Offensive, known as the "Bulge."

What made this so vivid in my memory was the rush to get there (infantry men do not normally ride to battle in trucks), the constant snow, freezing temperature, physical discomfort, and a most determined enemy resistance. This combat experience will never be forgotten.

Just getting to the battle can be frightening, according to **Philip Botwinoff** *of Valley Stream, New York.*

W E BOARDED a troopship on Christmas Day, 1944, heading for the European theater of operations.

The convoy seemed to stretch for miles as the massive Atlantic Ocean waves tossed the ships, much to the discomfort of the apprehensive troops. As the lead ship (The George Washington), we were faced with a near calamitous event while moving through the perilous U-Boat filled waters. Disaster loomed as a damaged rudder caused the ship to flounder, while the convoy continued on its journey.

Floating adrift and alone for 24 hours, the repair work continued—the troops anxious as full power was finally restored. When we eventually caught up to the convoy, submarine activities were intense—the destroyers weaved in and out, depth charges booming as they exploded below the surface.

It was with great relief that we spotted the English shorelines. As a 19 year old pfc, I awaited the European adventure.

Too often, the fear was justified, as **Paul L. Tilech** *of Pine City, New York, found out.*

O N DECEMBER 28, 1944, I, with my 20 men boarded a ship in England, named the Empire Javlin, headed for France. The Coast of England was out of sight when we hit a mine or were hit by a torpedo.

The Empire Javlin was sinking when a French frigate pulled along side. The French sailors placed a canvas over a life boat. We jumped from the sinking ship into the life boat where the French sailors grabbed us and threw us to the deck of the frigate.

After a while an American LST pulled along side of the frigate, we boarded the LST. That night we landed on LeHavre Beach in France. I believe we set some kind of record. We went from England to France on three ships, one was sunk and we didn't get our feet wet.

Some troops were killed with the explosion and some lost their lives jumping from one ship to the other. I'll never forget.

For many GIs, the Battle of the Bulge was their first taste of combat. According to **Philip E. Massie** *of Culver City, California, this was a real eye-opener!*

I T WAS MY FIRST DAY of actual combat. The 492nd Armored Field Artillery, 11th Armored Division, was detached with the 63rd Armored Infantry Battalion, Task Force BLUE, to guard a bridge over the Meuse River at the West tip of the Bulge.

The battalion was deep in several holes in the Givet "horn" of France. The L-4's needed a landing strip. The Air Section was isolated in a small valley in Belgium fringed by woods. Foot deep snow and cold. Rumors of infiltrating paratroops in American uniforms. Two pilots, two mechanics, two support EM's, two trucks and two airplanes. Late evening and the order came to report the L-4 to coordinates xxx-xx and pick up an observer. The crew and trucks departed in the dark.

30 Dec 1944. At daybreak the L-4's departed. As senior pilot I landed at the designated coordinates. Lt. Homer White, Battalion Forward Observer, with Jeep and driver, was waiting. We had flown together many times in training. The FO crawled in the back seat. I advanced the throttle, climbed to 700 feet and headed East by North.

I had never seen a war before. Snow covered everything. I flew and flew and flew. I figured the FO had the hot scoop and the maps. He figured I did. Five minutes out and I saw nothing in the air or on the ground.

Then streaks of red in front. Four big black balls, two above and two below. A half roll, a steep diving turn, a side slip. More red streaks. More big black balls.

In the turns I could see behind us there were many large cotton balls. Nose down, turns left and right, air speed on red line. One hundred and fifty miles an hour in a Piper Cub. From the back seat I heard, "Don't tear the wings off! Don't tear the wings off!" instead of "Our Father which art..."

At about two hundred feet the 88's quit. Somewhat lower the 40's stopped. At fifty feet the 20's quit. I leveled off at 15 feet and headed West by South, totally lost. We finally identified Newfchateau and turned to the new air strip.

It was a week before I took an observer near the front line. We had been at least five miles into German territory.

Lesson: Find out how much the observer knows before you take off.

Being lost in the sky can have tragic consequences to those on the ground, as **Larry L. Jones** *of Stone Mountain, Georgia, relates.*

O N CHRISTMAS DAY 1944, our own planes strafed and bombed an American combat team, of which I was a member, in the Battle of the Bulge, in Belgium.

The team had reached a strategic area on the front line the night before, and had dug in on the west bank of a stream. Fog enveloped the area overnight, suspending action until about noon Christmas Day. As the fog dissipated, the enemy was observed withdrawing from the area, and our air force was called in to strike a blow to the retreating enemy armor and personnel.

Unfortunately, many casualties and destruction were inflicted upon us simultaneously, mistakenly, by our planes. Personally, at age 21, I suffered instant loss of my right foot and severe injury to my left foot that day.

These were desperate times for both the Americans and the Germans, as **Leonard Paul Turner** *of Dundalk, Maryland, so graphically describes.*

I N THE BATTLE OF THE BULGE, my outfit was the 76th Infantry Division, 417th Infantry Regt. Signal section.

I remember the snow, the cold—no hot food and the uncertainty of what was going on. German soldiers dressed in American uniforms. Standing in our very long chow lines.

The passwords and counter passwords that only an American GI should have, "Daisy Mae Lil Abner."

It was very cold. Hardly anyone moved about, neither you nor the enemy. It was just as cold for them. Your M-1 bolt freezing up if you fired and you had to urinate on it to get it unfrozen.

We were on the flank of the Bulge on the Our River in a town called Echternach, Luxenborg. The town itself once served as headquarter for Marshal Von Rundstedt. It later was our jumping-off point for crossing the Seigfried Line into Germany and on to the city of Trier.

John C. Overman Jr. *of Apex, North Carolina, didn't experience a very cheery New Year.*

I T IS JANUARY 28, 1944 during the Battle of the Bulge, near Hofen, Germany. My infantry squad of the 99th Infantry Division, was given assignment to clear a path through a mine field for the tanks that were assigned to our company as we were to go on attack shortly.

The only equipment available to us were 3-prong hay forks that we found in a barn. As I was probing through the snow, a mine exploded.

At least one man was killed, and I was seriously wounded. Thank God for the Medics. They saved my life.

As I was on a stretcher to be evacuated, one of my men asked "Sgt. can I have the goodies in the package that you received"? I instructed him to divide it. The package contained mostly home-made country sausage.

*Another GI dealing with explosives at that time was **Eiler H. Drake** of Omaha, Nebraska.*

D URING THE BATTLE OF THE BULGE, everything was sent to the rear from Hagenau, France on the Rhine.

Our mission was to blow up the Free French Air Base and two abandoned "Spitfires". We whittled TNT blocks fitting 500 pound bombs in the runway. The Germans captured some "Thunderbolts" in Belgium, painted nose cones red and strafed us.

I high tailed to a bomb crater but it was occupied by a dud bomb so I took off for another. We blew the drome and Spitfires and got out of there as German patrols crossed the perimeter.

Since Sauverne and Colmar passes were captured by the Germans, we took a compass course west from the Vosges Mountains to our outfits. Missing our outfits morning reports five days, we were listed as deceased but ended up MIA's on our service records.

It was cold!!!

*Cold was only part of the problems facing **James M. Morgan** of Stanford, Kentucky.*

I WAS with the Med Det 319 Reg 80th Inf Div 3rd Army. I was a jeep driver. My job was to move the wounded from the front lines to the aid station.

During the battle of the Bulge in Heiderscheid, we went behind the enemy lines and cut the main highway on December 22, 1944, in the night and took the town. To hold it we had to call our own artillery on our own positions, there was only the 2nd battalion, but we held it against overwhelming odds.

My 2nd Lt. asked me if I would go pick up three wounded Germans. The road was a solid sheet of ice. It was down a hill about one and one-half miles under observation. There was a bomb crater, took half of the road where I was to turn in at the first house, and it was zeroed in. I put the jeep in second, then low and cut the the key off and jumped out. I outran the jeep, went through the door, no sooner than the door closed, a shell went off right behind my jeep. Blew all my tires but the left front, even my spare. I had 32 holes in my jeep.

I asked if the Germans had been searched? They said yes. We loaded them in the jeep, two were on stretchers, the other one sat up in the seat. I kept my eyes on him. Here was the problem. To drive a jeep one tire up and three flat. The only way it would pull itself was front wheel drive, and low range, wide open, 10 miles an hour. When I finally go to the aide station we searched them and found two loaded pistols on them. From then on I searched all POWs myself.

Roland Schump *of Iowa City, Iowa, says he got around during the Battle of the Bulge.*

I WAS with the 87th Infantry Division during the Battle of the Bulge. We fought in France, Germany, Belgium, and Luxumborg, all the way to the Czech border where we met the Russians. The Germans were not our only enemy, we fought the cold, snow, rain and terrain.

The 345th Infantry Regiment alone took 120 towns and cities, one of the largest being Koblenz, and were the first to break through the Seigfried line near Roth, Germany.

As we were about to go into the Seigfried line one of the most beautiful sights that I will never forget was our fighters and bombers coming back from bombing Berlin. For hours the sky was filled with planes.

The German Luftwaffe has been decimated by the war, but they manage to cobble together a force of aircraft with largely inexperienced pilots and launch a successful surprise bombing raid against airfields in Belgium, Holland, and northern France. The totality of the surprise allows the Germans to wreak 300 times more damage to their targets than to themselves.

However, as they return home, their own anti-aircraft units down several of their own, and these aircraft are irreplaceable.

In spite of this raid, the Allies have launched successful counterattacks in the Ardennes in all areas but Alsace, where Eisenhower orders the 7th Army to pull back.

By January 23, 1945, St. Vith is in Allied hands. At the same time, the Russian drive to Germany has led to massive evacuation of German troops from the Baltic. The German army is retreating on all fronts and the Allies smell the scent of victory.

Chapter 25
Final Push

On February 4 through February 11, 1945, Roosevelt, Churchill, and Stalin meet in Yalta and basically divide up Europe. Yet, though it is now obvious the Germans cannot last much longer, heavy fighting is still taking place.

From February 13 to February 15, RAF and US bombers wreak havoc on the city of Dresden. The bombing ignites a horrific firestorm and casualties are extremely high. Depending on whose figures are offered, anywhere from 30,000 to 200,000 are dead in the aftermath. Most estimates place the figure at 70,000. Most victims are German refugees.

On February 18, the Seigfried Line is breached at Echternacht by the 3rd Army. The Dragon's Teeth have shattered.

Yet, as the Ardennes fighting took place, Americans elsewhere in Europe were hardly comfortable, as **Dorothy Simpson** *of Everett, Washington, explains.*

C HRISTMAS, 1944 in Leghorn, Italy, we were tired and homesick. The holiday packages of crumbled cookies did little for our morale.

In the low depths of self-pity, we decided to visit the nearby army hospitals. Perhaps in the act of cheering the less fortunate, we would forget about ourselves and the loved ones we wanted to be with on this holiday.

Our idea was to visit as many hospitals as possible and return to our quarters just before the midnight curfew. We arrived home about 11:30 pm, exhausted. It had been a raw and freezing night. A few minutes after the 6x6 trucks had unloaded us at our gate we could hear the muted tones of a band playing Christmas carols.

Softly, with a gradual intensity, voices accompanied the brass instruments. We opened our windows. In the dark shadows of the street below stood the enlisted men we worked with every day. Suddenly we realized we were home and our families were around us every day.

William Curtis Smith *of Tallahassee, Florida, also saw the suffering taking place in Italy during the holidays.*

C HRISTMAS DAY, 1944, was a cold day with low hanging clouds hiding the Apennines of Northern Italy.

In a sea of mud, a line of ambulances were bringing in the wounded to an evacuation hospital. With tender care, nurses and medical personnel were greeting each patient with a "Merry Christmas". Christmas music was playing on the intercom as word spread from bed to bed, "our first hot meal in Italy, turkey with all the trimmings!"

Outside the tent city, in a large circle, sitting in the rain were women and small children, holding GI cans. Looking like walking skeletons, they were patiently waiting for the leftover dinner. With music playing "Silent Night", combat hardened GI's of Africa and Sicily went through the chow lines or left their beds, walked out of the tents, through the mud and with rain mixed with tears, placed in each can their Christmas dinner.

__Nash McKee__ of Weaverville, North Carolina, was in France for Christmas, but he didn't care much for it.

C HRISTMAS DAY, 1944, in the edge of a forest somewhere in Eastern France. A hundred yards away was hot Christmas dinner and packages from home. Coming toward us were columns of staggering, drunken German soldiers.

We had to get out in a hurry. Our retreat path was over an open area.With German bullets flying all around we returned fire as we ran. On the way to safety we fled past the company headquarters and the abandoned truck that held our dinner and packages.

For Christmas that year we were glad to get 'K' rations.

Still, Christmas is Christmas, as __Neil H. Johnson__ of Glenmora, Louisiana, discovered.

I WAS ASSIGNED to Headquarters and Headquarters 409th Infantry, 103rd Infantry Division as a first Lieutenant. On December 24, 1944, I found myself and a small group of GI's in a bunker of the Maginot Line, along with a group of French civilians.

Neither group was bilinguil, so we sang the familiar Christmas carols, we in English, they in French. I felt then and feel now, that despite all the horror of war we captured the true meaning of Christmas.

But the holidays soon were past and replacement troops were pouring in. __Harry H. Weineger__ of Yorktown Heights, New York, recalls that the Germans weren't the only enemy.

T HE DATE was January 8, 1945, when as an Infantry Replacement was placed on a French railroad boxcar called a 40 and 8 just outside of LeHarve, the temperature was at the zero mark and the ground was completely covered with about 6 inches of snow.

We were so packed in that when you sat down you had to bring your knees up to your chin, due to lack of space. Our food for the four day three night journey consisted of cold "C" rations, there was no heat and we had to use our steel helmets as toilets.

The only time we would stop, would be to let trains returning from the front lines carrying bodies of dead GIs, still in their winter overcoats, piled high in open gondolas pass. There were also German POWs who were crammed into completely wired cages transported in a standing position, due to lack of space.

We, as Infantry Replacements, proceeding to the front lines upon seeing these sights made the outlook for our survival very grim, but I guess I had luck and enough faith in my country, and God, for I am here to remember today.

Walter E. Little *of Providence, Rhode Island, also rode the train.*

I WAS EATING K-RATIONS the size of a Cracker Jack Box while riding along in a 40 by 8 (the old railroad European Box Car) freezing my butt off and realizing that we were the victorious troops and these were the same cars the Nazis used to transport the Jews going to their death camps during the Holocaust. Ironic.

It was ironic also that one of the prized ingredients of our K-Ration was the couple of cigarettes that we later found were injurious to one's life, yet when a GI was hit in combat, usually his dying act was to ask for a cigarette.

But I remember those days as happy because we shared these discomforts, had lots of laughs and made the best friends anyone could ever have—your G.I. buddy thru "thick or thin".

The Allies were facing heavy—almost desperate—resistance, and it was taking its toll. **Anton J. Rotchadl** *of North Mankato, Minnesota, was one of the victims.*

THE MEDIC who nudged my leg at about dusk said, "We've got to get you out of here, the shells are coming soon!"

He no more than helped me to a V-shaped machine gun dugout and said, "Stay here, I am getting another but I'll be back." And sure enough the shelling shook the entire area but the medic came to help me to the aid station.

Along the way he says, "Where you laid all afternoon is just a big hole."

To you and your counterparts I say, "You had a lot of guts, thank you!" The above occurred on February 25, 1945, during the attack on Hollen, Germany, after the Roer River crossing.

Meanwhile, even though most of the German navy had been decimated by mines when they tried to evacuate their ground troops from the Baltic, the waters of the Atlantic were by no means safe, as **Elmer E. Hoover** *of Hagerstown, Maryland, found out.*

ON THE NIGHT of March 8, the morning of March 9, 1945, P.C. 564 (USS Chadron) was on patrol off the Coast of Granville, France, when we got three radar contacts. We proceeded to investigate and contacted three German gun boats, firing six star shells, then the battle started.

Each of these gunboats were larger than the PC and each had more fire-power. In the ensuing battle, the Germans made a direct hit on our bridge, killing all but one. Hitting us on all sides, I was blown off the 40mm gun.

The skipper gave orders to abandon ship, which some men did, then later rescinded the order and decided to run the ship between the rocks onto the beach.

When we received help the morning of the 9th, there were 14 dead, 14 taken POWs (to Jersey Island) and 10 of us wounded. The wounded were taken to the 199th Army General Hospital in Rennes, France.

*William **Jurman** of Howard Beach, New York, has mixed memories of that time.*

I ENJOYED a 24 hour stay at a Rest Center in Huey, Belgium. It made me appreciate the ordinary everyday luxuries that we take for granted versus that of an infantryman in the field.

Several men from each line company were trucked in, our weapons were turned in to be checked by Ordinance, we showered, were issued clean clothes and given a Huey decal helmet liner. The decal guaranteed that if we were staggering drunk, the M.P.'s would know where to take us and put us to bed. We roamed the little town and I found a restaurant that offered steak and french fries.

It was delicious, even though I later discovered it was horse meat.

I remember seeing Bing Crosby in "Don't Fence Me In." Being able to stand erect safely rather than stooped in some cellar or dugout and to sleep, undisturbed, in a cot . . . that was living.

But things weren't so peaceful later, on March 2, 1945, when, at dawn, we entered the little town of Heimbach on the way to the Rhine. We had a Sherman tank in support, but they are very vulnerable in street fighting. Infantry had to check around corners before the tank can turn.

On a previous attack I saw three British Churchill tanks burning, with their ammunition popping off inside, so I understood their caution.

I just turned around the corner of a building and it felt as though a light bulb exploded in my face. A sniper's bullet had gone through the rim of my helmet, cut my eyebrow and went through the bridge of my nose.

Our medic was right there with the sulphur, bandage and Morphine. I was jeeped to an aid station and then to a hospital near Paris. Less than five weeks later I was back with the company.

*The Germans had destroyed bridges, mined roads, even opened dams, anything to slow or stop the Allied advance. Yet, somehow, they overlooked the key Ludendorff bridge at Remagen. But **Marcus L. Davis** of Christiansburg, Virginia, arrived just a little early.*

I WAS A FORWARD OBSERVER (Scout) in the 742nd F.A. under General Hodges. Our outfit was about 29 miles from the Rhine River. I was on a scouting mission for the purpose of sending back data to our guns to engage in battle for the purpose of crossing the bridge at Remagen.

Somehow I got lost and was behind the enemy lines. I noticed a house on a road nearby. Approaching the house with a firearm available I knocked on the door. A German woman opened the door. She said "me no hurt you."

This woman hid me in a water tower, and when it got dark at night time she would bring me a cooked meal. This lasted for about two weeks until my outfit arrived to help destroy the bridge at Remagen.

This evidently saved my life.

*Meanwhile **Clarence Taylor** of Lebanon, Indiana, and the men with him were about to make history at Remagen.*

I N THE EARLY MORNING HOURS, my unit crossed the Remagen Bridge over the Rhine River. My outfit was the Ninth Infantry Division which spearheaded the taking of and the subsequent crossing of the bridge.

Under intense mortar fire, coupled with incoming 88's, machine gun fire from the German side all made for and unforgettable moment in history. Establishing a bridge head on the east bank, we were under continuous shell fire from the enemy trying to slow our advance. This together with the aerial dog-fights between the Luftwaffe and American pilots made for the most hazardous conditions in and around the Ludendorff Bridge.

It was at the village of Erpel that my radio section chief was killed in action, while obtaining supplies from our supply vehicle. A spent 50 calibre round from an overhead dog-fight took his life.

*Incredibly, the bridge at Remagen withstood mortar and artillery and even attacks by the Me262 jet. When it finally did collapse, **Herbert Buchheit** of Perryville, Missouri, went to work.*

S OON AFTER THE COLLAPSE of the Ludendorff railroad bridge at Remagen Germany on March 17th, 1945, the 148th Engineer Combat Batalion began building a new bridge at 0730 hours March 18, 1945. The bridge was completed and opened to traffic at 0715 hours March 20, 1945. The type of bridge constructed was a 1258 foot class 40 floating Pontoon Bailey Bridge.

Then on 0700 hours March 26th, our Battalion the 148th Combat Engineers began work on one of its biggest engineering assignments construction of the eastern half of a 1180 foot dual Carriage Bailey bridge across the Rhine River at Bad Godesberg, Germany. This bridge is known as the Hodges Bridge commanding General of the first Army, and it was completed and open to traffic on April 6, 1945.

Crossing the Rhine, besides being a strategic necessity, was also a matter of morale. **William V. Harris** *of West Salem, Illinois, poetically explains.*

HITLER HAD BRAGGED this brag to the German people:
While flows one drop of German blood,
or sword remains to guard thy flood.
While rifle rests in patriots hand
No Joe shall tread thy sacred strand.

I was attached to the 9th Army commanded by Bill Simpson, as a machine gunner on the 743 Field Artillery. We were backed by the heaviest ring of steel the world has ever known.

At 0100 March 24th Major Warner snapped fire. For two hours and 29 minutes uninterrupted, unimaginable, incomparable, blast after blast tore the sky to shreds and pounded away at the eastern bank of the Rhine River yard by yard, the beachhead was expanded.

The Rhine had been breached.

Earl Prideaux *of Brighton, Colorado, was with Gen. Patton when he crossed the Rhine.*

I MET WITH GEN. PATTON at the 3rd Army assault bridge over the Rhine on March 24, 1945 near Oppenheim, Germany. I was in command of building the bridge, a 1,252-foot long structure which we constructed in 13 hours while under fire from air strikes and German 88s.

At 10 a.m., Patton, his aide, Col. Codman and Maj. Gen. Eddy arrived at the bridge in three jeeps and drove to its center. Patton remarked that Lord Haw Haw had announced on the radio that the Germans would kick our asses if we tried to cross the Rhine.

Patton answered that he would stand on the bridge and piss in the Rhine and defy the Germans to hit him. He then repeated Caesar's words: "I see in my hands the soil of Germany."

General Patton, Lt. Colonel Prideaux and Colonel Codman at the Rhine River (Photo provided by Earl Prideaux.)

Though the Rhine had been crossed, the fighting was vicious. **John H. Shue** *of York, Pennsylvania, had a close call.*

I T WAS A NIGHT PATROL. We "moved out" from a small town just across the Rhine river. We advanced only a hundred yards until Jerry sent up a flare.

The next clearly audible sounds were machine guns being put on "full load." The flare landed between five of us. As the flare burned, I reasoned that with the Krauts so close, we would surely be spotted.

After an eternity, the flare burned out and not a shot was fired in our direction. Word was immediately passed, "Get out of here."

I ran back to town and ducked into a doorway as tracer bullets seemed to be everywhere, illuminating the street. There was one minor casualty among the 32 men on that memorable mission. Only God knows why we weren't seen and the wiped out.

Donald Chase *of Framingham, Massachusetts, also saw fighting at the Rhine.*

I SURVIVED our assault crossing of the Rhine River at St Goar, March 26, 1945.

The second battalion had already crossed and rumor was that two companies had suffered heavy casualties. Now it was our turn and we were scared. Down to the river's edge, into small rubber assault boats, then paddling like wild men, driven by sheer terror, to get to the other side. With bullets cracking overhead, 88 shells exploding in the water, all of us trying not to panic, arms pumping like windmills, we finally reached the far shore.

A quick regrouping of the platoon, and then into the relative safety of the cellar of a nearby house, each of us in our own way happy to still be alive.

Even today, 45 years later, this scene remains as clear as the day it happened.

By the first of April, the 1st and 9th Armies have cut off a huge segment of the German army at the Ruhr. Some 325,000 men are trapped. The Allies push on.

Though the Luftwaffe has been almost totally destroyed, **William J. Falvey** *of Niles, Michigan, knows it wasn't completely out of commission.*

O N APRIL 2, 1945 the 358th Infantry advancing toward Czechoslovakia crossed the Werra River at VACHA, Germany and we had German Soldiers intermingled with our troops so much that we were actually fighting ourselves in some cases. (Even our own tanks against our own tanks)

Finally we got this stopped and captured the Germans in the middle.

Then, that same afternoon, an American plane was chasing a German plane and bullets exploded a railroad car full of black powder. It blew a large hole in the ground and even the railroad tracks were blown out of existence. The German plane was blown out of the air, 65 houses were demolished and there were many casualties, both civilian and military.

It was not an Atomic Bomb—But was the next thing to it all in all a day to remember.

Stanley J. Brown of Staten Island, New York, was getting ready to enter Europe about that time, but he, too, had his hands full.

THE 937TH FIELD ARTILLERY BN. fought during the entire winter campaign for the battle of Cassino. Afterward, we took invasion training on the Italian seashore, then were loaded aboard two landing craft for the invasion of southern France. We stood offshore from St. Raphael near the French Riviera all day.

I was on deck near dusk when a lone German plane approached. Undetected, it dropped a radio controlled missile which exploded amidships of our sister LST. The craft was fully loaded with troops and supplies and there were many casualties. Some of the survivors had to swim to shore.

When we landed and unloaded and proceeded inland, we were forced to delay until we could be resupplied and brought back up to full strength.

Eventually, we caught up to the 5th Army and Gen. George Patton to fight in France and Germany.

As US troops pushed deeper into Nazi territory, a gruesome story of sheer inhumanity began to unfold. Dominick A. Accetta of Fort Lee, New Jersey, begins the narrative.

IN APRIL 1945, our combat team, 89th Div. attached to the 4th Armored Division, came upon what we thought was a prison. It turned out to be a death camp, the first such camp the Allies came upon—Ohrdruf-Nord.

Dead bodies everywhere; the Germans tried to erase evidence of their brutality as American troops approached. Scores of dead in sheds were covered with lime, hundreds lay in huge pits where they were burned, some too slow to leave when the Nazis evacuated, were shot. Their bodies were still warm when our troops discovered them.

It is said that General Patton became sick when he visited the camp. The mayor and his wife committed suicide the night after he was forced to see this atrocity. Little attention was given to this death camp. At the same time a large amount of gold was found in another area.

It seems money was more important.

Frederick C. Enos of Utica, New York, was at another camp.

THE SIGHT of the soles of many bare feet protruding from under a tarpaulin covering dead bodies from Nazi inhumane treatment has never left me.

The truck was parked in the quadrangle of a Luftwaffe Barracks in Linz, Austria. One side of the quadrangle had a line of emaciated human beings patiently waiting for help from our army medics.

I recall the "old man" trudging down the road on spindle like legs. The "old man" was actually a boy about 14 years old. I visualize a man staring skyward oblivious of his surroundings, his death a few days away. The slaves starvation diet had claimed another victim. The ravages of Nazi slave labor were all around. Sights seen with the eyes of my youth, are mentally seen again by an aging man.

*Those who saw the camps, like **David D. Field** of Hampton, Virginia, were forever marked.*

I RECALL entering the concentration camp at Dachau the day after it was liberated in April, 1945.

Here, in this place of unspeakable horror, American doctors and nurses were exposing themselves to filth and disease as they went about the humanitarian mission of caring for the few pathetic remaining inmates who had somehow survived. To me Dachau symbolized what the war was all about.

On the one hand it represented all that was evil about Naziism, while on the other, the actions of those medical personnel represented all that was great about the ideals for which we had been fighting.

Ernest A. Moore *of Kearny, New Jersey, too, was moved.*

FOREVER BURNED INTO MY MIND are the visions of the mass destruction of human beings, the living dead, skin over bones. The piles of dead humans piled up like cords of wood. The ovens and the smell of death.

After 45 years, if I close my eyes, I can see it all over again, forever etched in my subconscious mind. I pray every day to God for America and our freedom.

Bernard (Barney) Zylka *of Duluth, Minnesota, says he spent almost three years overseas: Africa, Sicily, all over Europe, Belgium, Luxembourg, Austria, but it was Dachau that moved him most.*

THE MOST VIVID MEMORY was freeing the people at Dachau and Buchenwald concentration camps. I came in the first days here and people were still in the ovens burning with heads or feet sticking out of ovens. The stench was awful, I threw up miles before we reached the camps. I'll never forget it.

Dale K. Kaltved *of Lincoln, Nebraska, tells too of his visit to Dachau concentration camp.*

W E WERE MET at the entrance by a Polish guide, a former prisoner who spoke English well. We entered through an arched stone gate. Inscribed on the gate in German were the words, "Abandon hope all ye who enter here". As we entered the camp, the eerie silence was almost unbearable.

A tour of the camp followed. Most memorable was the crematory. A bronze tablet on the outside read, "Let not worms eat my body. Let it be light, therefore burn, do not bury me."

From the fake shower room where the prisoners were gassed, we were shown the four giant ovens where the bodies were burned. Flower wreaths hung on each oven. The death stench in the crematory is unforgettable.

The camps seemed to be located all over former Nazi territory. **Robert T. Johnson** *of Overland Park, Kansas, helped liberate one.*

O UR TANK went thru the gate of the Landsberg Concentration Camp, April 27, 1945.

Heading south, early in the morning, we crossed the RR bridge over the Lech River. We started smelling a terrible odor and suddenly we were at the concentration camp at Landsberg.

Forced the gate and faced hundreds of starving prisoners. Our first thought was to give them our K-Rations, but our medics stopped this, as their richness could have been deadly. Our cooks immediately started to make up a gruel that was offered a half cup at a time to those inmates that were able to walk.

We saw emaciated men whose thighs were smaller than wrists, many had bones sticking out thru their skin, and many crazed with fear and hunger. Also we saw hundreds of burned and naked bodies that were awaiting transportation to a crematory or mass burial site.

We stayed until an MP Battalion arrived to take charge of the chaos. While looking around a man in an inmate uniform came towards us. Our tank driver offered him a chocolate bar. Thinking he didn't understand, he grabbed the man's jacket, it ripped apart revealing a German Officer who was trying to escape. Needless to say he did not.

That evening I wrote my wife that "For the first time I truly realized the evil of Hitler and why this war had to be waged."

The masters of these camps got little sympathy, according to **Carl H. Asbury** *of Charleston, West Virginia.*

T HE ROAD leading to Buchenwald concentration camp was a nice road with grass growing wide on both sides of the road. As you get closer you could begin to smell burning flesh. When reaching the camp there were a lot of people on the outside of the gate. There were a pile of yellow bodies piled up like wood just inside the gate.

We talked to a French man who had just left the camp. He told us that the mistress of the camp was known as the Bitch of Buchenwald. That she would walk naked along the wall, when the men were marched out to work and any man that looked up at her was whipped. The French man also said that 10,000 Jews were taken out of the camp just before the Americans arrived.

We then went on into the camp. Just past the pile of bodies were the furnaces. There was still a body in the furnace. Moving on, we came to the mistress' office. On her desk she had a tattoo preserved in alcohol, also preserved in alcohol was a man's extra large sex organ.

Further on, we came to barracks where the men lived, on the right was a make shift bed made of a wood frame covered with straw. On another were three men, skin covered skeletons, one mustered a grin. The middle man was dead, the other two stayed alive by dividing the third's potato soup.

Further on was a temporary headquarters where the people of the camp set up. They had captured a SS Officer his head was swollen up about twice its normal size. This was because they were trying to get information out of him. Everytime some one passed him they would knock him down, holler "Achtune!" and he would jump up to be knocked down again.

When I was back at the camp the next day the SS officer's body was laying on top of the pile of bodies at the gate. They told us that they threw him a rope that night and he hanged himself. Some of the inmates of the camp went along with us, they carried wounded and help out.

Many camp guards were desperate to protect themselves, and atrocities took place. **Otto Schlavitti** *of Dunlap, Illinois, tells of one.*

I T WAS FRIDAY THE 13TH, 1945 when our XIII corps came upon the atrocity in a red barn in Gardelegen, Germany. A Hungarian who had survived the ordeal reported to us that about 2000 slave laborers (Polish, Russian, and Hungarians), who were making airplane parts in Germany, were put on a train traveling East. The train eventually reached Mieste, about 12 Kilometers from Gardelegen. From there they marched them to Gardelegen (minus about 300 political prisoners) but only 800 survived. The lame and sick were shot along the way.

At 6 P.M., they were herded into this red barn, ordered to sit down, as the SS troops spilled gasoline on the straw floor. An SS Corporal (16 years old) then struck a match and it became an inferno.

Those who tried to escape under the closed doors were machine-gunned as the SS troops laughed. Several days later the CG of the XIII Corps ordered all able males of the surrounding area to gather at the scene. He then ordered them to dig the graves, pick up the bodies with their hands and bury them.

After they were all buried, he spoke to the group. He said, "Don't ever say that the SS troops never committed atrocities, you have witnessed one of many!"

It made us all sick!

Still, the war went on. **C. Edwin Harp** *of Las Vegas, Nevada, saw action that month.*

O N 6 APRIL, 1945, my squad, along with other elements of the 261st Inf Division, were located just outside the town of Struth, Germany. At dawn we came under fire from a German counterattack involving a Battalion sized force of German Infantrymen along with sixteen Mark IV Panther Tanks and Seol Propelled Assult Guns.

At our location there was a large, fairly deep, roadside ditch which contained a lot of underbrush and small trees. Our squad fanned out in the ditch and waited for the German Tanks and Infantrymen coming up the slope toward us.

I had a bazooka. My ammo carrier and I crawled out beyond the front of the ditch so we could get a better shot at one of the tanks. We fired a round at one of the Mark IV Panter Tanks coming toward us. The round missed the target.

We then fired a second round and this one hit the tank and exploded. However, the tank kept on coming. By now, we were experiencing heavy incoming machine gun fire and were forced to with draw to the protection of the ditch.

Just as we did this a flight of P-47 Fighter-Bomber aircraft flew overhead. The P-47s formed into a circle and then started diving on the German tanks one at a time. They strafed the German Infantrymen with their 50 caliber wing guns and fired rockets at the tanks. When each pilot finished his dive he would climb back up into the circle of aircraft and wait his turn for the next dive.

Their continued strafing killed, or wounded a large number of the German infantrymen and their rockets knocked out 10 of their tanks. After suffering such heavy losses the remaining German forces started to withdraw. I remember thinking afterward, that we had really been saved by the bell, in this case, the P-47s.

But April 1945 would hold terrible news. **Betty J. Conrad** *of Canton, Illinois, was on quite a different battlefield when the news broke.*

W E CALLED IT the battle of Washington.
The war in Europe was winding down but the war with Japan was at its peak. Those of us who worked at the Navy Department were working long hours preparing for the final battles at sea. An invasion of Japan was advised by the top brass which meant a feverish preparation. We were not prepared for the news that came the afternoon of April 13. FDR was dead.

The following day a company of SPARS and a company of WAVES were asked to escort the caisson bearing the President's casket. We accepted the honor and silently marched down Pennsylvania Ave. The only sound was that of the hoofbeats of the riderless horse and the sobs of mourners. But the body in the casket was not only our leader but the bodies of all the men and women who had given their lives for freedom.

They must not and will not have died in vain.

Betty Lou Sherrell *of San Jose, California, witnessed the procession.*

IT IS A HOT SULTRY MORNING in Washington DC in April 1945. I was one of a group of SPARS in full dress uniform waiting as the funeral train from Warm Springs, Georgia rumbled into Union Station bearing the body of Franklin Delano Roosevelt.

The casket was loaded onto a caisson drawn by six white horses. Alongside was the saddled, riderless brown horse, symbol of a fallen chief. The slow march to the White House began, only the beat of a muffled drum for rhythm, and the slap-slap of feet on the hot pavement.

Marines lining the route snapped to attention with fixed bayonets, thousands of people stood silent except for an occasional sob.

At the White House, all the military contingents trooped on past, while the caisson turned into the circular drive.

For the troops in the field, even those in enemy hands, the word of Roosevelt's death was shocking. **J. Donald Griffin** *of Buffalo, New York, had problems of his own at that time. Yet...*

ON APRIL 12, 1945 when we received word of the death of President Roosevelt. We were POWs in Germany on a march from Muremburg to Mooseburg and numbered 700.

We received permission from the guards to hold a brief memorial service. Our camp leader brought us to attention, gave a right face to salute an American Flag placed in a nearby field and we stood at attention for the playing of Taps. The commands were executed with a precise military response, much to the surprise of the German guards who had only seen us in our normal, sloppy "POW" posture.

The precise execution of commands, the sight of our Flag deep inside Germany and the sadness over the death of a great leader still remain vivid in my memory.

Here's how **John W. Heisey** *of York, Pennsylvania, heard the news.*

I WOKE UP in a field hospital on 15 April 1945 after being wounded. I was starving and smelled food. Staggering out of the tent I looked around. An Army nurse came by and I asked her to help me find food. As she pointed out the mess tent, I noticed an American flag at half mast. Pointing to it I asked if that was for the soldiers who had died.

The nurse stared at me suspiciously and retorted: "Are you crazy? Don't you know President Roosevelt is dead?"

Still, the war went on, and for **Ross W. Smith** *of Brick, New Jersey, that day was doubly memorable.*

W E HAD RECEIVED NOTIFICATION of the death of President
Franklin D. Roosevelt.

Our ship was an Army Transport vessel, Y-103, on its way to the Pacific, via the Panama Canal. It was a hot Caribbean evening and thinking of Roosevelt's death made it hard to sleep below. I went up on deck
and fell asleep on the thwart in one of the lifeboats.

All of a sudden, I was jarred awake by the lowering of the lifeboat.
Was it a drill? No! Were we hit? No!

Thank god it was a false alarm. The bow watch had panicked and
pushed the alarm when he saw a porpoise breaking water and heading
towards the ship like a torpedo.

We were not to join our President that night!!

*For **Harry Arakelian** of Springfield, Pennsylvania, this should have
been a good day.*

I WAS SERVING in the replacements for the 10th Mountain Division
in Italy. When we fell out for formation on the morning of Thursday,
April 12, 1945, the Commanding Officer came out and said: "I have sad
news for you, guys. President Roosevelt has passed away."

There wasn't a dry eye in the formation.

I'll never forget that day because the next day, Friday, April 13th, was
my 24th birthday.

*Meanwhile, for men like **Henry M. Lagocki** of Philadelphia, Pennsylvania, the war went on.*

S PEEDING ALONG the Autobaun, in the turret of our halftrack. Fifty
cal in front, 4th Armed Div. and 3rd Army behind, no enemy in sight.
What could happen? We were to link up with the Russians at the Elbe
River.

We pulled along a woods to check it out, hell broke loose. My head felt
like it was in a vise with whirling lights in a tunnel. When it cleared I
found myself rolling on the ground with a head wound.

The Germans were firing 88s and whatever over our heads. Our
halftrack got a direct blast. Most of the squad were hit. The driver looked
bad, eyes open and quiet.

A half track pulled alongside and we crawled in. Before we could figure what happened, a plane full of wounded was landing near a hospital
in Nancy, France. The 4th Armored Div did not toast the Russians at the
Elbe.

*Probably, **Paul Pachowka** of Woodlyn, Pennsylvania, didn't toast the
Russians, either.*

I WAS STATIONED in Essen, Germany, in April 1945 with the 17th
Airborne. A couple of us were ordered to guard a mine with orders to
shoot anyone wanting to enter.

Four Russian officers joined us. We gave them cigarettes which they eagerly accepted. One of them spoke English. They moved off to the side and I heard an order being hissed. The order was to kill us and enter the mine for the gold buried there (of which we had no knowledge). A call to HQ gave me orders to kill them if they attempted to enter the mine. I gave orders to lock and load.

A jeep came to get the Russians. I'll never forget the look of astonishment on their faces. Just by dumb luck I didn't tell them I understood Russian! If I had, I would not be here writing this story.

Luck. Some have it, and others don't. **Warren O. McGuire** *of Fairfield, Connecticut, knows what that's about.*

HARRY GOODWIN was the first guy I became friends with at Camp Forrest in 1943. He was fun to be with on passes. More sophisticated than I, he approached girls with a good line and soon we would be enjoying ourselves.

He drank too much. I carried him back to camp many times. Sharing his packages, he'd laugh as I devoured his peanuts, and if he were feeling low, he'd send Duncan, a mutual friend with a message to "go into my act" and soon he would be laughing.

Our friendship continued as we followed Patton and Patch to Nuremburg. Then, on April 17, 1945, our fire mission was just completed when a sergeant said, "My God, number one just blew up!"

I ran to the pit. It was a mess of exploding powder and burning debris. "Where's Harry?" I asked. Someone pointed and I found Harry lying face-down about 25 feet from the gun. I will never forget that sight.

Others were lucky, like **John Baron** *of West Lafayette, Indiana.*

THIS TOOK PLACE on the island of Vis in Yugoslavia on the Dalmation Coast. I was serving in the OSS. We were bombed every night at 11 p.m. for a year, and "Bedtime Charley," on recon took pictures of us on the ground to determine the damage that had been done. Since we were well dug in to the side of the mountain, they couldn't get the best of us. If the Stukka dive bombers dove in any lower, they would end up in the bay behind us.

One of the most difficult times I faced while in Yugoslavia with an OSS team of Greek and Polish units was keeping the Germans at bay, blocking them from going through Brenner Pass. We harassed German units to prevent them from participating in the Normandy invasion.

They hit us one night with antipersonnel bombs that exploded four feet above the ground. Having saved some members of an allied air crew, one remarked they were happier in the air dropping their bombs than being on the ground listening to and watching them drop.

On more than one mission, the Lord looked after me and my number just wasn't up.

After a long time, exhaustion sets in. Perhaps that explains what happened to **Charles A. Goddard** *of Chaffee, Missouri.*

ABOUT MIDNIGHT on the top floor of the blacked-out, just-captured, stone German house, I flashed my light on the three loaves of bread that Harry Baker had brought up from Division Trains and some home-canned peaches deserted by the fleeing home owner.

Small arms firing had stopped but high scream and double "Boom!!" of 88s answered by Division Artillary sounded like we were nobody's target. Sound sleep came instantly, but then Bob Williams was shaking me awake and trying to get me to move "out of the shelling."

Thinking he was having a nightmare, I told Bob to go to the cellar, but to leave me alone. Next thing I knew, it was dawn, the sun was shining into my eyes, rubble from the wall that had been shelled into gravel while I peacefully slept, was all over the room—but neither I nor the three loaves of bread had a scratch. The jars of peaches were not as fortunate.

Some folks, like **J. Paul Heineman** *of Golden Valley, Minnesota, just aren't morning people.*

I AWOKE early one morning, at Dillingen, Germany, dressed, then looked out the window to see two German ME 109 planes straffing our troops 20 miles behind us, then watched them turn right for our position.

I ran across the farm yard to the mess-truck which had been backed halfway into the barn, with a .50 Cal. machine gun mounted on the cab.

I put a round into the chamber, figured I'd get at least 20 rounds into the ME 109 as it flew almost directly over me. I started to press the triggers when a voice hollered out, "DON'T FIRE THAT GUN!!!"

I hesitated just long enough to see the ME 109 disappear over the Danube River! When I asked the soldier why I shouldn't have fired the gun, his reply was, "The driver just cleaned it yesterday!!!".

Apparently, there was something about the Danube. **Robert F. Patton** *of Chapel Hill, North Carolina, had a strange experience there, too.*

IT WAS AFTERNOON before we were able to reach a small house after crossing the Danube River by pontoon boat. Inside we found everything as the German family left it, delicious wine and everything undamaged after many barrages of artillery fire.

We were tired, having had very little sleep the previous night. The Battalion Commander said, "Sergeant, how about some Boogie Woogie music?"

Surprised at such a suggestion, I checked for a booby trap in the piano and proceeded with a few notes. My fingers began to move with "Boogie Woogie Washer Woman."

The Radio Sergeant, unknown to me, broadcast the music over our network. No one will ever know how far it was retransmitted in our battle area.

Afterwards I enjoyed the inquiries about someone from our Regiment playing Boogie Woogie during the battle of the Danube River crossing, April 26, 1945 South of Regensburg, Germany.

Others, too, were seeing combat—men like **Alex Bourdas** *of Kinston, North Carolina.*

ON MAY 2, 1945 Task Force Smith, commanded by colonel Ridgeway P. Smith prepared an assault with companies A and B of the 67th Armored Division, on Adolph Hitler's famous birthplace city of Braunau, Austria.

Braunau is just across the Inn River from Simbach, Germany. The Germans had blown the bridge just before our forces were able to reach it. The German garrison at Braunau defied our order to surrender at first, but just before we were scheduled to pound the city with our artillery, the German command capitulated.

Companies B and A of which I was rifleman, crossed over the fast moving Inn River in leaky row boats and on a hastily improvised footbridge, and seized the city just before dark.

A counter attack by a force of German SS was beaten off that night, and some 20,000 allied prisoners of war were liberated at an aluminum factory jail at Ranshofen, Austria.

I remember manning my post beneath the second floor apartment where Hitler was born. On one corner of the building was a sign, "Adolph Hitler Strasse". The street had been renamed in his honor. Just across the street on the corner was an SS headquarters with the usual Nazi red banner and swastika.

Meanwhile, the German army is hastily retreating, taking with them POWs like **Weldon F. Phelps** *of Palm Harbor, Florida, who was a short distance away at the time.*

EARLY IN MAY 1945, approximately 4,000 American POWs were interned in a high forest on the Inn River near Braunau, Austria, Hitler's birthplace.

We were B-17 and B-24 non-commissioned officers (Gunners) who unfortunately had been shot down over Germany and France. Our internment followed a 17 day forced march across Austria from Stalag XVIIB, near Vienna.

The Russians were approaching Vienna from the West and the Germans wanted to use the Americans as a "Bargaining Chip" for the impending surrender to Patton's 13th Armored Division—hence the march to the Western Front.

One dark night a fellow crewman and I escaped when our guards converged for a smoke and conversation. With no food or water, we ran for miles. Finally, after near exhaustion, we approached a small farm house. The tenants recognized us as Americans and treated us royally.

Before we left, they requested we leave behind a note telling of our treatment for their protection against reprisal from approaching Allied Troops.

The farm tenants, like millions of others, knew the war was over.

Chapter 26
Captured

*Few things are more frightening or disheartening than to fall into enemy hands. Consider the sad tale **James T. Lingg** of Tacoma, Washington, has to tell.*

I WAS ON AN O.P. in France for 3 days. Then, just when I was to be relieved to go to the rear for a pancake breakfast, I was so hungry for those nice hot pancakes, I was sent out as point on a patrol.

I was hit in the chest, knocked into a ditch, started to crawl back to the rear, was hit again, in the spine and knocked out. When I came to, I looked up and all I could see was this forest of tall trees. After my eyes focused, I could see these trees were blades of grass.

I heard a guttural voice saying, "Comrad, Comraden" and turned to see a German pointing a machine pistol at me and decided I was a German Prisoner of War. God, how I missed those pancakes.

***Michael A. Cannella** of Riverview, Florida, remembers liberation.*

WHEN THE BRITISH 1ST ARMY came into the prison camp where I was held captive, April 16, 1945. Four months prior to that date on December 3, 1944, I was wounded and captured by the Germans along with other Americans in the Battle of the Bulge.

Many of had to walk and then were herded into box cars as they took us from camp to camp. We had nothing much to eat and many of us had dysentery and lice. I went from 170 lbs to 110 lbs.

It was a beautiful sight to behold that day when the British tanks under Field Marshall Montgomery rolled in. The tanks opened up their turrets and handed out loaves of bread to us.

I thank God every day for bringing me home safe.

*To be captured is bad, to live day by day not knowing if you are going to survive. That's what **Elmer R. Propst** of Cumberland, Maryland, experienced.*

FIVE AMERICANS, a Belgian captain of the underground and myself were captured December 23, 1944.

Were pinned down by tracer bullets of American scout car captured by

Germans. Knees of my pants worn out by crawling to keep from being captured lined up in front of a Mark V tank, part of the SS Panther Division. Tried three time to get us to a prison camp.

Christmas Eve lined up in front of a firing squad to be executed. After some discussion, Germans changed their minds.

Loaded on a truck and took back in woods near March. Christmas Day spent as German prisoner strafed by two American P38's, mortar fire and tanks using 30 caliber bullets.

Being pinned down, both Germans and American prisoners persuaded me to carry the white flag so they could surrender to the Americans, who stuck a 45 pistol in my belly till they could check my dog tags. Worn pants were replaced with a pair from salvage dump.

Kenneth W. Rees (deceased) told his wife Eloise R. Rees of Edmond, Oklahoma, about his experience negotiating.

HEADED FOR BERLIN, our jeep stopped. Bullets exploded, killing my driver.

Forced to surrender, I was prodded by Germans to a castle. As I removed my blood-soaked shirt, I saw my wounded shoulder and felt blood on my neck. When my dogtags dropped, I realized the bullet grazed my juggler before going through my shoulder. I shuddered. It could have severed my windpipe.

American tanks formed a barricade around the castle wall. I convinced the Germans to let me negotiate their surrender. Slipping toward a tank, I held the white flag.

But surprised soldiers fired shot through my wrist. With intense pain, I dropped. Losing consciousness, I prayed, "No fear in love. Perfect love casts out fear. John 4:18."

Suddenly, I found enough strength to stand the crossfire. I walked out of there alive — later learning if I had lost any more blood, I'd have died.

Thank God for protection!

Weldon Ulery of Miami Springs, Florida, probably doesn't appreciate the pleasure some people find in hiking.

I WAS MADE A GERMAN POW captured a week before Christmas. We were marched to Bittburg and bombed by U.S. planes on Christmas Day. About 500 of us were lined up and marched until liberated in April. Hardly any food and no shelter for four months. I lost 65 lbs. — but at least, I'm alive. I was in 109 Inf 28 Div.

Much of Europe and most of Germany was starving. This was bad news for prisoners like Joe Canavan of Brockton, Massachusetts.

WE WERE FREED on the morning of April 2, 1945. I was a POW in Stalag IX B at Bad Orb Germany. We were all suffering from acute malnutrition, and I myself was down to 93 pounds.

We had to line up by the side of the road every morning for the last few weeks to pay our respect to one, two or three of our comrades who had passed away the previous day.

On this morning, tanks from the 3rd Army crashed through the main gate and proceeded to throw us cigarettes, rations, and candy, which we hadn't seen for quite a while.

This was such an emotional experience that it will remain with me forever.

For American POWs, the sight of American tanks must have been a dream come true. **Robert Rodenbaugh** *of Norristown, Pennsylvania, was happy to see them.*

THE SIGHT of US tanks, as they entered Wetzler, Germany on 29 March 1945 meant liberation.

I was BAR man with 157th Inf, 45th Division Reg. I was to "take" three mountain tops to stop advance of Krauts, Alsace. Five companies took objective, two flanks failed. We were surrounded and cut-off. After six days of continuous mortar, artillery and infantry attacks, heavy casualties, both sides, Krauts sent in a white flag of surrender!

We tried to fight our way out, were caught under our own mortars. More casualties. Our officers said, "Lay down your arms".

Captors were 11th Div, 6th Regt SS.

Over 300 men, out of 800 were taken prisoner, five companies lost. Interred at Stalag XIIA. Taken from XIIA, boxcars to prevent liberation. Two P-51s knocked out the train. Forced to walk. Escaped, hid out in Wetzler.

Not everyone was liberated by armor units. **Robert M. Bowen** *of Linthicum Heights, Maryland, likes the Brits pretty well.*

WE CHEERED at the the sight of British troops advancing in a skirmish line toward our stalag at Bremervorde, Germany on April 29, 1945. Panzer troops had surrounded the camp several days before and had rebuffed the first attempt to liberate it.

I had been wounded and captured near Bastogne, Belgium on December 23, 1944, where I had served as a platoon leader in the 101st Airborne Division. I reached the Camp Lazarett a month before, moving from one hospital to another until I got there.

I was in poor physical shape, fifty pounds underweight and with a life threatening medical problem. Liberation meant life or death to me.

The British advanced behind an artillery barrage, driving the Germans away. Twenty-six American POWs died in the battle, but the rest of us were liberated to return home to decent medical treatment.

Kenneth L. Larson *of Los Angeles, California, remembers a holiday in prison.*

O N THE PHONOGRAPH RECORDING I heard the American entertainer Bing Crosby singing Irving Berlin's "Blue Skies" over a loudspeaker in a German prisoner-of-war camp. With the 106th "Golden Lion"
Infantry Division, I had been wounded and captured during the Battle of
the Bulge, December 18, 1944, and taken to a large camp some 40 miles
north of Hanover, Germany. Without essential food, all the prisoners lost
weight and worried about being taken away (as some had) and held as
bartering hostages. Dispirited and hungry, I took a walk one morning toward the main gate.

Suddenly, the German loudspeaker burst into sound and played
Crosby's wonderful recording of "Blue Skies." As I listened, my deadened
spirits lifted. I determined then and there to make it through to the end
of the war and to return to this choice land of America.

Like the Americans, the Russians, too, were on the move, and **Warren
W. Eddy** *of Los Angeles, California, doesn't seem to have trusted their
motives.*

J UST BEFORE THE WAR ENDED we were near Magdeburg on the
Elbe River and a guide from SHAFE was assigned to us with orders
to take a convoy across the Elbe, through the remaining German lines to
find a POW camp with Americans in it.

Off we went and almost immediately came face-to-face with a Russian
division. After negotiating our way through them (the guide spoke Russian), we eventually found the camp — just south of Berlin. The Russians
had taken over the camp and were unwilling to let us take anyone without 'orders'! They did agree to let us take those that were in the dispensary. When we went in to get them — we spread the word — if you want
to go home we'll be outside waiting — and out they came — over the fence
a platoon at a time — a beautiful sight.

The Russians were too amazed to do anything but talk — so we ig-
nored them and filled all our vehicles (80 plus). We brought out several
thousand that day and more came later. It was another example of
American ingenuity and bluff accomplishing a mission.

*Apparently, few things are stronger than a promise made to your
mother.* **Harry E. McCracken** *of Manor, Pennsylvania, made a promise.*

M Y BROTHER MILTON was shot down while flying missions over
Germany. He became a German prisoner.

I was a medic in the 99th infantry. We were advancing through Germany. We came to Mooseburg. I heard soldiers saying, "Let us hunt the
prison camp in this area." I volunteered to go with them. The tank and
vehicles crossed a field and through a fence, freeing this camp.

Some airmen were in the camp. I asked the American officer in charge
if there was a McCracken there. He was not sure. As I turned to leave, I
saw my brother standing in front of me. What a reunion.

The unusual part of this story is that I told my mother I was going overseas and that I would bring him back. I even ordered a set of clothing, including shoes his size. I took him to our aid station. He changed clothes.

Not only Americans were freed. **Lee E. Gingery** *of Shenandoah, Iowa, remembers a humanitarian mission he flew.*

E VERY COMBAT MISSION over Germany made an indelible impression in my memory, however, most vivid is a humanitarian mission performed two days after VE Day, May 10th, 1945.

Most of the operational B-17s of the 351st Bomb Group (as well as other 8th Air Force Groups in England) flew to Linz, Austria. There on the tarmac of the former Luftewaffe Air Field were gathered hundreds of French POWs, liberated from nearby Mauthausen.

Since each Flying Fortress carried a skeleton crew of five (I was the radio operator), we could carry 25 passengers. There was understandably some initial reluctance, bordering on fear, in the manner of the emaciated soldiers.

But on landing in Orleans, France there was no containing their emotions as the people of the city came forth to greet us. We proved to those people, that day, that Uncle Sam's mailed fist can indeed offer a velvet caress.

Donald D. Derrow *of Loudonville, Ohio, endured.*

I WAS IN 79TH DIV, 314th Inf, I & R Platoon. My regiment was surrounded, and most of us taken prisoners on Jan. 19, 1945.

We were marched and rode box cars in sub zero temperatures with inadequate clothing, very little food and no medical attention. After arriving at Stalag 7A, we continued on starvation diets; no heat or bedding, and covered with body lice.   Many bug tough, seasoned soldiers had tears in their eyes, when they saw that beautiful flag. . .

. . . seeing the American flag raised at prison camp a Stalag 7A, Mooseburg, Germany in early May 1945, when American 3rd Army, took over prison camps.

Now, we knew we were free.

Chapter 27
The Flag Is Raised

On May 8, 1945, the war was over in Europe. In the Pacific, however, fighting was still fierce. But US forces are making steady progress, penetrating ever deeper into what was once the domain of the Empire of the Rising Sun. But victory was far from assured and strategic bases still had to be secured.

__Leon Kogut__ of Arlington, Virginia, witnessed what would eventually play a part as a deciding factor in the war of the Pacific.

THE B-29 SUPERFORTS arrived on Saipan October 12, 1944. The airstrip was lined with spectators awaiting their arrival. Suddenly a B-29 appeared overhead, escorted by P-39 fighters. The fighters buzzed the strip, climbed and turned into the traffic pattern.

The B-29 came in, swooped low over the runway, climbed steeply, its wings actually shaking, then it too banked into the traffic pattern, turned toward the strip and came in for a smooth landing.

We'd witnessed its version of a victory roll. Everyone cheered and shouted in appreciation of the B-29's spectacular arrival. Shortly thereafter, the entire squadron of B-29s arrived.

That was the initial arrival of the Superforts, the aircraft which would bring the war to Japan.

According to __Weldon G. Jacobson__ of Milwaukee, Wisconsin, Saipan really wasn't much of an airport.

I USED TO WATCH the B-29's taking off from Saipan's airfield on their bombing runs to Japan. My vantage point was high atop the island at the 148th General Hospital.

The bombers were spaced only seconds apart, and as I look back on that scene it was similar to a tailgating line of traffic on today's freeway system. Their proximity to one another while thundering along that runway was awesome.

But the real scary part came when they literally dropped out of sight when they reached the end of the runway. The airstrip was considerably higher than sea level, and weighed down with their bomb loads, the planes actually lost elevation after being airborne.

I often wondered if the Air Force crews on those planes ever became accustomed to those erratic take-offs.

Albert Menaster *of San Francisco, California, watched Tinian being prepared for the big bombers.*

WHEN I WAS 21 years old, I was stationed as a Sgt Major, in charge of Army Ships Compliment, aboard the SS Cape Newenham and we arrived in the Southwest Pacific, Marinas Islands. We had left Seattle, WA, in June 1944 and arrived at Saipan Island in July, 1944.

We unloaded approximately 2,000 soldiers and their equipment. Most of them were engineers and they were to construct runways for the future bombing of Japan. Across from Saipan was the island of Tinian. That afternoon, the Navy began bombing Tinian from Saipan and I watched the bombing from our ship.

What I did not know at that moment was the US Air Force wanted Tinian in order to drop the first ATOMIC bomb. After Tinian was secured, the Air Force then flew the ENOLA GAY to Japan and did drop the first ATOMIC bomb.

Saipan was still within range of the enemy. **Robert Nelson Deal** *of Culpepper, Virginia, remembers a holiday air raid.*

IT WAS NEW YEARS NIGHT, 1944, on the Island of Saipan and we were having an air raid.

It was a most beautiful sight, seeing the tracers and the shells bursting. The sky was alive with lights. Everything on the island was shooting at those planes, even the Navy ships in the harbor were in the fight. They told us later that none of those planes went home. The planes did a little damage to the B-29 air base we were guarding.

Reinforcements disembark on Saipan, June 17, 1944.

I was in the Army AA and stayed on Saipan for 18 months. We were lucky that night for nobody got hurt. We had a lot of air raids, but that one I remember the most.

*Japan once ruled the air and the sea, but in part, men like **Arlo K. Johnson** of New Ulm, Minnesota, brought that to an end.*

A S A SUBMARINE SAILOR aboard the USS Seadragon our patrols were out in the Pacific. Doing our duty we torpedoed and sank any enemy boats in their shipping lanes.

One day we were depth-charged over 29 hours, and escaped from their 3 destroyers. Then we heard 'Tokyo Rose' come on the short-wave radio sending her sympathy to the many sweethearts, wives and orphans of the SeaDragon. The next day we torpedoed and sank several of their ships.

She then came over the waves calling us 'the dirty pink pirates', a name given us because the boat was given a coat of pink primer paint at Subic Bay, Philippines, and left in a hurry after the boat docked next to us was bombed at the beginning of the war.

We ate Christmas dinner at the entrance of Tokyo Bay in 1944; and headed for HOME.

For two days, carrier-based aircraft bomb Tokyo and Yokohama. Then, on February 19, 1945, Marines land on Iwo Jima, a tiny island consisting of only eight square miles. Though small, the island's defenses are formidable. But for about a half hour, there is little resistance to the landings.
***John J. Teuchert** of Barefoot Bay, Florida, was there.*

I FELT I was well trained for the invasion of Islands Marshall, Saipan Tinian and on D-Day 2-19-45, when our 4th Marine Division along with the 5th and 3rd Divisions saw their bloodiest fight.

It would prove costly before the Jap-held 3X8 the island fortress was secured on March 16, 1945.

On the first day an artillery shell hit me along with two of my buddies. While in the aid station on the beach Jap shells were making direct hits on the LST's unloading gear, etc, onto the beach. I have the greatest praise for the Navy, for the job they performed.

A Navy Coxswain lifted me about his L.C.V.P to be offloaded to the hospital ship solace offshore. There the medical staff on the USS Solace reset my right arm and operated on my right thigh.

After stays in Pearl Harbor and Oakland Naval Hospital, California, I was discharged a sergeant after 8 months of medical care and will never forget the fine doctors and all my buddies that paid a great price so that the Red, White, and Blue can fly in freedom.

Our division lost 3,928 killed and 14,424 wounded.

*Once the Japanese opened up, they really opened up, according to **Robert M. Kunkel** of Exeter, New Hampshire.*

M Y MOST MEMORABLE EXPERIENCE was the Battle of Iwo Jima. No question about it!

The very ground trembled constantly from the turbulence. The noise was overpowering — rifle fire whined, artillery boomed, and men screamed! The stench was overwhelming; all the common battlefield odors, plus the pungent scent of sulfur fumes which rose from the gaps in the rocky terrain.

Nightfall did not bring any relief from the violence, for darkness was sporadically interrupted by the eerie, glaring light of the flares which descended slowly on silken chutes; and by the abrupt flashes of exploding shells. Shadows moved!

And these were not split-second disturbances. The nightmare went on, without letup, for the better part of a month.

I can imagine nothing more vivid than this brief burst in history. It could well have been our hell on earth; for we are here now talking about it.

From all reports, nighttime on the island was an exercise in terror. **Walter H. Yocum** *of Hazleton, Pennsylvania, found a strange solace at night.*

O NE VERY SPECIAL NIGHT I became an old man at the unseemly age of 19. There I was, a technically trained non-combatant, soon to wish it were otherwise.

The fortunes of war being what they are, I found myself standing in a hole surrounded by inky blackness. Not being trained as a combatant I had a moment or two of outright terror. I sensed the three most life threatening conditions which I must come to terms with if I hoped to survive the night.

The first condition was the utter and absolute absence of any light and a stark blackness suggesting that evil has finally conquered. The second condition was a quiet deadly stillness wherein no sound dared exist. Finally there was the enemy swathed in his death dealing jungle expertise stealthily inching towards my termination.

Without warning a brilliant flash of light accompanied by an explosion of shocking proportions engulfed me. I was now in a suspended state of anticipation waiting for the unbearable pain that must surely follow.

I had just squatted down in the hole to check the time on my GI watch with the snap-down leather cover when the enemy struck . . . We all have experienced that worst of all nightmares, only to awaken in the nick of time and rejoice in our deliverance. So it was with this brave soldier that morning as I wonderingly snapped and unsnapped that leather cover on my radium faced illuminated dial GI wristwatch.

Sometimes, only words and music can describe an event. **John C. Love** *of Oklahoma City, Oklahoma, shares one.*

THE PLATOON HYMN

At the Fourth Division graveyard
In Iwo's bloody sands
I strolled between the crosses
Of Marines who'd met their end
Fighting for each other . . .
And a land they'd left behind
And as I wandered there among them
A hymn ran through my mind
It had become a daily journey
As the battle raged and roared
When I'd look along the new days rows
For a name I'd known before
As I worried for old comrades
Up there in the fray
Whom I'd known before, in a better place
Than we were in that day
And there was Ross, and there was Rhodes
Just a grave apart
The tears just hung there in my eyes
And anguish filled my heart
We'd sung the hymn, those two and I
With others of our platoon
On another isle, they call "P.I."
To drive away the gloom
It was a bond we understood
As each man was alone
With thoughts of those he'd left behind
In a place that he called "home"
And when I saw their faces
Smiling at me, from the sand
I cried as if my heart would break
Then Jesus took my hand
He held my hand and spoke to me
In a voice with golden tones
"Don't cry, my son . . . they walk with me
Where they'll never be alone
They're in a place where my Father dwells
In a land so far above
In a special place, made just for those
Who know you special love"
So now, whenever I hear the hymn
I feel a special pride
For those who've gone before me
And now walk at Jesus' side
For I know their trials are over
And a smile is on each face
As they walk there "In the Garden"
Of that very special place

Mrs. Bob Hultquist of Ganado, Texas, tells what happened to her brother.

MY BROTHER, Clifford J. H. Youngdale a Seabee in the Navy, who is now deceased, jumped in a pill box they had just finished digging after landing on Iwo Jima with several other boys.

When the shelling ceased and the smoke and dust settled he looked across and saw a Navy officer who he thought resembled himself. During the conversation that followed they discovered they were first cousins, he from Iowa and my brother from Texas. They had only seen each other once at age 3 years other than pictures.

Plans were made to have breakfast on his cousin's ship, but shortly after daybreak, creeping out there was no sign of the ship on the horizon. Seconds later another shelling took place and only my brother and two other boys survived. They were after the ship.

Choking back a tear of pride is hard when you read of the sacrifice on Iwo Jima. James W. Thomas of Houghton Lake, Michigan, would understand.

I WAS HAVING BREAKFAST the morning of the invasion of Iwo Jima. Sitting at the table with me were Sgt. Leonard O. Tiner, Sgt. Anthony A. Yuch, Sgt. Douglas M. Knowles, Pfc. Ernest Sharp Jr., Pfc. Robert G. Jozwiak, and Cpl. George Weigle.

We laughed and joked about everything except the imminent Invasion. Sgt. Tiner, veteran of Guadalcanal and Bouganville, whispered to the others, then they all shouted, "Thomas, you're now a Leatherneck."

This moment was not only a thrill, an experience, but an honor. To be called a Leatherneck by a veteran Marine, just prior to my first battle, was really something to remember. This would be our last breakfast together, because the 'Angel of Death' kissed Sgt. Tiner, Sgt. Yuch, Sgt. Knowles, and Pfc. Ernest Sharp Jr. on the Island of Iwo Jima.

The situation offshore was not altogether safe as A. H. Kuehn of Burke, Virginia, can confirm.

IN FEBRUARY 1945 during the Iwo Jima Campaign while I was stationed aboard an attack cargo ship, the USS Artemis (AKA-21). We remained in the area for about 10 days.

Every evening around dusk all non-combat ships would leave the area in formation and at sunrise the next morning we would return. Our ship carried approximately 250 Marine Reserves with full equipment needed for a beach invasion. On the fourth day of the operation we were ordered to release the Marines for the beach in small boats.

One evening just before departing the fighting area the combat ships picked up approaching planes on radar. Minutes later Japanese fighter planes from the mainland were in the area and were after the aircraft.

Anti-aircraft shooting started as they searched a baby carrier (Bismarck "C") only about 1000 yards away from our ship. The carrier was sunk in about 15 minutes.

This incident has remained with me since that day.

John H. Spenard *of Wingdale, New York, was more than a little concerned about this idea of withdrawing each night.*

FEBRUARY 1945: Our LST (Landing Craft Tanks) was sailing from Saipan to the Volcanic Islands. We had only recently been briefed as to what lay ahead — invasion of Iwo Jima.

We found ourselves part of so huge a fleet one might conjecture, it was moving on Japan itself. Arriving at Iwo, the on-going American bombardment was incredible. After dark on the evening of D-Day, I left the sick bay area and went on deck. To my surprise the waters around the sinister island were now mostly empty, the majority of the vessels having distanced themselves for the night.

I inquired of an officer why only we and several other craft were in close.

"Oh", he replied, "we are one of a few ships selected to draw fire."

Iwo Jima will forever live as a symbol of the war in the Pacific because of the raising of an American flag. ***Benny J. Gross*** *of Onida, South Dakota, witnessed it.*

I SAW the American flag being raised on top of Mt. Suribachi on the island of Iwo Jima, a small island in the Pacific. This rock mountain is 556 feet high.

The Sixth Fleet advances on Iwo Jima, with Mt. Suribachi in the background.

We made a beach landing with well trained troops on February 19, 1945. I served in the 5th Marine Division landing on the island with the initial forces the 27th Marines. Admiral Nimitz said of the men who served on Iwo Jima, "Uncommon valor was a common virtue."

The island was captured after 36 days of bitter fighting. The price for Iwo was 6,821 Marines killed and 18,000 wounded. I was twice wounded for which I received two Purple Hearts months later at a citation at Mare Island, California.

Offshore, a young **Wilbert L. Beggs** *of Camarillo, California, witnessed history.*

I N DECEMBER 1945, I was assigned to the newly christened USS Carteret APA 70 attack transport, as a radarman. After the shakedown we sailed west to Oahu where we took on a detachment of Marines. From there we continued to Saipan to join a convoy.

On D-Day, H hour February 19, 1945, the Carteret arrived at an island called Iwo Jima where our landing boats (LCVPs) transported the Marines ashore to engage the enemy in fierce and deadly battle. Casualties were unexpectedly heavy. The Cargeret stood by for several days to take on the wounded.

One day the crew was piped on deck to witness one of the most dramatic and memorable events of World War II, the raising of our American flag on Mount Suribache by a group of US Marines.

Like many legends, there are a few questions about the Iwo flag incident, as **Norman D. Syse** *of Chicago, Illinois, notes.*

T HE SIGHT of the American flag on Mount Suribachi from the deck outside the radio room of the USS Cecil, anchored off the east coast of Iwo Jima, was impressive.

Was it the battalion flag raised by 5th Division Marines who took the mountain?

Or was it the second flag in the photograph shot by Joe Rosenthal of The Associated Press nearly two hours later?

After the first flag went up the battalion commander was afraid "some son of a bitch is going to want that flag. But he's not going to get it. That's our flag." And a corporal was sent looking for a replacement which he found in LST 779 on the beachhead next to the mountain.

Either way one thing is certain: The flag I saw was a welcome sight in the early going of the fight for the island.

Wesley J. Hiles *of Summit Hill, Pennsylvania, had an excellent view.*

I SERVED aboard U.S.S. Nevada for two and one-half years, from Oct 1943-Mar 1946.

The morning February 23, 1945, Mt Surabachi, Iwo Jima. As a signalman, I had access to the Long Glass on the Signal Bridge.

The word was passed over the ship's PA-system that the Marines were nearing the summit of Surabachi. I immediately focused on the summit, and shortly thereafter through the smoke and dust I could view perfectly the historic flag raising on the summit of Mt Surabachi, by these brave Marines.

After all these years, I can truly say everytime I see our Flag fly in the breeze or hear our National Anthem, pride swells in my heart and I ask God to bless America and all veterans of all wars for making America the Greatest country in the world.

*To **James Edwin Smith** of Greenville, North Carolina, it was an unforgettable moment.*

O N A LITTLE 500 X 5000 yard island in the South Pacific, silence suddenly came — for 30 seconds. The sudden hush "All Quiet" — you looked up and looked around, then saw the US flag being raised on Iwo Jima. Mt. Serabachi was for all eyes.

Tears, Yes.

*Pride is evident in the words of **Raymond C. Goron** of Greensburg, Pennsylvania.*

I WITNESSED our flag raised on Mt. Suribachi during the Iwo Jima Campaign. Thousands of our service men started jumping for joy at the sight, then the awful realization that the flag was no more as the Japanese overran the mountain.

Later on the Marines recaptured Mt. Suribachi and re-raised the flag. Telling any of these men that some day the United States would be fighting for the right to burn our flag, would have been the same as suicide, no one would have believed you.

War always brings out the best in every man; don't let any or of our veterans die in vain.

***Winfred Leon Strain** of Rensselaer, Indiana, may have been a little too busy to realize he had witnessed history.*

I WAS SERVING on the USS Bolivar (APA 34) as a Coxswain in the small boat crew (LCM). I had unloaded troops and supplies for the invasion of Iwo Jima.

On one of the runs to the beach with a load of supplies, I had to wait several hundred yards off the island because the beach area was congested with other small boats. I happened to look up toward the island and could see some movement at the highest point. I looked through my binoculars, and watched the "raising of the American Flag."

It was a great feeling to know another island was secure. I didn't even realize until much later that I had witnessed a very historic event.

*Casualties were high, but for men who had spent what seemed like a lifetime in the jungle, like **Roy Parks** of Gleason, Tennessee, it didn't take much to make them happy.*

AFTER 2 YEARS of jungle and 2 wounds, we entered the Lyquean Gulf, in route to Monela, the first civilized place on Rozell Avenue in Manila, beside a large cemetery. I got wounded again. Then in route back to the gulf through two field hospitals by Cub plane then on a Navy barge lit up so bright and wide open, then one of the strangest thing there was a 10 gal garbage can filled with Baby Ruth Bars slightly molded. Were they ever good.

After a few hours we came up on the prettiest white ship. It was lit up like a Christmas tree. We were taken a board at 11:00 PM. There were white sheets and pillow cases, all dressed out nurses served hamburgers and ice cream, in route to New Guinea. This was the greatest time of my Army career.

***John A. Adams** of Provo, Utah, offers this:*

THERE IS A MARKED CONTRAST between those fighting in far-away places and those living back home.

We stood on the deck of an attack transport ship and watched the heavily laden shoulders descend into small boats in the darkness off some distant shore. These somber men had just a few days earlier pitied the men in the Navy, having to always cope with life on water. Many had been sea-sick and others in the Sick Bay because of injuries incurred from gear, not properly stowed away, that had fallen on them during heavy seas.

The unhappy plight of these soldiers and the squalid conditions they faced on small Pacific Islands was compared with the business as usual we found back home. Returning to Seattle at Christmas time was like entering a fairy land. Life seemed to go merrily on in all of the cities and towns across the United States, with only radios and newspapers to serve as daily reminders of a distant war.

Fighting continues off Iwo Jima, but it becomes obvious the Japanese position is hopeless. At the same time, in early March, a devastating attack against Tokyo by 279 Superfortresses ignites a firestorm that kills at least 80,000, but more likely resulted in the deaths of 120,000. The bombing will prove, in lives, more devastating than either atomic bomb.

Worse, more incendiary raids will follow.

***R.A. Duvanich** of Mission Viejo, California, tells what it was like in the sky.*

IT WAS MY FOURTH BOMBING MISSION over Japan. Ours was a B-29 crew and this was the first of five consecutive fire bomb missions over major Japanese cities. Armageddon, this night, had come to Tokyo.

I remember the firey inferno below and the glow of embers that burst through the acrid stench of black smoke. It was as if Dante's words had come alive and he stood by in silent approval. Wandering search light sought to silhouette the night marauders in its beacons. I heard the sound of flak, like pebbles raining on a tin roof. The smoke filled thermal clouds tossed the plane around like so much fluff.

Our bombs fell merciless into the firestorm below as we slipped into the darkness and headed home.

It was another seven hours before we put down on our island base. I reached for my book of poetry and found these lines.

You smug-faced crowds with
   kindling eye
Who cheer when soldier lads
   march by
Sneak home and pray you'll never
   know
The hell where youth and laughter
   go.

Merle E. Bouges *of Lincoln, Nebraska, suddenly became aware of his own mortality.*

M Y FIRST B-29 MISSION over Japan was in May 1945. We were going in at 25,000 feet, in tight formation, that beautiful sunlit morning. Miles ahead a wall of anti-aircraft explosions rose into the sky. Moments later we were in it. Flack shells were bursting everywhere.

Carefully searching the sky for Japanese aircraft from my top gunner's sighting station, I was suddenly shocked to see a hole through our left wing. It looked like a small splash in a pool of calm water.

A cold chill came over me. My hair seemed to stand on end. They were trying to kill us, I realized. This wasn't fun and games anymore, I thought. This was for keeps!

As the weeks wore on, we sustained other and more severe battle damage. But there is nothing — ever — like the first shot fired.

On Iwo Jima, a suicide attack takes place on March 26. Of the Japanese garrison of 20,700, only about 200 survive. US losses number 6,000 dead and 17,000 wounded.

On April 1, 1945, on the back of the largest naval armada ever assembled, the US attacks the Japanese island of Okinawa. The Japanese are entrenched along what is called the Shuri Line and Kamikaze attacks step up, but little resistance to US forces is encountered until April 4.

The calm is short-lived. *Eugene J. Klingele* *of Quincy, Illinois, tells of a sea disaster.*

I SAW THE AFTERMATH of damage inflicted on our carrier USS Franklin (Ap. 1945 — 832 killed).

While on duty with the Navy 128, SRU Pearl Harbor Navy Yard, I saw this ship as it was tied up there. It came back listing badly burned, a mass of twisted steel. Standing only a gang-plank distance away, I saw first hand the damage. The ship was completely blackened by fire and smoke, flight deck burned, hangar deck in bad shape, anti-aircraft batteries hanging over the side and so on.

I salute the men who served and saw combat on this ship. They have the most vivid memories, they are the real heroes.

Yet, the Japanese fight on, as **Phillip H. Klenman** *of Seattle, Washington, bears witness.*

H ORROR was my witnessing the execution by handgun of an enemy. I was a crew member of the USS Ralph Talbot (DD390) during the Okinawa Campaign, May 1945. We had encountered and sunk an explosives-laden suicide boat that attempted to ram us. The enemy sailors were thrown into the water and we attempted to rescue them. One of them swam to our ship and we helped him climb a cargo net tied to the ship.

As he was climbing aboard, he suddenly produced a grenade and attempted to arm it. He was immediately met by a continuing fusillade of bullets from our sailors who were attempting to help him. Bullet after bullet crashed into him. Slowly his bullet-ridden body, spewing and spurting blood, slipped over the side and into the now reddened water. A sickening sight that haunted me for years.

The fighting through the islands has taken its toll. **John A. Snyder** *of Monessen, Pennsylvania, describes the horror.*

O UR MACHINE GUN SQUAD of five, positioned itself one night in a Japanese anti-aircraft emplacement near Motoyama Airfield #2 giving us high ground visibility. Close-by a cave was on fire and ammunition was exploding.

Some Japs came out, spotted us and lobbed a concussion grenade that rolled into our position. Since we had no cover, Sgt. George L. Barlow crawled toward the grenade. It exploded beneath him saving us from injury but critically wounding him. I cradled his head in my arms and he was bleeding profusely.

He begged, "Please don't leave me here to die".

Amid total confusion, we exchanged hand grenades but the Japs used the cave for cover and concealment. A second grenade wounded PFC O'Dwyer. Sgt Barlow died.

Realizing this position was extremely vulnerable, we carried his body to the base of the emplacement abandoning our position.

Julio Sanchez Jr. *of Tampa, Florida, went ashore the first day.*

I WAS 17 in 1943, had volunteered for the Navy and taken communications training at the Naval Armory in Indianapolis, Indiana. I was assigned to the Amphibious Forces, sent to Guadalcanal, then placed on a convoy that sailed north. On Easter Sunday, April 1, 1945, with a radio pack on my back, our team landed on the southwestern tip of Okinawa and encountered heavy enemy fire.

We were ordered to drop equipment and return to the ship. The following months were filled with airplane battles, constant bombardment from our ships, lighting smog pots to hide our ships from enemy aircraft, Kamikaze attacks, shooting at planes as they flew low between our ships, the surrender of Japanese vessels after the atomic bomb was dropped on Nagasaki on August 5, 1945, and the surrender of a Japanese soldier still hiding in Guam's jungles in the spring of 1946.

To this day, I still remember my serial number and International Morse Code.

Glenn E. Miller *of Palm Bay, Florida, offers his impressions.*

TWO DISTINCT SCENES join to form my most vivid recollections of WWII. First, I saw ships of all shapes and sizes spread out clear to the horizon and as far around as could be seen. It was an awesome sight. Seemed like all the ships in the world had converged on a small island in the vast Pacific called Okinawa. I later learned it was the largest task force ever assembled.

Second, the sky pock-marked with exploding anti-aircraft shells and third, heading for shore in a landing craft and passing directly under the thundering 14 inch guns of the Battleship New York. Possible point of interest: Hollywood star William Lundigan was in that same boat. He was a Marine photographer.

A GI's job is often to kill, but nothing says he has to like it. **Elmer A. Mapes** *of Bettendorf, Iowa, remembers Okinawa.*

I HEARD a baby's cry in the night — April, 1945 — northern end of Okinawa. Fourth Regiment Marines readied fox-holes, set roadblocks and established a defense perimeter as the sun disappeared.

The silence of that night seemed particularly "loud". A few hours elapsed. Suddenly, bursts of machine-gun and rifle fire split the silence seam at the road-block. Just as suddenly the shooting stopped and was replaced by screams, moans and an unnerving baby's cry.

Sleep was unattainable as the solitary cry of that baby pierced the quiet of the night's carnage greeted us, but there was no baby.

Why did those Okinawan civilians attempt to filter through the lines at night after being repeatedly warned by the Allied authorities to attempt no nighttime travel?

Was that baby's mother killed there?

Did the baby survive?

Perhaps **Raymond G. Stramel** *of McCook, Nebraska, was nearby.*

W AR CAN BE CRUEL. Not only to the military, but to civilians as well.

As my Company was moving to the south of the island, to do battle, we marched through several residential areas, that had been devastated and demolished by naval gun fire, artillery, bombings, etc.

This one home in particular, had a large fish pond, and there in the middle of the pond was a young mother, with her small baby tied to her back, lying face down in about 12" of water. Of course, the poor souls were dead.

One can lose some very close buddies in battle, but to see such a sight of a helpless mother and her baby in such a situation; Well — War is Hell.

The episode still haunts me at times, and nothing can erase it from my mind.

The fighting in the Pacific would take its toll. **Jacob D. Dunbar** *of North Liberty, Indiana, remembers the aftermath of some of it.*

I WAS ON IE SHIMA off Okinawa. The island had been secured, and I was walking up a path, and there in the middle was a Japanese leg sticking up in the air with the legging and tennis shoe on.

Also, I was on the LSM 136 on the beach. I saw Ernie Pyle get killed. I also saw the LSM 135 go out to pick up survivors and was hit by two suicide planes.

No one survived.

A few days later, they had dead Japanese soldiers piled up on the beach like cord wood. A bulldozer dug a hole and pushed a hundred or more of them in. Two destroyers came in tied together, one with a hole in it large enough to drive a car in.

War has a price to pay, as **Albert J. Hassett Jr.** *of Woodside, New York, found.*

I WAS AN ARMY ENGINEER working to repair the badly deteriorated surface of the highway that paralleled the beaches. I noticed an approaching USMC International truck which had a white painted wooden cross wired to the radiator.

Puzzled, I watched as the vehicle jolted past and saw that the contents in the back of the truck were covered by a loosely secured tarp. I was horrified to see that the "cargo" comprised the bodies of Marines killed in the bloody fighting along the Shuri Escarpment. They were stacked like cordwood, their booted feet protruding from beneath the tarp. Some of the boots were well worn but I saw others showing barely any sign of wear belonging to replacements landed shortly before from one of the transports still at anchor off the invasion beaches.

The Japanese are becoming desperate and the final Kamikaze attacks take a toll. Somerset, Kentucky's **Lee G. "Hap" Johnson** *and his shipmates paid the price.*

OKINAWA, MAY 9, 1945. I was a crew member on a 20 mm anti-air craft gun on the bridge of the USS England (D.E.635) assigned picket line duty for defense of larger ships from Japanese Kamikazie planes.

Sunset brought three Val bombers on attack. Two fell to an American fighter plane and another ship. The third, bullet riddled by our gunfire, hit just forward and below our gun.

The blast and shrapnel left me the sole survivor at our station. Nearly helpless from a shattered hip and shrapnel wounds I was rescued by shipmates who jumped from the flying bridge above onto the blazing deck. They helped me overboard as a gamble for survival. Rescue came from a seagoing tug. More than a year was spent in Navy hospitals.

Thirty-seven shipmates were killed or missing from the attack.

*Nor is the enemy always directly the culprit, as **Richard M. McCluskeY** of Brooklyn, New York, explains.*

I WAS A CREWMAN aboard the battleship USS Alabama BB60 and cruising off Formosa. We were called to Air Attack Station because of an emminent Japanese air attack. All ships made sudden turns and the Alabama's starboard side became awash.

One of the crewmen named Olsen was washed overboard. Our ship came under air attack for over two hours, zigzagging back and forth and incredibly passed the spot in the sea where Olsen went overboard.

Incredibly Olsen was picked up by destroyer Olsen and ultimately returned to the Alabama. Olsen was brought to the bridge and with tears in his eyes he was welcomed back aboard the ship by our captain.

*Casualties were not confined to the sea or the ground. **Florian Tomkowiak** of Cudahy, Wisconsin, tells about some lucky fliers.*

I WAS INVOLVED with the rescue of 3 USAAF airmen; 2nd Lieutenant James New, Sergeant Isidore Barrack, and Corporal Louis Branch on June 15, 1945.

USS Underhill was enroute from Leyte, Philippine Island to Hollandia, New Guinea and searched for the airmen for two days. By order of Commander, Philippine Sea Frontier at 0545, June 115, 1945, USS Churchill DE682 secured from search, 13.5 miles from Merir Island and departed for Hollandia. At 0725 a green sea marker was sighted and at 0735 objects in water were identified as human beings. All engines were stopped to lower whaleboat and rescue men. At 0751 survivors came aboard and one airman said, "OH, BOY SAILORS."

*Eventually, the sea war came to the Japanese mainland. **Gerald J. Turner** of Staten Island, New York, was . . .*

A GUNNERS MATE 2nd class assigned to the USS brush DD 745, a destroyer of 2250 ton Flecher class with Admiral Halsey's 3rd fleet.

We were assigned to enter Tokyo Bay for a sneak attack at night. We entered in a column of nine destroyers at midnight on July 22, 1945.

The mission was to destroy anything visible on radar. Upon a surface contact each destroyer fired 2 torpedoes and then we opened fire with our twin 5" guns, three gun mounts fired approximately six hundred rounds.

We hit a convoy of three merchant ships and an escort believed to be a destroyer. Officially two ships and one possibly sunk and the destroyer damaged. We had no casualties to our ships or men. This was the first surface attack inside Tokyo Bay. At entering the Navy at age 19 and now at age 67, this will live in my memory till my end.

Herbert L. Mastin *of Lakeland, Florida, believed caution wasn't a bad idea.*

I WAS A YOUNG 18 year old sailor, assigned to USS LCT 463, stationed in Okinawa.

After the invasion of Okinawa our duty was to go to anchorage area off the island and unload ships and bring supplies to the beach, or other ships.

One particular time, we were along side a liberty ship unloading ammunition on to our deck heard a plane approaching. I looked up and saw a Japanese Kamikaze swooping down on us. He was coming in fast and low.

I sprung to the side and jumped overboard, never thinking that I couldn't swim. Then to my surprise the plane passed over our ship and crashed into a larger tender ship which was probably the original target to begin with.

Needless to say I was given a reprimand for leaving the ship without permission.

Fate has held sway for five long years . . . and as far as ***John R. Beuler*** *of Livonia, New York, knows it still does.*

THE JOHN W. WEEKS (DD701) was doing radar picket duty 50 miles ahead of Task Force 38 on August 9.1945. I was on the bridge with the Captain as his phone talker when five planes, strafed, bombed and attempted suicide crash dives on the four destroyers in our division.

The Borie (DD704) was badly damaged when the first plane crashed on their bridge. I had been asked to transfer earlier to the Borie, had I done so I surely would have been killed since I would have been on that bridge.

We had taken part, from December 30, 1944 to this date, in the Invasion of Luson, Battles of Iwo Jima and Okinawa and the Japanese Raids during which time other destroyers had received hits. Would our luck hold out?

The other four planes were downed without damaging the remaining three destroyers.

On this same day, an A-Bomb was dropped on Nagasaki and the Weeks was at general quarters for more than 13 hours.

Louis Russo *of Glenolden, Pennsylvania was . . .*

WORKING IN A BATTERY SHOP when a crew member came in for a battery and said that they just dropped a bomb and they didn't know what damage it did. All they saw was smoke and fire.

This was the Atomic Bomb that was just dropped on Hiroshima.

Melvin A. Erickson *of Clinton, Iowa says . . .*

I VIEWED the ruins, the destruction and chaos of dropping the first atomic bomb on Hiroshima on August 6, 1945. This scene is branded in my memory.
Over the city
B-29s glided;
and as they dropped
their payload,
the rising mushroom danced
among its victims,
softly sighing:
"Dust to dust."

Lotus H. Fultz *of Madison, Indiana, was another who was in the sky on August 7.*

IT WAS AUGUST 7, 1945 on Ie Shima, a tiny island of the Ryukyu Chain. We were being briefed for a bombing strike in the Sea or Straits of Japan. Our Squadron of black Liberators, the 63rd of the 42nd BG in the 5th Air Corps had sunk more Japanese shipping than any other whole Air Corps! The briefing officer revealed that a B-29 had unloaded a huge devastating bombing device literally wiping out Hiroshima.

In case our secondary objective, the Pusan Air Docks, was to be our target we were to fly a 100 mile detour. It was because of turbulence and something called "fall-out." Ours could quite possibly have been the last regular mission flown in WWII. The next day Nakasaki was cremated.

I said a prayer for Harry Truman, his crew and the crews of the Enola Gay and Bockscar then . . . and to this day I still say a big thank you and a prayer for them all . . . .

The atomic bomb. Was it necessary? Were two necessary? No one will ever know. **Joe D. Lawhn** *of Port Lavaca, Texas, made a fly-over of the area.*

AUGUST 9, 1945, we passed over Nagasaki, Japan, 3 to 5 minutes after the atomic bomb had dropped. The plutonium cloud, (The most dangerous bomb dropped) was 35,000 to 40,000 feet high, and we passed thru the fall-out of radiation. The cloud was everywhere.

We were in the 43rd Bomb GP, 403rd Sqdn, stationed in Ie Shima, off Okinawa, and our target for that day was Iwakuni, about 30 miles south of Hiroshima, atomic bombed August 6th.

After dropping our bombs on Iwakuni, we proceeded south on our same route, was back over Nagasaki which was -2° (degrees), due south to IE Shima.

Lt. Yeager was our plane pilot, flying B-24 #621. It was an 8 hour, 20 minute mission and we had fire and flak. In retrospect of what happened to Chernobyl and its people, I wonder how many have died from cancer of our group that day.

*The destruction of the atomic bombs was incredible, but most believe it was the only thing that would have forced Japan's surrender. The attitude of **David B. Kinsey Jr.** of Taft, Texas, is shared by many of his fellow veterans.*

I LANDED D-Day at Sasebo, Japan, about 25 miles from Nagasaki. After a couple of weeks, I was taken on a sightseeing tour of Nagasaki. We stopped at "ground-zero" for about an hour. It was hard to imagine that one bomb could be so destructive. I realized then, that the bomb had probably saved my life and a lot of other Americans. If we had invaded Japan, we would have had to kill women and children because they were trained to kill us. Hooray for Harry Truman!!

*The world was about to change very rapidly. **Elmer A. Mapes** of Bettendorf, Iowa, thought he was part of an invasion force.*

GUAM, AUGUST 15, 1945. We, members of the 4th Marine Regiment, were on the beach in full combat gear, preparing to board ship for yet another combat campaign. We had returned to Guam after completing our role in the capitulation of Okinawa. Guam served us as a "Rest" area and as a base for preparations for the dreaded invasion of Japan.

August brought word of Hiroshima and Nagasaki: this led to temporary jubilation. Still — no surrender. Thus we found ourselves on the beach in our "going to battle" status. Memories of campaigns at Bougainville, Guam and Okinawa vividly reminded me of the tenuousness of life.

At that moment the Fleet suddenly signalled that Japan had sued for peace! The possibility of returning HOME became much less remote and the grim forebodings of moments before were replaced by anticipations more pleasant.

*Perhaps others had the same feeling. **Cecil F. Ashmore** of Tucson, Arizona, did.*

BY THE END of July 1945 some of us in my 90mm AAA Gun Bn. had the required 38 months overseas and enough "points' for our first leave of the war. Some had enough points for discharge. Those of us eligible for R&R leave boarded a Navy AKA in Buckner Bay about 3rd of August.

A few days out there were rumors going round about an atom bomb. None of us had ever heard of an atom bomb. Few days later over the ships PA came, "Now hear this . . . Now hear this . . . B-29's have dropped atomic bombs on two Japanese cities . . . the Japanese have surrendered . . . the war has ended."

I felt empty, sort of cheated. Guess we all did. No clapping, yelling or cheering on deck of that ship. Just silence. This wasn't the way it was supposed to end.

But it did.

Chapter 28
The War Is Over

The war in Europe was over. **Anthony C. Trojan** *of Bayside, New York, remembers Hitler and his mistress, dead, their charred bones and bunker, as objects of curiosity.*

A WEEK after the surrender, I went on an Army three day tour to Hitler's home in Berchesgarden. It had been bombed by the USAF and by RAF by night. The house was built of stone and concrete, and its interior had been burned out.

Looking through the glassless picture window, I observed a most magnificent view on this beautiful day in May 1945. I can never forget the fact that I stood on the same spot where Hitler stood, the man who started the war and now it was ended. It was here that such a catastrophic world history had its beginning and end.

As I stood there, it was unbelievable that in these beautiful surroundings any man could have such destructive thoughts.

Richard M. Wray *of Colonial Heights, Virginia, is still far from home.*

A S A MEMBER of the 104th Infantry Division (the Timberwolves), I was crossing the border of Belgium near the town of Wuustwezel into Holland with members of my platoon.

After a mile or two we took a break along the tree-lined narrow road. Scattered nearby were a few Dutch houses. Suddenly, a window in one of the houses opened and the handsome face of a young boy appeared. He smiled at me, proceeded to sing one verse of "America" in perfect English, smiled again, and closed the window.

This was my first impression of Holland and the Dutch people. I might add that it was a lasting impression. Before I could get his name, we were given the order to proceed to join the Canadian First Army.

For **Gerald C. Myers** *of Jeanerette, Louisiana, VE-Day is mixed with other memories.*

F IRST, was being witness to the tragedy of the torpedoing of the troop ship "LEOPOLDVILLE" in the English Chanel Christmas Eve, 1944, with a loss of 802 members of the 66th Infantry, (Black Panther) Division of which I as a member.

Secondly, being on telephone duty while manning outpost 55 in the Lorient-St Nazaire sector and receiving a telephone call from the battalion on our right (about 6:00 AM May 6th, 1945) stating that a German staff car was approaching their positions with a white flag. A delegation of German Army officers stated that they wanted to negotiate a surrender of some 50,000 German troops, signalling the end of the war for the 66th infantry division.

Joseph Laska of Schenectady, New York, took it upon himself to make sure folks knew the Americans had been there.

I WAS WITH THE INFANTRY and waited at the Elbe River for the Russians that ended the war in Germany. It was near Magdeburg about 48 miles from Berlin. The Russian soldiers laughed when we said we were with the Infantry. They laughed because they felt that the US had no Infantry as every soldier had a jeep and no one walked.

Only the front line Russian soldier had a Russian uniform, all others had parts of various US uniforms which they were grateful to the US for and commented on it. We all congratulated each other for lasting to the end of the war especially those of us who landed at Cherbourg and were still on our feet.

Also, the American flag was prominent in the war with Japan but not a single one was to be seen in Europe so I decided to make one. Problems arose. Everyone knows the American flag but no one, including myself, knows how many short red and white stripes are in the flag or how far across the flag the blue goes.

An Army manual had the answer. All the material needed was obtained from bombed out German homes. I carried it with me until I finished it, in spite of being called Betsy Ross. Forty-eight stars, a blue field and stripes on each side called for lots of hand sewing. I hung the flag over a schoolhouse on a lightning rod made into a flagpole. Unfortunately, the red shrunk in the rain and the wind tore the old thread apart so it had to be repaired each evening until I gave up and soon moved on.

After the battle is over, decorating those GIs and units who had distinguished themselves is traditional. That's how Richard A. Gardener of Oakland, New Jersey, recalls the end of the war.

I WAS VERY PROUD when my Unit was received by General Patton after the War was over. As a Sergeant in the 83rd Infantry, I was wounded three separate times and hospitalized on two of those occasions. When the General got to our unit he looked for Purple Heart ribbons to be displayed. We had been ordered to wear all our decorations. Suddenly, he was in front of me and he asked me if I was ok now and to tell him how and where I was wounded.

When I finished he looked me in the eye and patted me on the shoulder and said I was a good soldier.

That moment made the Blood, Sweat and Tears worthwhile. I shall always remember that special moment.

Timing is everything. **Mike Sandella** *of Kansas City, Missouri, probably wonders why the war couldn't have ended just a little sooner.*

I WAS in the European theater for 30 months. My company was stationed in a German town close to the Austrian border.

Four men were sent to a nearby barn to get water for the kitchen. We had gotten one-third of a tank and I went back in the barn to get one more bucket of water after putting the water in the tank.

As we were leaving, about 50 feet from the barn, an incendiary bomb hit and destroyed it. Upon returning to camp, Sergeant asked if I wanted to go to Paris on a 7 day furlough.

While in Paris, the war ended and there were celebrations all over that city.

The war was over, and **John R. Austin** *of Cockeysville, Maryland, took a few moments to contemplate.*

IT HAPPENED while I was serving with the 94th Division attached to Patton's 3rd, somewhere between Pilsen and Prague on the first night at the end of the war.

I was on top of a hill overlooking a small village when the lights started coming on slowly. One at a time until the valley was well lighted.

It was at that time I vividly recalled the song "When the Lights Come on Again All Over the World"; a night I'll never forget!

At war's end, is your enemy still your enemy? **DeWitt W. Welch** *of Stone Mountain, Georgia, had to answer that question.*

WE WERE ON OUR WAY to Split, Yugoslavia with a cargo of wheat and a deck load of trucks for the army to unload in Brendisi, Italy. We stopped in Sicily for orders. They told us that the Adriatic Sea was clear of German U-boats.

A few days out of Sicily early in the morning of May 6, 1945, we had heard that the war with Germany was over. We saw a group of boats coming toward us, when they were close enough for us to see what they were; they were five U-boats and eight E-boats all flying a black surrender flag. They passed to starboard, they dipped their colors and so did we.

We went on to Split and were told we were the first American ship to come in since the war started. The ship we were on was the S.S. Big Foot Wallace, Captain John Hansen Master.

Ralph G. Vaccaro *of Miramar, Florida, found himself wondering this, too.*

A FTER THE WAR in Europe was over, shortly before Christmas, I was on the platform of the train station in Baden Baden. I had permission from my CO and the French Command in Karlsruhe to visit a town called Trossingen in the Black Forest.

As I waited for my connection, a long, slow freight pulled in. Suddenly I was in the middle of returning German POWs. My ODs and Eisenhower Jacket stood out like a sore thumb amid a sea of gray-green.

While in the past I had frightening moments from the noise of artillery, tanks of planes, now I was frightened by the silence and my thoughts. Hundreds of POWs passed by. Not one said a word or made a threatening gesture. In about five minutes I was once again alone.

*Perhaps **Leroy N. Stewart** of Washington, Kansas, speaks for everyone who fought. Who will be the last one to die?*

I HAD TAKEN PART in the Omaha Beach operation and as a member of Co. K., 26th Regt., First Division, was in every battle the rest of the war.

May 7, we were in Czechoslovakia where the war was to end the next day. At that time I was the only one in the Co. that had made it all the way. We were to attack the next day and I didn't get much sleep that night. I kept wondering if my luck would last one more day.

The first town we came to was flying white flags. Our last objective was Abrsroth, which like all day, was taken without a shot being fired by either side.

After we outposted the town, our job was done. The war was over. I had made it.

*The war ends when enemies become friends, sharing a common concern. **John R. Winslow** of Eugene, Oregon, met his enemy.*

O MAHA BEACH, Caumont, St Lo, St Bartholomew, Aachen, The Hurten Forest, Battle of the Bulge, Langendorf Hill, and the Rhine River—I was there and remember.

One of my customers (a German tank mechanic in WWII) one evening and after a few beers including a chorus of the song "Ang Zine" at the piano Bar, we discovered we were across from each other on the Rhine during WWII.

Vietnam came along and his son was a helicopter pilot for the good ole USA and my son a Sgt in the Army, both decorated several times.

Of course the German Tank Mechanic of WWII and I are the best of friends. He tells of backing a tank over his best friend. So, you see the world is a small place after all. We never quit suffering the mental anguish of war.

*In spite of the anguish, VE-Day was a time of celebration. **William S. Pfriender** of Spring Lake, New Jersey, was in a city that knows how to celebrate.*

I WAS IN PARIS as a Master Sergeant, in the spring of 1945, when victory came to the Allied armies in Europe, the imminent fall of Berlin an added joy to the city that had already observed its liberation from German occupation.

Late in the afternoon of May 7, French newspapers sold like beer in Bizerte, with one banner headlines screaming: CAPITULATION SANS CONDITIONS. Nonstop demonstrations of pent-up emotions went on for several days and nights, and Paris once again, for the first time in five long years, fully recaptured its fame as the "City of Light."

Multi-colored flares fell from low-flying planes, a thrilling display of fireworks reminiscent of Fourth-of-July pyrotechnics back home, while a potpourri of popular patriotic tunes filled the air: "It's A Long Way To Tipperary," "Over There," "Madelon," and the martial "Marseillaise."

Little wonder, then, why this WWII scenario remains indelibly inscribed in my memory.

Ultimately, VE-Day meant going home. Some had no home to go to. **Karl L. Gaber** *of Bulger, Pennsylvania, was . . .*

RIDING ON A TROOP TRAIN (box cars) after Germany had surrendered. We were on our way home, at last. Traveling slowly, we were passing another train, sidetracked to let us by. Its passengers were displaced persons, coming from probably Hitler's work camps, gaunt, dirty, dressed in rags. One woman was squatted, urinating in the snow.

Did I feel ashamed to see her? I don't know. I've often wondered how she felt, being seen by all us men, or had her captivity left her completely empty of feelings?

Today, years later I'm sure the same events are happening to the refugees, trying to pass through Jordan in the mideast.

Will this same sad story of good people, just wanting to live a happy, peaceful life never end? I think not.

Men in high places whether in government or big business, who are greedy for power and wealth, will continue to ruin the lives of nations and people.

Though the war in Europe was over, the grim reality was that more wars would follow. **Sidney R. Moore** *of Cohasset, Minnesota, knows what that's like.*

THE AIR was tense in our little town. Suddenly, all the people, mostly women, burst out of their houses into the middle of our street. They were cheering, crying and hugging. Sirens and whistles blew. A pretty young woman that lived across the street from us was beating two big pans together over her head.

This surprised me because she was usually quite serious and dignified. Sometimes she used to sit on her front steps and talk to me about her husband who was an infantryman with the 101st Airborne Division.

Twenty years later I was saying good-by to my young wife and two sons ages five and three as I left for Vietnam. My five year old hugged me and said, "Hide good over there, Dad."

I realized at that moment that he had taken more interest in our adult conversations than I thought.

Perhaps no one suffers more from war than children. **Maurice Aiken** *of Charlestown, New Hampshire, is plagued with the memory of young-sters.*

A FTER THE DEFEAT of Germany, I was part of the occupation army. Still sharp in my memory was when the little children lined up to get our left-overs after we ate.

The haunted and hungry look in their eyes was the most vivid.

For some, there was more than a haunted, hungry look. **Albert James** *of North Babylon, New York, must worry about modern politics in Europe.*

I WAS IN GERMANY just after the war was over and my platoon was sent to occupy a town (Hachtetiou) south part of Germany. One day I noticed some of the men talking to a young German boy, about 15 years old. He could speak very good English. I noticed he was wearing a Hitler youth belt buckle. I questioned him about his teaching. He told me he was taught much about America, and after the war was to be Mayor of Balti-more.

So I said, "It didn't turn out that way."

His reply? "Next time, it will."

At first, I was angry and was about ready to do him some bodily harm, but I thought, if I was in his place and was taught that way for years, I would think that way also. (There but for the grace of God, go I.) So I just turned my back and walked away.

Kids are always affected by war, sometimes long after it's over. **Paul V. Campbell** *of Wayne, Nebraska, is one of them.*

F OR THOSE OF US too young to have experienced World War II our-selves, our remembrance of the war is through the lives of those who did.

Sitting at the table eating dinner one night in 1954, Dad winced, grabbed his jaw and his napkin, and spent the next couple of minutes pulling out of his gumline a half inch piece of metal, all covered with blood. Dad said this was a souvenir of North Africa (where he was wounded the first time) and he went back to his meal. This man had shrapnel in his jaw, in both legs, in his back. His teeth were all gone, his knees were bad and he spent the rest of his life in pain, and in the Army.

To a wide eyed little boy of six, this was Audie Murphy and John Wayne all in one. I'm, proud of his service, I'm proud to have followed in his footsteps by joining the Army when it became my time to serve. And I was proud to hear Taps played over his grave at Ft. Donnelson National Cemetery, when, for Dad, World War II finally ended in 1974.

And what of those who had seen war's devastation with their own eyes? **Henry L. Stark** *of El Paso, Texas, was one who did.*

AFTER a severe bombing raid, my family was evacuated to a small farming community near my hometown of Ulm in Southern Germany.

Sometime in late April or early May of 1945, an American armored unit entered our small village spearheaded by a jeep and a tank. Not knowing what to do we continued our lunch and were soon visited by a soldier who was riding in the jeep.

He opened the door showing a .45 cal. pistol, said, "Hi", took a look around the room, closed the door, and proceeded to the next house.

Toward evening the town filled up with troops and I earned my first candy bar by helping to unload a truck full of 5 gallon cans of gasoline.

At the time I was 11 years old and had never tasted chocolate before.

Of course, there were also other reasons to celebrate war's end, says **Dorthea Gavron** *of Oscoda, Michigan.*

I WAS A STUDENT NURSE with the United States Cadet Nurse Corps working in the pediatric ward, midnight shift, when I heard the announcement, "The war is over!" No more late curfews or rationed cigarettes.

For those coming home, it was, according to **Bernard M. Boone** *of West Avoca, Pennsylvania, a royal celebration.*

WE ARRIVED unannounced in Hoboken, New Jersey, six troop transport ships converted to hospital ships carrying the war wounded soldiers back from the war zones.

I'll never forget the reverent hush that fell over the city as hundreds and hundreds of Red Cross ambulances sped to load, with many salutes, at the ship's dock and hastily departed without even speaking a word. It was the most carefully synchronized military operation that I've ever seen in my life, including my own Korean War service.

Everyone was praying with thankfulness to Almighty God for their safe return and very joyful that these GI's loved ones would soon be reunited with them —even though some of us had lost loved ones in action.

None of the media were told about the soldiers arrival except the state and local police when the military decided.

When VE-Day was announced in the United States, it affected everyone. **Leonard C. Meyer** *of Indianapolis, Indianapolis, remembers that day well.*

IT WAS A MOMENTOUS DAY in May, 1945, when my mother interrupted the daily routine at our one-room school. In a hushed voice she told us that the War was over in Europe. We all went outside and said the Pledge of Allegiance, offered a prayer of thanksgiving, reverently took down the Flag and went home.

Although still children, we felt that we were a part of that victory. We picked up scrap iron, plucked milkweed pods (used in making parachutes), saved tin cans, and willingly accepted rationing of sugar, gasoline, and meat. We saved our pennies to buy Savings Stamps and Bonds. Also, we each knew individuals who were serving our country overseas; some of us had friends or family members who were not coming back.

Little wonder that these simple acts performed in this tiny school yard remain in our hearts.

Simple acts mean a lot. **Abel John Tesdall** *of Jewell, Iowa, witnessed one.*

O UR TANK DESTROYER BATTALION had landed on D-Day at Utah Beach, we had been battling along for many weeks.

We finally rolled into a small town in Belgium in a column of tanks and were stopped in a residential district. A middle aged woman came out of her house with a look of pure joy on her face. She came over to our tank carrying an unopened box of Fanny Farmer candy. In a rush of emotional tears, she told us she had been saving it since 1939 for the day they would be freed! She opened it and passed it to us. It seemed to put things in perspective!

No matter where American GIs may go, a special lady is always waiting to greet them when they come home, says **Darwin K. Pelz** *of Blairsburg, Iowa.*

W AS IT the landing at Oran, Africa, November 8th, 1942, my first real taste of the war? Or was it the first dead German soldier I saw? Was it going through the desert of Africa to Bizzerti, when General Patton gave me hell for not having the cover on the windshield of my jeep?

The landing at Gela, Sicily; the march to Polarmo and on to Maccina? The landing at Salerno, Italy or the landing at Anzio, where the fighting was so desperate? The sight as we lay on a hillside watching the bombing of the Monastery, we could see the pilots in the planes as they locked in dog fights over head.

There was the fierce fighting at Cassino, and the crossing of the Vaulterno river at 2:00 AM so cold our wet clothes froze on our bodies, then sleeping in water filled foxholes with just our heads out.

Being wounded four times, spending endless hours recovering in the 45th General Hospital in Naples, Italy.

My favorite and most vivid memory was when we arrived in New York Harbor aboard a hospital ship. We felt the ship stop and were told to go top-side.

There she was, the most beautiful girl in the world, the Statue Of Liberty. We were home.

Kenneth Wermager *of Elkton, Minnesota, wondered if he'd see her again.*

I WAS AS A CREW MEMBER on a Liberty Ship in the Merchant Marines when the war ended in Europe. This ship had been converted to carry 400 troops besides cargo. We were anchored in the Holland River, with orders to go to Cherborg, France and pick up German prisoners, but the war ended. We instead went to La Harve and picked up boys whom had just been released from prison.

Coming back through the North Atlantic, we hit a very dense fog. The convoy Commodore gave a change of course due to ice bergs. The ship's skippers got them mixed up and the ships were going in different directions. We almost hit two ships and our ex-prisoners thought they still wouldn't make it home.

But, I'll never forget the happy looks on the faces of those guys as we steamed into New York Harbor with all flags flying.

A grateful nation offered more than a statue, says **Phyllis Stankovic** *of Mesa, Arizona.*

I WAS A PETTY OFFICER in the Navy, stationed at the Oakland Supply Depot.

As I was walking down the street in San Francisco, the news broke that the war was over and we had won. I was embraced by both civilians and serviceman every step I took as I was heading for the USO club.

I will always cherish that memory and the memory of how the civilians helped in every way possible way, showing their appreciation for our time spent in the service of our country.

Some would never receive that welcome home. For some, according to **John P. Montrose** *of Melbourne, Florida, all they could offer was . . .*

A SIMPLE MEMORIAL DAY SERVICE in 1945.
The European war had ended and there was little likelihood that we of the 29th Infantry Division would face further combat. A fitting time to pay tribute to our fallen comrades. Each unit of the Division was represented by a Guidon Bearer, Officer, Non-com and Private.

This relatively small group assembled in a field outside Bremen, Germany with the Division Commander, Major General Charles Gearhardt, other Staff Officers and the Division Band. With no spectators a genuine atmosphere of intimacy prevailed.

As the organization, rank and name of each deceased man was called it was answered by a lowering of the unit guidon and a lusty, "HERE SIR!!!", from his fellow Officer, Noncom or Private.

Only we privileged few present could appreciate the emotional sentiment experienced from answering for those lost buddies.

Ultimately, the nightmare had to end. **Lucie Clemens** *of Little Neck, New York, knows when it ended for her.*

A S A CHILD I suffered many heart-rending separations caused by the war. We lived in Cologne, Germany. Day and night, horrifying air-raids hit the city and I was taken out of harms way to live with a large family on a farm, far away from home.

My father had been drafted by the German army, also my two older sisters, and later even some of the farmer's horses, plus their German-Shepherd. I hated this war. Nothing in my life was secure anymore. When it finally was over the Americans occupied the Bavarian region around the farm.

Life went on without much change. The blueberries were ripe again and if we wanted pies, we children had to bring home the berries. Deep in the forest we became alarmed by a noise. Behind us we saw an African-American soldier cutting himself a walking-stick from a branch. Petrified we watched him come towards us.

"Guten Morgen", he said with an accent, and when a friendly smile lit up his face, we relaxed. He picked berries for awhile and seemed as glad as we were that the war had ended.

He said, "Peace", when he walked away.

Chapter 29
Final Victory

Atomic weapons had been tested on July 16, 1945, in Alamagordo, New Mexico, and preparations are made to drop the weapons on Japan. Before this happens, however, President Harry Truman wants assurances from Stalin that the USSR will join in the fight in the Pacific. To this end, Churchill, Stalin, and Truman meet at Potsdam.

The Potsdam Declaration is broadcast to Japan, telling them to surrender or face destruction that will reduce them to total poverty. It is pointedly not mentioned whether the Japanese emperor will be allowed to remain in power if Japan surrenders.

On July 28, Premier Suzuki goes on the air and tells his people to ignore the Potsdam threat. Later, some will speculate whether the translation of the demand was slanted or accurate.

On August 6, 1945, the first atomic bomb is dropped on the city of Hiroshima by elements of the 20th Air Force. The aircraft is piloted by Col. Paul Tibbets. Sixty percent of the city is destroyed.

Like D-Day, this had been another closely guarded secret. Only later did **Charles W. Rode** *of Annandale, Minnesota, realize what he'd been involved with.*

I WAS IN THE NAVY in WWII in a secret unit called ComSerRon 10. We worked with proximity fuses and got our orders direct from Washington.

When we were in Leyte Gulf in the Philippines a civilian electronic technician came over from the US with some electronic testing equipment. We were on an ammunition barge that had separate rooms. He and I were the only ones allowed in this room as we were testing the proximity fuses that were used on the atom bombs that were dropped on Hiroshima and Nagasaki.

They were picked up by an officer that I was told not to salute but to shake his hand, because nobody was to know he was there. I am sure it was Colonel Tibbets.

On August 8, the USSR declares war on Japan because of its refusal to accept the Potsdam Declaration and launches a massive attack on the

Japanese in Manchuria. They have mustered more than one-and-a-half million troops and literally annihilate the one million Japanese located there.

When Truman issues a statement saying the bombing would continue, the Japanese War Council convenes and decides late at night to accept the Potsdam terms. However, there is much political in-house wrangling and finally, in disgust, Emperor Hirohito tires of the dialogue and records an unprecedented radio message which is broadcast to the Japanese people. He tells them to "bear the unbearable."

The next day, August 15, 1945, is VJ-Day.

It is too late for those **George A. Sutton Jr.** *of Westmont, New Jersey, tells about.*

THE EVENING of August 10, 1945, I was part of a Naval Detachment on Tsugen Shima, a small Island in Buckner Bay, off the coast of Okinawa. A radio broadcast announced the Japanese would surrender with conditions.

The celebration started. Troops ashore and ships in the bay started firing guns, filling the air with shrapnel. This was stopped by a raid alert.

Two evenings later August 12th, I was on the beach washing clothes in the bay, when I heard then saw a plane coming in low off the ocean on the far side of the bay, where a large number of ships were anchored.

Suddenly, there was aloud explosion at the stern of one of the ships. The next day I heard the USS Pennsylvania was hit by an aerial torpedo. The Japanese surrendered August 15th, 1945. Three days too late for the USS Pennsylvania. One of the first and last casualties of the war.

Arthur W. Johnson *of Lynnwood, Washington, was already heading home.*

I WAS A MEMBER of US Navy CB Det # 1007, the date August 8, 1945. We were out in the middle of the Pacific Ocean heading back to the good old USA aboard a huge luxury liner President Monroe.

The public address system blurted out that an atom bomb was dropped on Japan. We didn't know what an atom bomb was, but we soon learned that was the beginning of the end of the war. A few days later we came under the Golden Gate bridge and pleasure craft of all size's were circling our big ship their were bands playing and can can girls were dancing on these little boats, a lump in my throat and tears in my eyes.

It was the proudest moment in my life just to be a small part of this war, and glad to be an American.

Mrs. Ellen Tucker *of Tifton, Georgia, thought her hospital was being attacked.*

I WAS ATTACHED to the 74th Field Hospital on Okinawa. I was on duty that evening in August. Everything was quiet when all of a sudden we heard gunfire bursting all around us. The only thing we could think of was that the Japanese had broken through our lines and were headed for our hospital. We were all concerned. One young soldier panicked and flipped out of his cot and hid under it.

Then over the loud speaker came, "Attention, attention".

We held our breath waiting to hear what came next, fearing the worst.

Then came these beautiful words, "The war is over, the Japanese have surrendered."

The gunfire we heard was from other installations that had already heard the news. Looking up into the sky, I saw tracer bullets in the form of a "V" for VICTORY.

Some, like the officer described by **Robert R. Hansen** *of Sioux City, Iowa, found it hard to believe.*

I ANNOUNCED the end of the war via Armed Forces Radio Station WVTI, Cebu City, Philippines.

The station broadcast world events on a regular schedule, receiving news from short wave, slow dictation originating in San Francisco. When word came on August 15, 1945 that Japan had capitulated, as Staff Sergeant Program Director, I immediately broke into our programming with the good news.

It soon brought the commanding general of the Island of Cebu to the station to seek verification. He and his staff joined our crew in jubilation. It was an exciting and unforgettable moment.

The war ended in a nick of time for **Edmond C. Ward** *of Kentfield, California, and thousands more like him.*

ON JULY 3, 1945, I shipped out of Seattle as an 18 year old infantry replacement. Our first stop was the 13th Replacement Depot near Schofield Barracks in Hawaii, where we were briefed on Pacific warfare and trained in amphibious landings, weapons and related subjects. We all accumulated a layer of red dust on our fatigues and were still training during the first week of August.

While attending weapons training at Helemano, several of us were marched through the pineapple fields back to the repple deppel and alerted for shipment. We read in Stars & Stripes about the atomic bomb which was dropped on Japan. Wearing full field pack and helmet and carrying our M-1 rifles and duffle bags we piled onto the back of a 2 1/2 ton truck.

We had no idea where we were going, but when we rolled through the gates at Hickam Field it appeared that we would fly to someplace. Instead, we passed beyond Hickam Field to Fort Kamehameha, a beautiful Coast Artillery Post at the entrance to Pearl Harbor. There we were greeted by high point men who had been awaiting their replacements. Some had been there since before December 7, 1941.

They helped us with our gear and we traded our dusty fatigues for clean khakis. At dusk we watched a company of Infantry man machine guns on the beach.

And then the war was over. We settled down to a year of garrison duty, the luckiest replacements of all.

Eduardo Alequin *of Hormigueros, Puerto Rico, remembers when the word reached his island.*

I T WAS ABOUT NINE O'CLOCK that August 9, 1945. I was on the sidewalk of Luna Street in old San Juan looking at the stars in the sky when the thunder of cannons and horns of the automobiles, suddenly broke the silence.

The people on the streets began shouting, "Japan surrendered, Japan surrendered".

It was indescribable the euphoria on their faces, because the war had come to an end. Many people with tears in their eyes were running up and down the streets. That was unforgettable and still vivid in my mind.

Circumstances wouldn't let some participate in the celebration directly. **Thomas Clair Knapp** *of Apache Junction, Arizona, didn't mind.*

T HE PENT UP EMOTIONS of the Army, Navy and Marine personnel, who made up our manifest, overflowed with cheers and shouts of joy intermingled with manly tears of thanksgiving as we passed beneath the Golden Gate Bridge toward a berthing spot.

We docked too late to transfer the passengers, so all were given liberty; the ship's company was given port and starboard liberty. I chose to swap my liberty for duty as I wanted to read my mail. Rumors of Japan's surrender were many.

I had just sorted my mail when I heard the PA systems on nearby ships come to life with the announcement that Japan had surrendered! Immediately ship whistles sounded, sirens wailed and soon the strains of church bells ringing throughout the bay area could be heard above all.

I missed all the excitement on shore, but enjoyed some of the most awesome moments of my life.

Ironically, the war's end had tragic results, too, as **Fred C. Murphy** *of Upland, California, describes.*

I WAS A CREW MEMBER on a ship in Buckner Bay, Okinawa when the war ended on 8-15-45. The night of the day this news was received. Gunners on many of our ships opened up with small caliber anti-aircraft weapons to celebrate the end of the war. I was on the exposed bridge of our ship when tracers started flying almost horizontally. I ducked inside for cover.

The next day word was passed that at least six men had been killed as a result of the wild firing of weapons. Considering the fact that many of the men on our ships had been in a lot of combat and the war had finally ended, it was a sad event.

*Nor was it much better on shore, according to **Sidney R. Branson** of Windham, Maine.*

I WAS WITH THE US ARMY in the Pacific for two and one-half years. Our last campaign was on Okinawa, and after it was secured we started training for invasion of the homeland of Japan.

We were assigned to the 5th amphibious corps. In early evening we got word that the Japanese surrendered after we dropped the two A-bombs on Hiroshima and Nagasaki—then all hell broke loose on the island and on the ships in the harbor—everybody started shooting their weapons in celebration. All types of ammo, and star shells lit up the sky, a tremendous "4th of July" celebration occurred—a sight and sound never to be forgotten. We had over 30 casualties on Okinawa that night, luckily no fatalities. One GI in our outfit got a spent bullet in the shoulder.

*In some case, the celebrating got out of hand. **Bruno L. Kearns** of New Port Richey, Florida, seems to be describing a combat zone.*

I T'S WHAT San Francisco newspapers called the "invasion of Market Street."

My ship had just pulled into port and we were on our way for a 3-day pass when the message came that Japan had surrendered. Within minutes, the city's air raid sirens were blaring. Thousands of honking horns and screaming throngs which soon reached 100,000 jammed downtown San Francisco. The two-day celebration which included an estimated 40,000 service personnel, caused 7 deaths, 1200 injuries and millions of dollars in damage.

All policeman and firemen were called to duty. Trolleys and vehicles were turned over. Chinatown was ablaze. Businesses bolted their doors as thousands of windows were broken. Booze was taken from the windows of liquor and drug stores and sailors paraded around in display clothing, carrying mannequins with them. The drunken and bleeding were lying in store entry areas.

At the request of city officials, the Navy cancelled all leaves.

On the quiet Wednesday morning of August 15, 1945, Old Glory waved atop the Native Sons Monument, while Market Street looked like and invading force had just made a path of death and destruction.

*Still, the celebrations took place. **Donald J. Hertrich** of Weaver, Alabama, was just a child at the time.*

I USED TO STAND in the yard looking at a sky blackened by large numbers of airplanes flying overhead. Our home was about 15 miles from the Glenn L. Martin Airplane Company, (known today as Martin Marietta Corporation).

Whenever another batch of planes were ready for delivery, they would "formup" over our area before flying off to some unknown war zone. It was a thrilling sight for a boy between seven and 10 to watch those low flying planes, waving frantically to the pilots as they passed overhead.

V-J Day also has special meaning for me. My dad owned an ancient "MACK", chain drive, open cab, truck. When news reached us that the Japs had surrendered, my father, mother and I rode through the streets of Baltimore in that old truck. Blowing the horn, shouting with joy, and banging on the side of the truck with our shoes.

Warren E. Peterson *of Omaha, Nebraska, remembers the morning after.*

I WAS ON THE NAVAL AIR BASE on the Island of Tinian. Two days after the second Atomic Bomb was dropped on Japan. Every available B-29 was loaded with fuel and bombs and made a mass bomb run on Japan.

The B-29's started to return to the base around 10 P.M. that evening. There were hundreds of them over the Island with their lights on—making it seem like day.

They were running low on fuel and landing as many as three planes on one strip at a time—parking them anywhere and everywhere; on the sides of the strip, in the ditches, between the strips and over the end of the runway.

At 3 A.M. the following morning, over the loud speaker—voice blasted out—"The War Is Over."

As soon as daylight arrived, I walked down to the airstrip to observe the sight of the planes parked everywhere. Everything was quiet and peaceful. It reminded me of the old saying, "The big party is over and everyone is sleeping in."

Leland Sveum *of Richfield, Minnesota, knew a man who was probably representative of every GI in the war.*

A BOARD the USS Kasaan Bay, CVE-69, somewhere off Okinawa, August 1945, Japan surrendered, and the old man, Capt Perkins broke out the beer, one bottle per man, to celebrate the occasion.

Down the flight deck walked Curly, ships water tender. No dungarees for Curly. From bottom to top, Curly was dressed in two toned shoes, plaid slacks, Hawaiian shirt, straw hat and cane. The war was over and Curly was again a civilian.

Captain Perkins took one look from the bridge, called the Master-at-Arms, and had Curly thrown in the brig. Then he called the ships photographer to take pictures of Curly behind bars before he released him.

I'll never forget the sight of Curly in his civvies walking down the flight deck. For surely, Curly epitomized what all of us were thinking. Thank God, it's finally over and we can go home.

Or was it? War memories never really go away. **Lewis M. Romans** *of Littleton, Colorado, is not alone.*

D ARKNESS. The strange sounds of ships navigating at night still haunt me. The swish of water against the sides, the fear of Japanese submarines, not knowing if your ship is going to get a torpedo in its side. And at dawn, the Kamikazes always seemed to spot us.

It was fitting that when President Roosevelt announced Japan had surrendered, all the naval ships turned on their lights.

For men like **Arnold A. Bocksel** *of Syosset, New York, surrender meant life itself.*

O N AUGUST 17, 1945, the day I was liberated after three and one-half years as a Japanese prisoner of war in Mukden, Manchuria.

We were startled to see Russian Tanks and Vehicles enter the prison compound. Russians rounded up all the Japanese in the camp and the Russian Commander announced that Mukden had been secured and "from this hour, all prisoners of war are free". The moment we had hoped for had actually arrived.

After the Japs were marched off and our initial shouts of joy and unbelief had quieted, many of us burst into tears. We were given the gift of life again and the great gift of freedom which you can only appreciate, if it is taken away from you. We would see our loved ones again; we made it!

Tears were the only possible way to release the years of pent up emotions; tears of joy for ourselves and tears of sorrow for those who had died among us and were not here to share in this day.

Robert J. Huelsbeck *of Appleton, Wisconsin, helped fly the former POWs home.*

T HE HAPPY EXPRESSION on the faces of American POWs when we arrived at Atsugi Airbase in Japan in 1945 to fly them back to the United States was unforgettable.

As one of the early arrivals in Japan bringing in barrels of gasoline to get the airbase started we encountered the distraught appearing POW's clutching their Japanese ditty bags and tin cups. I said, "Throw those things away, we will get you all new equipment."

They seemed amazed at the size of our airplanes. One said, "Can that plane fly us back to the States?"

I felt satisfaction that this was my greatest contribution to the war effort as an Air Force pilot.

Incredibly, the ordeal of the American POWs wasn't quite over, according to **Lillian Meyer Carr** *of Chardon, Ohio.*

T HE TROOP TRAIN arrived October 1945 at Fletcher General Hospital, Cambridge, Ohio with 150 POWs.

One POW was ordered off the train in his back yard in Galipolis. Two weeks later he arrived, signed in AWOL. I arrived on duty, contacted the Colonel in charge, ordered him to send my patient up to my ward NOW. He did not deserve to be in the Brig an AWOL after three and one-half years a Jap POW.

Picture a 2nd Lt ordering a Colonel to release an AWOL POW. Minutes later the POW arrived on my ward. Twenty-nine years later at a National American Defenders Bataan-Corregidor Convention, I was questioned, "Why do POWs make a fuss over you?"

I explained about the Troop Train. The POW shouted "My God, I was the train master who delivered them to you that night."

But there is more to surrender than a radio message. **Frank J. Messina** *of Whitehall, Pennsylvania, recalls his feelings.*

JOY? FEAR? Or both?

As Assistant Construction Supervisor with the 805th Engineer Aviation Battalion, there was a special significance to my feelings of joy as the Japanese surrender party landed their two white "Betty" bombers marked with green crosses on "B" runway at Ie Shima.

Ie Shima is a very small island three miles across the China Sea from Okinawa. Joy was clouded with fear that some vengeful G.I. might, with violence, thwart the Japanese surrender party's success on its way to General MacArthur in the Philippines. The Japanese delegation did get off the island, however, and continued on its way to its rendezvous with history without mishap.

Richard T. Baker *of Frederick, Maryland, was there . . .*

WHEN GENERAL DOUGLAS MCARTHUR ordered the Japanese Government to send their envoys to land on the tiny island of Ie Shima on August 20, 1945, for surrender talks.

The Japanese planes carrying the envoys were to be painted white with green crosses over the insignias, and would be safely escorted by our fighter planes. They would then proceed to Manila to meet with him.

I was at the air-strip when they landed and was only a few feet from the envoys as they transferred to American C-54's. Knowing that the hostilities finally had ended was an historical event I will always remember.

Ebbert H. Hopper *of Oklahoma City, Oklahoma, remembers that event, also.*

I WAS ON MORATI. We saw a Japanese plane painted white with a red cross on it landing on the air strip. Then came in a large American plane and landed close by the red cross plane and out stepped General Douglas McArthur to accept the surrender of the Halmaheras.

My tent was next to the air strip, so naturally a group of us guys got our cameras and went up and took pictures of the Jap surrender.

Tables were set up in the middle of the runways. There were chairs for the generals to sit at the tables and the papers were signed for the Surrender and the Acceptance of the Surrender.

After the preliminaries, they saluted each other and then went back to their planes and took off again.

After so many years, trusting the people who used to be the enemy is hard. **Arvid J. Houglum** *of Grandview, Texas, tells of one more mission.*

I WAS A B-24 PILOT and flight leader with the 64th Squadron, 43 Bomb Group. My task for the day was to "check out" a newly arrived B-24 crew.

As far as the nation was concerned, the war was essentially ended when the second atomic bomb exploded over Nagasaki on August 9th. General MacArthur remained unconvinced that that the Japanese were serious in the peace overture. He wanted further assurances. The Far East B-24 Bomb Groups stationed on Ie Shima and Okinawa were directed to test the Japanese resolve.

On a normal combat mission involving coastal cities, our B-24's would be loaded with four tons of bombs. After takeoff we would circle while gaining altitude and assemble into our assigned combat formations. We would fly over water until close to our target. From an altitude of 15 to 20,000 feet, we would turn toward the target area, drop our bombs in sequence, then fly back toward the sea to put distance between us and any ground based anti-aircraft guns.

Plans for the August 25th Bombing Mission were radically changed. First of all, our bomb load was reduced from 4 tons to 3 five hundred pound bombs.

Second, we were to fly no higher that 4000 feet.

Third, as soon as we reached the south end of Kyushu, we were to fly over all cities with known anti-aircraft guns and combat fighter planes and proceed northward toward the main island of Japan, i.e. Honshu. If we were fired upon or intercepted by fighter planes, we were instructed to pick targets of opportunity, drop our bombs, and return.

August 25th was a beautiful day and only a few clouds greeted us as we took off from the island airbases. After flying over a few cities at 3,500 feet we began to relax. No black ack-ack puffs were greeting us and no Zeros were taking off from airports below.

We flew on, reached the southern tip of Honshu, then flew for a few more minutes until the stark black and white of a destroyed Hiroshima appeared below. We made a slow turn over the city, then headed back to sea.

Our bombadiers disarmed our three 500 pound bombs. We opened the bomb bay doors and dropped the bombs into the sea. By now all tension was gone and grins covered the faces of crew members.

We had just participated in the very last combat mission of WWII. No shots were fired, no bombs were detonated. WWII really was over.

The B-24 Liberator had carried its last load of bombs.

However, there was still the matter of the formal surrender. Men like **Robert E. Kastner** *of Torrington, Wyoming, helped pave the way.*

I WAS SERVING as Radioman aboard the Destroyer/Minesweeper— USS Fitch (DMS-25). We were the first ship entering Tokyo Bay to sweep mines about three weeks before Japan's official surrender aboard the Battleship Missouri.

During the minesweeping operation I'll never forget the sight of "white flags" flying on every gun emplacement built in the mountains and on the shoreline. The guns were aimed to fire directly at our ship. I saw Japan's intent to surrender but was not convinced enough to trust their actions. The mines we couldn't see remained a threat as did suicide planes, torpedo boats and submarines all still manned by the Japanese.

Our mission was completed, we were privileged to witness the signing of peace first hand on the Battleship Missouri. Then we celebrated the end of World War II.

William E. Stone *of Bethlehem, Pennsylvania, agrees that this was a nervous time.*

ON AUGUST 28, 1945, after countless encounters with Kamikaze attacks, we approached the entrance to Tokyo Bay. The first two vessels in were small wooden minesweeps followed by our squadron flagship USS Ellison, we the USS Hambleton, became the second man-of-war to enter Tokyo Bay.

No one knew for certain what would happen as we anchored in Conestoga fashion between the base at Yokosuka and the docks of Yokihama. The USS San Diego was the command ship until the main fleet arrived with the USS Missouri, where the final unconditional surrender ceremony took place on September 1945.

Erwin Scholtz *of Laurel, Maryland, was another early arrival at Tokyo Bay.*

I WAS PROUD to be present in Tokyo Bay when the Japanese signed the surrender terms.

I was a torpedoman on the USS Lansdowne, one of the first ships into Tokyo Bay when the war ended. Several days later she would transport the Japanese surrender party out to the USS Missouri for the formal ceremony.

Along the way the USS Lansdowne had endured bitter cold weather off Alaska. Tropic heat of the Solomon Islands baked her decks. Typhoons in the Philippines caused dangerous rolls. Mines, planes and shells tried to sink her. The nickname "Lucky L" came into being. Months of sea duty turned into years. The crew was at the breaking point. Japan finally surrendered and we were ordered to head for Tokyo Bay.

I returned home and got on with my life. Memories keep those days alive.

Harold T. Bradbury *of San Diego, California, remembers one incident in particular.*

I WAS BMC—Chief Master-at-Arms on the Battleship USS South Dakota. (1942-1946)

About a month before the "Signing" aboard the USS Missouri, I was detached with 48 men to prepare for the initial landing on Japan at the Yokosuka Naval Base. We set up a motor pool for Admiral "Bull Halsey", who was aboard the USS South Dakota. We were on the beach when USS Missouri arrived in Tokyo Bay.

We sailed for the USA where Admiral Bull Halsey retired. He shook my hand and wished me a happy career before I "piped" him over the side. When I returned to the Master-at-Arms shack, there was a line of shipmates to shake the hand that shook the had of Admiral Bull Halsey.

The war was over!

Harvey D. Larson *of Sheldon, Wisconsin, was aboard still another ship.*

I WAS SERVING with our great Naval Forces in the Pacific Ocean. When the Japanese Empire decided to give up or surrender our ship the Seaplane tender the Cumberland Sound was the seventh major ship to enter Tokyo Bay.

I was chosen by the Warrant Officer in charge of my quarters to go to the seaplane that we all called the Black Cat (as that was the color of the sea plane) that the great Admiral Nimitz was on when he did land in Tokyo Bay to sign all the surrender papers aboard the Battleship Missouri.

I was one of the crew to greet him. The great admiral. The great admiral did shake all of our hands and thanked us very much for meeting him. It was a great thrill for me. I was in charge of the crew on our motor launch that we used for the trip. We then proceeded to take and escort him to the huge battleship Missouri that was anchored in Tokyo Bay.

Our ship was the seaplane tender the USS Cumberland Sound. This was on my most vivid memory of WWII.

The Americans will hold a formal presence in Japan for decades to come. **Joe Smith Jr.** *of Paducah, Kentucky, will be one of the first.*

I WAS ONE of about 150 air corps technicians that landed at Atsugi Air Base 2 days before the occupation troops. We flew in C-46's and C-47's and was escorted in our landing by Navy fighter planes. We had fork lifts and 2½ ton airborne trucks that had to be assembled to help unload the equipment of the occupational troops.

The largest weapon were Thompson sub-marine guns. We didn't know what the Japs would do and we would have been sacrificed if they had turned on us. We were guarded by Jap troops and were restricted to the base until our occupational troops arrived.

The Japs welcomed us very humbly and had officers and laborers to assist us in unloading our planes if needed.

On September 2, 1945, the formal Japanese surrender is signed aboard the USS Missouri. **Flin Crawford King** *of Columbia, Tennessee, was nearby.*

I WAS ABOARD the USS Knapp DD 653, when the Japanese delegation went aboard the USS Missouri to sign the documents declaring the end of World War II.

The Knapp was 150 yards off starboard bow of USS Missouri. Our crew heard the program. My thoughts "Thank God, it's over, AMEN."

Jim Carothers *of West Hyattsville, Maryland, was there, too.*

WE CAME in to the harbor at Yokohoma after the war and set down near the Missouri where surrender signing took place.

During signing a couple hundred B-29's flew over as we stood at attention. We went over the side on nets and into boats that took us to Yokohoma. We could see the ceremony on the Missouri.

Very impressive.

Clifford W. Malson *of Denver, Colorado, offers details of the surrender.*

AS I LOOK across the bay, I can see the USS Missouri off our port beam. General MacArthur, Admiral Nimitz, Admiral Halsey, General Wainwright and many others are either on board or going aboard.

Boats of all types are crowded around the ladders of the big ship. Their passengers anxiously waiting to be piped aboard.

The surrender in its entirety is being recorded and will be played back to all of the fleet, later this morning. We, aboard the Iowa are getting detailed descriptions of what is taking place, as it can be seen from the bridge. Scores of giant B-29's have just flown over and now hundreds of carrier based planes are coming in. I can see another wave of B-29's coming in even lower than before. They seem to blot out a dreary sky.

It has just been announced that the surrender has been signed by the Japanese. It seems that everything has been timed to the second, as just now the sun has broken through the clouds as if to say, "God approves of what has taken place here today."

This is truly a big moment in my life! I feel rather frightened as I listen to President Truman, as he speaks from the White House.

For millions of GIs, it was time to go home.

Chapter 30
Coming Home

It's time to go home. How many GIs have waited to hear those words? **Willard A. Heath** *of Boise, Idaho, must have been glad when he rotated back to the United States.*

I T IS NOVEMBER 6, 1944. We were on troopship, the SS Monterey, returning from three years overseas in the Southwest Pacific area: Java, New Guinea and Australia.

Up early one morning, everyone acting as look-outs. Looking not for enemy aircraft or submarines this time. We are all looking for our first glimpse of land after a nonstop voyage from Brisbane, Australia. A shout goes up! There it is! California, the United States of America!

What a glorious sight—what a glorious feeling. In no time at all we are sailing back under the Golden Gate Bridge, through the San Francisco Bay and up to the dock. We'll be home this Christmas.

Sure enough, after a couple of days processing, we were given leave, and I was on my way to Portland by train.

Even though a war may be declared over, for those who fought and those who waited, it is never over until home is in sight. The war was over for **George J. Davis** *of Rhinebeck, New York, but getting home was something else again.*

T WO OF US were liberated in Czechoslovakia. The war sputtered on as we made our way into Prague after V-E Day. The nearest Americans were in Pilsen, 70 miles away.

Our aim was to get there posthaste. Walking Prague's streets, we spotted three jeeps and a staff car opposite the Hotel Alcron. Couldn't bum a ride as they were escorting Lt. General Huebner, who was in the Alcron discussing the repatriation of Russian and Allied POWs.

Shortly, the general appeared. As we executed snappy salutes, my buddy asked plaintively, "How about a lift to Pilsen, sir?" No response.

As the convoy revved up, Huebner's aide came running, asking if we could prove we were Americans. Lee Rubin hastily produced a fraternity card; I flashed my Franklin D. Roosevelt High School ring.

Satisfied, the aide announced, "The general would like you to accompany him to Pilsen".

What a way to return to American control—with a three-star general.

*Homecoming was especially joyous for **Joe Canavan** of Brockton, Massachusetts.*

M Y RETURN from the E.T.O. into New York Harbor on May 15, 1945 was unforgettable.

I was returning on the hospital ship George Washington from Camp Lucky Strike in LeHavre, France after being liberated from a POW Camp; Stalag IX B at Bad Orb, Germany. As we approached the harbor before daybreak, word had spread throughout the ship that we were entering New York. While standing at the rail, just as dawn was breaking, there in the gray mist was the Statue of Liberty silhouetted in the early morning light.

I was amazed at the eerie silence that occurred at that moment. I believe that most of the guys felt as I did.

***E.A. Humphrey** of Lodi, California, came home on the other coast.*

Y OU SHOULD HAVE SEEN the sight of big, strong combat infantry men of the 201st Infantry Regiment, lined up and weeping freely at the railing of our troopship as it entered Puget Sound (Seattle) following 30 months duty in the Aleutian Islands.

Overwhelmed by the tree studded view of the beautiful shoreline, obliterated and almost destroyed by their many months overseas in one of the most remote, uninhabited and weathered theaters of operations better known as the cradle of the storms.

Bold and brave, yes, but bent on being home and allowing their emotions to spill over.

*The tension of waiting for months after the war had ended must have been nerve-wracking for men like **Mancel Kirk** of Bethel Springs, Tennessee.*

I WAS STANDING on the deck of USS Randolph air plane carrier, December 15, 1945. As she pulled slowly out of the Naples Harbor and Naples disappeared, 23 months of life had vanished.

I joined CG 168th Infantry 34 Division February 1944. We got to the top of Cassino. Rain, snow and German forced us off. We went to Anzio Beachead, March 21, 1944, for two months we were dug in casualties were high.

On May 23, we pushed off for Rome. June 5th we went thru Rome we took Leghorn Risa Florence Gothlic line late Oct. 1944 only 15 miles from Po Valley on north slopes of Appines Mt snow, rain and winter Germans stop us far the next six months we dug in on April 17, my 21st birthday.

I had made Platoon Sergeant and led my platoon into Po Valley was in Bella, Italy, May 2, 1945 when war ended. I never forgot the boys that never made it back and so many close calls. I arrived back in New York on Christmas Day 1945.

Sure was nice to see the Statue of Liberty and be home again.

William A. Wolf *of Ocean City, Maryland, wondered at the sanity of war surplus.*

A FTER THE SURRENDER of Germany, many Gi's were shipped home from the European Theater, myself included.

I was on a troop ship, and on the way back to the United States we saw numerous cargo vessels anchored in the middle of the Atlantic Ocean which were dumping material and food overboard.

This was an appalling sight to many of us, because we all realized that this "surplus" food and equipment could have been put to good use by the starving people of Europe and the United States.

This practice was never brought to the people's attention, and whenever I mention it to folks, they don't believe that it happened.

For some, like **Edward A. Kennedy** *of Westminster, Maryland, a fair amount of red tape had to be to attended to.*

"Y OU ARE A WHAT on a B-26?" the WAC personnel officer exclaimed. I knew I was in trouble, but I'm getting ahead of myself.

In 1943, a 9th Air Force memorandum was issued requesting volunteers for flight training on the Martin B-26 aircraft. I volunteered and was accepted. After completing intensive training on bombing techniques, I became a "toggler," the title that elicited the response from the WAC.

A toggler is the guy who releases the bombs.

After 33 missions, I was shot down and became a POW. When you don't return from a mission, your records are forwarded to permanent storage, making it became necessary to create separation papers. However, there is no classification for a toggler. I was a non-entity.

The personnel officer finally informed me that my MOS was bombadier, and my WD-AGO form 53-55 now states that.

Charles R. Webb *of Mundelein, Illinois, also faced some red tape.*

T HE WAR WAS OVER and most of my outfit was shipped home. I was the only one left with our mascot, a black and white cocker spaniel dog named Duffy, when I got my orders to be shipped home.

I wanted Duffy to be cared for and tried to give her away to a Red Cross worker. I boarded the ship and Duffy made several attempts to follow me up the gangplank only to be pushed back to shore. No animals were allowed on the ship. The ship was set to sail and Duffy made such a racket that the Red Cross worker and some buddies tossed Duffy to me aboard ship. Once the ship was sailing, animals could stay.

We docked and at the discharge center, and Duffy was discharged, inoculated, dog-tagged before I could bring her home.

Hugh L. Bryan *of Hartsville, South Carolina, remembers coming home.*

A S I STOOD on the pier at LeHarve and looked up at the troopship
that was to take me home, I had a feeling that I will never forget. I
could feel the tensions and fatigue that I had lived with for so long leaving me. I was no longer facing the unknown; it was all behind me.

I remember the moisture in my eyes when the ship came into Boston
Harbor and we saw the large wooden letters "Welcome Home" on the side
of a hill.

I remember when I finally got home it was dark. As I reached the front
door the light came on and there were my wife and seven year old daughter whom I hadn't seen in three years. I can't describe what my feelings
were then if I tried.

Other veterans will understand.

There are also a few doubts, as **Quinton F. Reams** *of Punxsutawney,
Pennsylvania, recalls.*

I T'S NOT that I didn't have lots of memorable days. The day I went
overseas. Three invasions, eight campaign's and all those days of combat with the 1st Infantry Division 18th Regiment 3rd BN Hqt Co.

I was one of the first to go in the service from my hometown after war
was declared and one of the first to come home after V-E Day.

How would people feel about my return? There was a lot of fellows
killed and wounded, and I was coming home and the war was still going
on in the Pacific. Would people be glad to see me? Would my family accept me back? Would I fit in? Could I get a job?

A million things went through my mind and I was scared to death.

But I was home.

How do you know you're home? **James R. Warnke** *of Boynton Beach,
Florida, answers.*

W E WERE RETURNING from Bremerhaven, Germany on the
Antioch.

Victory.

After days of being storm-tossed in the North Sea and a very rough
crossing of the Atlantic with most of the troops continuously seasick, we
approached New York.

The radios finally picked up American stations and we heard commer-
cials! Ipana toothpaste, Fleer's Gum, Lucky Strikes! The years overseas
faded away as we realized that we were close to home.

The next morning we went on deck as we entered New York harbor.
And there She was, the Statue of Liberty. The men leaned on the ship's
rail and were silent. All of us had lumps in our throats and there were a
few tears. If we hadn't thought about it too much before, we all realized
while gazing on Her beauty how much it means to be an American.

Today I remember those wonderful words, "For those who have fought for it, Freedom has a taste that the protected will never know."

*The country rolled out the red carpet, according to **Vincent J. Gittins** of Staten Island, New York.*

U PON MY RETURN from overseas on the Queen Mary and upon passing through the Narrows, it was noticed that on the banks of Brooklyn was a huge American Flag made out of flowers and underneath were the words, "WELCOME HOME, JOB WELL DONE".

I saw that many others were crying as well as myself. I don't know what their thoughts were at the time for crying, but I'll always remember mine.

They were just being home, the sight of OUR FLAG, and more importantly for those who did not make it

To this day, every time I think of it —I see it—and every time I see it, I cry.

*That majestic lady in the harbor, symbol to the world, meant a lot to men like **Al Swenson** of Osage, Iowa.*

I SAW the Statue of Liberty as we returned home after the war was over. The date was 1945. It as a beautiful day with the sun shining on that beautiful lady. It seemed to us that she was giving us a special welcome home.

Most of us had been in combat and had seen the destruction that comes from war. Our bombers and combat units had destroyed many German cities such as Hamburg, Duren and Aachen.

We had walked through the streets of Aachen, with its almost complete ruin. We saw and heard people talking and coming out of homes that were just a pile of rubble. We saw little French kids, using discarded food tins, filling them out of our garbage cans and taking our garbage home to eat. Many stood shivering in the cold with no coat and very poor shoes.

We saw tough battle-hardened Veterans cry when they returned to their tent and remembered the buddy whose ships left our formation in a cloud of smoke.

The lady greeting us in the harbor meant peace and a return to those we left behind. She was beautiful and still is.

*The Statue of Liberty has special meaning to **Leroy D. "Whitey" Schaller** of Bolivar, Pennsylvania, too.*

T HERE WERE TEARS in the eyes of returning veterans. Recently repatriated from Stalag IX B, I was aboard a hospital ship in New York harbor. Because of the fog, we were at anchor in the bay. It was May 5, 1945. The joyous sounds of participants celebrating V-E Day were heard.

We were in sight of the Statue of Liberty as, one-by-one, nurses brought blinded veterans to the railing, "to see the Lady in the harbor."

There has never been a "dear John" from this girl, according to **Samuel P. Saunders** *of Norfolk, Virginia.*

I RETURNED HOME after nearly 5 years in the Army. From the deck of our troop ship I saw for the first time in my life the Statue of Liberty, that majestic lady and her torch aloft. I thought to myself, "I know you have been carrying that torch for a long time, but you don't know how long I have been carrying a torch for you."

But it was not only a statue that bid welcome to homecoming GIs, according to **Kathleen E. Yiengst** *of Lebanon, Pennsylvania.*

WHEN THE QUEEN MARY sailed into New York harbor on June 20, 1945, she was given a tremendous welcome. This was her first trip back from Europe after V-E Day.

It was one of the proudest moments of my life as I joined 15,000 soldiers, doctors and nurses as we shouted and cheered from her decks. The trip apparently was well publicized because every boat that could float came out to meet us. Our triumphant homecoming was summed up by one exuberant blond Army nurse who waved a pair of black lacy panties from a porthole shouting, "Hey, we won"! She was the delight of the photographers on the pier and the picture ended up in the current issue of "LIFE" magazine.

I'm sure other troops were given a hearty welcome on their return but that first one seemed a bit more glamorous and will remain outstanding in my memory.

Anthony J. Salerno *of Jacksonville, Florida, may have been one of the passengers that day.*

I RETURNED HOME after spending 90% of my service overseas. December 5, 1942, ninety days after entering the army, I was ETO bound on the Queen Mary, with 17,000 others. June 15, 1945, again on the Queen, we departed, expecting to reach New York on the 20th.

At 5 AM that final morning, the decks were jammed, all craning for a glimpse of "HOME." A native New Yorker, my heart pounded in expectation. Ever so S-L-O-W-L-Y, something arose on the horizon.

"What is it?" My heart soared. "The Parachute Jump!" I cried out. It was the ride brought to Coney Island, Brooklyn, after the 1939-40 New York World's Fair.

Everyone was crying, copious tears streaming down our cheeks, our trials and tribulations of the past three years forgotten in the joy of being home again. I shall never forget that day as long as I live.

*The nation rolled out the welcome mat and the celebrations would continue for months. **Monroe O. Slater** of Pasadena, Texas, tells of a proud, grateful nation.*

"NAVY DAY", October 27, 1945. From the Observation deck on my ship, President Harry S. Truman received 7 miles of warships anchored in the Hudson River in NY.

After the President's luncheon on the USS Missouri, his party of dignitaries, which included heads of state of several nations, top officials of our Armed Forces, came aboard the Renshaw. As the Renshaw, followed by other destroyers a Destroyer Escort, carrying all these officials and the press, passed the 47 fighting ships, there was a 21-gun salute from each ship to the Commander-in-Chief.

While these guns were fired with utmost precision, each ships companies stood at rigid attention at the rails as the Presidential Destroyer passed. During the fleet review there were 1,200 planes that circled twice overhead in an orbit of about 12 miles. The procession took 40 minutes to pass a single point.

The 2 million people that lined the river in New York and the 500,000 in New Jersey were treated to a spectacle not ever seen in the two cities history.

What a Sound! What a Sight! What an Occasion! I shall treasure it all my life.

*As peace seemingly settled over the world, GIs came home, including **Edward K. Fox** of Topeka, Kansas.*

I WAS RELIEVED when I was notified that I was on the rotation list to go home, after three and a half years overseas. I was on Luzon in the Philippines with the 39th Fighter Squadron, 5th Air Force, ground crew.

Six men of my squadron and 19 from another unit were on the list. We left Mangalden Field and past Manila. We could see smoke curling skyward. First day we landed at Tacloben, Leyte, on a C-46 Commando transport. After flying to Palau and Biak Islands.

We flew on a C-47 on the last leg to Hollandia, New Guinea. We had to circle the field for sometime as the landing gear would not lower. They finally got it cranked down and we sat in crash position. Bless the pilot as he made a fine landing without mishap. We were 25 very happy men to survive this last leg. We were all happy to return to the good old USA.

*Those who returned after the celebrations, like **William J. McLaughlin** of Marstons Mills, Massachusetts, had something of a let-down.*

THE WAR ENDED and I was back in Boston after years of Pacific fighting.

Guadalcanal to the Philippines, five bitter campaigns. August 1945 found us veterans headed home, but before the 33 day cruise ended the war and celebrations were long over. With an overnight pass from Fort Devens I left the North Station to walk across town thinking, "Surely someone will say, `Hi, Bill' welcome home . . . "

I studied the faces. None was familiar. On the El train the bus, again a blank. An old man sat smoking his pipe outside a three decker. "Edson Street?" I asked.

"Next on the left," pointing with his pipe, "Know someone there?"

"My mother," then lamely, "She moved while I was gone."

"Oh," glancing at my Army uniform, "Have ye been long away?"

"Three years and seven months," half bitterly after the disappointing trek.

"God bless you lad," he said warmly, reaching out a huge fist, "Welcome home."

*Sometimes, greetings were found from some unlikely sources, as **Tony A. Kozach** of Taunton, Massachusetts, relates.*

THE FOUR-ENGINE C-54 Skymaster was over San Francisco Bay at 2,000 feet and was in the process of letting down for a landing at Hamilton Field, California.

Down below and dead ahead was the Golden Gate Bridge. A few miles beyond that "Scenic Span of Steel" lay the sparkling Bay City of San Francisco, clearly visible in the `dawn's early light'. To the World War II GI's aboard the aircraft who had spent several seemingly endless years in the Southwest Pacific, this was a dream come true—a most impressive, sentimental and memorable sensation.

However, one of the most thought-provoking sights that caught the eye and held the attention of the returning serviceman was not located on the mainland. It was a sight that was spelled out in a beautiful and colorful floral design that was embedded in there ground on the island of Alcatraz.

The message which was about 50 yards long and about 10 yards wide read: "Welcome Home"!

***W.B. Stanford** of Hartselle, Alabama, also saw a welcome home sign.*

AS WE WERE SAILING under the Golden Gate Bridge out of the Pacific and I could see a big sign on the ground, made out of rock and painted, saying "Welcome Home Boys".

In a few minutes as we were docking, a band on the dock was playing "The Battle Hymn of the Republic". I never felt more American in all my life. Of all the battles I saw and the metal I won, that was my most vivid memory of World War II.

*Apparently, San Francisco knew how to welcome GIs home, according to **John L. Bill** of Powell, Ohio.*

I WAS RETURNING to the United States from the Southwest Pacific on a troopship. We anchored outside of the Golden Gate Bridge our last night at sea and the communication section piped in the San Francisco Radio stations throughout the ship. It was a real thrill to hear the music and the words of welcome back to the U.S. from the stations. But the best was yet to come.

The next morning we proceeded under the Golden Gate Bridge into the harbor. As we tied up to the dock we were met by a barge loaded with a full big band and the most beautiful female singer I had ever seen. The opening song was "Sentimental Journey" and it just got better after that.

There were many, many moist eyes along the railings of our ship. What a wonderful welcome home. I have never forgotten that moment in my young life.

But the military could awe the city, too. **Grace L. Looney** *of Mountain View, Arkansas, saw the return of the Task Force.*

THE DAY I witnessed the awe-inspiring, glorious and triumphant return of Task Force 58 from the South Pacific Theater in to Pearl Harbor after the Japanese surrender in 1945 was unforgettable.

Task Force 58 in all its might and splendor was escorted by the USS Missouri with Admiral William B. "Bull" Halsey in command, and all of the ship's personnel were lined on deck in dress whites at parade rest as they steamed into harbor.

It was both a sad occasion as we reflected on the casualties that had been involved, but also a grateful, glorifying experience to greet the returning fleet as they sailed into port on their way home with their mission victoriously accomplished.

The Statue of Liberty isn't necessary to welcome the troops home. America offers her own splendor regardless of the port of entry, according to **Art Bundrock** *of Troy, Montana.*

AFTER THREE AND A HALF YEARS of mostly combat in Central and South Pacific, we were sent home from the Philippine Islands. Eight hundred wounded and high point service men, after 30 days in the fog and slow-moving ship, the General Bratford "a troop ship" we came into Puget Sound near Seattle.

It was evening, the weather had just cleared, and there in the distance was snow capped Mt Rainier, and lights coming on all along the shores of Puget Sound.

Then to our surprise came a beautiful ship full with beautiful girls singing, "Sentimental Journey", many tears were shed right then.

Some who came home, however, according to **Alvin Del Vechio** *of Indianapolis, Indiana, were met with tears.*

IN MY MIND, I can still picture my tour of duty in Escort Co. bringing back the war dead to the next of kin to be buried with full honors in National and Private Cemeteries.

The terrible sadness I felt for the Mothers and Fathers when they shed tears over their lost son who died in battle defending his country. I was discharged from the Army as 2nd Lt. Infantry in October of 1946. Reenlisted as M/Sgt. in Escort Co. at Ft. Sheridan, Ill.

After training I began bringing back the War Dead to next of kin. We picked up the War Dead at a depot in Chicago and delivered them by train to 32 different states. I met many Fathers, Mothers, and wives who looked at me through tears when I presented them our flag.

Many times I also cried with them.

James S. Foster of Grand Island, Nebraska, tells of waiting for a friend.

SHORTLY AFTER THE CLOSE of the war, seven other discharged servicemen and I, all in uniform, stood near the railway depot in a small rural southern Iowa town. We were awaiting the arrival of the "local" train from around the bend to the west. My college roommate and friend for four years was returning on that train from the Normandy invasion.

Except for the train's noise as it slowly approached and stopped, there was absolute silence. The eight of us, his family and a host of friends escorted him from the train and up a steep hill to his church, and its cemetery.

As "Taps" was played, I had to wonder why it was him, not one of us, who had made the supreme sacrifice. Why had there been such a waste of this promising young man?

*For others, like **Virginia Counts** of Belvidere, Tennessee, the waiting and wondering ended.*

MY BROTHER returned home on the third Sunday in May 1945. I noticed a truck coming down the land approaching my parents home with a soldier inside. I yelled, "It's Buddy."

We met him halfway down the lane, Dad was shaving and Mother was frying chicken. Dad came running with shaving cream on his face and Mother was wiping her hands on her apron. My brother, William T. Swafford, enlisted in the Army, July 1, 1944, before his eighteenth birthday. After boot training, he came home on a three day pass, before his assignment overseas.

On October 14, 1944 he was taken prisoner by the Germans. The only word we received concerning him for seven months was, "Missing in Action." His return was as though he had returned from the dead.

I praise and thank my God everytime I see my brother or hear his name called.

__Robert Phillip Owen__ of El Dorado, Arkansas, might argue there are things worse than getting wounded in battle.

I HAD A WIFE and two small children when I volunteered for the U.S. Navy Reserve in August 1942 and had many harrowing experiences flying the North Pacific over the Kuriles logging radar information.

In September 1944, I returned to the states for more training and was granted a short delay. All the way home I dreamed of seeing my wife and children again. I could picture my young son and daughter rushing to my arms when they saw me.

As I stepped from the taxi, my four-year-old daughter was on the porch. I went toward her with outstretched arms and she ran into the house and grabbed her mother's skirt. After embracing my wife, I went into the bedroom where my two and a half year-old son was standing in his baby bed. When I approached him with my arms outstretched, he screamed and ran from me to the other side of the bed.

This is a memory I can never forget.

James T. Barr of Lexington, South Carolina, knew what he was fighting for, and when he returned, it was to the best welcome a GI could ask for.

O N 25 MARCH 1945, I was assigned to the 109th Finance Disbursing Section, US Army, Finance Department. On 9 July, 1944, the unit sailed for its assigned duty station in Bristol, England.

My wife, Jo, was staying with her mother in Omaha, Nebraska. She was pregnant with our first child. Our daughter, Helen, was born 12 November 1944 just a few months after our unit arrived in Bristol. Jo kept pictures of me scattered about the house and would show them to Helen, saying, "That is Daddy."

The 109th FDS returned to the States on 10 Sept 1945. I arrived in Omaha 13 Sept, Jo met me at the train and we walked to the car where 10 month old Helen was waiting with her Grandmother. I looked at Helen for the first time , she looked at me, and with outstretched arms she said, "Daddy".

This certainly is my most vivid memory of World War II.

Yes, the war is over.

Contributors

The following individuals have shared their memories through letters to The American Legion. Their generous contributions have made this publication possible, and we thank them.

AAROE, Paul	*Belvidere, New Jersey*
AASER, Morris	*McVille, North Dakota*
ABBOTT, Lester B.	*Somerset, Kentucky*
ACCETTA, Dominick A.	*Fort Lee, New Jersey*
ACEE, Joe G.	*Sulligent, Alabama*
ACOSTA, Jim V.	*Hightstown, New Jersey*
ADAMS, Harry Giles	*Blackshear, Georgia*
ADAMS, John A.	*Provo, Utah*
AFOS, Blas B.	*Surallah, South Cotabato, Philippines*
AGEN, William J.	*Wrightstown, Wisconsin*
AIKEN, Maurice	*Charlestown, New Hampshire*
ALARIE, Richard J., Sr.	*Putnam, Connecticut*
ALDRIDGE, George W., Jr.	*Chevy Chase, Maryland*
ALEQUIN, Eduardo	*Hormigueros, Puerto Rico*
ALEXANDER, Earle W.	*Minneapolis, Minnesota*
ALIX, Ulysse	*Milford, New Hampshire*
ALLENDER, Chester	*Jeffersonville, Indiana*
ALLMAN, Le Roy	*Garden City, Kansas*
ALMANDARES, D.B.	*Tampa, Florida*
AMGWERT, John B. (Burt)	*Lincoln, Nebraska*
ANDERSON, Joe Nathan	*Marysville, California*
ANDERSON, Reynold Anderson	*Hamburg, New York*
ANDERSON, Richard B.	*Toms River, New Jersey*
ANDERSON, Richard L.	*Baltimore, Maryland*
ANDERSON, Robert H.	*Los Angeles, California*
ANDREWS, Don	*Valley, Nebraska*
ANTHONY, Luke	*Fort Recovery, Ohio*
ARAKELIAN, Harry	*Springfield, Pennsylvania*
ASBURY, Carl H.	*Charleston, West Virginia*
ASHMORE, Cecil F.	*Tucson, Arizona*
ATKINSON, Thomas R. Sr.	*Lakeville, Pennsylvania*
AUCOIN, Raoul N.	*Baton Rouge, Louisiana*
AUSTIN, John R.	*Cockeysville, Maryland*
AUSTIN, Paul	*Grafton, Virginia*
AYERS, Ralph H.	*Cedartown, Georgia*
BACHNER, Joel E.	*Reading, Pennsylvania*
BACON, Melvin Delaine	*Cape Girardeau, Missouri*
BAHORED, Isaac R.	*Flushing, Michigan*
BAILEY, Michael E.	*Orange, California*
BAILEY, Raymond	*Searcy, Arkansas*
BAKER, Kenneth L.	*Walnut Creek, California*
BAKER, Richard T.	*Frederick, Maryland*
BAKER, Robert J.	*Webb City, Missouri*
BALL, James R.	*Hertford, North Carolina*
BANGERT, Earl J.	*Hillside, New Jersey*
BARBS, Ross	*Newburgh, Indiana*
BARNWELL, Charles B., Sr.	*Bamberg, South Carolina*
BARON, John	*West Lafayette, Indiana*
BARR, James T.	*Lexington, South Carolina*
BARRERA, Carlos D.	*San Antonio, Texas*
BARTON, Robert E.	*Garden City, Kansas*
BEARD, Clifton R.	*Cumberland Furnace, Tennessee*
BEATTIE, David D., Sr.	*Oak Hill, Florida*
BECKER, George	*Skokie, Illinois*
BEDNARCYK, John W.	*Simsbury, Connecticut*
BEE, Earle R.	*Parkersburg, West Virginia*
BEGGS, Wilbert L.	*Camarillo, California*
BELL, Earl D.	*Hartford City, Indiana*
BENNETT, David	*Cohasset, Minnesota*
BENSEN, Benny	*New Orleans, Louisiana*
BENSINGER, Guy A., Jr.	*Palm Beach Gardens, Florida*
BERGDOLLM, James O.	*Madison, Indiana*
BERKEY, Maurice E., Jr.	*Salem, Indiana*
BERNICE, John B.	*Columbia, Maryland*
BILL, John L.	*Powell, Ohio*
BILLS, Richard S.	*St. Benedict, Pennsylvania*
BISHOP, Worden F.	*Spokane, Washington*
BITTCK, Bob Sr.	*Tulsa, Oklahoma*
BOCKSEL, Arnold A.	*Syosset, New York*
BONDS, Ed	*Hesperia, California*
BOONE, Bernard M.	*West Avoca, Pennsylvania*
BORNN, Arthur V.	*Victoria, Texas*

BOSTON, Glen I.	*Franklin, Illinois*
BOTWINOFF, Philip	*Valley Stream, New York*
BOUGES, Merle E.	*Lincoln, Nebraska*
BOURDAS, Alex	*Kinston, North Carolina*
BOVEE, Elmer	*Addison, New York*
BOWEN, Robert M.	*Linthicum Heights, Maryland*
BOWERS, Joy Patterson	*Littleton, Colorado*
BRADBURY, Harold T.	*San Diego, California*
BRADFORD, Norman C.	*La Habra, California*
BRADSTREET, Kenneth G.	*Emporia, Kansas*
BRANSON, Sidney R.	*Windham, Maine*
BRANTLEY, Hattie R.	*Jefferson, Texas*
BREYFOGLE, Melvin S.	*Estherville, Iowa*
BRIDGES, Margie Ann	*Harrisburg, Arkansas*
BROCK, Leonard	*Phoenix, Arizona*
BROCKMAN, L.W.	*Hinsdale, Illinois*
BROSIUS, Steward S.	*Strasburg, Pennsylvania*
BROWN, Dwight C.	*Arlington, Virginia*
BROWN, James H.	*Benton Harbor, Michigan*
BROWN, Jewell	*Anna, Texas*
BROWN, Stanley J.	*Staten Island, New York*
BROWN, Walter H.	*Tarpon Springs, Florida*
BROWNLOW, Ken	*Spring Hill, Florida*
BRYAN, Franklin A.	*Fort Wayne, Indiana*
BRYAN, Hugh L.	*Hartsville, South Carolina*
BUCHHEIT, Herbert	*Perryville, Missouri*
BUCKLEY, Francis X.	*Malden, Massachusetts*
BUCKHOUT, Arthur I.	*Sea Cliff, New York*
BUMPUS, Robert E.	*Maynard, Massachusetts*
BUNDROCK, Art	*Troy, Montana*
BURKE, Mrs. Anne	*Hellertown, Pennsylvania*
BURKETT, Louis	*Parrish, Alabama*
BUSE, Howard L.	*Hershey, Pennsylvania*
BUTLER, John W.	*Oxford, Massachusetts*
BYRD, William E.	*Redwood City, California*
CALDWELL, Derwood	*Spring, Texas*
CALDWELL, William N.	*Phoenix, Arizona*
CALLAGHAN, Francis J.	*LaGrange, Illinois*
CALLAHAN, Harry L.	*East Meredith, New York*
CALLENTINE, Helen L.	*Jefferson City, Missouri*
CAMARATA, Jasper (Jeep)	*Souderton, Pennsylvania*
CAMERON, William H.	*Nashville, Tennessee*
CAMPBELL, Paul V.	*Wayne, Nebraska*
CAMPBELL, Thomas D. Sr.	*Junction City, Kansas*
CANNELLA, Michael A.	*Riverview, Florida*
CARL, John A.	*Vestaburg, Pennsylvania*
CARLSON, Stan W.	*Minneapolis, Minnesota*
CAROTHERS, Jim	*West Hyattsville, Maryland*
CARR, Lillian Meyer	*Chardon, Ohio*
CARR, Tom	*Merrick, New York*
CARRICK, Homer K.	*Oceanside, California*
CARROLL, Ernie	*Ticonderoga, New York*
CARUBIA, Joseph	*Montgomery, New York*
CARUK, Frank H.	*Palatine, Illinois*
CASPERSON, Ralph A.	*Niles, Michigan*
CAULFIELD, Charles J.	*Clearwater, Florida*
CHASE, Donald	*Framingham, Massachusetts*
CHILD-TAYLOR, Sarah G.	*Aurora, Indiana*
CHILDS, Wayne	*Edina, Minnesota*
CHYBRZYNSKI, Frank J. Jr.	*Natrona Heights, Pennsylvania*
CLARK, Joseph R.	*Bella Vista, Arkansas*
CLARK, L. W.	*Westminster, Texas*
CLEMENS, Lucie	*Little Neck, New York*
COCARUS, James	*Rochester, New Hampshire*
COLLINS, Robert M. (Rip)	*West Palm Beach, Florida*
CONNALLY, Joseph R.	*Geneva, Illinois*
CONRAD, Betty J.	*Canton, Illinois*
COOK, Harold F.	*Seminole, Florida*
COOPERIDER, Walt	*Lompoc, California*
CORNISH, Vernon F.	*Fort Worth, Texas*
COTTEN, Patricia	*Rio Oso, California*
COUNTS, Virginia	*Belvidere, Tennessee*
COZZI, Rocco	*Rahway, New Jersey*
CRUDO, Mary Villella	*Erie, Pennsylvania*
CRUMP, Elizabeth E.	*Albany, Georgia*
CUDDINGTON, Edward C.	*Sparta, Michigan*
CURRELL, Bill M.	*Saginaw, Michigan*
DAHLIA, Joseph A.	*Chicago, Illinois*
DAURIAM, B.J.	*Bronx, New York*
DAVENPORT, Tom	*Bellevue, Ohio*
DAVID, Kathryn	*Sandusky, Ohio*
DAVIS, D. Allen	*Lemoyne, Pennsylvania*

DAVIS, George J.	*Rhinebeck, New York*
DAVIS, Hugh M.	*Iselin, New Jersey*
DAVIS, James Robert	*Mishiwaka, Indiana*
DAVIS, Mr. June G.	*Shelbyville, Kentucky*
DAVIS, Marcus L.	*Christiansburg, Virginia*
DAVIS, Stan	*Kissimmee, Florida*
DAWSON, George	*Wantagh, New York*
DE COSTE, Edward	*Clearwater, Florida*
DEFRIES, Delbert H.	*Bloomington, Minnesota*
DEHART, Gordon F.	*Aurora, Illinois*
DEL VECHIO, Alvin	*Indianapolis, Indiana*
DELANOY, Robert V.	*Kingston, New York*
DENNY, John Robert	*Tallahassee, Florida*
DEPUTY, Harry D., Jr.	*San Bernadino, California*
DERROW, Donald D.	*Loudonville, Ohio*
DERRYBERRY, William A.	*Columbia, Tennessee*
DEVERE, Carl M. (Bud), Sr.	*Alexandria, Virginia*
DICKENS, Burns R.	*Mt. Pleasant, South Carolina*
DIEFENBACH, John A.	*San Antonio, Texas*
DILKS, Claude F.	*Hawthorne, Florida*
DIMEDIO, Carl M.	*Bronx, New York*
DISCO, Steve	*Chapmanville, West Virginia*
DOJKA, Edwin S.	*Niagara Falls, New York*
DOLAN, John	*Whiting, Maine*
DOLAN, William	*Owego, New York*
DONAHUE, Michael J.	*Midland, Michigan*
DOOLEN, Roy G.	*Kinmundy, Illinois*
DOUCETTE, Concetta	*South Windsor, Connecticut*
DOUGLAS, Barbara R.	*Emerson, Iowa*
DRAKE, Eiler H.	*Omaha, Nebraska*
DRAUGHN, Homer E.	*El Centro, California*
DRENNAN, John F.	*Dallas, Texas*
DRUM, Marvin C.	*Jackson, Missouri*
DUCKETT, Iva Faye Burden	*Holt, Michigan*
DUCLOS, Veda	*Prairie du Rochet, Illinois*
DUNBAR, Joseph E.	*Midland, Michigan*
DURST, Murray	*Randolph, New Jersey*
DUTTON, Jack S.	*Normandy, Missouri*
EDDY, Warren W.	*Los Angeles, California*
EICHELBERGER, William B.	*Venice, Florida*
EISING, Eugene	*Miami Beach, Florida*
ELLIS, Robert F.	*Nashua, New Hampshire*
ENABNIT, Elgin G., Jr.	*Fairfield, Connecticut*
ENNIS, Teresa O'Connell	*Bronx, New York*
ENOS, Frederick C.	*Utica, New York*
ERHARDT, Robert	*Fort Plain, New York*
ERICKSON, Melvin A.	*Clinton, Iowa*
ERLICK, Samuel	*Cherry Hill, New Jersey*
ERSLEY, Helen	*Okeechobee, Florida*
ESSICK, Alonzo E.	*Promise City, Iowa*
ESTEBAN, Florencio	*Baguio City, Philippines*
EVANS, J.M.	*Falls Church, Virginia*
EVANS, Willard F. (Bill)	*Tucker, Georgia*
FAHEY, John J.	*Broadview Heights, Ohio*
FALVEY, William J.	*Niles, Michigan*
FARMER, Mary	*Leesburg, Florida*
FASIG, Gene H.	*Camp Hill, Pennsylvania*
FAY, Howard K., Jr.	*Westborough, Massachusetts*
FERGUSON, Richard F.	*Carthage, Missouri*
FETHERLIN, R.E.	*Lola, Kansas*
FIELD, David D.	*Hampton, Virginia*
FINLEY, Marjorie Barnes	*Arcadia, Nebraska*
FINNEGAN, Peter	*Caldwell, New Jersey*
FINNEY, Norma A.	*Floodwood, Minnesota*
FITZGERALD, James Howard	*Lockport, New York*
FLEENER, Gene A.	*Big Bear Lake, California*
FLYNN, William J.	*Philadelphia, Pennsylvania*
FOGLE, Kenneth E.	*Frederick, Maryland*
FORTIN, Clement G.	*Rockwell, North Carolina*
FOSTER, James S.	*Grand Island, Nebraska*
FOX, Edward K.	*Topeka, Kansas*
FOX, Nelson Brambier, Sr.	*Caryville, Florida*
FOX, Vincent L.	*Sebring, Florida*
FRANZ, Merle T.	*Yelm, Washington*
FRANZEN, Delores	*Melbourne, Kentucky*
FREDERICK, Douglas W.	*Superior, Nebraska*
FREEMAN, George B.	*Orangeburg, South Carolina*
FREIM, Martin G.	*Zephyr Cove, Nevada*
FRISBY, John C.	*Forestville, Maryland*
FRITZ, Harry	*Philadelphia, Pennsylvania*
FULMER, Robert L.	*Spring Mount, Pennsylvania*
FULTZ, Lotus H.	*Madison, Indiana*

FYHRIE, Lambert W.	*Duluth, Minnesota*
GABER, Karl L.	*Bulger, Pennsylvania*
GAINOR, Robert	*Port Richey, Florida*
GALEAZ, Phyllis T. Santaglo	*Lynn, Massachusetts*
GALPIRINO, Harry	*Buffalo, New York*
GARATE, Patricia P.	*Beowawe, Nevada*
GARBARINO, Albert N.	*San Diego, California*
GARDNER, Richard A.	*Oakland, New Jersey*
GARR, Margaret H.	*Springfield, Illinois*
GATES, Henry D.	*Middleboro, Massachusetts*
GAVITT, Leo C.	*Stanton, Michigan*
GAWRILUK, Raymond S.	*Naperville, Illinois*
GAY, Edward F.	*Harrisburg, Pennsylvania*
GENGEL, Frank C.	*Bellevue, Nebraska*
GERSTAN, Al	*Garden Grove, California*
GILLION, Robert W.	*Paoli, Indiana*
GILLMARTIN, David W.	*Sag Harbor, New York*
GINGERY, Lee E.	*Shenandoah, Iowa*
GITTINS, Vincent J.	*Staten Island, New York*
GIUSTO, Edward J.	*Augusta, Georgia*
GLICK, Wayne	*Wichita, Kansas*
GODDARD, Charles A.	*Chaffee, Missouri*
GOFF, Myron V.	*Livonia, Michigan*
GOMES, Joseph Santos	*Santa Maria, California*
GOODENKAUF, Arley L.	*Table Rock, Nebraska*
GOODWIN, Gilbert A., Jr.	*East Dennis, Massachusetts*
GORCH, Edward F.	*Maspeth, New York*
GORDON, Charlene Buckman	*Camp Point, Illinois*
GORON, Raymond C.	*Greensburg, Pennsylvania*
GORR, Walter R.	*Tracy, California*
GOULD, Lewis J.	*St. Charles, Michigan*
GRABER, Norman	*Encinitas, California*
GRABOWSKI, Stanley	*Rutland, Vermont*
GRAEWIN, Erwin A.	*Norwalk, Wisconsin*
GRAY, Constance Krasowska	*Union, New Jersey*
GRAY, James	*Hallandale, Florida*
GREINER, Loren M.	*Emmetsburg, Iowa*
GREIVELL, Richard H.	*Thomaston, Georgia*
GRESHAM, James W.	*Princeton, Kentucky*
GRIFFIN, J. Donald	*Buffalo, New York*
GRONECK, George M.	*Cloverdale, California*
GROSS, Benny J.	*Onida, South Dakota*
GROSS, Leo	*Pound, Wisconsin*
GROTHOUSE, Arthur J.	*Delphos, Ohio*
HALL, Hugh L.	*Asheville, North Carolina*
HALL, Marion C., Jr.	*Deltaville, Virginia*
HALLAND, Oreal H.	*Thief River Falls, Minnesota*
HAMILTON, Worth O.	*Monroe, North Carolina*
HANGARTNER, Elmer	*Fairfield, California*
HANSEN, Robert R.	*Sioux City, Iowa*
HANST, Kenneth F., Jr.	*Naples, Florida*
HARDER, Fitzgerald F.	*Arkansas City, Kansas*
HARDY, Joe R.	*Ft. Worth, Texas*
HARMELINK, Maurice	*Grand Rapids, Michigan*
HARP, C. Edwin	*Las Vegas, Nevada*
HARPER, Bill R.	*Cookville, Texas*
HARRIS, William V.	*West Salem, Illinois*
HARTLEY, Robert W.	*Wellington, Kansas*
HARVEY, Samuel R.	*St. Cloud, Minnesota*
HASKELL, Milton	*Beaver Dam, Wisconsin*
HASSETT, Albert J., Jr.	*Woodside, New York*
HATHAWAY, Mildred Smith	*Edgartown, Massachusetts*
HAWKES, L. Everett	*Windham, Maine*
HAWKINS, James F.	*Fresno, California*
HAWKINS, L.J.	*Maxwell, Texas*
HAYES, Sherrill W.	*Nashville, Tennessee*
HAYS, T.	*Portland, Oregon*
HEACOCK, Nan Wilkinson	*Bradyville, Tennessee*
HEATH, Willard A.	*Boise, Idaho*
HECHT, R.O.	*Highland, Illinois*
HEFFERN, William R.	*Shively, Kentucky*
HEINEMAN, J. Paul	*Golden Valley, Minnesota*
HEINLE, Edwin L.	*Lewiston, Idaho*
HEINZ, Karl G.	*Indian Harbour Beach, Florida*
HEISEY, John W.	*York, Pennsylvania*
HELLER, Henry F.	*Fond du Lac, Wisconsin*
HENDERSON, William G.	*St. Peters, Missouri*
HENDRIX, William A.	*St. Joseph, Michigan*
HERBSTER, Ken	*Milford, Iowa*
HERNON, Peter J., Sr.	*St. Louis, Missouri*
HERTRICH, Donald J.	*Weaver, Alabama*
HILES, Wesley J.	*Summit Hill, Pennsylvania*

HILLIS, Harry, Jr. — *Olney, Illinois*
HODGENS, Robert J., Sr. — *Ridge, New York*
HOHENSEE, William — *Munith, Michigan*
HOLLAND, Elmer C. — *Jonesboro, Arkansas*
HOLLEN, Kermit C. — *Philippi, West Virginia*
HOLMES, J.K. — *Oneida, New York*
HOLTCAMP, Clem H. — *Denver, Colorado*
HOOVER, Elmer E. — *Hagerstown, Maryland*
HOPPER, Ebbert H. — *Oklahoma City, Oklahoma*
HOSKINS, John William — *Kilmichael, Mississippi*
HOUGLUM, Arvid J. — *Grandview, Texas*
HOWE, Gary C. — *Steeleville, Illinois*
HUDSON, Lola M. — *Ferndale, Pennsylvania*
HUELSBECK, Robert J. — *Appleton, Wisconsin*
HUGGINS, Lloyd G. — *Petersburg, Virginia*
HUGHES, Mary Hannah Hitchcock — *Lake Worth, Florida*
HULTQUIST, Mrs. Bob — *Ganado, Texas*
HUMPHREY, E.A. — *Lodi, California*
HUNT, Raymond J. — *Glenview, Illinois*
IMMASCHE, Vic — *Lawrence, Kansas*
JACKSON, Delwood S. — *Cincinnati, Ohio*
JACKSON, Jim — *Prunedale, California*
JACOBSON, Weldon G. — *Milwaukee, Wisconsin*
JACOBSON, Lloyd A. — *Swan Valley, Idaho*
JAMES, Albert — *North Babylon, New York*
JANTZ, Edmund — *Heber Springs, Arkansas*
JARRETT, Luther J. — *St. Alban, West Virginia*
JARVIS, Harry J. — *Ayden, North Carolina*
JARVIS, Hobart A. — *Barbourville, Kentucky*
JENSEN, Alton C. — *Grantsburg, Wisconsin*
JESSO, Harold E. Jr. — *Gloucester, Massachusetts*
JIMENEZ, Ramon F. — *Leyte, Philippines*
JOHNSON, Arlo K. — *New Ulm, Minnesota*
JOHNSON, Arthur W. — *Lynnwood, Washington*
JOHNSON, Lee G. (Hap) — *Somerset, Kentucky*
JOHNSON, Neil H. — *Glenmora, Louisiana*
JOHNSON, Robert F. — *Green Bay, Wisconsin*
JOHNSON, Robert T. — *Overland Park, Kansas*
JONES, Larry L. — *Stone Mountain, Georgia*
JONES, Oliver J. — *Garden City, New York*
JORDAN, Gladys — *Robbinsville, North Carolina*
JORGENSEN, James R. — *Sioux Falls, South Dakota*
JOULES, Lily G. — *Rochester, New York*
JURMAN, William — *Howard Beach, New York*
JUSTICE, Donald B. — *Lusby, Maryland*
KALTHOFF, Raymond E. — *Marshall, Missouri*
KALTVED, Dale K. — *Lincoln, Nebraska*
KALUSTIAN, Harry — *Fresno, California*
KAMINSKY, Philip — *Wantagh, New York*
KANARKOWSKI, Phillip J. — *West Newton, Pennsylvania*
KANOUR, William W. — *Naples, Florida*
KAPEC, Joseph E. — *Spring Hill, Florida*
KARETKA, Peter — *Chicopee, Massachusetts*
KASSAY, Ernest J. — *Tonawanda, New York*
KASTNER, Robert E. — *Torrington, Wyoming*
KATZ, Lawrence C. — *Blytheville, Arkansas*
KAVONIAN, Harold — *Milford, Massachusetts*
KEAGLE, Paul E. — *Pasadena, Maryland*
KEAN, Jeanne Steele — *Bridgeville, Pennsylvania*
KEARNS, Bruno L. — *New Port Richey, Florida*
KELLER, Frank J. — *Tonawanda, New York*
KELLY, Paul T. — *Tulsa, Oklahoma*
KENNEDY, Edward A. — *Westminster, Maryland*
KERTESZ, Emery P. Jr. — *Ottsville, Pennsylvania.*
KILEY, William D. — *Arcadia, Florida*
KIME, Lewis W. — *Matawan, New Jersey*
KING, Flin Crawford — *Columbia, Tennessee*
KINSEY, David B., Jr. — *Taft, Texas*
KIRK, Mancel — *Bethel Springs, Tennessee*
KITCHEN, David — *Poplar Bluff, Missouri*
KLEIN, Jerome — *Sarasota, Florida*
KLENMAN, Phillip H. — *Seattle, Washington*
KLINGELE, Eugene J. — *Quincy, Illinois*
KLISIEWICZ, Edward — *Temple, Texas*
KLOSS, David S. — *Somerdale, New Jersey*
KNAPP, Thomas Clair — *Apache Junction, Arizona*
KNAPP, Tom — *Brooklyn, New York*
KNIGHT, James E. — *Brunswick, Maine*
KODISH, Eleanor — *Lock Haven, Pennsylvania*
KOGUT, Leon — *Arlington, Virginia*
KOLGER, Louis — *Cincinnati, Ohio*
KOMRO, Raymond E. — *Durand, Wisconsin*

KOMSTOHK, Thomas H.	Indianapolis, Indiana
KOWAL, Joseph M.	Reading, Pennsylvania
KOZACH, Tony A.	Taunton, Massachusetts
KRAMER, Michael P.	Bath, Pennsylvania
KRANS, John T.	Galesburg, Illinois
KRASHEFSKI, Leonard A.	Moodus, Connecticut
KRUSE, James V.	Elkhart, Indiana
KUDLA, Lillian P.	Chicago, Illinois
KUEHNA, H.	Burke, Virginia
KUHLOW, Edgar L.	Sheboygan Falls, Wisconsin
KUHN, Adolph	Manteca, California
KUNKEL, Robert M.	Exeter, New Hampshire
LABELLE, Viola L.	Worcester, Massachusetts
LABOUR, Wilson J.	Berwick, Pennsylvania
LAGOCKI, Henry M.	Philadelphia, Pennsylvania
LAGUTAN, Pedro P.	San Jose, Montalban Rizal, Philippines
LAMB, George F.	Pittsburgh, Pennsylvania
LANDON, Edith Stoessel	Fayetteville, North Carolina
LANGFORD, Shelby V.	Hemet, California
LARSON, Kenneth L.	Los Angeles, California
LASHLEY, Mary B.	Hagerstown, Maryland
LASKA, Joseph	Schenectady, New York
LAWRENCE, Leo B.	Pipersville, Pennsylvania
LEAMING, Jack	Wildwood, New Jersey
LEBAR, Leola R.	Norfolk, Nebraska
LEDBETTER, Edward Warren	Phoenix, Arizona
LEE, Robert J.	Kailua, Hawaii
LEE, Roy G.	Indianapolis, Indiana
LEE, Ruth	Phillips, Wisconsin
LEIGH, Miles J.	Sioux City, Iowa
LEVANDOSKI, Leonard S.	Wilkes-Barre, Pennsylvania
LEVIN, Phillip	Bay Harbor Islands, Florida
LEVY, Robert W.	Las Vegas, Nevada
LINDSAY, David F.	Sierra Vista, Arizona
LINGG, James T.	Tacoma, Washington
LIPPERT, Mrs. William	West Amherst, New York
LIT, Nathan	Philadelphia, Pennsylvania
LITTLE, Walter E.	Providence, Rhode Island
LITTMAN, Abraham	Tamarac, Florida
LLOYD, Warren R.	Altamonte Springs, Florida
LOEBL, William F.	Chanhassen, Minnesota
LOMAESTRO, Benjamin J.	Troy, New York
LOONEY, Grace L.	Mountain View, Arkansas
LOPIANO, Robert R.	Rochester, New York
LOVE, John C.	Oklahoma City, Oklahoma
LOVEJOY, Marjorie McDonough	Buffalo, New York
LUCAS, Charles	Detroit, Michigan
LUCIANO, Michael	Westport, Connecticut
LUEDEMANN, Clarence	Indianapolis, Indiana
LUND, Edward	Menomonie, Wisconsin
MACE, Frank	Providence, Rhode Island
MACELWEE, Paul T.	Shamokin, Pennsylvania
MACHOLL, Earl M.	Marietta, New York
MAGUIRE, John J.	Wallingford, Pennsylvania
MAHNKEN, Marion H.	Port St. Lucie, Florida
MAIER, Robert O.	Oak Harbor, Washington
MALON, Virginia Ford	Oklahoma City, Oklahoma
MALSON, Clifford W.	Denver, Colorado
MANCINI, Anthony	Boca Raton, Florida
MANCUSO, Joseph D.	Washington, Pennsylvania
MAPES, Elmer A.	Bettendorf, Iowa
MARGE, Gabriel	Augusta, Georgia
MARION, Theodore A.	Shirley, Massachusetts
MARQUARDT, A.G. (Mark)	Lancaster, California
MARRON, Bernard J.	Sheridan, Wyoming
MARRONE, Stephen	Maspeth, New York
MARSE, George Sr.	Harahan, Louisiana
MARTINEZ, John U.	Hemet, California
MARTS, Opal R.	Park Rapids, Minnesota
MASSIE, Philip E.	Culver City, California
MASTIN, Herbert L.	Lakeland, Florida
MAY, Joseph R.	Malad City, Idaho
MCALLISTER, James E.	Kalamazoo, Michigan
MCCALLION, A.G.	New York, New York
MCCAULEY, Lawrence H.	Columbus, Ohio
MCCLUSKEY, Richard M.	Brooklyn, New York
MCCLUSKY, Mary B.	Port Charlotte, Florida
MCCRACKEN, Harry E.	Manor, Pennsylvania
MCDONOUGH, George E.	Brownsville, Pennsylvania
MCFERREN, Alvin H.	Shreveport, Louisiana
MCGORAN, John H.	Corte Madera, California
MCGUIRE, Warren O.	Fairfield, Connecticut

MCHARRY, Bill	*Anderson, Indiana*
MCKEE, Nash	*Weaverville, North Carolina*
MCKEOWN, Thomas E.	*Scituate, Massachusetts*
MCLAUGHLIN, William J.	*Marstons Mills, Massachusetts*
MCLEIEER, Joy	*Boynton Beach, Florida*
MEEHAN, Raymond J.	*Lewisburg, Pennsylvania*
MEIER, Rexall L.	*Wisconsin Rapids, Wisconsin*
MELLO, Anibel	*West Warwick, Rhode Island*
MENASTER, Albert	*San Francisco, California*
MENKER, Raymond L.H., Jr.	*Dayton, Ohio*
MERCURIO, Dante J.	*Marlboro, New Jersey*
MESSINA, Frank J.	*Whitehall, Pennsylvania*
METZLER, Allan	*Oakhurst, New Jersey*
MEYER, Donald L.	*Boone, Iowa*
MEYER, Leonard C.	*Indianapolis, Indianapolis*
MEYER, Virginia	*Mount Gilead, Ohio*
MICKIEWICZ, Adam S.	*Meriden, Connecticut*
MIKA, Mary L.	*Florissant, Missouri*
MILLER, Glenn E.	*Palm Bay, Florida*
MILLER, Richard H.	*Amherst, Virginia*
MILLS, Charlie W.	*Louisville, Kentucky*
MINETOLA, Irene	*Allentown, Pennsylvania*
MINOR, Carl A.	*Maysville, Missouri*
MONTGOMERY, David	*Petersburg, Illinois*
MONTGOMERY, James W.	*Wichita, Kansas*
MONTGOMERY, Thelma	*Des Moines, Iowa*
MOORE, Charles	*Ft. Wayne, Indiana*
MOORE, Ernest A.	*Kearny, New Jersey*
MOORE, Sidney R.	*Cohasset, Minnesota*
MORANTTE, Claro C.	*Tanauan, Leyte, Philippines*
MORGAN, James M.	*Stanford, Kentucky*
MORGAN, Richard V.	*Waynesburg, Pennsylvania*
MORRIS, Jack B.	*Cape Coral, Florida*
MORTON, Ohland F.	*Eufala, Oklahoma*
MOSTELLER, Roscoe	*Greenville, South Carolina*
MOTUSH, Stanley C.	*New Lisbon, Wisconsin*
MULLER, Steven G.	*East Northport, New York*
MUNK, A.F. Munk	*Baltimore, Maryland*
MURPHY, Fred C.	*Upland, California*
MUSSO, Peter	*Orland Park, Illinois*
MYERS, George L.	*Cedarburg, Wisconsin*
MYERS, Gerald C.	*Jeanerette, Louisiana*
MYHAND, Sirl	*Orleans, California*
MYKITA, Mytro	*Carnegie, Pennsylvania*
MYSAK, Bru	*Jackson Heights, New York*
NAPER, J. N.	*Westchester, California*
NEEDLEMAN, Robert	*Chicago, Illinois*
NELSON, Robert	*Cincinnati, Ohio*
NELSON, Robert Deal	*Culpeper, Virginia*
NELSON, Victor H.	*Richland, Washington*
NEWTON, Grace Cornell	*Beaumont, Texas*
NEWTON, J. Byron	*Powder Springs, Georgia*
NEWTON, Jerry	*Beaumont, Texas*
NICHOLS, Joseph E.	*North Creek, New York*
NICOLAI, Joseph P., Jr.	*Charlevoix, Michigan*
NOACK, Robert C.	*Celina, Ohio*
O'GRADY, James P.	*Rochester, New York*
O'GRADY, Thomas E.	*Saginaw, Michigan*
OAKMAN, Dorothy J.	*Lake View, Iowa*
OEHLERICH, Lucille	*Keystone, Iowa*
OGLE, Clifford H.	*Tampa, Florida*
OLSON, Bud C.	*Choteau, Montana*
OLSON, Dennis H.	*Nevada City, California*
OLSON, Robert G.	*Park Hill, Oklahoma*
OLSON-FOUST, Carmen	*Booneville, Arkansas*
ONLYDIDOF, Harry	*Annandale, Minnesota*
OOTON, Scottie	*Effingham, Illinois*
OVERMAN, John C., Jr.	*Apex, North Carolina*
OWEN, Robert Phillip	*El Dorado, Arkansas*
PACHENKER, William	*Brooklyn, New York*
PACHOWKA, Paul	*Woodlyn, Pennsylvania*
PAINE, Harold W.	*Mason City, Iowa*
PAISLEY, Paul K.	*Newton Falls, Ohio*
PARK, Edward	*Big Pine, California*
PARKS, Roy	*Gleason, Tennessee*
PASAPORTE, Santiago L.	*Iloilo City, Philippines*
PASSOW, Harold W.	*Hazelhurst, Wisconsin*
PATON, John E.	*Brandon, Florida*
PATTON, Robert F.	*Chapel Hill, North Carolina*
PEARSON, Earl O.	*Fox Lake, Illinois*
PEARSON, Irene Rachko,	*Clifton, New Jersey*
PELLINO, Frank	*Ridgefield, New Jersey*

SCHAAF, Bob Vander	*Alton, Iowa*
SCHALLER, Leroy D. (Whitey)	*Bolivar, Pennsylvania*
SCHLAVITTI, Otto	*Dunlap, Illinois*
SCHMIDT, Andrew	*Iron River, Michigan*
SCHNABEL, Hugo	*Aberdeen, South Dakota*
SCHOCK, Ernest	*Forbes, North Dakota*
SCHOENER, Raymond J.	*Ironton, Ohio*
SCHOEWE, William A.	*Milton, Florida*
SCHOLTZ, Erwin	*Laurel, Maryland*
SCHOOFS, Louis G.	*Harlingen, Texas*
SCHUH, Robert J.	*Chilton, Wisconsin*
SCHULER, William G.	*Souderton, Pennsylvania*
SCHUMP, Roland	*Iowa City, Iowa*
SCHWANTES, Irma M.	*Fulda, Minnesota*
SEKERAK, Betty	*Columbus, Ohio*
SEMBOWER, Charles W.	*Bloomington, Indiana*
SEVEC, Andrew W., Sr.	*Clarksville, Pennsylvania*
SHANNON, Dorothy	*Clinton, Indiana*
SHAPIRO, Murray	*Chatsworth, California*
SHEPHERD, Mrs. Walter	*Noel, Missouri*
SHERRELL, Betty Lou	*San Jose, California*
SHIMKUS, George H.	*Webster Grove, Missouri*
SHOOP, Dale L.	*Fayetteville, Pennsylvania*
SHUE, John H.	*York, Pennsylvania*
SIEGEL, Helen Weiss	*Amory, Massachusetts*
SIEMINSKI, Marie Keno	*Grand Rapids, Michigan*
SIMMONS, Betty L.	*Ravenel, South Carolina*
SIMPSON, Dorothyy	*Everett, Washington*
SIMPSON, George E.	*San Angelo, Texas*
SLATER, Monroe O.	*Pasadena, Texas*
SMITH, Jack	*Dallas, Texas*
SMITH, James Edwin	*Greenville, North Carolina*
SMITH, Joe Smith Jr.	*Paducah, Kentucky*
SMITH, Melvin	*Scottsdale, Arizona*
SMITH, Ross W.	*Brick, New Jersey*
SMITH, William Curtis	*Tallahassee, Florida*
SNIDER, Nathan Hale	*Mandeville, Louisiana*
SNOWDEN, Jack	*Upland, California*
SOCKOL, Lois	*Needham, Massachusetts*
SOERGEL, Estelle H.	*Lake Park, Minnesota*
SOKEL, Saul	*Boca Raton, Florida*
SOLKER, Barbara S.	*Bath, Pennsylvania*
SOLOMON, Anthony	*Glenshaw, Pennsylvania*
SOLOMON, Gustav	*Bronx, New York*
SOUTHERN, Ira W.	*Princeton, West Virginia*
SPADACCINO, Dominick C.	*Langhorne, Pennsylvania*
SPENARD, John H.	*Wingdale, New York*
SPISKOK, George	*Pricedale, Pennsylvania*
SPONAUGLE, Helen	*Fontana, California*
SPRAGUE, Carlton B. Sr.	*Island Pond, Vermont*
SPROWLS, Donald	*Salem, South Carolina*
STANFORD, W.B.	*Hartselle, Alabama*
STANKEY, Kep	*Yankton, South Dakota*
STANKOVIC, Phyllis	*Mesa, Arizona*
START, Henry L.	*El Paso, Texas*
STEDLER, Dick	*Tonawanda, New York*
STEPHENS, James Darwin	*Georgetown, Kentucky*
STEVENS, William A.	*Greensburg, Pennsylvania*
STEWART, E.W.	*San Francisco, Calfifornia*
STEWART, Leroy N.	*Washington, Kansas*
STOLICKER, Mrs. Mildred D.	*Holly, Michigan*
STONE, Edward W.	*Syracuse, New York*
STONE, William E.	*Bethlehem, Pennsylvania*
STOTT, Lloyd	*LeRoy, New York*
STRAIN, Winfred Leon	*Rensselaer, Indiana*
STRAMEL, Raymond G.	*McCook, Nebraska*
STUART, Allen	*Baudette, Minnesota*
STULL, Charles William	*Buchanan, Virginia*
SULLIVAN, Thomas	*Raytown, Missouri*
SUPINSKI, John X., Jr.	*Rockville, Maryland*
SUTTON, George A. Jr.	*Westmont, New Jersey*
SVEUM, Leland	*Richfield, Minnesota*
SWANSON, Mrs. Elman	*Bedford Park, Illinois*
SWENSON, Al	*Osage, Iowa*
SYNDER, John A.	*Monessen, Pennsylvania*
SYSE, Norman D.	*Chicago, Illinois*
TABER, Robin E.	*Fairfield, California*
TALBOTT, Vivian T.	*Humboldt, South Dakota*
TAYLOR, Clarence	*Lebanon, Indiana*
TAYLOR, Richard E.	*Wenatchee, Washington*
TESDALL, Abel John	*Jewell, Iowa*
TEUCHERT, John J.	*Barefoot Bay, Florida*

THACH, John O.	*Westminster, Colorado*
THOMAS, Charles R.	*Margate, New Jersey*
THOMAS, James W.	*Houghton Lake, Michigan*
THOMPSON, Martin D.	*Sarasota, Florida*
TILECH, Paul L.	*Pine City, New York*
TOMAINO, Jospeh R.	*Monroeville, Pennsylvania*
TOMKOWIAK, Florian	*Cudahy, Wisconsin*
TRAVIS, William W.	*Birmingham, Alabama*
TREATMAN, Paul	*Brooklyn, New York*
TROIDL, Charles F.	*Cheektowaga, New York*
TROJAN, Anthony C.	*Bayside, New York*
TUCKER, Mrs. Ellen	*Tifton, Georgia*
TUPPER, Ted	*Massapequa, New York*
TURNER, Gerald J.	*Staten Island, New York*
TURNER, Leonard Paul	*Dundalk, Maryland*
TURNER, William A. Sr.	*Valdosta, Georgia*
TURNO, Al	*Inverness, Florida*
ULAN, Sidney M.	*Wallingford, Pennsylvania*
ULERY, Weldon	*Miami Springs, Florida*
UPHAM, James R.	*Grand Blanc, Michigan*
URICCHIO, William A.	*Southwick, Massachusetts*
VAAS, David C.	*Ashland, Ohio*
VACARRO, Ralph G.	*Miramar, Florida*
VALLO, Lawrence J.	*Jemez Pueblo, New Mexico*
VANDA, K.W.	*Endicott, New York*
VARNER, Leo L.	*Rome, New York*
VASSEY, Howard M.	*Lancaster, South Carolina*
VELTMAN, Ronald H.	*New Hyde Park, New York*
VILLARIAL, Thomas	*Forest Heights, Maryland*
WADE, Victor E.	*Cromwell, Connecticut*
WAGNER, Marilyn Lane	*Columbus, Ohio*
WAGNER, O. Jerry	*Belmont, Michigan*
WALL, William T.	*Sun City, Arizona*
WALSH, Michael T.	*Phillipsburg, New Jersey*
WANGSVICH, Delmar H.	*Key West, Florida*
WARD, C. Edwin	*Little Falls, New Jersey*
WARD, Edmond C.	*Kentfield, California*
WARNKE, James R.	*Boynton Beach, Florida*
WARREN, Richard L.	*Warrenton, Missouri*
WATTERS, Joseph A.	*Friesland, Wisconsin*
WEBB, Barnes S.	*Madison, Tennessee*
WEBB, Charles R.	*Mundelein, Illinois*
WEIDEMOYER, Kenneth C.	*Perkasie, Pennsylvania*
WEINEGER, Harry H.	*Yorktown Heights, New York*
WELCH, DeWitt W.	*Stone Mountain, Georgia*
WELLS, Walton E.	*Arivaca, Arizona*
WESTERHAUS, Marlin A. H.	*Winside, Nebraska*
WHITE, Clifton L.	*Brewer, Maine*
WHITE, J. Oreo	*Kaplan, Louisiana*
WHITE, Violet	*Titusville, Florida*
WHITESIDE, Betty R.	*Potwin, Kansas*
WHITNEY, Irving	*Pembroke, Massachusetts*
WHITTAKER, Harry J.	*St. Johns, Michigan*
WILKUM, Lester R.	*Milwaukee, Wisconsin*
WILSON, J.A.	*McAlester, Oklahoma*
WILSON, Kermit T.	*Guthrie, Oklahoma*
WILSON, William	*Livingston Manor, New York*
WINDT, Irwin	*Liberty, New York*
WINSLOW, John R.	*Eugene, Oregon*
WOJTOWICZ, Edward A.	*South St. Paul, Minnesota*
WOLF, Herbert R.	*Lancaster, Pennsylvania*
WOLF, Vincent E.	*Venice, Florida*
WOLF, William A.	*Ocean City, Maryland*
WOOD Clyde (Pete)	*Moorhead, Mississippi*
WOODLAND, Wesley	*Lake Ronkonkoma, New York*
WRAY, Richard M.	*Colonial Heights, Virginia*
WRIGHT, Mrs. Robert D.	*Venice, Florida*
WYSOCKI, Charles, Jr.	*Green Valley, Arizona*
YARWOOD, William R. (Bill)	*Anaheim, California*
YIENGST, Kathleen E.	*Lebanon, Pennsylvania*
YLAGAN, Pedro Y.	*Pacoima, Californian*
YOAKUM, Woodrow W.	*Hobbs, New Mexico*
YOCUM, Walter H.	*Hazleton, Pennsylvania*
YOUNG, Kenneth B. Young	*Ft. Wayne, Indiana*
YOUNG, R. Tom	*Louisville, Kentucky*
YULE, George P.	*Lakeside, California*
ZELINSKI, Norbert	*Manitowoc, Wisconsin*
ZIPES, Mel	*Wappingers Falls, New York*
ZOWNIR, Myron	*Long Island City, New York*
ZYLKA, Bernard (Barney)	*Duluth, Minnesota*
ZYWIEC, Lonnie	*Columbus, Nebraska*